AS LEVEL SOCIOLOGY

The complete course for the AQA specification

Rob Webb   Hal Westergaard   Keith Trobe   Liz Steel

NAPIER PRESS *Sociology*

Published by Napier Press
PO Box 6383
Brentwood CM13 2NQ
Tel: 01277 260653
Email: napierpress@aol.com
Website: www.sociology.uk.net

Second Edition © Napier Press 2008

First Edition published in 2004 by Napier Press; Reprinted 2005
Second Edition published in 2008 by Napier Press

ISBN-10: 0954007956
ISBN-13: 978-0954007959

The authors assert the moral right to be identified as the authors of this work.

British Library Cataloguing in Publication Data
A catalogue record for this book is available from the British Library

Edited by Rob Webb
Design by HL Studio
Picture research by Hal Westergaard
Printed and bound by Butler and Tanner

Acknowledgements
Guardian Newspapers Ltd for the extract from The Observer, 30 August 1978, and from the article 'Today's Special' by Rebecca Smithers in The Guardian, 19 July 2001. Extract by David Morgan 'Risk and Family Practices' reprinted by permission of Sage Publications Ltd from E. Silva et al, 'The New Family' (1999) (© David Morgan 1997). Extract from Stephen Wagg, 'I Blame the Parents' (1992), Blackwell Publishing Ltd. Extracts from Liz Steel and Warren Kidd, 'The Family' (2001), Palgrave Macmillan. Sharon Gewirtz for extract from S. Gewirtz et al, 'Markets, Choice and Equity in Education', Open University (1995). Extract from Karen Chapman, 'The Sociology of Schools', Tavistock (1986) by Thomson Publishing Services. Extract from Debbie Epstein 'Boys' Under-achievement in Context' in D. Epstein et al, 'Failing Boys?' (1998) Open University Press is reproduced by kind permission of the Open University Press/McGraw-Hill Publishing Company. Extract from Social Trends by kind permission of the Office for National Statistics. Extract from Sarah Thornton, 'Club Cultures' (1995), Polity Press, Cambridge.

Every effort has been made to contact the holders of copyright material, but if any have been inadvertently overlooked the publishers will be pleased to make the necessary arrangements at the first opportunity.

The publishers would like to thank the following for permission to reproduce pictures. Alamy Images: pages 3, 4, 6, 8, 18, 22, 25, 36, 38, 56, 60, 61, 65, 73, 74, 75, 80, 85, 92, 97, 109, 110, 112, 116, 124, 138, 144, 152, 161, 162, 168, 170, 191, 194, 204, 220 and 237; Berwick Street Film Collective (Mark Karlin, Mary Kelly, James Scott, Humphrey Trevelyan), LUX, London: page 70; Corbis: pages 28, 148, 150 and 184; Daniel Bridge: page 227; Don Rutledge: pages 210 and 211; Getty Images: pages 46, 67 and 223; Imperial War Museum: page 42; Mary Evans Picture Library: page 121; Mirrorpix: page 91; Photofusion: pages 33, 86, 94, 100, 102, 103, 115, 119, 126, 131, 133, 134, 164, 172, 180, 182, 186, 202, 206, 218 and 230; Wikipedia: page 30.

NAPIER PRESS *Sociology*

Go to www.sociology.uk.net
On-line support for Sociology teachers and students using this book.

CONTENTS

What is Sociology?

CHAPTER 1

What is sociology?

Sociology is the study of society and of people and their behaviour.

Sociologists study a wide range of topics. For example, the AQA AS and A level specification includes topics such as those in Box 1.

In studying topics like these, sociologists create **theories** to explain human behaviour and the workings of society. Theories are explanations of the patterns we find in society. For example, we may have a theory as to why there are differences in girls' and boys' achievement levels in school.

A theory tries to make **generalisations**. That is, it tries to explain all similar cases, not just a single case. For example, it tries to say why boys in general do less well at school than girls, rather than why simply this or that individual boy does less well.

Box 1	Some topics in sociology

GENDER   STEREOTYPING   RACE & ETHNICITY

CLASS   PEER GROUPS

RACISM   SEXISM   SAME SEX RELATIONSHIPS

RESEARCHING SOCIAL BEHAVIOUR   SOCIAL INEQUALITY

MARRIAGE & DIVORCE   DOMESTIC VIOLENCE

SCHOOLS   CHILDHOOD   LONE PARENTS

Sociology is an **evidence-based** subject. This means it is not just about the sociologist's personal opinion or pet theory – our opinions and theories must be backed up by facts about society. Sociologists therefore collect evidence methodically by carrying out **research** to establish whether their theories are correct. A good theory is one that explains the available evidence.

As well as producing theories about society, sociology has practical applications. For example, if we know the causes of social problems such as educational under-achievement, we may be able to use this knowledge to design social policies to improve children's educational opportunities. A **social policy** is a programme or plan introduced by government that aims to achieve a particular goal, such as raising educational standards or reducing crime rates. Governments may use the findings of sociological research to develop more effective policies.

Nature or nurture?

People disagree about whether our behaviour is somehow 'natural' or innate (inborn), or whether it is the result of nurture – that is, our upbringing in society.

Some biologists argue that behaviour is mainly shaped by natural **instincts**. An instinct is an innate, fixed, pre-programmed pattern of behaviour shared by all members of a given species. For example, all blackbirds are 'programmed' to produce the same song patterns, and a blackbird reared in isolation from others will still produce the same song.

In other words, instinctive behaviour doesn't have to be learned. Many instincts are an automatic response to particular stimuli in the environment, such as birds migrating as the seasons change. These behaviours are not learned and the animal apparently has no control over them.

Many biologists argue that, like animal behaviour, our behaviour too is governed by instinct. For example, they claim that humans have natural instincts for reproduction and self-preservation, and that women have a maternal instinct for childbearing and rearing.

However, sociologists question whether human behaviour really is governed by instincts. They point out that on the whole our behaviour is not fixed biologically.

Although we may all possess the same biological urges or drives, the way we satisfy them varies between individuals and societies. For example:

- Although we all have a sex drive, the way we satisfy it can vary: from promiscuity to monogamy, polygamy etc – or we may choose to remain celibate.
- We have a drive for self-preservation, yet some people choose to commit suicide or risk their lives in war.
- Women are said to have a maternal instinct, yet some choose to abandon or abuse their children – and today over a fifth of all women in Britain choose not to have children at all.

If our behaviour really was determined by instincts, we would not expect to find such enormous variations in behaviour between individuals and societies.

Sociologists argue that the reason for these variations is that our behaviour is **learned** rather than instinctive. Much of this learning occurs in our early years through contact with others and this has an enormous influence on our behaviour and development.

For example, language, knowledge of right and wrong, practical skills such as dressing oneself, table manners and so on all have to be learnt from other members of society. Box 2 shows some of the harmful effects that lack of social contact in our early years can have on human development.

Sociologists therefore argue that biology and instincts cannot explain our behaviour, because most of it is learned not inborn, and because it is not fixed for all members of our species, but varies between societies. As an alternative way of explaining human behaviour, therefore, sociologists use the two related ideas of culture and socialisation.

▲ Much of our learning occurs in our early years.

Culture, norms and values

Sociologists define **culture** as all those things that are learned and shared by a society or group of people and transmitted from generation to generation. Culture includes all the things that a society regards as important, such as customs, traditions, language, skills, knowledge, beliefs, norms and values.

For example, the culture of societies whose way of life is based on hunting will include hunting skills and techniques, knowledge of the habits and movements of game animals and so on. Similarly, such cultures often contain shared beliefs about the spirits of the animals they hunt and how they should be treated.

Members of a society also share norms and values. **Values** are general principles or goals. They tell us what is good and what we should aim for. For example, modern American society places a high value on individual achievement and the accumulation of personal wealth. By contrast, societies such as those of Native American Indians place a high value on individuals fulfilling their duties to the group, including the duty to share their wealth rather than keep it for themselves.

Box 2	The effects of extreme isolation

Over the years, there have been several cases of 'feral' (wild) children found in forests and elsewhere who had apparently been reared by wolves or other animals. There is no way of knowing for sure if such children really had been nurtured by animals, but it is certain they had had little contact with other humans. One case was that of Shamdev, an Indian boy aged about five found in a forest playing with wolf cubs. When first found:

> 'Shamdev cowered from people and would only play with dogs. He hated the sun and used to curl up in shadowy places. After dark he grew restless and they had to tie him up to stop him following the jackals which howled around the village at night. If anyone cut themselves, he could smell the scent of blood and would scamper towards it. He caught chickens and ate them alive, including the entrails. Later; when he had evolved a sign language of his own, he would cross his thumbs and flap his hands: this meant "chicken" or "food".' (The Observer, 30 August 1978)

Of course, it is possible that parents abandon children like Shamdev precisely because they are abnormal, and such children may not have developed normally even if they had been raised in human company. However, the case of Isabelle suggests otherwise. Discovered at the age of six, Isabelle was the child of a deaf mute single mother. Both mother and child had been kept shut up by the family in a darkened room for most of the time. According to Kingsley Davis (1970):

> 'Her behaviour towards strangers, especially men, was almost that of a wild animal, manifesting much fear and hostility. In place of speech she made a strange croaking sound. In many ways she acted like an infant... At first it was even hard to tell whether or not she could hear, so unused were her senses. Many of her actions resembled those of deaf children.'

She was also unable to walk properly, and at first it was thought she might have severe learning difficulties. However; in two years of intensive training, Isabelle was able to cover the stages of learning that normally take six years and she went on to develop normally. These examples show that basic human social characteristics are not inborn or instinctive. We have to learn to be 'normal human beings' through contact with others in our early years.

While values lay down general principles or guidelines, **norms** are the specific rules that govern behaviour in particular situations. For example, cultures that place a high value on respect for elders usually have specific rules on how they are to be approached or addressed. It may not be permissible to look directly at them when speaking to them, or openly disobey or disagree with them.

Each culture has detailed rules or norms governing every aspect of behaviour, from food and dress to how we perform our jobs or who we may marry. Some norms, such as written laws or rules, are formal. Other norms are informal, such as table manners.

If we fail to keep to a norm, others may punish us. For example, stealing may result in a fine or imprisonment. Likewise, when we uphold a norm, we may be rewarded. For example, obeying the norm that we should work hard at school may earn us a place at university.

Sociologists use the term **sanctions** to describe anything that encourages people to conform to norms. Rewards are positive sanctions, while punishments are negative sanctions. Sanctions are a form of **social control**. That is, they are a way of ensuring that society's members behave as others expect them to.

Cultures and their norms vary greatly. What one culture considers normal or desirable, another may see as unacceptable. For example, in some cultures it is permitted to have several spouses at the same time (polygamy), whereas in others only one is allowed (monogamy).

Activity

Working alone or in small groups:

1 Make a list of all the characteristics of Shamdev and Isabelle that might be described as 'non-human'.

2 What 'human' characteristics, skills and abilities would you expect a normal five or six year old child to possess? Are any of these inborn?

3 What conclusions would you draw about the importance of nurture and nature in human development?

Similarly, some cultures have taboos on specific foods, or rules about what foods may be eaten together.

There may also be cultural variations within a society, especially a large complex one such as Britain. Different groups may have their own **subcultures** that vary significantly from the mainstream culture. For example, different religious groups may have different dietary norms as well as different beliefs about the afterlife.

Cultures and their norms and values may change over time. For example, attitudes to a wide range of behaviour, including smoking, homosexuality, married women working, cohabitation and sex before marriage have all changed in the recent past.

▲ *Every culture has detailed norms governing all aspects of daily life.*

■ **Secondary socialisation** takes place later, at school and in wider society.

Through primary socialisation, we learn what is expected of us as members of a family, but secondary socialisation introduces us to the more impersonal adult world. As well as the family and school, there are other agencies of socialisation, including peer groups, the mass media and religion. Each of these plays a part in transmitting the norms, values and skills we need in order to perform our roles in society.

Activity

Ask your parents for examples of things that are acceptable today that were frowned upon when they were young – and vice versa. Then repeat with a member of your grandparents' generation. What norms have changed?

Activity

In small groups, discuss the following questions. Compare your answers with the other groups in the class.

Food norms

1 Are there any things that other cultures consider to be food that your culture would not and vice versa?

2 What norms do our culture and others have governing:

    (a) how to eat (implements, manners etc)?

    (b) what should be eaten when (time of day/year, special occasions etc)?

Bus norms

1 To get from home to school or college, you might need to take a bus. Make a list of all the norms you can think of that the passengers, the driver and other road users will have to follow if you are to get to your destination safely and on time.

2 What norms govern whether or not we should sit next to someone else?

3 What norms govern the kind of communication permitted between passengers sitting next to one another?

4 Imagine you were taking a three year old on a bus. What sort of things might they do that you would not dream of doing? What does this tell us about norms?

Socialisation

As the examples of feral children show (see Box 2), we are not born knowing right from wrong, how to speak a language or what type of food we should eat. That is, we are not born with a culture – instead we must learn it from other members of society.

Sociologists refer to this process of learning one's culture as socialisation – learning all the things that are necessary for us to be accepted as full members of society. Another way of describing socialisation is to say it is a process of 'internalising' the culture, whereby society 'gets into' and becomes part of us.

Socialisation begins when we are born and continues throughout life. Sociologists distinguish between primary and secondary socialisation:

■ **Primary socialisation** takes place in the early years of life and occurs largely within the family, where we learn language, basic skills and norms.

Status and role

A **status** is a position in society. We can think of society as made up of lots of different positions or statuses. Some statuses are **ascribed**: based on fixed characteristics that we are born with and cannot normally change, such as our sex or ethnicity. Other statuses are **achieved** through our own efforts, such as getting into university or being promoted at work.

Those who occupy a given status are expected to follow particular norms of behaviour. For example, someone occupying the status of teacher is expected to mark students' work, treat them fairly, start lessons punctually, know their subject and so on. This set of norms together makes up the **role** of teacher.

Socialisation involves not only learning the general culture of society as a whole, but also the things we need to perform our particular roles within society. For example, boys and girls may be socialised differently to prepare them for different gender roles in adulthood.

1 What norms make up the role of (a) student (b) employee?

2 In what ways does the socialisation of boys and girls differ?

Individual and society

So far, we have assumed that individuals are shaped by the socialisation process to ensure that they perform the roles society requires of them. However, this implies we are simply the products of society and have no choice in how we act. How true is this? There are two main views:

- the structural view
- the social action view.

The structural view sees us as entirely shaped by the structure of society (the way society is organised or set up). It sees us as behaving according to society's norms and expectations, which we internalise through the socialisation process.

In this view, society determines our behaviour – we are like puppets on a string, manipulated by society. This is sometimes described as a 'macro' (large-scale) approach because it focuses on how wider society influences us. The emphasis is firmly on the power of society to shape us.

The social action view sees us as having free will and choice. It emphasises the power of individuals to create society through their actions and interactions. This is sometimes described as a 'micro' approach because it focuses on small-scale, face-to-face interactions between individuals. An example is the study described in Box 3, which shows how the beliefs we hold about others, influence how we interact with them.

In practice, most sociologists accept that individuals do have some degree of choice, as the social action view argues, but that their choices are limited by the structure of society, as the structural view argues.

Activity

Think about your own educational experiences and choices.

- In what ways do you have freedom of choice about your education?

- In what ways are your choices shaped by wider society (e.g. by your parents' views or income, the job market, your school or college)?

Box 3	Shoplifting in Chicago

Interactionist sociologists take a social action approach to crime. Rather than seeing crime as caused by 'society', they see it as the outcome of the labels people apply to others in their interactions with them. Mary Cameron's (1964) study of shoplifting in Chicago department stores is a good example of this approach.

Cameron found that stores didn't automatically prosecute everyone they suspected of shoplifting. They were often reluctant to prosecute because of the difficulty of proving the case and the cost of releasing employees to be witnesses. They were inclined to let suspects off with a warning, particularly if they were willing and able to pay for the goods.

1 What evidence does Cameron give of suspects being able to negotiate an outcome other than prosecution?

2 Apart from being young and black, what other characteristics do you think store detectives might see as typical of shoplifters?

3 How could you apply Cameron's ideas to explaining the fact that the working class are more likely to be convicted of crimes than the middle class?

However, not everyone was treated in the same way. According to Cameron, store detectives made assumptions about what the 'typical shoplifter' is like. They believed adolescents and black people were more likely to be shoplifters and kept them under surveillance when they were in the store. By contrast, the detectives were unlikely to be suspicious of people they saw as 'respectable'. These people tended to be middle-class and white. Even when the detectives witnessed an offence, they were less likely to report it if the suspect was of a similar background to themselves.

When arrests were made, the stores were more likely to press charges if the suspects were black. For example, only 9% of arrested white women were charged, but 42% of black women. Furthermore, when cases went to court, not only were black women more likely to be found guilty; they were six times more likely to be jailed than white women.

Cameron's study shows how people's beliefs about others influence how they act towards them. In this case, the ideas of the store detectives and others about the 'typical shoplifter' affected which groups they chose to pursue, and this in turn criminalised more blacks than whites.

Consensus or conflict?

Although structural sociologists agree that society shapes our behaviour, there are disagreements among them about the kind of structure society has. Functionalist sociologists see society as based on value consensus; that is, harmony and agreement among its members about basic values. By contrast, Marxist sociologists see society as based on conflict.

According to **functionalists**, society is held together by a shared culture into which all its members are socialised. Sharing the same culture integrates individuals into society by giving them a sense of solidarity or 'fellow feeling' with others. It enables members of society to agree on goals and how to achieve them and so allows them to cooperate harmoniously.

Functionalists see society as like a biological organism such as the human body. Like a body whose parts (organs, cells etc) fit together and depend on one another, society too is a system of interdependent parts. Each part performs functions that contribute to the well being of society as a whole. For example, the family reproduces the population and performs the function of primary socialisation, while the education system equips us with the knowledge and skills needed for work.

Marxists disagree with the functionalist view. They see society as based on class conflict, not consensus. They argue that society is divided into two social classes:

- The minority capitalist class, or bourgeoisie, own the means of production such as the factories, raw materials and land.
- The majority working class, or proletariat, own nothing but their own labour, which they have to sell to the bourgeoisie in order to survive.

The bourgeoisie exploit the workers and profit from their labour. This exploitation breeds class conflict, which Karl Marx (1818-83) believed would eventually lead to the working class overthrowing capitalism and creating a classless, equal society. In the Marxist view, all social institutions – such as religion, the media and the education system – serve to maintain capitalism, for example by promoting the idea that inequality is inevitable and fair.

Feminist sociologists agree with Marxists that there are fundamental divisions and conflicts in society, but they see gender rather than class as the most important division. They regard society and its institutions as male-dominated or *patriarchal*. For example, they see the family as unequal and oppressive, with women doing most of the housework and childcare.

Diversity and identity

According to Marxists and functionalists, in modern society the individual's identity is largely fixed. Marxists see our identity as stemming from our class position, while functionalists see it as the result of being socialised into the shared culture.

However, **postmodernist** sociologists argue that we are now living in a postmodern society (see Box 4). Unlike modern society, where individuals share a common culture or class identity, postmodern society is fragmented (splintered) into a wide variety of different groups.

These groups are based on differences in ethnicity, age, religion, region, nationality, sexuality and so on. This diversity gives individuals greater freedom to 'pick and mix' their identities from a wide variety of sources.

However, critics argue that postmodernists exaggerate how far things have really changed. In particular, postmodernists ignore the continuing importance of social inequality and the ways this limits people's choices and shapes their lives.

> In what ways does poverty limit people's choices and shape their lives?

Inequality

Britain remains an unequal society. For example, in 2003 the richest 5% of people in Britain owned 40% of the nation's total wealth, while the poorest half of the population shared only 7% of total wealth.

▲ *Why do the police target some groups more than others?*

Box 4	Social change and types of society

Sociology as a subject first developed in response to major changes that began to take place in western society from the 18th century onwards. One key change was **urbanisation** – the shift from a largely rural society where people lived in villages, to an urban society where they lived in towns and cities. The process of urbanisation was paralleled by one of **industrialisation**, in which the workforce increasingly moved out of agriculture and into factory production.

These changes had an enormous impact on all areas of social life and to understand them, many sociologists made a distinction between two types of society:

- **traditional society:** a rural-agricultural society where there was little social change, a strong sense of community and religion dominated people's view of the world.
- **modern society:** an urban-industrial society with social and technological change and a belief in progress and science.

However, some sociologists argue that we now live in a new type of society:

- **postmodern society:** a post-industrial society in which change is increasingly rapid but uneven, and where people have lost faith in the ability of science to bring about progress.

In postmodern society, information technology and the media play a central role. The world moves towards a single global economy and culture. Sources of individual identity become more diverse.

Critics argue that this change has been exaggerated and that we are still living in the modern rather than a postmodern era. For example, Marxists argue that society is still capitalist and class inequality remains its key feature.

Sociologists are interested in social stratification – that is, inequalities between groups such as social classes, men and women, ethnic groups and age groups. They use the concept of 'life chances' to describe these inequalities. Life chances refer to the chances of enjoying the 'good things', such as educational success, a long and healthy life, high quality housing, and well-paid, interesting work. Different classes, genders, ethnic groups and age groups tend to have different life chances.

Gender

Although there have been major changes in recent years, such as girls overtaking boys at school, men and women still do not occupy equal positions in society.

- More women than men are in poverty. Most low-paid workers and poor pensioners are women.
- On average, women earn only about four fifths of what men earn.
- Women do more housework and childcare than men.

Social class

Sociologists usually define a person's class in terms of their occupation. Those in non-manual jobs such as doctors, teachers and office workers are defined as middle-class, while those in manual jobs such as electricians, bus drivers and street sweepers are defined as working-class. Class has a major effect on many aspects of our lives, as the following examples show:

- Manual workers earn less than non-manual workers and are more likely to become unemployed.

- Men in class V (unskilled manual workers such as cleaners) are three times as likely to be heavy smokers and nearly five times as likely to die of lung cancer, compared to men in class I (professionals such as doctors).
- The infant mortality rate (deaths during the first year of life) is twice as high for babies in class V as for those in class I.

Ethnicity

Ethnicity refers to shared culture and identity. An ethnic group is one whose members see themselves as a group with a shared heritage and cultural background, often including the same language and religion. Ethnicity doesn't just refer to minority groups – most societies also have an ethnic majority.

- Unemployment is three times higher for African and Bangladeshi/Pakistani people than for whites.
- Minority employees tend to earn less than whites and are more likely to work shifts.
- The infant mortality rate of African Caribbean and Pakistani babies is double that of whites.

Age

Age is an important factor affecting a person's status and age stratification is a basic feature of many societies.

- In many traditional societies, the old are accorded high status. By contrast, in today's society, they have a low status.
- Children in today's society are economically dependent on adults and legal restrictions prevent them from working. This is not the case in all societies.
- The old and the young are more likely to be poor, compared with other age groups.

These different forms of inequality often overlap. For example, gender and age inequalities may reinforce one another. Women are likely to have smaller pensions in old age because they have not worked full-time for as long, due to family responsibilities.

1 Suggest two reasons for social class differences in death rates.

2 Suggest two reasons why women earn less than men.

3 Suggest two reasons why members of ethnic minority groups are more likely than whites to be unemployed.

How do sociologists study society?

As we saw earlier, sociologists create theories to explain society and human behaviour. To be of any value, these theories must be based on evidence about the real world.

Sociologists have to collect this evidence. To do so, they carry out research using a variety of methods and sources of evidence. These include:

- **social surveys**, which involve asking a sample of people a series of questions in an interview or a written questionnaire
- **participant observation**, where the sociologist joins in with the group they are studying in order to gain deeper insight into their lives
- **official statistics** compiled by the government (for example on educational achievement, family size, unemployment and crime rates).

When choosing a method of research, sociologists need to be aware that every method has its particular strengths and limitations. For example, a social survey can usually gather information from a large cross-section of the population, but often the results will lack depth and detail, compared for example with a study using participant observation. However, research that uses participant observation can usually only study small numbers of people.

Summary

Sociology is the study of society and human behaviour. Sociologists construct **theories** – general explanations of social patterns. They conduct research to collect **evidence** to support their theories. Governments may use sociologists' findings to develop **social policies**.

Human behaviour is not instinctive, but **learned** through contact with others, as the examples of feral children show. **Culture** includes all those things learned and shared by a group, including knowledge, beliefs, norms and values. **Values** are general principles. **Norms** are specific rules of behaviour. Complex societies may contain many **subcultures**. **Socialisation** is the process of learning one's culture. Sociologists distinguish between **primary** and **secondary** socialisation.

Society is made up of **statuses**, some of which are **ascribed** (fixed at birth) while others are **achieved**. A **role** is the set of norms that govern how a person in a particular status should act.

The **structural view** sees society as shaping the individual. The **social action view** sees individuals as having choice, creating social reality through their interactions. **Functionalists** see society as based on **value consensus**, with interdependent parts performing functions for the good of the whole. **Marxists** see society as based on **class conflict**, in which the bourgeoisie exploit the proletariat. They believe capitalism will ultimately be replaced by a classless society. **Feminists** see society as **patriarchal** or male dominated.

Postmodernists believe we have moved to a more **fragmented** society in which there are diverse sources of identity. Critics argue that they ignore important **class**, **gender**, **ethnic** and **age inequalities**. These have a powerful effect on people's **life chances**.

Sociologists use a variety of **methods** and sources, such as surveys, participant observation and official statistics to gather evidence to test their theories.

QuickCheck Questions

1 Explain what is meant by a social policy.

2 What do the examples of 'feral' children show about human behaviour?

3 Explain what is meant by: (a) culture; (b) norms; (c) socialisation.

4 Explain the difference between ascribed status and achieved status.

5 True or false? The social action approach believes that individuals are like puppets on a string, manipulated and shaped by society.

6 True or false? The bourgeoisie is another name for the working class.

7 Explain what is meant by 'value consensus'.

8 According to functionalists, what is the advantage of members of society sharing the same culture?

9 Explain what is meant by 'patriarchal society'.

10 Explain the difference between urbanisation and industrialisation.

11 In which types of society (traditional, modern or postmodern) are the following features likely to be found: (a) belief in progress; (b) little social change; (c) diverse sources of identity?

12 True or false? Conducting a social survey normally involves joining in with the group you are studying.

 Check your answers at www.sociology.uk.net

What does AS level sociology involve?

AS level sociology gives you an understanding of important aspects of society, and of how sociologists study and explain people's behaviour. Studying AS sociology will enable you to discuss social issues in a more informed and systematic way and it will help you to make sense of your own and other people's experiences.

The skills you develop will help you to think logically about the world. AS level will give you a firm foundation if you want to study sociology at A2 or degree level.

Topics and exams

If you are doing AQA AS sociology, you have to study three topics. The three topics you will be studying if you are using this textbook are:

- Unit 1: Families and Households (one topic) – one hour written exam
- Unit 2: Education *plus* Sociological Research Methods (two topics) – two hour written exam.

What the examiners are looking for

When you sit an exam, your work is assessed in terms of two aims or 'assessment objectives', each worth approximately half the marks

- Assessment Objective 1 (AO1): Knowledge and Understanding
- Assessment Objective 2 (AO2): Interpretation, Application, Analysis and Evaluation

Knowledge and Understanding means you need to know and understand some of the main ideas and methods sociologists use, and what they have discovered as a result of their studies.

Interpretation involves selecting information that is appropriate to the question. This can come from your own knowledge and from the stimulus items in the exam paper.

Application involves linking ideas, theories and studies to the question, clearly showing their relevance to what you have been asked about.

Analysis involves explaining things in detail, showing how ideas fit together, comparing and contrasting, organising answers logically and drawing conclusions.

Evaluation involves judging something, such as the advantages and disadvantages of different research methods, or the arguments for and against a sociologist's views.

For further details of the exams and assessment objectives, see chapter 5.

Developing your knowledge and skills

Developing your knowledge and understanding of sociology and your skills of interpretation, application, analysis and evaluation is a gradual process and something you will need to work at throughout your AS course. There is no quick fix. However, here are some pointers that will help you:

- **Keep up with your course:** attend regularly, do the work your teacher sets you, pay attention to the feedback you receive, keep your folder well organised.
- **Work with others:** join in class discussions, form study groups with classmates, discuss sociology topics outside class, revise together, talk to friends who have already done AS sociology.
- **When you don't understand, ask** your teacher or classmates, or look it up. Don't be shy – you're probably not the only one who doesn't get it.
- **Use your textbook:** it contains thorough coverage of the topics you're studying and detailed guidance on exam success.
- **Apply what you learn:** sociology is about the real world, and you'll find lots of examples of sociological ideas all around you – in the news, on the street, at home, in school or college. Use examples in your writing. This will help you with the skills of Interpretation and Application.
- **Be critical:** when you come across new information, don't take it at face value. Look for the strengths and weaknesses of ideas; ask what evidence there is for someone's argument. This will help you develop the skill of Evaluation.
- **Take ideas apart** to see how they 'tick'. Try to make comparisons and contrasts between the different ideas, theories and methods you study. This will help you develop the skill of Analysis.
- **Answer the question:** when doing written work, keep focused on what you've actually been asked. Make a plan, and keep checking back to it and the question. Make it clear why you're including the material.

1 Analysis: Using information from the section on 'Consensus or conflict?' (page 8), state one similarity and one difference between Marxists and feminists.

2 Evaluation: Using information from the section on 'Diversity and identity' (page 8), state one criticism of the postmodernist view.

Tour of the book's features

Before starting to use the book, we invite you to come on a quick tour to show you some of the book's features and help you get the most out of it.

A growing gender gap in educational achievement.

Topic 4 Gender differences in education

Along with social class and ethnicity, gender has a major impact on people's experience of education. In recent years, there have been some important changes in this area. In particular, while both sexes have raised their level of achievement, girls have now overtaken boys.

On the other hand, one area where gender patterns have been slower to change is in subject choice, with boys and girls often opting to study traditional 'sex-typed' subjects and courses. Similarly, there is also evidence that schooling continues to reinforce differences in gender identity between boys and girls.

The main questions that interest sociologists in the study of gender differences in education are:

■ Why do girls now generally achieve better results than boys?
■ Why do girls and boys opt to study different subjects?
■ How does schooling help to reinforce gender identities?

This Topic examines some of the answers that sociologists have given to these questions.

Learning objectives

After studying this Topic, you should:

■ Be able to describe the patterns of gender differences in educational achievement.
■ Understand and be able to evaluate the explanations for these differences.
■ Understand and be able to evaluate the explanations for gender differences in subject choice.
■ Understand the effect of school experiences in shaping gender identities.

Topics

Each chapter is divided into manageable sized topics, each covering a separate issue in sociology.

The AQA Specification

The specification is the syllabus produced by the exam board, telling you what you have to study. The AQA specification for Families and Households requires you to examine the following:

■ The relationship of the family to the social structure and social change, with particular reference to the economy and to state policies.
■ Changing patterns of marriage, cohabitation, separation, divorce and childbearing and the life-course, and the diversity of contemporary family and household structures.
■ The nature and extent of changes within the family, with reference to gender roles, domestic labour and power relationships.
■ The nature of childhood, and changes in the status of children in the family and society.
■ Demographic trends in the UK since 1900; reasons for changes in birth rates, death rates and family size.

For full details of the specification, visit www.aqa.org.uk

The AQA Specification

At the start of each chapter, this tells you what you are required to study for the exam.

Activity

Go to the website of the British Sociological Association and follow the link to their Statement of Ethical Practice. In that statement, find examples of circumstances where it is acceptable to ignore any of the ethical principles listed above.

www.britsoc.co.uk

Activity

These develop your knowledge, understanding and skills by giving you a task to carry out, either on your own or with classmates. Some involve research outside class, carrying out small surveys or searching the library and the Internet, including the book's own dedicated website.

Learning objectives

After studying this topic, you should:

■ Know what the main types of data are and what research methods sociologists use.
■ Understand the practical, ethical and theoretical factors influencing choice of method and topic, and be able to assess their relative importance.
■ Understand the difference between positivist and interpretivist approaches to research.

Learning objectives

These spell out what you are going to learn in each topic.

Explain briefly Keddie's arguments that:

1 'a child cannot be deprived of its own culture'.
2 cultural deprivation theory 'blames the victims'.
3 it is the education system that is at fault.

Question panels

In each topic there are short questions on what you are reading about for you to answer on your own or with others. They are very similar to the short questions in the exam.

Boxes

These contain extra information, such as examples, details of important sociological ideas or studies, or relevant policies and laws. Some have questions to get you thinking further.

QuickCheck Questions

These test-yourself questions come at the end of each topic to test your understanding of what you have read and reinforce your knowledge of key ideas. You can check your answers on our website.

QuickCheck Questions

1 According to Parsons, which role do men perform – the instrumental or the expressive?

2 Complete the sentence: Symmetrical families involve .... conjugal roles.

3 Gershuny believes that men are more likely to do domestic labour if their wives are: (a) working full-time (b) working part-time (c) not working.

4 Give two examples of the commercialisation of housework.

5 Explain what is meant by 'gender scripts'.

6 Name one sociologist whose findings indicate that family resources are not shared equally.

 Check your answers at www.sociology.uk.net

Summary

Sociologists disagree as to whether couples are becoming more equal. **Functionalists** and the **New Right** argue for the necessity of **segregated conjugal roles** based on biological differences between the sexes. However, 'march of progress' sociologists argue that the family is becoming more **symmetrical**, with joint conjugal roles. **Feminists** disagree, arguing that men's contribution remains minimal and women now shoulder a **dual burden** of paid and unpaid work, or even perform a **triple shift** that also includes emotion work.

Couples remain unequal in terms of **decision making** and **control of resources**. Men earn more and are more likely to take the major decisions, even where incomes are pooled. **Radical feminists** argue that **domestic violence** is an extreme form of **patriarchal power** over women. However, though most victims are female, not all women are equally at risk.

Summary

Each topic ends with a summary that picks out the most important points. This at-a-glance overview will help you consolidate what you have learned and revise for the exam.

Examining experiments

(a) Explain what is meant by a 'control group'. (2 marks)

(b) Explain the difference between the dependent variable and the independent variable in an experiment. (4 marks)

(c) Suggest **two** criticisms of field experiments. (4 marks)

(d) Examine the reasons why some sociologists choose not to use experiments when conducting research. (20 marks)

The examiner's advice

Every exam question has its own examiner's advice panel to guide you and help you plan your answers.

Exam questions

At the end of every topic there is a practice question based on those you'll find on the exam papers. At the end of the chapter, there is a full exam question for you to try, plus a mock exam for both units.

The examiner's advice

Part (d) is an 'Examine' question of the type you will see in the exam. It carries 12 AO1 marks (knowledge and understanding) and 8 AO2 marks (interpretation, application, analysis and evaluation).

Focus mainly on *laboratory* experiments, but remember to discuss *field* experiments and the *comparative method* too.

Most of the AO1 marks are for knowledge of practical, theoretical and ethical *limitations*. With *laboratory* experiments, practical problems include controlling all the possible variables, studying the past or large-scale social phenomena. Theoretical problems include representativeness, validity, artificiality and the Hawthorne Effect. You should relate these points to the positivist-interpretivist debate (see Box 22). Ethical limitations include deceiving and potentially harming participants. For *field* experiments, the main limitations are deception and reduced control over variables. The *comparative method* also cannot control variables.

You can gain AO2 marks by referring briefly to the *strengths* of experiments by linking a strength to each limitation in turn (rather than listing all the strengths at the end). For example, an ethical problem is that experimenters may have to deceive participants, but in so doing they may overcome the Hawthorne Effect.

METHODS IN CONTEXT

The Sociological Methods chapter has special *Methods in Context* sections that show you how each method can be used to study topics in Education.

Methods Link: group interviews

Willis carried out unstructured group interviews to uncover the counter-school culture of the 'lads'. These interviews allowed the lads to talk freely in their own words about the way they viewed school, teachers and work. The interviews gave Willis an insight into their world.

However, critics argue that unstructured group interviews are an unreliable method – they cannot be repeated in exactly the same way with other groups. Also, the meaning of what is said in a group interview is so open to the researcher's own biased interpretation that the results may be of little value.

Read more about using interviews to research education in **Methods in Context** on pages 202-5.

SPECIAL *METHODS IN CONTEXT* FEATURES

- A big feature of the AS exam is the compulsory Methods in Context question, where you have to apply a given research method to a topic in Education. This book has a series of unique features devoted to preparing you to tackle this question successfully.
- Each *Methods in Context* section has its own practice question just like those in the exam.
- All practice questions have the examiner's advice to guide you.
- The Education chapter has *Methods Links* boxes throughout that deal with the way sociologists apply different research methods to educational topics.

ADDITIONAL FEATURES

Key concepts – a list of essential terms you need to be familiar with, defined briefly and clearly, often with links to other concepts to help you develop your understanding. Use it as a quick reference section to check the meaning of key terms. Also good when revising for the exam!

Preparing for the exam – Chapter 5 tells you what the examiners are looking for. It gives detailed advice on exam technique and how to tackle questions effectively.

Mock exam papers for you to try – plus students' answers and the Examiner's marks and advice on how to score top marks.

 www.sociology.uk.net This book has its own dedicated website where you can find additional activities, questions, answers and examiner's advice – plus lots more to help you succeed.

Examining methods in context

Researching labelling in schools

Interactionist sociologists such as Becker claim that teachers label different groups of pupils and treat them unequally. This affects pupils' self-esteem and educational achievement.

Teachers are required to treat pupils fairly and so are unlikely to admit that they label them. If teachers are aware that they are being studied, they may avoid saying or doing anything that could be taken as 'labelling'.

Whether or not a particular action by a teacher is part of a labelling process is open to interpretation. For example, one researcher might see telling off a pupil as 'labelling', while another might view it as 'justifiable classroom discipline'.

Researchers not only want to know whether labelling occurs. They also want to measure its effect on pupils' self-esteem and achievement.

Question

Using material from **Item A** and elsewhere, assess the strengths and limitations of experiments for the study of labelling in schools. (20 marks)

The examiner's advice

This question requires you to apply your knowledge and understanding of different types of experiments – laboratory, field **and** the comparative method – to the study of the **particular** issue of labelling in schools. It is not enough simply to discuss experiments in general.

For example, Item A suggests teachers are unlikely to admit that they label pupils and are likely to change their behaviour when researched. Covert field experiments overcome this 'Hawthorne Effect' because teachers and pupils, unaware of the research purpose, will act normally.

However, covert experiments mean that informed consent cannot be obtained and participants have no opportunity to withdraw from the research. Other ethical problems of experiments include risk of harm to vulnerable young people.

You should consider how useful laboratory experiments are in studying labelling in school. How likely are teachers and pupils to act as they normally would in class? Schools are large institutions – can their scale and complexity be reproduced in a laboratory?

You need to keep a reasonable balance between the strengths and limitations of different types of experiments. You can also refer to studies that have used this method (e.g. Rosenthal and Jacobson) and to any relevant research you have been involved in.

Families and Households
CHAPTER 2

What is a family? What is a household?

A household is a person living alone or a group of people living together (e.g. sharing meals, bills, housework etc). This group may or may not be related to one another.

Defining the family is harder. One definition is that it involves monogamous marriage between a man and a woman, plus their child(ren), all sharing the same residence. This *nuclear* family is often held up as the ideal. However, this definition rules out groups that many would see as families, such as unmarried cohabiting couples.

At the other extreme is the idea that any set of arrangements that those involved see as a family, *is* a family. This has the advantage of not requiring us to make judgements about other people's lifestyles: if you define your own personal set-up as a family, sociologists have no right to disagree.

However, some would see this approach as too broad, since literally any group can count as a family – so it may include households that some would not see as 'proper' families. For example, some regard gay relationships in this way.

Key questions about the family

In this chapter, we shall be examining some of the different aspects of family life that sociologists are interested in. These include:

- Are husbands and wives today equal?
- How far has the position of children and our attitudes towards childhood changed?
- Changes in the size of families, birth and death rates, and in the population as a whole.
- Changes in marriage, cohabitation, divorce and parenthood, and the increasing diversity of family types today.
- The impact on families of government policies and laws.

The AQA Specification

The specification is the syllabus produced by the exam board, telling you what you have to study. The AQA specification for Families and Households requires you to examine the following:

- The relationship of the family to the social structure and social change, with particular reference to the economy and to state policies.
- Changing patterns of marriage, cohabitation, separation, divorce and childbearing and the life-course, and the diversity of contemporary family and household structures.
- The nature and extent of changes within the family, with reference to gender roles, domestic labour and power relationships.
- The nature of childhood, and changes in the status of children in the family and society.
- Demographic trends in the UK since 1900; reasons for changes in birth rates, death rates and family size.

For full details of the specification, visit: www.aqa.org.uk

Topic 1 Couples

In the 19th century, the Victorian family was very patriarchal – that is, the man was in every sense the head of the household. For example, on marrying, a woman's property became her husband's. Similarly, grounds for divorce were very unequal – a man could gain a divorce on the grounds of his wife's adultery, but a woman had to prove her husband's cruelty or another 'matrimonial offence' in addition to adultery

This Topic is about married and cohabiting couples. It looks at equality and inequality in families and households. Sociologists are interested in how far couples have a more equal relationship today. Some of the key questions they ask about couples are:

- Do men and women share housework and childcare equally?
- Do men and women have an equal say in family decisions and do they get equal shares of the household's income?
- Why does domestic violence occur and who commits it?

Learning objectives

When you have studied this Topic, you should:

- Know about gender roles in the domestic division of labour.
- Know about power relationships between couples, including decision-making, control of resources and domestic violence.
- Be able to analyse how far these roles and relationships have changed over time.
- Be able to evaluate different sociological views on couples' roles and relationships.

The domestic division of labour

The domestic division of labour refers to the roles that men and women play in relation to housework, childcare and paid work. Sociologists are interested in whether men and women share domestic tasks equally.

Parsons: instrumental and expressive roles

In the traditional nuclear family, the roles of husbands and wives are segregated – separate and distinct from one another. In Talcott Parsons' (1955) functionalist model of the family, for example, there is a clear division of labour between spouses:

- The husband has an instrumental role, geared towards achieving success at work so that he can provide for the family financially. He is the breadwinner.
- The wife has an expressive role, geared towards primary socialisation of the children and meeting the family's emotional needs. She is the homemaker, a full-time housewife rather than a wage earner.

Parsons argues that this division of labour is based on biological differences, with women 'naturally' suited to the nurturing role and men to that of provider. He claims that this division of labour is beneficial to both men and women, to their children and to wider society. Some conservative thinkers and politicians, known as the New Right, also hold this view.

However, other sociologists have criticised Parsons:

- Michael Young and Peter Willmott (1962) argue that men are now taking a greater share of domestic tasks and more wives are becoming wage earners.
- Feminist sociologists reject Parsons' view that the division of labour is natural. They argue that it only benefits men.

Joint and segregated conjugal roles

Elizabeth Bott (1957) distinguishes between two types of conjugal roles; that is, roles within marriage:

- **Segregated conjugal roles**, where the couple have separate roles: a male breadwinner and a female homemaker/carer, as in Parsons' instrumental and expressive roles. Their leisure activities also tend to be separate.
- **Joint conjugal roles**, where the couple share tasks such as housework and childcare and spend their leisure time together.

Young and Willmott identify a pattern of segregated conjugal roles in their study of traditional working-class extended families in Bethnal Green, east London, in the 1950s. Men were the breadwinners, most often working in the docks. They played little part in home life and spent their leisure time with workmates in pubs and working men's clubs. Women were full-time housewives with sole responsibility for housework and childcare, helped by their female relatives. The limited leisure that women had was also spent with female kin.

The symmetrical family

Young and Willmott (1973) take a 'march of progress' view of the history of the family. They see family life as gradually improving for all its members, becoming more equal and democratic. They argue that there has been a long-term trend away from segregated conjugal roles and towards joint conjugal roles and the 'symmetrical family'.

By the symmetrical family they mean one in which the roles of husbands and wives, although not identical, are now much more similar:

- Women now go out to work, although this may be part-time rather than full-time.
- Men now help with housework and childcare.
- Couples now spend their leisure time together instead of separately with workmates or female relatives. They are more home-centred or 'privatised'.

In their study of families in London, Young and Willmott found that the symmetrical family was more common among younger couples, those who are geographically and socially isolated, and the more affluent (better off). For example, the young couples who had moved away from Bethnal Green and were living at a distance from the extended family and workmates were more likely to have a symmetrical relationship. Young and Wilmott see the rise of the symmetrical nuclear family as the result of major social changes that have taken place during the past century:

- **Changes in women's position**, including married women going out to work
- **Geographical mobility** – more couples living away from the communities in which they grew up
- **New technology** and labour-saving devices
- **Higher standards of living.**

Many of these factors are inter-linked. For example, married women bringing a second wage into the home raises the family's standard of living. This enables the couple to make the home more attractive, and therefore encourages men to spend time at home rather than in the pub with their workmates. It also means the couple can afford more labour-saving devices. This makes housework easier and encourages men to do more.

> Explain how geographical mobility might help to give rise to symmetrical families.

A feminist view of housework

Feminist sociologists reject this 'march of progress' view. They argue that little has changed: men and women remain unequal within the family and women still do most of the housework. They see this inequality as stemming from the fact that the family and society are male-dominated or patriarchal. Women occupy a subordinate and dependent role within the family and in wider society.

The feminist Ann Oakley (1974) criticises Young and Willmott's view that the family is now symmetrical. She argues that their claims are exaggerated. Although Young and Willmott found that most of the husbands they interviewed 'helped' their wives at least once a week, this could include simply taking the children for a walk or making breakfast on one occasion. For Oakley, this is hardly convincing evidence of symmetry.

In her own research on housewives, Oakley found some evidence of husbands helping in the home but no evidence of a trend towards symmetry. Only 15% of husbands had a high level of participation in housework, and only 25% had a high level of participation in childcare.

Husbands were more likely to share in childcare than in housework, but only in its more pleasurable aspects. Most couples defined the father's role as one of 'taking an interest'. A good father was one who would play with the children in the evenings and at weekends and 'take them off her hands' on Sunday morning. However, this could mean that mothers lost the rewards of childcare, such as playing with the children, and were simply left with more time for housework.

Later research supports Oakley's findings. Mary Boulton (1983) found that fewer than 20% of husbands had a major role in childcare. She argues that Young and Willmott exaggerate men's contribution by looking at the tasks involved in childcare rather than the responsibilities. A father might help with specific tasks, but it was almost always the mother who was responsible for the child's security and well-being.

Similarly, research conducted in Manchester by Alan Warde and Kevin Hetherington (1993) shows that sex-typing of domestic tasks remains strong. For example, wives were

30 times more likely to have been the last person to have done the washing, while husbands were four times more likely to have been the last person to wash the car.

In general, Warde and Hetherington found that men would only carry out routine 'female' tasks when their partners were not around to do them. Nevertheless, they did find evidence of a slight change of attitude among younger men. They no longer assumed that women should do the housework, and were more likely to think they were doing less than their fair share.

This generational change is partially supported by other research. For example, Future Foundation's (2000) study of 1,000 adults found that 60% of men claimed to do *more* housework than their father, while 75% of women claimed to do *less* housework than their mother.

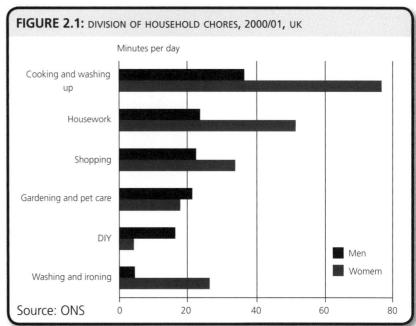

FIGURE 2.1: DIVISION OF HOUSEHOLD CHORES, 2000/01, UK

Minutes per day

Source: ONS

However, women still do more housework than men and, as Figure 2.1 shows, there are also still gender differences in the amounts of time spent on particular household chores. According to the Office for National Statistics, on average women spend over two and a half hours per day on housework, cooking, washing up, cleaning and ironing, compared with men's one hour a day.

In general, car maintenance and DIY are the only chores that men spend more time on. Men have an extra half hour's free time per day compared with women. Although some studies have found a narrowing of the gender gap in terms of time spent on housework in recent decades, overall it is clear that women still do more domestic labour than men.

Oakley: the rise of the housewife role

Rather than seeing a march of progress towards symmetry since the 19th century as Young and Willmott do, Oakley describes how the housewife role has become the dominant role for married women.

Industrialisation and the rise of factory production in the 19th century led to the separation of paid work from the home. Although women had initially been part of the industrial labour force, they were gradually excluded from the workplace and confined to the home with sole responsibility for housework and childcare, while men became the sole breadwinners.

This enforced women's subordination and economic dependence on men. In this way, the housewife role was socially constructed, rather than being women's 'natural' role, as Parsons claims.

In Oakley's view, even though the 20th century saw an increase in the number of married women working, the housewife role is still women's primary role. Also, women who work are concentrated in low-paid jobs that are often an extension of the housewife role, such as nursing, secretarial work or childcare.

Activity

Many studies have attempted to measure the extent of symmetry in relationships.

1 In groups of four, devise a set of questions that you will use to ask a sample of couples about their relationship. You will need to include questions about women working, the contribution of each partner to housework and childcare, and joint and separate leisure activities.

2 Each member of the group should interview at least two couples.

3 When you have completed the interviews, get back together in your group to discuss the results. Did the answers vary a great deal? If so, why? What factors seem to be important in influencing how symmetrical the relationship is?

The impact of paid work

Most of the women in Oakley's study in the 1970s were full-time housewives, but many more households now have a second income from the wife's full- or part-time work. Today, three-quarters of married or cohabiting women in the UK are economically active, as against fewer than half in 1971.

Sociologists are interested in whether this trend towards both partners working is leading to a more equal division of domestic tasks, with a 'new man' doing his fair share of the housework and childcare: or whether it simply means that women now have to carry a 'dual burden' of paid work as well as domestic work.

For example, Man-Yee Kan (2001) found income from employment, age and education affected how much housework women did: better-paid, younger, better-educated women did less housework. For example, every £10,000 increase in the woman's annual income reduces her weekly housework time by two hours.

Gershuny: the trend towards equality

Some sociologists argue that women working full-time is leading to a more equal division of labour in the home.

Jonathan Gershuny (1994) found that wives who worked full-time did less domestic work:

- Wives who did not go to work did 83% of the housework and even wives who worked part-time still did 82%.
- Wives who worked full-time did 73% of the housework. The longer the wife had been in paid work, the more housework her husband was likely to do.
- Couples whose parents had a more equal relationship were likely to share housework more equally themselves.

Why might men's higher earnings mean they are able to do less housework than women?

Gershuny explains this trend towards greater equality in terms of a gradual change in values and parental role models. He argues that social values are gradually adapting to the fact that women are now working full-time. However, he found that even though men are now doing more housework, they still tend to take responsibility for different tasks, as Figure 2.1 shows.

Similarly, Oriel Sullivan's (2000) analysis of nationally representative data collected in 1975, 1987 and 1997 found a trend towards greater equality as men did more domestic labour. In particular, there was an increase in the numbers of couples with an equal division of labour and men were participating more in traditional 'women's' tasks.

The views of Sullivan and Gershuny are optimistic ones, similar to Young and Willmott's 'march of progress' view that conjugal roles are becoming more symmetrical.

Rosemary Crompton (1997) accepts Gershuny's evidence. However, she explains it differently, in terms of economic factors rather than changing values or role models. As women's earning power increases relative to men's, so men do more in the home.

However, earnings remain unequal. On average, women's earnings are only about three-quarters those of men. Crompton therefore concludes that as long as earnings remain unequal, so too will the division of labour at home.

▲ Literally, 'ready to eat'. Fast food is a major aspect of the commercialisation of housework.

The commercialisation of housework

Another approach that emphasises economic factors is that of Hilary Silver (1987) and Juliet Schor (1993). They stress the importance of two major economic developments in reducing the burden of housework on women:

- **Housework has become 'commercialised'**. Goods and services that housewives previously had to produce themselves are now mass-produced and supplied by supermarkets, fast food outlets and so on. Freezers, microwave ovens, 'ready meals' etc all reduce the amount of domestic labour that needs to be done.
- **Women working** means that they can afford to buy these goods and services.

As a result, Silver and Schor argue, the burden of housework on women has decreased. Schor even goes so far as to claim that these developments have led to 'the death of the housewife role'.

However, critics argue that for many poorer women, buying in expensive goods and services is not an option. Also, even if commercialisation has reduced the amount of housework to be done, this does not prove that couples are sharing the remaining chores equally.

1 What is meant by the 'commmercialisation of housework'?

2 Make a list of all the services you can think of that families can buy in instead of providing themselves.

3 Why is the disappearance of housework more likely to be a middle-class phenomenon?

The dual burden

Many feminists argue that, despite women working, there is little evidence of a 'new man' who does an equal share of domestic work. They argue that women have simply acquired a dual burden of paid work and unpaid housework. In the view of feminists, the family remains patriarchal: men benefit both from women's earnings and from their domestic labour.

Elsa Ferri and Kate Smith (1996) provide evidence of the dual burden. They found that increased employment of women outside the home has had little impact on the domestic division of labour. Based on a sample of 1,589 33-year-old fathers and mothers, they found that the father took the main responsibility for childcare in fewer than 4% of families.

Even where a woman works and her husband is unemployed, there is little evidence of husbands doing more at home. Lydia Morris (1990) found that men who had suffered a loss of their masculine role as a result of becoming unemployed saw domestic work as women's work and therefore to be avoided. However, Xavier Ramos (2003) found that in families where the man is not in paid work and his partner works full-time, male domestic labour matches that of his partner (19 hours per week).

For many women, access to full-day childcare is essential. However, as Sara Arber and Jay Ginn (1995) point out, middle-class women may be able to afford this, but many working-class women cannot. As a result, they remain trapped in a vicious circle of childcare responsibilities and low-paid, part-time employment.

These class differences between women are well illustrated by Nicky Gregson and Michelle Lowe's (1994) study of the employment of domestic 'help' by dual-earner middle-class families. These couples found it more economical to employ working-class women as nannies and cleaners than for the wife to stay at home doing the housework. Unlike the middle class, of course, most working-class women cannot afford to employ someone to do their housework for them and so have to carry a dual burden of paid and unpaid domestic work.

Emotion work

'Emotion work' describes work whose main feature is the management of one's own and other people's emotions. Arlie Hochschild (1983) originally used the concept to describe jobs such as airline stewardesses. She notes that women are more likely than men to be performing jobs involving emotional labour.

Other sociologists have applied this idea to the family. David Morgan (1997) illustrates this with the example of caring for a sick child. This involves:

'physical care and monitoring, handling the fears and frustrations experienced by the sick child, handling the adjustments required on behalf of other members of the family who may be resentful of the attention being accorded to the sick child, and drawing upon one's own emotional resources and exercising emotional control while doing all of this.'

Emotion work is usually seen as a 'labour of love' because it involves caring for other family members. Nevertheless, it *is* work, and work done mainly by women. Jean Duncombe and Dennis Marsden (1995) argue that women are expected not only to do a double shift of both housework and paid work, but also to work a triple shift that includes emotion work.

> Suggest four situations in which women might carry out emotion work within their families.

Lesbian couples and gender scripts

Why has there been so little change in the division of labour, despite the increase in the number of women working? Gillian Dunne (1999) argues that the division of labour continues because of deeply ingrained 'gender scripts'. These are expectations or norms that set out the different gender roles men and women in heterosexual couples are expected to play.

Dunne contrasts this with the situation among lesbian couples, where gender scripts do not operate to the same extent. In her study of 37 cohabiting lesbian couples with dependent children, Dunne found evidence of symmetry in their relationships. Compared with heterosexual women, lesbians are more likely to:

- Describe their relationship as equal and share housework and childcare equally.
- Give equal importance to both partners' careers.
- View childcare positively.

Dunne argues that this is because lesbian and heterosexual partners interact in different ways. Heterosexuals are under pressure to conform to masculine or feminine 'gender scripts' by performing different kinds of domestic tasks that confirm their gender identities.

In lesbian relationships, however, household tasks are not linked to particular gender scripts. This allows lesbian couples to create a more equal relationship. For example, as one of the women in Dunne's study commented, in heterosexual relationships there is always a subconscious belief that women are supposed to do the housework.

This supports the radical feminist view that relationships between men and women are inevitably patriarchal and that women can only achieve equality in a same-sex relationship.

Similarly, Jeffrey Weeks (1999) argues that same-sex relationships offer greater possibilities of equality because the division of labour is open to negotiation and agreement, and not based on patriarchal tradition.

However, Dunne found that where one partner did much more paid work than the other, the time that each partner spent on domestic work was likely to be unequal. This suggests that paid work exerts an important influence on the division of labour even in same-sex relationships.

Summary

- There is some evidence that a woman being in paid work leads to more equality in the division of labour, though probably only if she is in full-time work.
- Many feminists argue that, in reality, the effect of this is limited: women still continue to shoulder a dual or triple burden. And even if men are doing more in the home, domestic tasks themselves remain gendered.
- Feminists argue that the root of the problem is patriarchy. Patriarchal gender scripts shape society's expectations about the domestic roles that men and women ought to perform. Patriarchy also ensures that women earn less at work and so have less bargaining power in the home. Until patriarchy is successfully challenged in the home and in the workplace, therefore, the domestic division of labour is likely to remain unequal.

Resources and decision-making in households

As we have seen, there is inequality in who does what in the home. There is also inequality in who gets what – in how the family's resources are shared out between men and women. This is linked to who controls the family's income and who has the power to make decisions about how it is spent.

Michelle Barrett and Mary McIntosh (1991) note that:

- Men gain far more from women's domestic work than they give back in financial support.
- The financial support that husbands give to their wives is often unpredictable and comes with 'strings' attached.
- Men usually make the decisions about spending on important items.

Research shows that family members do not share resources such as money and food equally. For example, Elaine Kempson (1994) found that among low-income families, women denied their own needs, seldom going out, and eating smaller portions of food or skipping meals altogether in order to make ends meet.

Similarly, in Hilary Graham's (1984) study, over half the women who were living on benefits after separating from their husbands said that they and their children were actually better off. Although their husbands' earnings had not necessarily been low, they found that benefits were a more reliable source of income.

In many households, a woman has no entitlement to a share of household resources in her own right. As a result, she is likely to see anything she spends on herself as money that ought to be spent on essentials for the children. Even in households with apparently adequate incomes, resources may be shared unequally, leaving women in poverty.

Decision-making and paid work

One reason why men often take a greater share of the family's resources is because they usually contribute more money, due to their higher earnings. The feminist sociologists Jan Pahl and Carolyn Vogler (1993) focus on how each partner's contribution to family income affects decision-making within the family. They identify two main types of control over family income:

- **Pooling** – where both partners have access to income and joint responsibility for expenditure; for example, a joint bank account
- **Allowance system** – where men give their wives an allowance out of which they have to budget to meet the family's needs, with the man retaining any surplus income for himself.

Pooling is on the increase. Comparing a sample of 1,211 couples with their parents, Vogler (1994) found a large increase in pooling (from 19% to 50%), and a sharp decline in the housekeeping allowance system (from 36% to 12%).

Pahl and Vogler found that pooling was more common among couples where both partners work full-time. However, they found that even here, the men usually made the major financial decisions.

This is supported by Irene Hardill's (1997) research. In her study of 30 dual-career professional couples, she found that the important decisions were usually taken either by the man alone or jointly and that his career normally took priority when deciding whether to move house for a new job. This supports Janet Finch's (1983) observation that women's lives tend to be structured around their husbands' careers.

Similarly, Stephen Edgell's (1980) study of professional couples found that:

- **Very important decisions** – such as those involving finance, a change of job or moving house – were either taken by the husband alone or taken jointly but with the husband having the final say.
- **Important decisions** – such as those about children's education or where to go on holiday – were usually taken jointly, and seldom by the wife alone.
- **Less important decisions** – such as the choice of home decor, children's clothes or food purchases – were usually made by the wife.

Like Pahl and Vogler, Edgell argues that the reason men are likely to take the decisions is that they earn more. Women usually earn less than their husbands, and being dependent on them economically, have less say in decision-making.

However, other feminists argue that inequalities in decision-making are not simply the result of inequalities in earnings. They argue that in patriarchal society, the cultural definition of men as decision-makers is deeply ingrained in both men and women and instilled through gender role socialisation. Until this definition is challenged, decision-making is likely to remain unequal.

---

1 How might employment outside the home affect power over the family's resources?

2 Why do you think 'pooling' is more likely to be found among younger couples than among their parents?

3 Pahl interviewed couples both together and separately. This was rather expensive to do, so why do you think she felt it was necessary?

Domestic violence

The Women's Aid Federation (2008) defines domestic violence as:

'physical, psychological, sexual or financial violence that takes place within an intimate or family-type relationship and forms a pattern of coercive and controlling behaviour. It may involve partners, ex-partners, household members or other relatives.'

A common view of domestic violence is that it is the behaviour of a few disturbed or 'sick' individuals, and that its causes are psychological rather than social. However, sociologists have challenged this view:

- Domestic violence is far too widespread to be simply the work of a few disturbed individuals. According to the British Crime Survey (2007), domestic violence accounts for almost a sixth of all violent crime. Catriona Mirrlees-Black's (1999) survey of 16,000 people estimates that there are 6.6 million domestic assaults a year, about half involving physical injury.

- Domestic violence does not occur randomly but follows particular social patterns and these patterns have social causes. The most striking of these patterns is that it is mainly violence by men against women. For example, Kathryn Coleman et al (2007) found that women were

more likely than men to have experienced 'intimate violence' across all four types of abuse – partner abuse, family abuse, sexual assault and stalking.

Similarly, Mirrlees-Black found that:

- most victims are women
- 99% of all incidents against women are committed by men
- nearly one in four women has been assaulted by a partner at some time in her life, and one in eight repeatedly so.

This is confirmed by Russell and Rebecca Dobash's (1979) research in Scotland, based on police and court records and interviews with women in women's refuges. They cite examples of wives being slapped, pushed about, beaten, raped or killed by their husbands. Dobash and Dobash found that violent incidents could be set off by what a husband saw as a challenge to his authority such as his wife asking why he was late home for a meal. They argue that marriage legitimates violence against women by conferring power and authority on husbands and dependency on wives.

Official statistics

Official statistics on domestic violence understate the true extent of the problem for two main reasons. Firstly, victims may be unwilling to report it to the police. Stephanie Yearnshire (1997) found that on average a woman suffers 35 assaults before making a report. Domestic violence is the violent crime least likely to be reported.

Secondly, police and prosecutors may be reluctant to record, investigate or prosecute those cases that are reported to them. According to David Cheal (1991), this reluctance is due to the fact that police and other state agencies are not prepared to become involved in the family. They make three assumptions about family life:

- that the family is a private sphere, so access to it by state agencies should be limited
- that the family is a good thing and so agencies tend to neglect the 'darker side' of family life
- that individuals are free agents, so it is assumed that if a woman is experiencing abuse she is free to leave. However, this is not true. Male violence is often coupled with male economic power: abused women are often financially dependent on their husbands and unable to leave.

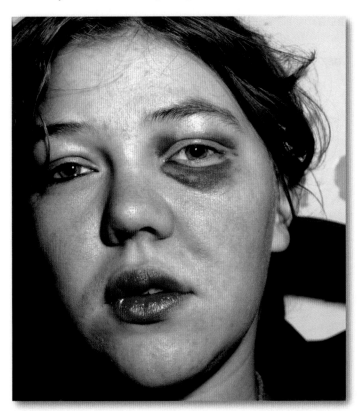

▲ *Nearly one in four women has been assaulted by a partner.*

Activity **The problems of studying domestic violence**

Go to www.sociology.uk.net

The radical feminist explanation

Radical feminists interpret findings such as those of Dobash and Dobash as evidence of patriarchy. For example, Kate Millett (1970) and Shulamith Firestone (1970) argue that all societies have been founded on patriarchy. They see the key division in society as that between men and women. Men are the enemy: they are the oppressors and exploiters of women.

Radical feminists see the family and marriage as the key institutions in patriarchal society and the main source of women's oppression. Within the family, men dominate women through domestic violence or the threat of it.

For radical feminists, widespread domestic violence is an inevitable feature of patriarchal society and serves to preserve the power that all men have over all women. Furthermore, in their view, male domination of state institutions helps to explain the reluctance of the police and courts to deal effectively with cases of domestic violence. (For more details of the radical feminist perspective, see Topic 3, page 43.)

Radical feminists help to explain why most domestic violence is committed by men. They argue that violence against women is part of a patriarchal system that maintains men's power. They give a sociological, rather than a psychological, explanation by linking patterns of domestic violence to dominant social norms about marriage.

However, Faith Robertson Elliot (1996) rejects the radical feminist claim that all men benefit from violence against women. Not all men are aggressive and most are opposed to domestic violence. Radical feminists ignore this.

Radical feminists also fail to explain female violence, including child abuse by women and violence against male partners. For example, Mirrlees-Black found that about one in seven men has been assaulted, and one in 20 repeatedly so.

Activity

In small groups, answer the following questions, then report back to the whole class and compare your answers with other groups.

1 Dobash and Dobash identified the following as common 'triggers' to domestic violence: jealousy; money; children; drunkenness; arguments over food. Explain why each of these might trigger violence, linking them where possible to ideas about gender roles.

2 Suggest reasons why many battered wives remain with their violent husbands.

3 In what ways apart from physical violence may men be able to dominate their wives?

4 Give examples of ways in which other areas of society, such as the media, education and the law, can be seen as patriarchal.

Other groups at risk

Sociologists have identified other patterns of domestic violence in addition to male violence against women. According to Mirrlees-Black, social groups at greater risk of domestic violence include:

- children and young people
- those in the lowest social classes
- those who live in rented accommodation
- those on low incomes or in financial difficulties
- those with high levels of alcohol consumption and users of illegal drugs. According to the British Crime Survey (2007), the offender was under the influence of alcohol in 39% of cases.

Some of these groups overlap. For example, statistics show that children from lower social classes appear at higher risk of abuse and violence.

Suggest reasons why poorer families are more likely to end up in the child abuse statistics than better-off families.

Wilkinson: domestic violence, inequality and stress

Richard Wilkinson (1996) offers an explanation of these patterns. He sees domestic violence as the result of stress on family members caused by social inequality.

Inequality means that some families have fewer resources than others, such as income and housing. Those on low incomes or living in overcrowded accommodation are likely to experience higher levels of stress. This reduces their chances of maintaining stable, caring relationships and increases the risk of conflict and violence. For example:

- Worries about money, jobs and housing may spill over into domestic conflict as tempers become frayed.
- Lack of money and time restricts people's social circle and reduces social support for those under stress.

The findings of Wilkinson and Mirrlees-Black show that not all people are equally in danger of suffering domestic violence: those with less power, status, wealth or income are often at greatest risk.

Wilkinson's approach is useful in showing how social inequality produces stress and triggers conflict and violence in families. As those in lower social classes face greater hardship and thus stress, this helps to explain the class differences in the statistics on domestic violence.

However, unlike the radical feminist approach, Wilkinson does not explain why women rather than men are the main victims.

For more activities on Couples...

Go to www.sociology.uk.net

Summary

Sociologists disagree as to whether couples are becoming more equal. **Functionalists** and the **New Right** argue for the necessity of **segregated conjugal roles** based on biological differences between the sexes. However, **'march of progress'** sociologists argue that the family is becoming more **symmetrical**, with joint conjugal roles. **Feminists** disagree, arguing that men's contribution remains minimal and women now shoulder a **dual burden** of paid and unpaid work, or even perform a **triple shift** that also includes emotion work.

Couples remain unequal in terms of **decision making** and **control of resources**. Men earn more and are more likely to take the major decisions, even where incomes are pooled. **Radical feminists** argue that **domestic violence** is an extreme form of **patriarchal power** over women. However, though most victims are female, not all women are equally at risk.

QuickCheck Questions

1 According to Parsons, which role do men perform – the instrumental or the expressive?

2 Complete the sentence: Symmetrical families involve .... conjugal roles.

3 Gershuny believes that men are more likely to do domestic labour if their wives are: (a) working full-time (b) working part-time   (c) not working.

4 Give two examples of the commercialisation of housework.

5 Explain what is meant by 'gender scripts'.

6 Name one sociologist whose findings indicate that family resources are not shared equally.

7 What reason does Edgell give for why men have more power to influence family decision-making?

8 Suggest two reasons why domestic violence is not simply the behaviour of a few psychologically disturbed individuals.

9 Identify two other groups apart from women who are at risk of domestic violence.

Check your answers at www.sociology.uk.net

Examining couples

Item A   According to Young and Willmott, there has been a long-term trend towards the symmetrical nuclear family in Britain since around the beginning of the 20th century, with more and more families taking this form. Initially, the symmetrical family was more common among the middle class, but it has now spread to the working class too – a process that Young and Willmott call 'stratified diffusion'.

However, the view that the nuclear family is now symmetrical is widely criticised by feminists and other sociologists. They argue that there is still an unequal gender division of labour in the family that disadvantages women. Not only do women remain responsible for most of the   5 housework and childcare, but increasingly they are now also expected to go out to work as well, meaning that in effect they have to work a double shift. Others go further, arguing that women have to work not a double but a triple shift.

(a) Explain what is meant by the term 'triple shift' (**Item A**, line 7).   (2 marks)

(b) Identify **two** reasons why a 'gender division of labour' continues to exist among many couples (**Item A**, line 5).   (4 marks)

(c) Suggest **three** reasons why the symmetrical family may have become more common over the last century (**Item A**, line 3).   (6 marks)

Essay   Examine the patterns of, and reasons for, domestic violence in society.   (24 marks)

The examiner's advice

The essay carries 14 AO1 marks (knowledge and understanding) and 10 AO2 marks (interpretation, application, analysis and evaluation). The emphasis is on showing a sound, detailed sociological knowledge, but to score high marks you must also demonstrate AO2 skills.

A good start would be a definition of domestic violence. Note that the question asks about patterns and reasons, so make sure you deal with both. For patterns, the main focus needs to be on gender – in terms of both victims and abusers. For reasons why women are more likely to be victims, you can use Dobash and Dobash and radical feminism – and also Ansley's Marxist feminist view (see Topic 3, page 43). Mention other patterns too: social class differences, and also non-partner violence (e.g. against children, elders), using Mirrlees-Black and Wilkinson. These can also be used to evaluate radical feminism (it only explains violence against women). You can also show evaluation by raising problems about the validity of the statistics. Write a conclusion summing up the patterns and reasons.

Topic 2 Childhood

Sociologists are interested in how the status of different family members has changed over time. For example, as we saw in Topic 1, there have been debates about whether couples have become more equal today than they were in the past.

In this Topic, we look at changes in childhood and the position of children in the family and society, as well as the factors responsible for these changes.

We examine three major issues:

- How childhood is socially constructed – that is, how it is created and defined by society.
- Is the position of children better today than it was in the past?
- What is the future of childhood likely to be?

Learning objectives

When you have studied this Topic, you should:

- Understand why sociologists see childhood as a social construction.
- Know the reasons for the emergence of the modern notion of childhood.
- Be able to analyse and evaluate different views of the position of children today.
- Be able to analyse and evaluate different views of the future of childhood.

Childhood as a social construct

Sociologists see childhood as socially constructed; in other words, as something created and defined by society. They argue that what people mean by childhood, and the position that children occupy in society, is not fixed but differs between different times, places and cultures. We can see this by comparing the western idea of childhood today with childhood in the past and in other societies.

The modern western notion of childhood

It is generally accepted in our society today that childhood is a special time of life and that children are fundamentally different from adults. They are regarded as physically and psychologically immature and not yet competent to run their own lives. There is a belief that children's lack of skills, knowledge and experience means that they need a lengthy, protected period of nurturing and socialisation before they are ready for adult society and its responsibilities.

As Jane Pilcher (1995) notes, the most important feature of the modern idea of childhood is separateness. Childhood is seen as a clear and distinct life stage, and children in our society occupy a separate status from adults.

This is emphasised in several ways, for instance through laws regulating what children are allowed, required or forbidden to do. Their difference from adults is also emphasised through differences in dress, especially for younger children, and through products and services specially for children, such as toys, food, books, entertainments, play areas and so on.

Related to the separateness of children's status is the idea of childhood as a 'golden age' of happiness and innocence. However, this innocence means that children are seen as vulnerable and in need of protection from the dangers of the adult world and so they must be kept 'quarantined' and separated from it. As a result, children's lives are lived largely in the sphere of the family and education, where adults provide for them and protect them from the outside world. Similarly, unlike adults, they lead lives of leisure and play and are largely excluded from paid work.

However, this view of childhood as a separate age-status is not found in all societies. It is not universal. As Stephen Wagg (1992) puts it:

'Childhood is socially constructed. It is, in other words, what members of particular societies, at particular times and in particular places, say it is. There is no single universal childhood, experienced by all. So, childhood isn't "natural" and should be distinguished from mere biological immaturity.'

This means that, while all humans go through the same stages of physical development, different cultures construct or define this process differently.

In western cultures today, children are defined as vulnerable and unable to fend for themselves. However, other cultures do not necessarily see such a great difference between children and adults. We can see this by looking at examples both from other cultures today and from European societies of the past.

> 1 Explain in your own words the meaning of the statement that childhood is a 'social construct'.
>
> 2 Suggest three examples of ways in which childhood today 'is seen as a clear and distinct life stage'.

Cross-cultural differences in childhood

A good way to illustrate the social construction of childhood is to take a comparative approach – that is, to look at how children are seen and treated in other times and places than our own. The anthropologist Ruth Benedict (1934) argues that children in simpler, non-industrial societies are generally treated differently from their modern western counterparts in three ways:

- They take responsibility at an early age. For example, Samantha Punch's (2001) study of childhood in rural Bolivia found that, once children are about five years old, they are expected to take work responsibilities in the home and in the community. Tasks are taken on without question or hesitation.
  Similarly, Lowell Holmes' (1974) study of a Samoan village found that 'too young' was never given as a reason for not permitting a child to undertake a particular task: 'Whether it be the handling of dangerous tools or the carrying of extremely heavy loads, if a child thinks he can handle the activity, parents do not object'.
- Less value is placed on children showing obedience to adult authority. For example, Raymond Firth (1970) found that among the Tikopia of the western Pacific, doing as you are told by a grown-up is regarded as a concession to be granted by the child, not a right to be expected by the adult.
- Children's sexual behaviour is often viewed differently. For example, among the Trobriand Islanders of the south-west Pacific, Bronislaw Malinowski (1957) found that adults took an attitude of 'tolerance and amused interest' towards children's sexual explorations and activities.

Benedict argues that in many non-industrial cultures, there is much less of a dividing line between the behaviour expected of children and that expected of adults. Such evidence illustrates the key idea that childhood is not a fixed thing found universally in the same form in all human societies, but is socially constructed and so differs from culture to culture.

Historical differences in childhood

The position of children differs over time as well as between societies. Many sociologists and historians argue that childhood as we understand it today is a relatively recent 'invention'.

The historian Philippe Ariès (1960) argues that in the Middle Ages (from about the 10th to the 13th centuries), 'the idea of childhood did not exist'. Children were not seen as having a different 'nature' or needs from adults – at least, not once they had passed the stage of physical dependency during infancy.

In the Middle Ages, childhood as a separate age-stage was also short. Soon after being weaned, the child entered wider society on much the same terms as an adult, beginning work from an early age, often in the household of another family. Children were in effect 'mini-adults' with the same rights, duties and skills as adults. For example, the law often made no distinction between children and adults, and children often faced the same severe punishments as those meted out to adults.

As evidence of his view, Ariès uses works of art from the period. In these, children appear without 'any of the characteristics of childhood: they have simply been depicted on a smaller scale'. The paintings show children and adults dressed in the same clothing and working and playing together.

> What problems might there be in using evidence such as paintings and diaries, as Ariès does, to understand childhood or family life in the past?

Parental attitudes towards children in the Middle Ages were also very different from those today. Edward Shorter (1975) argues that high death rates encouraged indifference and neglect, especially towards infants. For example, it was not uncommon for parents to give a newborn baby the name of a recently dead sibling, to refer to the baby as 'it', or to forget how many children they had had.

▲ *Adults and children are barely distinguishable from each other in Bruegel's famous 16th century painting.*

According to Ariès, however, elements of the modern notion of childhood gradually began to emerge from the 13th century onwards:

- Schools (which previously adults had also attended) came to specialise purely in the education of the young. This reflected the influence of the church, which increasingly saw children as fragile 'creatures of God' in need of discipline and protection from worldly evils.
- There was a growing distinction between children's and adults' clothing. By the 17th century, an upper-class boy would be dressed in 'an outfit reserved for his own age group, which set him apart from adults'.
- By the 18th century, handbooks on childrearing were widely available – a sign of the growing child-centredness of family life, at least among the middle classes.

According to Ariès, these developments culminate in the modern 'cult of childhood'. He argues that we have moved from a world that did not see childhood as in any way special, to a world that is obsessed with childhood. He describes the 20th century as 'the century of the child'.

Some sociologists have criticised Ariès for arguing that childhood did not exist in the past. Linda Pollock (1983) argues that it is more correct to say that in the Middle Ages, society simply had a different notion of childhood from today's.

However, Ariès' work is valuable because it shows that childhood is socially constructed: he demonstrates how ideas about children and their social status have varied over time.

Reasons for changes in the position of children

There are many reasons for the changes in the position of children. These include the following changes during the 19th and 20th centuries:

- Laws restricting child labour and excluding children from paid work. From being economic assets who could earn a wage, children became an economic liability, financially dependent on their parents.

- The introduction of compulsory schooling in 1880 had a similar effect, especially for the children of the poor (middle- and upper-class children were already receiving education). The raising of the school-leaving age has extended this period of dependency.

- Child protection and welfare legislation, such as the 1889 Prevention of Cruelty to Children Act. Exactly a century later, the 1989 Children Act made the welfare of the child the fundamental principle underpinning the work of agencies such as social services.

- The growth of the idea of children's rights. For example, the Children Act defines parents as having 'responsibilities' rather than 'rights' in relation to children, while the United Nations Convention on the Rights of the Child (1989) lays down basic rights such as entitlement to healthcare and education, protection from abuse, and the right to participate in decisions that affect them, such as custody cases.

- Declining family size and lower infant mortality rates. These have encouraged parents to make a greater financial and emotional investment in the fewer children that they now have.

- Children's health and development became the subject of medical knowledge. Jacques Donzelot (1977) observes how theories of child development that began to appear from the 19th century stressed that children need supervision and protection. (See also Topic 7, page 86 on Donzelot.)

- Laws and policies that apply specifically to children, such as minimum ages for a wide range of activities from sex to smoking, have reinforced the idea that children are different from adults and so different rules must be applied to their behaviour.

Activity

Make a list of all the activities that the law prevents children from engaging in. Find out the age limits for each of these. For example, what are the age restrictions governing access to alcohol?

Most sociologists agree that the process of industrialisation – the shift from agriculture to factory production as the basis of the economy – underlies many of the above changes. For example, modern industry needs an educated workforce and this requires compulsory schooling of the young. Similarly, the higher standards of living and better welfare provision that industry makes possible lead to lower infant mortality rates. Industrialisation is thus a key factor in bringing about the modern idea of childhood and the changed status of children.

Has the position of children improved?

As we have seen, childhood is socially constructed and varies between times, places and cultures. There are important differences between childhood in western societies today as compared with both present-day Third World countries and European societies in the past. For example, in the Middle Ages, child labour was a basic fact of life for almost all children, while schooling was available only to the wealthy.

The march of progress view

These differences raise the question of whether the changes in the status of childhood that we looked at earlier represent an improvement. The 'march of progress' view argues that, over the past few centuries, the position of children in western societies has been steadily improving and today is better than it has ever been. This view paints a dark picture of the past. As Lloyd De Mause (1974) puts it:

"The history of childhood is a nightmare from which we have only recently begun to awaken. The further back in history one goes, the lower the level of childcare, and the more likely children are to be killed, abandoned, beaten, terrorised and sexually abused."

Writers such as Ariès and Shorter hold a 'march of progress' view. They argue that today's children are more valued, better cared for, protected and educated, enjoy better health and have more rights than those of previous generations.

For example, children today are protected from harm and exploitation by laws against child abuse and child labour, while an array of professionals and specialists caters for their educational, psychological and medical needs. The government spends huge sums on their education – an estimated £64 billion in 2007/8.

Better healthcare and higher standards of living also mean that babies have a much better chance of survival now than a century ago. In 1900, the infant mortality rate was 154 per 1,000 live births; today, it is 5 per 1,000. (See Topic 4, page 47).

Higher living standards and smaller family sizes (down from 5.7 births per woman in the 1860s to 1.84 in 2006) also mean that parents can afford to provide for children's needs properly. According to one estimate, by the time a child reaches their 21st birthday, they will have cost their parents £186,000 (Liverpool Victoria, 2007).

March of progress sociologists argue that the family has become child-centred. Children are no longer to be 'seen and not heard', as they were in Victorian times. Instead they are now the focal point of the family, consulted on many decisions as never before. Parents invest a great deal in their children emotionally as well as financially, and often have high aspirations for them to have a better life and greater opportunities than they themselves have had.

Furthermore, it is not just the family that is now child-centred; so is society as a whole. For example, much media output and many leisure activities are designed specifically for children.

The conflict view

The march of progress view is that the position of children has improved dramatically in a relatively short period of time. However, conflict sociologists such as Marxists and feminists dispute this. They argue that society is based on a conflict between different social groups such as social classes or genders. In this conflict, some groups have more power, status or wealth than others. Conflict sociologists see the relationship between groups as one of domination and subordination, in which the dominant group act as oppressors.

Conflict sociologists argue that the 'march of progress' view of modern childhood is based on a false and idealised image that ignores important inequalities. They criticise the 'march of progress' view on two grounds:

- There are inequalities *among children* in terms of the opportunities and risks they face: many today remain unprotected and badly cared for.
- The inequalities *between children and adults* are greater than ever: children today experience greater control, oppression and dependency, not greater care and protection.

Inequalities among children

Not all children share the same status or experiences. For example, children of different *nationalities* are likely to experience different childhoods and different life chances. 90% of the world's low birth-weight babies are born in the Third World.

There are also *gender* differences between children. For example, according to Mayer Hillman (1993), boys are more likely to be allowed to cross or cycle on roads, use buses, and go out after dark unaccompanied. Jens Bonke (1999) found that girls do more domestic labour – especially in lone-parent families, where they do five times more housework than boys.

Similarly, there are *ethnic* differences: Julia Brannen's (1994) study of 15-16 year olds found that Asian parents were more likely than other parents to be strict towards their daughters. Similarly, Ghazala Bhatti (1999) found that ideas of *izzat* (family honour) could be a restriction, particularly on the behaviour of girls.

Table 2A	Children registered on child protection registers during the year ending 31 March 2006: England	
Type of abuse	**numbers**	**percentages**
Neglect	13,700	43
Physical injury	5,100	16
Sexual abuse	2,600	8
Emotional abuse	6,700	21
Mixed	3,300	11

Source: Clarke (2006)

1 What difficulties might there be in defining child abuse?

2 Suggest reasons why statistics on the numbers of children on child protection registers might not be an accurate measure of child abuse.

There are also important *class* inequalities between children:

- Poor mothers are more likely to have low birth-weight babies, which in turn is linked to delayed physical and intellectual development.
- According to Caroline Woodroffe (1993), children of unskilled manual workers are over three times more likely to suffer from hyperactivity and four times more likely to experience conduct disorders than the children of professionals.
- According to Marilyn Howard (2001), children born into poor families are also more likely to die in infancy or childhood, to suffer longstanding illness, to be shorter in height, to fall behind at school, and to be placed on the child protection register.

Thus we cannot speak of 'children' in general as if they were all equal – social class, gender and ethnic differences affect their life chances.

Inequalities between children and adults

There are also major inequalities of power between children and adults. March of progress writers argue that adults use this power for the benefit and protection of children, for example by passing laws against child labour.

However, critics such as Shulamith Firestone (1979) and John Holt (1974) argue that many of the things that march of progress writers see positively as care and protection are in fact just new forms of oppression and control. For example, Firestone argues that 'protection' from paid work is not a benefit to children but a form of inequality. It is a way of forcibly segregating children, making them more dependent, powerless and subject to adult control than previously.

These critics see the need to free children from adult control, and so their view is described as 'child liberationism'. Adult control takes a number of forms.

▲ *Constant supervision?*

neglect and abuse

Adult control over children can take the extreme form of physical neglect or physical, sexual or emotional abuse. In 2006, 31,400 children were on child protection registers because they were deemed to be at risk of significant harm – most often from their own parents (see Table 2A). The charity ChildLine receives over 20,000 calls a year from children saying that they have been sexually or physically abused. Such figures indicate a 'dark side' to family life of which children are the victims.

controls over children's space

Children's movements in industrial societies such as Britain are highly regulated. For example, shops may display signs such as 'no schoolchildren'. Children are told to play in some areas and forbidden to play in others. There is increasingly close surveillance over children in public spaces such as shopping centres, especially at times when they should be in school.

Similarly, fears about road safety and 'stranger danger' have led to more and more children being driven to school rather than travelling independently. For example, Hillman found that, in 1971, 80% of 7-8 year olds were allowed to go to school without adult supervision. By 1990, this had fallen to just 9%. According to Hugh Cunningham (2007), the 'home habitat' of 8 year olds (the area in which they are able to travel alone) has shrunk to one-ninth of the size it was 25 years ago.

This control and surveillance contrasts with the independence of many children in Third World countries today. For example, Cindi Katz (1993) describes how rural Sudanese children roam freely both within the village and for several kilometres outside it.

controls over children's time

Adults in modern society control children's daily routines, including the times when they get up, eat, go to school, come home, go out, play, watch television and sleep. Adults also control the speed at which children 'grow up'. It is they who define whether a child is too old or too young for this or that activity, responsibility or behaviour. This contrasts with Holmes' finding that among Samoans, 'too young' is never given as a reason for not letting a child undertake a particular task.

Activity

In pairs, describe a day in the life of a five-year-old in Britain today. How many times during that day might that child be controlled by adults? Use the headings control over time, space and bodies and access to resources to classify these instances.

controls over children's bodies

Adults exercise enormous control over children's bodies, including how they sit, walk and run, what they wear (sun hats, make-up, glasses), their hairstyles and whether or not they can have their ears pierced. It is taken for granted that children's bodies may be touched (in certain ways by certain adults): they are washed, fed and dressed, have their heads patted and hands held, are picked up, cuddled and kissed, and they may be disciplined by smacking.

At the same time, adults restrict the ways in which children may touch their own bodies. For example, a child may be told not to pick their nose, suck their thumb or play with their genitals. This contrasts with the sexual freedoms enjoyed by children in some non-industrial cultures such as the Trobriand Islands.

control over children's access to resources

In industrial societies, children have only limited opportunities to earn money, and so they remain dependent economically on adults:

- Labour laws and compulsory schooling exclude them from all but the most marginal, low-paid, part-time employment.
- Although the state pays child benefit, this goes to the parent not the child.
- Pocket money given by parents may depend on 'good behaviour' and there may be restrictions on what it can be spent on.

All this contrasts with the economic role of children in Third World societies and in European societies in the past. For example, Katz found that Sudanese children were already engaged in productive work from the age of three or four.

Activity

If you have any younger brothers or sisters, ask them for their views on childhood – what they like and don't like about being a child, and how they resist adult control (parents, teachers). Alternatively, think back to your own experiences as a child.

Age patriarchy

Diana Gittins (1998) uses the term 'age patriarchy' to describe inequalities between adults and children. Just as feminists use the concept of patriarchy to describe male domination and female dependency, Gittins argues that there is also an age patriarchy of adult domination and child dependency. In fact, patriarchy means literally 'rule by the father' and as Gittins points out, the term 'family' referred originally to the power of the male head over all other members of the household, including children and servants as well as women.

Today this power may still assert itself in the form of violence against both children and women. For example, according to Cathy Humphreys and Ravi Thiara (2002), a quarter of the 200 women in their study left their abusing partner because they feared for their children's lives (See Topic 1, page 25 for further discussion of domestic violence.) Such findings support Gittins' view that patriarchy oppresses children as well as women.

Evidence that children may experience childhood as oppressive comes from the strategies that they use to resist the status of child and the restrictions that go with it. Jennifer Hockey and Allison James (1993) describe one strategy as 'acting up' – acting like adults by doing things that children are not supposed to do, such as swearing, smoking, drinking alcohol, joy riding and under-age sexual activity. Similarly, children may exaggerate their age ('I'm nearly 9').

'Acting down' – behaving in ways expected of younger children – is also a popular strategy for resisting adult control (e.g. by reverting to 'baby talk' or insisting on being carried). Hockey and James conclude that modern childhood is a status from which most children want to escape.

However, critics of the child liberationist view argue that some adult control over children's lives is justified on the grounds that children cannot make rational decisions and so are unable to safeguard their interests themselves.

Critics also argue that, although children remain under adult supervision, they are not as powerless as the child liberationists claim. For example, as we saw earlier, the 1989 Children Act and the United Nations Convention on the Rights of the Child establish the principle that children have legal rights to be protected and consulted.

Activity

Draw up a two-column table entitled, 'Has the position of children improved?' Head the left-hand column 'Yes' and the right-hand column 'No'. In each column, list evidence and arguments in support of that view.

Then write a brief conclusion saying whether on balance you think the position of children has improved, giving your reasons.

The future of childhood

If the idea of children's rights is gaining ground, could this be a sign that children are becoming more powerful and that the distinction between childhood and adulthood is breaking down? Is childhood as we know it in western society disappearing? Sociologists and others have put forward several different answers to these questions. We examine these now.

The disappearance of childhood

Neil Postman (1994) argues that childhood is 'disappearing at a dazzling speed'. He points to the trend towards giving children the same rights as adults, the disappearance of children's traditional unsupervised games, the growing similarity of adult and children's clothing, and even to cases of children committing 'adult' crimes such as murder. In his view, the cause both of the emergence of childhood, and now its disappearance, lies in the rise and fall of print culture and its replacement by television culture.

- During the Middle Ages, most people were illiterate, and speech was the only skill needed for participation in the adult world. Children were able to enter adult society from an early age. Childhood was not associated with innocence, nor the adult world with mystery. There was no division between the world of the adult and that of the child.

- Childhood emerged as a separate status along with mass literacy, from the 19th century on. This is because the printed word creates an information hierarchy: a sharp division between adults, who can read, and children, who cannot. This gave adults the power to keep knowledge about sex, money, violence, illness, death and other 'adult' matters a secret from children. These things became mysteries to them, and childhood came to be associated with innocence and ignorance.

- Television blurs the distinction between childhood and adulthood by destroying the information hierarchy. Unlike the printed word, TV does not require special skills to access it, and it makes information available to adults and children alike. The boundary between adult and child is broken down, adult authority diminishes, and the ignorance and innocence of childhood is replaced by knowledge and cynicism. The counterpart of the disappearance of childhood is the disappearance of adulthood, where adults' and children's tastes and styles become indistinguishable.

Postman's study is valuable in showing how different types of communication technology, such as print and television, can influence the way in which childhood is constructed. However, he over-emphasises a single cause – television – at the expense of other factors that have influenced the development of childhood, such as rising living standards or changes in the law.

> Suggest three examples of ways in which children's activities, leisure, dress or food and those of adults have become similar in recent years.

A separate childhood culture

Unlike Postman, Iona Opie (1993) argues that childhood is not disappearing. Based on a lifetime of research into children's games, rhymes and songs, conducted with her husband Peter Opie, she argues that there is strong evidence of the continued existence of a separate children's culture over many years.

Their findings contradict Postman's claim that children's own unsupervised games are dying out. Their studies show that children can and do create their own independent culture separate from that of adults.

The globalisation of western childhood

As we saw earlier, child liberationists argue that modern western childhood is oppressive and children today are subject to adult authority. They also argue that, far from disappearing, western notions of childhood are being globalised. International humanitarian and welfare agencies have exported and imposed on the rest of the world, western norms of what childhood should be – a separate life stage, based in the nuclear family and school, in which children are innocent, dependent and vulnerable and have no economic role.

For example, campaigns against child labour, or concerns about 'street children' in Third World countries, reflect western views about how childhood 'ought' to be – whereas in fact, such activity by children may be the norm for the culture and an important preparation for adult life. In this view, 'childhood' is not disappearing, but spreading throughout the world.

Contradictory trends – the reconstruction of childhood?

Some writers suggest that children in the UK today are experiencing what Sue Palmer (2006) calls 'toxic childhood'. She argues that rapid technological and cultural changes in the past 25 years have damaged children's physical, emotional and intellectual development. These changes range from junk food, computer games, and intensive marketing to children, to the long hours worked by parents and the growing emphasis on testing in education.

Concerns have also been expressed about young people's behaviour. For example, Julia Margo and Mike Dixon (2006), drawing on recent studies, report that UK youth are at or near the top of international league tables for obesity, self-harm, drug and alcohol abuse, violence, early sexual experience and teenage pregnancies. A UNICEF survey in 2007 ranked the UK 21st out of 25 for children's well being.

Such concerns reveal an anxiety that the modern notion of childhood as an innocent and protected stage is under threat. However, it is hard to draw firm conclusions about this, for two reasons.

Firstly, not all children are affected equally by these negative trends. Sarah Womack (2007) quotes the head of the Children's Society as saying:

"Rather than childhood being generally miserable, there are clusters of young people, namely those growing up on the poorer end of the social scale, who live desperate lives, while others do not".

Secondly, it depends on which aspect of childhood we look at. Some aspects suggest the continuation of childhood as a separate age-status, while others suggest it may be disappearing or changing. For example:

- Children today have more rights, but they still do not have equal rights with adults and they remain subject to adult authority.
- There are growing similarities between children and adults in leisure activities, dress, diet etc.
- The extension of compulsory and post-compulsory education has made young people economically dependent 'children' for longer and longer.
- Children's freedom of movement has become more restricted with fears over road safety and 'stranger danger'.

▲ *Street child, San Cristobal de las Casas, Mexico. Is this oppression, or preparation for adult life?*

- However, children now have greater access to means of communication.
- Many adults remain concerned about children's behaviour and discipline and about exposure to media sex and violence.

Finally, childhood may be 'disappearing' because of falling birth and death rates. These two trends are producing an ageing population with more old people and fewer young ones. Jens Qvortrup (1990) argues that, as the number of people who are parents with dependent children falls, so there will be fewer voices calling for resources to go to children. This may also make childhood a more isolating experience, as families become smaller and there are fewer children in the neighbourhood. However, it could also be that children's relative scarcity will make them more valued and powerful.

Although it is difficult to predict how our notion of childhood will develop in the future, we have seen that there are a number of trends that may re-shape children's future position. These possibilities of change demonstrate that childhood is not a fixed, universal fact but a status that is socially constructed. Whether it will be reconstructed as something that segregates children further, or as a status that gives them greater freedom, remains to be seen.

For more activities on Childhood...

Go to www.sociology.uk.net

Summary

Childhood is a **social construction** and varies between times, places and groups. Most sociologists see our idea of childhood as a fairly recent one, the result of **industrialisation** and other social changes. Modern society constructs childhood as a time of **vulnerability, innocence and segregation** from the adult world.

'March of progress' sociologists believe we live in an increasingly **child-centred society**. They state that children have never had it so good. Critics argue that this ignores the continued existence of child poverty, abuse and exploitation.

Child liberationists argue that children in modern western society are victims of **age patriarchy** and are subject to adult control. Some argue that we are witnessing the **disappearance of childhood** as the media erode the boundary between childhood and adulthood. Others argue that the West is imposing its ideas of childhood on the Third World.

QuickCheck Questions

1 Explain what is meant by the 'social construction of childhood'.

2 Ruth Benedict identifies three ways in which childhood in non-industrial cultures often differs from childhood in the west. State two of these.

3 Edward Shorter gives examples of parental neglect or indifference towards children in the Middle Ages. State one of these.

4 Why are children less of an economic asset to their parents today than they were in the past?

5 Give one example of class differences between children.

6 What is age patriarchy?

7 Why does Neil Postman believe childhood is disappearing?

8 What is meant by the 'globalisation of western childhood'?

 Check your answers at www.sociology.uk.net

Examining childhood

Item A   According to some sociologists, children in today's supposedly child-centred society lead lives that are segregated and controlled, but childhood was not always like this. For example, Ariès describes a medieval world in which, if children were not actually the equals of adults, they nevertheless mixed freely with adults in both work and leisure. Little distinction was drawn between adults and children.

According to this view, however, industrialisation brought major changes to the position of children. The development of industrial society meant that their lives were increasingly confined, disciplined and regulated by adults. The result is that in the West today, adults exercise a   5 control over children's time, space and bodies that would have been unimaginable to medieval society.

Not all sociologists share this view of modern childhood, however. Some argue that the distinction between childhood and adulthood is once again becoming blurred.

(a) Explain what is meant by the term 'child-centred society' (**Item A**, line 1).   (2 marks)

(b) Suggest **two** examples of ways in which the distinction between childhood and adulthood is 'becoming blurred' (**Item A**, line 8).   (4 marks)

(c) Identify **three** changes linked to industrialisation that have led to changes in the position of children (**Item A**, line 4).   (6 marks)

Essay   Using material from **Item A** and elsewhere, assess sociological explanations of changes in the status of childhood.   (24 marks)

The examiner's advice

The essay carries 10 AO1 marks (knowledge and understanding) and 14 AO2 marks (interpretation, application, analysis and evaluation). The emphasis is on showing well developed AO2 skills, but to score high marks you must also show a good sociological knowledge. You must also make sure you use the Item.

The key idea is the social construction of childhood. You need to be able to explain this concept and to give some historical and cross-cultural examples of how the position of children varies; use the Item to help you (e.g. Ariès). Describe the modern notion of childhood (as innocent, needing protection etc) and examine the factors that led to its emergence (e.g. industrialisation, legislation, literacy etc). You can show analysis and evaluation by discussing conflicting views of the status of childhood today, such as 'march of progress' (e.g. De Mause, Shorter) versus 'child liberationist' approaches (e.g. Firestone, Holt). You can also assess different views of whether childhood is now changing again, or even disappearing (e.g. Postman, Opie, the globalisation of western childhood). Write a separate conclusion.

Topic 3 The functions of the family

So far in this chapter, we have looked at some of the key members of the family – husbands and wives, parents and children – and at how far their roles and relationships may have changed. We now turn our attention to how the family fits into wider society.

This Topic deals with the role or purpose of the family – what it does for its members and for society. It looks at the answers sociologists have given to the question, 'What are the functions of the family?'

Sociologists have studied the family from a number of different perspectives or viewpoints and reached different conclusions as to its role or functions. In this Topic, we shall examine the following sociological perspectives on the family:

- **Functionalism** – a consensus perspective
- **Marxism** – a class conflict perspective
- **Feminism** – a gender conflict perspective

Learning objectives

When you have studied this Topic, you should:

- Understand the functionalist, Marxist and different types of feminist perspectives on the family.
- Be able to analyse the similarities and differences between these perspectives.
- Be able to evaluate the usefulness of these perspectives on the family.

The functionalist perspective on the family

Functionalists believe that society is based on a value consensus – a set of shared norms and values – into which society socialises its members. This enables them to cooperate harmoniously to meet society's needs and achieve shared goals.

Functionalists regard society as a system made up of different parts or sub-systems that depend on each other, such as the family, the education system and the economy. Functionalists often compare society to a biological organism like the human body. For example, just as organs such as the heart or lungs perform functions vital to the well being of the body as a whole, so the family meets some of society's essential needs, such as the need to socialise children.

Functionalists see the family as a particularly important sub-system – a basic building block of society. For example, George Peter Murdock (1949) argues that the family performs four essential functions to meet the needs of society and its members:

- **Stable satisfaction of the sex drive** with the same partner, preventing the social disruption caused by a sexual 'free-for-all'.
- **Reproduction of the next generation**, without which society could not continue.
- **Socialisation of the young** into society's shared norms and values.
- **Meeting its members' economic needs**, such as food and shelter.

Criticisms of Murdock

Murdock accepts that other institutions could perform these functions. However, he argues that the sheer practicality of the nuclear family as a way of meeting these four needs explains why it is universal – found in all human societies.

However, while few sociologists would doubt that most of these are important functions, some argue that they could be performed equally well by other institutions, or by non-nuclear family structures.

Other sociologists have criticised Murdock's functionalist approach. Marxists and feminists reject his 'rose-tinted' harmonious consensus view that the family meets the needs of both wider society and all members of the family. They argue that functionalism neglects conflict and exploitation:

- **Feminists** see the family as serving the needs of men and oppressing women.
- **Marxists** argue that it meets the needs of capitalism, not those of family members or society as a whole.

Both these views are examined later in this Topic.

1. What similarities can you see between society and an organism such as the human body? What differences are there between the two?

2. What other institutions apart from the family might be able to perform any of the functions that Murdock identifies? Do you think they would be as effective as the family?

Parsons' 'functional fit' theory

Apart from the functions identified by Murdock, the family may meet other needs too. For example, it may perform welfare, military, political or religious functions. In the view of Talcott Parsons (1955), the functions it performs will depend on the kind of society in which it is found.

Furthermore, the functions that the family has to perform will affect its 'shape' or structure. Parsons distinguishes between two kinds of family structure:

- **The nuclear family** of just parents and dependent children
- **The extended family** of three generations living under one roof.

Parsons argues that the particular structure and functions of a given type of family will 'fit' the needs of the society in which it is found.

According to Parsons, there are two basic types of society – modern industrial society and traditional pre-industrial society. He argues that the nuclear family fits the needs of industrial society and is the dominant family type in that society, while the extended family fits the needs of pre-industrial society.

In Parsons' view, when Britain began to industrialise, from the late 18th century onwards, the extended family began to give way to the nuclear. This was because the emerging industrial society had different needs from pre-industrial society, and the family had to adapt to meet these needs. Parsons sees industrial society as having two essential needs:

1 A geographically mobile workforce

In traditional pre-industrial society, people often spent their whole lives living in the same village, working on the same farm. By contrast, in modern society, industries constantly spring up and decline in different parts of the country, even different parts of the world, and this requires people to move to where the jobs are.

Parsons argues that it is easier for the compact two-generation nuclear family, with just dependent children, to move, than for the three-generation extended family. The nuclear family is better fitted to the need that modern industry has for a geographically mobile workforce.

2 A socially mobile workforce

Modern industrial society is based on constantly evolving science and technology and so it requires a skilled, technically competent workforce. It is therefore essential that talented people are able to win promotion and take on the most important jobs, even if they come from very humble backgrounds.

In modern society, an individual's status is achieved by their own efforts and ability, not ascribed (fixed at birth) by their social and family background, and this makes social mobility possible. For example, the son of a labourer can become a doctor or lawyer through ability and hard work.

For this reason, Parsons argues, the nuclear family is better equipped than the extended family to meet the needs of industrial society. In the extended family, adult sons live at home in their father's house – where the father has a higher ascribed status as head of the household. However, at work, the son may have a higher achieved status (a more important job) than his father. This would inevitably give rise to tensions and conflict if they both lived under the same roof. The solution therefore is for adult sons to leave home when they marry and form their own nuclear family. The nuclear family therefore encourages social mobility as well as geographical mobility.

The result is the mobile nuclear family, which is 'structurally isolated' from its extended kin (relatives). Though it may keep in touch with them, it has no binding obligations towards them – unlike the pre-industrial extended family, where relatives had an overriding duty to help one another, for example at harvest or in times of hardship or crisis.

Loss of functions

The pre-industrial family was a multi-functional unit. For example, it was both a unit of production in which family members worked together on the family farm, and a unit of consumption, feeding and clothing its members. It was

---

Box 5	The evidence against Parsons

Other sociologists and historians have produced evidence that contradicts Parsons' claims of a 'functional fit' between the extended family and pre-industrial society, and between the nuclear family and industrial society. We can summarise these criticisms in terms of the following three questions:

1 Was the extended family dominant in pre-industrial society?

According to Young and Willmott (1973), the pre-industrial family was nuclear, not extended as Parsons claims, with parents and children working together, for example in cottage industries such as weaving. Similarly, Peter Laslett's (1972) study of English households from 1564 to 1821 found that they were almost always nuclear. A combination of late childbearing and short life expectancy meant that grandparents were unlikely to be alive for very long after the birth of their first grandchild.

2 Did the family become nuclear in early industrial society?

According to Parsons, industrialisation brought the nuclear family. However, Young and Willmott argue that the hardship of the early industrial period gave rise to the 'mum-centred' working-class extended family, based on ties between mothers and their married daughters, who relied on each other for financial, practical and emotional support.

The idea that individuals break off or maintain family ties because of the costs or benefits involved is called exchange theory. Michael Anderson's (1980) study of mid-19th century Preston uses exchange theory to explain the popularity of the working-class extended family. He shows how the harsh conditions of the time – poverty, sickness, early death and the absence of a welfare state – meant that the benefits of maintaining extended family ties greatly outweighed the costs. These benefits included using older kin for childcare while parents worked, and taking in orphaned relatives to produce extra income and help towards the rent.

Similarly, Tamara Hareven (1999) concludes that the extended family, not the nuclear, as Parsons claims, was the structure best equipped to meet the needs of early industrial society. Her study of French Canadian migrants in the American textile industry, from 1880 to 1930, shows how it acted as a source of security and mutual aid, as well as promoting geographical mobility by helping newcomers to find work.

3 Is the extended family no longer important in modern society?

There is partial support for Parsons' claim that the nuclear family has become the dominant family type today. Young and Willmott argue that, from about 1900, the nuclear family emerged as a result of social changes that made the extended family less important as a source of support. These changes included geographical mobility, higher living standards, married women working, the welfare state and better housing.

However, the extended family has not disappeared. Studies show that it continues to exist because it performs important functions, for example providing financial help, childcare and emotional support (see Topic 5, page 67).

a more self-sufficient unit than the modern nuclear family, providing for its members' health and welfare and meeting most individual and social needs.

However, according to Parsons, when society industrialises, the family not only changes its structure from extended to nuclear, it also loses many of its functions. For example, the family ceases to be a unit of production: work moves into the factories and the family becomes a unit of consumption only. It also loses most of its other functions to other institutions, such as schools and the health service.

In Parsons' view, as a result of this loss of functions, the modern nuclear family comes to specialise in performing just two essential or 'irreducible' functions:

- **The primary socialisation of children** to equip them with basic skills and society's values, to enable them to cooperate with others and begin to integrate them into society.
- **The stabilisation of adult personalities:** the family is a place where adults can relax and release tensions, enabling them to return to the workplace refreshed and ready to meet its demands. This is functional for the efficiency of the economy.

Activity

In groups, discuss Parsons' ideas. Consider each of the two 'irreducible' functions suggested by Parsons and answer the following questions:

1 What is meant by primary socialisation?

2 Can primary socialisation be provided by anyone other than the family?

3 Is the family helped by any other organisations in limiting stress and conflict?

4 Does the family always *reduce* stress for its members?

5 Parsons might argue that a one-parent family cannot adequately perform these functions. Do you agree with this view?

Activity   Strengths and weaknesses of functionalism

Go to www.sociology.uk.net

The Marxist perspective on the family

While functionalists see society as based on value consensus (agreement), Marxist sociologists see capitalist society as based on an unequal conflict between two social classes:

- the capitalist class, who own the means of production
- the working class, whose labour the capitalists exploit for profit.

Marxists see all society's institutions, such as the education system, the media, religion and the state, along with the family, as helping to maintain class inequality and capitalism. Thus, for Marxists, the functions of the family are performed purely for the benefit of the capitalist system. This view contrasts sharply with the functionalist view that the family benefits both society as a whole and all the individual members of the family.

Marxists have identified several functions that they see the family as fulfilling for capitalism:

1 Inheritance of property

Marxists argue that the key factor determining the shape of all social institutions, including the family, is the mode of production – that is, who owns and controls society's productive forces (such as tools, machinery, raw materials, land and labour). In modern society, it is the capitalist class

that owns and controls these means of production. As the mode of production evolves, so too does the family.

Marx called the earliest, classless society, 'primitive communism'. In this society, there was no private property. Instead, all members of society owned the means of production communally. At this stage of social development, there was no family as such. Instead, there existed what Friedrich Engels (1891; 1978) called the 'promiscuous horde' or tribe, in which there were no restrictions on sexual relationships.

However, as the forces of production developed, society's wealth began to increase. Along with increased wealth came the development of private property, as a class of men emerged who were able to secure control of the means of production. This change eventually brought about the patriarchal monogamous nuclear family.

In Engels' view, monogamy became essential because of the inheritance of private property – men had to be certain of the paternity of their children in order to ensure that their legitimate heirs inherited from them.

In Engels' view, the rise of the monogamous nuclear family represented a "world historical defeat of the female sex". This was because it brought the woman's sexuality under male control and turned her into "a mere instrument for the production of children".

Marxists argue that only with the overthrow of capitalism and private ownership of the means of production will women achieve liberation from patriarchal control. A classless society will be established in which the means of production are owned collectively, not privately. There will no longer be a need for the patriarchal nuclear family, since there will be no need to have a means of transmitting private property down the generations.

2 Ideological functions

Marxists argue that the family today performs key ideological functions for capitalism. By 'ideology', Marxists mean a set of ideas or beliefs that justify inequality and maintain the capitalist system by persuading people to accept it as fair, natural or unchangeable.

One way in which the family does this is by socialising children into the idea that hierarchy and inequality are inevitable. Parental (especially paternal) power over children accustoms them to the idea that there always has to be someone in charge (usually a man) and prepares them for a working life in which they will accept orders from their capitalist employers.

According to Eli Zaretsky (1976), the family also performs an ideological function by offering an apparent 'haven' from the harsh and exploitative world of capitalism outside in which workers can 'be themselves' and have a private life. However, Zaretsky argues that this is largely an illusion – the family cannot meet its members' needs. For example, it is based on the domestic servitude of women.

3 A unit of consumption

Capitalism exploits the labour of the workers, making a profit by selling the products of their labour for more than it pays them to produce these commodities. The family therefore plays a major role in generating profits, since it is an important market for the sale of consumer goods:

- Advertisers urge families to 'keep up with the Joneses' by consuming all the latest products.
- The media target children, who use 'pester power' to persuade parents to spend more.
- Children who lack the latest clothes or 'must have' gadgets are mocked and stigmatised by their peers.

Thus, Marxists see the family as performing several functions that maintain capitalist society: the inheritance of private property, socialisation into acceptance of inequality, and a source of profits. In the Marxist view, while these may benefit capitalism, they do not benefit the members of the family.

Criticisms of the Marxist perspective

- Marxists tend to assume that the nuclear family is dominant in capitalist society. This ignores the wide and increasing variety of family structures found in society today.

- Feminists argue that the Marxist emphasis on social class and capitalism underestimates the importance of gender inequalities within the family. In the feminist view, the family primarily serves the interests of men rather than capitalism.
- By contrast, functionalists argue that Marxists ignore the very real benefits that the family provides for its members, such as intimacy and mutual support.

Activity

Which of the following statements about the family are likely to be put forward by (a) a functionalist (b) a Marxist (c) both?

1 It fulfils the needs of its individual members.

2 It is important in socialising children.

3 Its structure is determined by economic factors.

4 It provides consumers to buy goods.

5 It provides a 'safety valve' away from work.

6 It fulfils its functions for society.

7 It is universal and necessary everywhere.

8 It has an important reproductive role.

9 It keeps women under patriarchal control.

10 It performs its functions for capitalism.

▲ *Women as a reserve army of labour*

Feminist perspectives on the family

Like Marxists, feminists take a critical view of the family. They argue that it oppresses women – as we saw in Topic 1, they have focused on issues such as the unequal division of domestic labour and domestic violence against women. They do not regard gender inequality as natural or inevitable, but as something created by society.

However, feminism is a broad term covering several different types. Each of these approaches the family in a different way and offers different solutions to the problem of gender inequality. We shall examine four main types of feminism here:

1 Liberal feminism

Liberal feminists are concerned with campaigning against sex discrimination and for equal rights and opportunities for women (e.g. equal pay and an end to discrimination in employment).

- They argue that women's oppression is being gradually overcome through changing people's attitudes and through changes in the law such as the Sex Discrimination Act (1975), which outlaws discrimination in employment.
- They believe we are moving towards greater equality, but that full equality will depend on further reforms and changes in the attitudes and socialisation patterns of both sexes.

In terms of the family, they hold a view similar to that of 'march of progress' theorists such as Young and Willmott (see Topic 1, page 19). Although liberal feminists do not believe full gender equality has yet been achieved in the family, they argue that there has been gradual progress. For example, some studies suggest that men are doing more domestic labour, while the way parents now socialise their sons and daughters is more equal than in the past and they now have similar aspirations for them.

However, other feminists criticise liberal feminists for failing to challenge the underlying causes of women's oppression and for believing that changes in the law or attitudes will be enough to bring equality. Marxist feminists and radical feminists believe instead that far-reaching revolutionary changes to deep-rooted social structures are needed.

2 Marxist feminism

Marxist feminists argue that the main cause of women's oppression in the family is not men, but capitalism. Women's oppression performs several functions for capitalism:

- **Women reproduce the labour force** through their unpaid domestic labour, by socialising the next generation of workers and maintaining and servicing the current one.

- **Women absorb anger** that would otherwise be directed at capitalism. Fran Ansley (1972) describes wives as 'takers of shit' who soak up the frustration their husbands feel because of the alienation and exploitation they suffer at work. For Marxists, this explains male domestic violence against women.
- **Women are a 'reserve army' of cheap labour** that can be taken on when extra workers are needed. When no longer needed, employers can 'let them go' to return to their primary role as unpaid domestic labour.

Marxist feminists see the oppression of women in the family as linked to the exploitation of the working class. They argue that the family must be abolished at the same time as a socialist revolution replaces capitalism with a classless society.

3 Radical feminism

Radical feminists argue that all societies have been founded on patriarchy – rule by men. For radical feminists, the key division in society is between men and women:

- **Men are the enemy:** they are the source of women's oppression and exploitation.
- **The family and marriage are the key institutions** in patriarchal society. Men benefit from women's unpaid domestic labour and from their sexual services, and they dominate women through domestic and sexual violence or the threat of it.

For radical feminists, the patriarchal system needs to be overturned. In particular, the family, the root of women's oppression, must be abolished. They argue that the only way to achieve this is through *separatism* – women must organise themselves to live independently of men.

Many radical feminists argue for 'political lesbianism' – the idea that heterosexual relationships are inevitably oppressive because they involve 'sleeping with the enemy'. Similarly, Germaine Greer (2000) argues for the creation of all-female or 'matrilocal' households as an alternative to the heterosexual family.

However, for liberal feminists such as Jenny Somerville (2000), radical feminists fail to recognise that women's position has improved considerably – with better access to divorce, better job opportunities, control over their own fertility, and the ability to choose whether to marry or cohabit. Somerville also argues that separatism is unlikely to work – heterosexual attraction makes it unlikely that the conventional nuclear family will disappear.

However, Somerville does recognise that women have yet to achieve full equality. She argues that there is a need for 'family friendly' policies, such as more flexible working, to promote greater equality between partners.

4 Difference feminism

The feminist approaches we have considered so far all tend to assume that most women live in conventional nuclear families and that they share a similar experience of family life.

However, difference feminists argue that we cannot generalise about women's experiences in this way. They argue for example that lesbian and heterosexual women, white and black women, middle-class and working-class women, and so on, have very different experiences of the family from one another.

For example, black feminists argue that by regarding the family solely as a source of oppression, white feminists neglect black women's experience of racial oppression. Instead, black feminists view the black family positively as a source of support and resistance against racism.

However, other feminists argue that this approach neglects the fact that, despite such differences, women do in fact share many of the same experiences. For example, compared with men, they face a greater risk of domestic violence and sexual assault, low pay and so on.

Criticisms of perspectives on the family

As we have seen, there are major differences between functionalist, Marxist and feminist theories of the family. However, other sociologists argue that they all suffer from two weaknesses:

1 They all assume that the traditional nuclear family is the dominant family type

This ignores the increased diversity of families today. Although the nuclear family remains important, it is by no means the only family type. Compared with 40 years ago, many more people now live in other families, such as lone parent families, stepfamilies and so on. We examine family diversity in Topic 5, *Changing family patterns*.

2 They are all structural theories

That is, they assume that families and their members are simply passive puppets manipulated by the structure of society to perform certain functions – for example, to provide the economy with a mobile labour force, or to serve the needs of capitalism or of men. (For more details of structural theories, see Chapter 1, page 7.)

Sociologists influenced by the social action view of society (see page 7) and by postmodernism reject this view. They argue that structural theories ignore the fact that we have some *choice* in creating our family relationships. In fact, the diversity of family types found today reflects the fact that we can choose our domestic set up for ourselves.

These sociologists argue that to understand the family today, we must focus on the meanings family members give to relationships and situations, rather than on the family's supposed 'functions'. We examine this view in Topic 6, *Family diversity and the life course*.

Activity

Different feminists hold different views about the root cause of women's oppression and what is needed to remove it. Complete the following table in order to analyse these differences:

Type of Feminism	What is seen as the main cause of oppression?	What needs to happen in order to remove this oppression?
Liberal Feminism		
Marxist Feminism		
Radical Feminism		

For more activities on The functions of the family...

 Go to www.sociology.uk.net

Summary

Functionalists take a **consensus** view of the role of the family. They see it as a **universal** institution that performs essential functions for society as a whole and all members of the family. Parsons sees a **functional fit**, with the nuclear family fitting modern society's need for a geographically and socially **mobile labour force**. However, critics argue that he is wrong about the relationship between **industrialisation** and family structure.

Marxists see the family as serving the economic and ideological needs of **capitalism**. **Feminists** see the family as serving the needs of **men** and perpetuating **patriarchal control** of women. **Liberal, radical and Marxist feminists** differ over the cause of women's subordination and the solution to it. Functionalist, Marxist and feminist theories have all been criticised for neglecting family **diversity** and individuals' capacity to **choose** their family arrangements.

QuickCheck Questions

1 What is meant by ascribed status?

2 Explain the difference between geographical mobility and social mobility.

3 According to Young and Willmott, what factors led to the nuclear family becoming dominant in modern society?

4 According to Anderson, why did working-class people maintain extended family ties during the early industrial period?

5 What is meant by 'patriarchal ideology'?

6 According to Marxists, how does the family perform an ideological function?

7 Explain the difference between Marxist feminism and radical feminism.

8 Suggest two ways in which women have gained more equality in the last 40 years.

 Check your answers at www.sociology.uk.net

Examining the functions of the family

Item A According to functionalist sociologists, the family is a key institution of society. It performs vital functions for the maintenance of society as a whole and for the benefit of all its individual members. For example, according to George Peter Murdock, it provides for the stable satisfaction of the sex drive and thus avoids the social disruption and conflict that could be caused by a sexual 'free for all'. Similarly, the family reproduces the next generation and thereby ensures the continuation of society over time.

Functionalists tend to see the nuclear family as the ideal family type for modern society. For example, Talcott Parsons argues that it is the family structure best equipped to meet the need of industrial society for a mobile labour force. Similarly, the nuclear family performs two essential functions for its members and for society as a whole.   5

However, not everyone accepts the functionalist view of the family and its role. Marxists and feminists reject its consensus assumptions about who benefits from the family. Similarly, historians and sociologists have put forward evidence to challenge Parsons' view that there is a 'functional fit' between the type of society and the type of family structure found within it.   10

(a) Explain what is meant by 'consensus' (**Item A**, line 8).   (2 marks)

(b) Identify the 'two essential functions' that Parsons sees the nuclear family as performing (**Item A**, lines 6-7).   (4 marks)

(c) Suggest **three** functions that the family might perform **apart from** those referred to in **Item A**.   (6 marks)

Essay Using material from **Item A** and elsewhere, assess the contribution of functionalism to our understanding of families and households.   (24 marks)

The examiner's advice

The essay carries 10 AO1 marks (knowledge and understanding) and 14 AO2 marks (interpretation, application, analysis and evaluation). The emphasis is on showing well-developed AO2 skills, but to score high marks you must also show a good sociological knowledge. You must also make sure you use the Item.

You need to identify and describe some of the main features of the functionalist approach to the family. These should include Murdock's view that the nuclear family is universal because of its 'sheer practicality' in performing four essential functions. Use Item A to identify two of these and add the other two yourself. Examine Parsons' idea that there is a 'functional fit' between the extended family and pre-industrial society, and between the nuclear family and industrial society.

It's essential that you evaluate (make judgments about) the functionalist contribution. Use the final paragraph of Item A as a starting point from which to contrast functionalism with 'conflict' perspectives (especially Marxism and feminism), and then to consider the historical evidence on Parsons' 'functional fit' theory. You can also consider functional alternatives to the family, and note that functionalists ignore family and household diversity today. Write a separate conclusion.

A Victorian-style funeral – but death rates today are far lower than the 19th century.

Topic 4 Demography

Learning objectives

When you have studied this Topic, you should:

- Know the main population trends in the UK since 1900.
- Understand and be able to evaluate the reasons for population changes, including birth and fertility rates, family size, death rates, ageing and migration.
- Understand and be able to evaluate the consequences of these changes.

Family and population are closely linked. For example, new members of the population are mostly born into and raised by families, while the kind of care they receive from their family affects their chances of survival. Similarly, as the studies by Anderson and Hareven show (Topic 3, page 40), when people migrate from country to country or from region to region, they often rely on kinfolk to facilitate their move.

The study of populations and their characteristics is called demography. These characteristics include:

- Size: is the population large or small, growing or declining?
- Age structure: is the average age of the population rising or falling?

As Figure 2.2 shows, the factors that most directly affect the size of a country's population are:

- Births: how many babies are born.
- Deaths: how many people die.
- Immigration: how many people enter the country from elsewhere.
- Emigration: how many people leave the country to live elsewhere.

In this Topic, we examine some of the main features of the UK population and how it has changed. Britain in 1801 had a population of 10.5 million. By 1901, this stood at 37 million. By 2007, the population of the UK had reached nearly 61 million and one projection is that it will rise to 71 million by 2031.

Until the 1980s, UK population growth was largely the product of **natural change** – that is, the result of there being more births than deaths. However, since the 1980s, most of the growth has come from **net migration** – that is, more immigration than emigration.

Births

The number of births obviously affects population size. Sociologists use the concept of **birth rate** to measure births. The birth rate is defined as the number of live births per 1000 of the population per year.

As Figure 2.3 on page 48 shows, there has been a long-term decline in the number of births since 1900. In that year, England and Wales had a birth rate of 28.7, but by 2007 it had fallen to an estimated 10.7.

However, as Figure 2.3 shows, there have been fluctuations in births, with three 'baby booms' in the 20th century. The first two came after the two world wars (1914-18 and 1939-45), as returning servicemen and their partners started families that they had postponed during the war years.

There was a third baby boom in the 1960s, after which the birth rate fell sharply during the 1970s. The rate rose during the 1980s, before falling again after the early 1990s, with a recent increase since 2001.

The total fertility rate

The factors determining the birth rate are, firstly, the proportion of women who are of childbearing age (usually taken to be aged 15-44) and, secondly, how fertile they are – that is, how many children they have. The total fertility rate (TFR) is the average number of children women will have during their fertile years.

The UK's TFR has risen since 2001, but it is still much lower than in the past. From an all-time low of 1.63 children per woman in 2001, it rose to 1.84 by 2006. However, this is still far lower than the peak of 2.95 children per woman reached in 1964 during the 1960s baby boom.

These changes in fertility and birth rates reflect the fact that:

- More women are remaining childless than in the past.
- Women are postponing having children: the average age for giving birth is now 29.6, and fertility rates for women in their 30s and 40s are on the increase. Older women may be less fertile and have fewer fertile years remaining, and so they produce fewer children.

Reasons for the decline in the birth rate

Sociologists have identified a number of reasons for the long-term decline in the birth rate since 1900. These reasons involve a range of social, economic, cultural, legal, political and technological factors.

1 Changes in the position of women

There were major changes in the position of women during the 20th century. These include:

- Legal equality with men, including the right to vote.
- Increased educational opportunities – girls now do better at school than boys (see Chapter 3, Topic 4).
- More women in paid employment, plus laws outlawing unequal pay and sex discrimination.
- Changes in attitudes to family life and women's role.
- Easier access to divorce.
- Access to abortion and reliable contraception, giving women more control over their fertility.

As a result of these changes, women now see other possibilities in life apart from the traditional role of housewife and mother. Many are choosing to delay childbearing, or not to have children at all, in order to pursue a career. For example, in 2006, one in five women aged 45 was childless – double the number of 20 years earlier.

2 Decline in the infant mortality rate

The infant mortality rate (IMR) measures the number of infants who die before their first birthday, per thousand babies born alive, per year. Many sociologists argue that a fall in the IMR leads to a fall in the birth rate. This is because, if many infants die, parents have more children to replace those they have lost, thereby increasing the birth rate. By contrast, if infants survive, parents will have fewer of them.

In 1900, the IMR for the UK was 154. In other words, over 15% of babies died within their first year. These figures are higher than those of less developed countries today. For

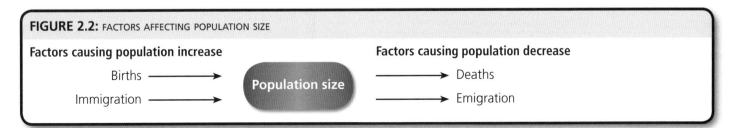

FIGURE 2.2: FACTORS AFFECTING POPULATION SIZE

Factors causing population increase

Births ⟶

Immigration ⟶

Population size

⟶ Deaths

⟶ Emigration

example, in 2003, the world's highest recorded IMR was that of Liberia, at 144.

During the first half of the 20th century, the UK's IMR began to fall. This was due to several reasons:

- Improved housing and better sanitation, such as flush toilets and clean drinking water, reduced infectious disease. Infants are much more susceptible to infection because of their less developed immune system.
- Better nutrition, including that of mothers.
- Better knowledge of hygiene, child health and welfare, often spread via women's magazines.
- A fall in the number of married women working may have improved their health and that of their babies.
- Improved services for mothers and children, such as antenatal and postnatal clinics.

Before the mid-20th century, it is doubtful whether specifically medical factors had much effect on the IMR – although indirectly, the medical profession had a significant impact through its campaigns to improve public health measures.

However, from about the 1950s, medical factors began to play a greater role. For example, mass immunisation against childhood diseases such as whooping cough, diphtheria and later measles, the use of antibiotics to fight infection and improved midwifery and obstetric techniques, all contributed to a continuing fall in the IMR.

As a result of all the above developments, by 1950 the UK's IMR had fallen to 30 and by 2007 it stood at 5 – less than one thirtieth of its 1900 figure.

However, while many sociologists claim that the falling IMR led to a fall in birth rates, others reject this view. For example, Brass and Kabir (1978) argue that the trend to smaller families began not in rural areas, where the IMR first began to fall, but in urban areas, where the IMR remained higher for longer.

Activity Births and deaths

Go to www.sociology.uk.net

3 Children have become an economic liability

Until the late 19th century, children were economic assets to their parents because they could be sent out to work from an early age to earn an income. However, since the late 19th century children have gradually become an economic liability: (See Topic 2, page 31.)

- **Laws** banning child labour, introducing compulsory schooling and raising the school leaving age mean that children remain economically dependent on their parents for longer and longer.
- **Changing norms** about what children have a right to expect from their parents in material terms mean that the cost of bringing up children has risen.

As a result of these financial pressures, parents now feel less able or willing than in the past to have a large family.

4 Child centredness

As we saw in Topic 2, the increasing child centredness both of the family and of society as a whole means that childhood is now socially constructed as a uniquely important period in the individual's life. In terms of family size, this has encouraged a shift from 'quantity' to 'quality' – parents now have fewer children and lavish more attention and resources on these few.

Future trends in birth rates

As a result of the above factors, birth rates, fertility rates and family sizes have fallen over the last century. However, as we saw earlier, there has been a slight increase in births since 2001.

One reason for this is the increase in immigration because, on average, mothers from outside the UK have a higher fertility rate than those born in the UK. Babies born to mothers from outside the UK accounted for 22% of all births in 2005. However, as Figure 2.3 shows, the projection for the period up to 2041 expects the annual number of births to be fairly constant, at around 700-720,000 per year.

FIGURE 2.3: BIRTHS AND DEATHS IN THE UK, 1901-2041

Births

Projections

Millions

Deaths

1.20 · 1.00 · 0.80 · 0.60 · 0.40 · 0.20 · 0.00

1901 · 1921 · 1941 · 1961 · 1981 · 2001 · 2021 · 2041

Effects of changes in fertility

Changes in the number of babies born affect several aspects of society. These include the family, the dependency ratio, and public services and policies.

The family

Smaller families mean that women are more likely to be free to go out to work, thus creating the dual earner couple typical of many professional families. However, family size is only one factor here. For example, better off couples may be able to have larger families and still afford childcare that allows them both to work full-time.

The dependency ratio

The dependency ratio is the relationship between the size of the working or productive part of the population and the size of the non-working or dependent part of the population. The earnings, savings and taxes of the working population must support the dependent population. Children make up a large part of the dependent population, so a fall in the number of children reduces the 'burden of dependency' on the working population.

However, in the longer term, fewer babies being born will mean fewer young adults and a smaller working population and so the burden of dependency may begin to increase again.

Public services and policies

A lower birth rate has consequences for public services. For example, fewer schools and maternity and child health services may be needed. It also has implications for the cost of maternity and paternity leave, or the types of housing that need to be built. However, we should remember that many of these are political decisions. For example, instead of reducing the number of schools, the government may decide to have smaller class sizes instead.

Activity **Effects of China's one-child policy**

Go to www.sociology.uk.net

Deaths

In the UK, the overall *number* of deaths has remained fairly stable since 1900, at round about 600,000 per year – although of course in 1900, this number of deaths was out of a much smaller population than today. However, there have been some important fluctuations. For example, the two world wars (1914-18 and 1939-45) brought a rise in the number of deaths, while the influenza epidemic of 1918 brought deaths to a record level of 690,000.

However, the death *rate* has fallen since 1900. The death rate is the number of deaths per thousand of the population per year. In 1900, the death rate stood at 19, whereas by 2007 it had almost halved, to 10.

The death rate had already begun falling from about 1870 and continued to do so until 1930. It rose slightly during the 1930s and 1940s – the period of the great economic depression, followed by World War II – but since the 1950s it has declined slightly.

Reasons for the decline in the death rate

There are several reasons why the death rate declined during the 20th century.

According to N.L. Tranter (1996), over three-quarters of the decline in the death rate from about 1850 to 1970 was due to a fall in the number of deaths from infectious diseases such as diphtheria, influenza, scarlet fever, measles, smallpox, diarrhoea, typhoid and above all tuberculosis (TB). Since deaths from infectious disease were commonest in the young, it is not surprising that most of the decline in the death rate occurred among infants, children and young adults.

By the 1950s, so-called 'diseases of affluence' (wealth) such as heart disease and cancers had replaced infectious diseases as the main cause of death. These degenerative diseases affect the middle aged and old more than the young.

There are several possible reasons for the decline in deaths from infection. It is possible that the population began to develop some natural resistance as a result of natural selection (that is, those who were most susceptible died off and did not reproduce), or that some diseases became less virulent (powerful).

However, social factors probably had a much greater impact on infectious diseases. These include the following:

Improved nutrition

Thomas McKeown (1972) argues that improved nutrition accounted for up to half the reduction in death rates, and was particularly important in reducing the number of deaths from TB. Better nutrition increased resistance to infection and increased the survival chances of those who did become infected.

However, others have challenged McKeown's explanation. For example, it does not explain why females, who receive a smaller share of the family food supply, lived longer than males, nor why deaths from some infectious diseases, such as measles and infant diarrhoea, actually rose at a time of improving nutrition.

Medical improvements

Before the 1950s, despite some important innovations, medical improvements played almost no part in the reduction of deaths from infectious disease. For example, as Tranter observes:

"As late as the 1930s, levels of obstetric knowledge and technique were so poor that they were more likely to increase rather than decrease death rates in childbirth."

However, after the 1950s, improved medical knowledge, techniques and organisation did help to reduce death rates. Advances included the introduction of antibiotics, widespread immunisation, blood transfusion, higher standards of midwifery and maternity services, as well as the setting up of a single publicly funded National Health Service in 1949. More recently, improved medication, by-pass surgery and other developments have reduced deaths from heart disease by one-third.

Public health measures and environmental improvements

In the 20th century, more effective central and local government with the necessary power to pass and enforce laws led to a range of improvements in public health and the quality of the environment.

These included improvements in housing (producing drier, better ventilated, less overcrowded accommodation), purer drinking water, laws to combat the adulteration of food and drink, the pasteurisation of milk, and improved sewage disposal methods. Similarly, the Clean Air Acts reduced air pollution, such as the smog that led to 4,000 premature deaths in five days in 1952.

Other social changes

Other social changes also played a part in reducing the death rate during the 20th century. These included:

- The decline of more dangerous manual occupations such as mining
- Smaller families reduced the rate of transmission of infection

- Greater public knowledge of the causes of illness
- Higher incomes, allowing for a healthier lifestyle.

Life expectancy

Life expectancy refers to how long on average a person born in a given year can expect to live. As death rates have fallen, so life expectancy has increased. For example:

- Males born in England in 1900 could expect on average to live until they were 50 (57 for females).
- Males born in England in 2003-5 can expect to live for 76.9 years (81.2 for females).

If we take the past two centuries, life expectancy has increased by about two years per decade.

One reason for lower average life expectancy in 1900 was the fact that so many infants and children did not survive beyond the early years of life. As we saw earlier, in 1900 over 15% of babies died in their first year. To put the improvement in life expectancy into perspective, we can note that a newborn baby today has a better chance of reaching its 65th birthday than a baby born in 1900 had of reaching its *first* birthday.

Class, gender and regional differences

Despite the overall reduction in the death rate and the increase in life expectancy over the last 100 years, there are still important class, gender and regional differences. For example, women generally live longer than men – although the gap has narrowed due to changes in employment and lifestyle (such as women smoking).

Similarly, those living in the North and Scotland have a lower life expectancy than those in the South, while working-class men in unskilled or routine jobs are nearly three times as likely to die before they are 65 compared with men in managerial or professional jobs.

Suggest three reasons why manual workers have higher death rates than professionals.

The ageing population

The average age of the UK population is rising. In 1971, it was 34.1 years. By 2007, it stood at 39.6. By 2031, it is projected to reach 42.6. There are fewer young people and more old people in the population. As Figure 2.4 shows, the number of people aged 65 or over is projected to overtake the number of under-16s for the first time ever in 2014.

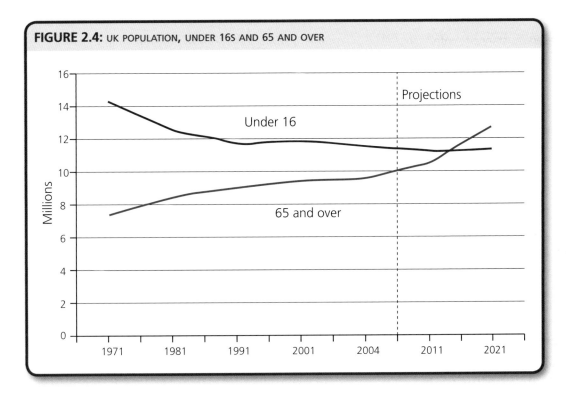

FIGURE 2.4: UK POPULATION, UNDER 16S AND 65 AND OVER

Public services

Older people consume a larger proportion of services such as health and social care than other age groups. This is particularly true of the 'old old' (usually defined as 75 or over) as against the 'young old' (65-74). However, we should beware of over-generalising, since many people remain in relatively good health well into old age.

In addition to increased expenditure on health care, an ageing population may also mean changes to policies and provision of housing, transport or other services.

Activity The UK's ageing population

www.sociology.uk.net

Another way of illustrating the changing age-profile of the population is by means of 'age pyramids' such as the ones in Figure 2.5 on page 52. These show how older age groups are growing as a proportion of the population, while younger groups are shrinking. In fact, as Donald Hirsch (2005) notes, the traditional age 'pyramid' is disappearing and being replaced by more or less equal-sized 'blocks' representing the different age groups. For example, on current projections, by 2041 there will be as many 78 year olds as five year olds.

This ageing of the population is the result of several factors:

- Increasing life expectancy – people are living longer into old age
- Declining infant mortality, so that nowadays hardly anyone dies early in life
- Declining fertility – fewer young people are being produced in relation to the number of older people in the population.

Effects of an ageing population

We have already examined the reasons for changes in life expectancy, infant mortality and fertility. We shall focus here on the effects or consequences of an ageing population.

One-person pensioner households

The number of pensioners living alone has increased and one-person pensioner households now account for about 14% of all households. Most of these are female, both because women generally live longer than men, and because they are usually younger than their husbands.

The dependency ratio

Like the non-working young, the non-working old are an economically dependent group who need to be provided for by those of working age, for example through taxation to pay for pensions and health care. As the number of retired people rises, this increases the dependency ratio and the burden on the working population.

However, it would be wrong to assume that 'old' necessarily equals 'economically dependent'. For example, the age at which people retire can vary – about one in ten men in their 50s is no longer working, while recent changes mean that women will soon have to wait until they are 65 to access the state pension (previously women's pensions began at 60, men's at 65). Others carry on working into their 70s.

Also, while an increase in the number of old people raises the dependency ratio, in an ageing population this is offset by a declining number of dependent children.

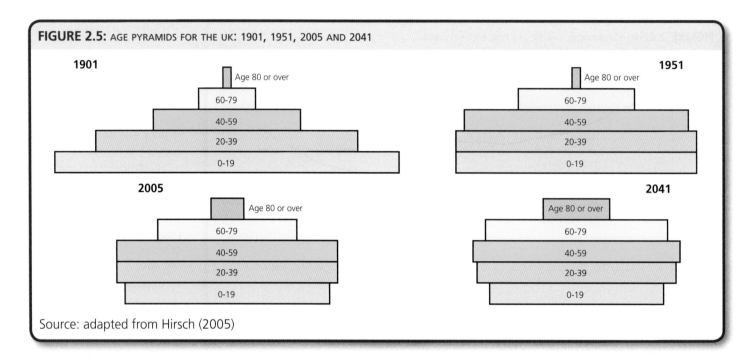

FIGURE 2.5: AGE PYRAMIDS FOR THE UK: 1901, 1951, 2005 AND 2041

Source: adapted from Hirsch (2005)

The social construction of ageing as a 'problem'

As we saw in the case of childhood (Topic 2), age statuses are socially constructed. This also applies to old age. Much of the 'discourse' (way of speaking and thinking about something) about old age and ageing is negative and has constructed it as 'problem'. For example:

- The Griffiths Report (1988) on the care of the elderly saw society as facing the problem of meeting the escalating costs of health and social care for the growing numbers of old people.
- Recently, there have been concerns about the 'pensions time bomb', with fears about how society will meet the cost of providing pensions for the elderly.

More broadly, in modern societies, 'ageism' – the negative stereotyping of people on the basis of their age – often portrays the old as vulnerable, incompetent or irrational, and as a burden to society. This contrasts with the view of the elderly found in traditional societies. In these cultures, the old are revered and respected; ageing is associated with a rising status.

> What are the similarities and the differences in social attitudes towards old people and children?

According to Peter Townsend (1981), one reason for negative attitudes to the elderly in our society is that old age has been socially constructed as a period of dependency by creating a statutory retirement age at which most people are expected or required to stop working and are forced to rely on inadequate benefits that push many into poverty.

Policy implications

Donald Hirsch (2005) argues that a number of important social policies and trends will need to change to tackle the new problems posed by an ageing population. The main problem will be how to finance a longer period of old age. This can either be done by paying more from our savings and taxes while we are working, or by continuing to work for longer, or a combination of both.

Hirsch therefore argues that we need to reverse the current trend towards earlier retirement. One way of doing this is by redistributing educational resources towards older people so that they can retrain and improve their skills and so continue earning.

Similarly, there may need to be changes in housing policy to encourage older people (who are more likely to be living in larger houses than they need) to 'trade down' into smaller accommodation and retirement homes. This would release wealth to improve their standard of living and free up housing resources for younger people.

As Hirsch recognises, many of these policy changes require a cultural change in our attitudes towards old age. His view illustrates the notion that old age is a social construct – that is, not a fixed, purely biological fact, but something shaped and defined by society. For example, in an ageing society, we may find changes in our idea of how old is 'old enough' to retire, or our beliefs about what share of society's resources should go to people at different stages of their lives.

Migration

In addition to natural change (births and deaths), the other factor affecting the size and age of the population is migration.

Migration refers to the movement of people from place to place. It can be internal, within a society, or international.

- **Immigration** refers to movement into an area or society.
- **Emigration** refers to movement out.
- **Net migration** is the difference between the numbers immigrating and the numbers emigrating, and is expressed as a net increase or net decrease due to migration.

For most of the 20th century, the growth of the UK population was the result of natural increase (more births than deaths), rather than the numbers of people immigrating and emigrating.

This was because, until the 1980s, the numbers immigrating were lower than those emigrating. For example, in every single year from 1946 to 1978, more people left the UK to settle elsewhere than arrived to live in the UK.

From 1900 until the Second World War (1939-45), the largest immigrant group to the UK were the Irish, mainly for economic reasons, followed by Eastern and Central European Jews, who were often refugees fleeing persecution, and people of British descent from Canada and the USA. Very few immigrants were non-white.

By contrast, during the 1950s, black immigrants from the Caribbean began to arrive in the UK, followed during the 1960s and 1970s by South Asian immigrants from India, Pakistan, Bangladesh and Sri Lanka, and by East African Asians from Kenya and Uganda.

One consequence of this immigration was that it produced a more ethnically diverse society. By 2001, minority ethnic groups accounted for 7.9% of the total population. One result of this has been a greater diversity of family patterns in Britain today. (See Topic 5, page 66.)

However, as noted earlier, throughout this period, more people left the UK than entered. Nor did non-white immigrants make up the majority of settlers. During the 1950s, the Irish were the largest single group (with over a third of a million) and almost as many again arriving from continental Europe.

Despite this, however, a series of immigration and nationality acts from 1962 to 1990 placed severe restrictions on non-white immigration. By the 1980s, non-whites accounted for little more than a quarter of all immigrants, while the predominantly white countries of the European Union became the main source of settlers in the UK.

Emigration

From as early as the mid-16th century until the 1980s, the UK has almost always been a net exporter of people: more have emigrated to live elsewhere than have come to settle in the UK. Since 1900, the great majority of emigrants have gone to the USA and to the Old Commonwealth countries (Canada, Australia and New Zealand) and South Africa.

The main reasons for emigration have been economic – both in terms of 'push' factors such as economic recession and unemployment at home, and even more so in terms of 'pull' factors such as higher wages or better opportunities abroad.

In the earlier part of the century, there were often labour shortages in the destination countries, while after 1945, the relatively poor performance of the British economy compared with that of other industrial countries acted as an incentive to emigrate. These economic reasons for migration contrast with those of some other groups, who have been driven to migrate by religious, political or racial persecution.

We should also note the existence of assisted passage schemes, by which the UK or receiving country's government paid part or all of the costs of migration. These schemes were particularly important in encouraging emigration to the Old Commonwealth countries, such as Australia, and they were often introduced partly for political or ideological reasons, such as to strengthen the ties with the 'mother country' or to boost the white population of the former colonies.

Activity

In pairs, read through the section on Migration. Now make a list of all the factors that might lead people to move from one country to another. Identify each one as either a 'push' factor (moving away from something), a 'pull' factor (moving to gain something), or both.

Recent and future migration patterns

Recent years have seen increasing levels of both immigration and emigration. Between 1994 and 2004, immigration rose from 314,000 to 582,000 annually, while emigration rose from 238,000 to 360,000.

In 2004, there was a net migration of 223,000 people into the UK. This was the highest net inflow of people since 1991, and considerably higher than for the previous year.

The key reason for the increase was the expansion of the European Union in 2004 to include ten new member states, mostly in Eastern Europe, giving their citizens the right to live and work in the UK. Four fifths of the increase in net migration in 2004 came from these ten states, with Poland accounting for the biggest share.

Both immigrants and emigrants were generally young, and slightly more likely to be male than female. The main reasons for migration are study or work, with about a quarter of all immigrants coming to study in the UK and over a fifth coming to take up a specific job.

However, a significant number of emigrants from the UK are older. Forty per cent of British emigrants were moving to other EU countries such as Spain, in many cases to retire there.

The UK's low fertility rate of 1.84 children per woman means that the existing population is not able to replace itself. Conventionally, it is assumed that each woman needs to produce 2.1 children in order to keep population at current levels. Thus, if it were not for net migration, the UK population would be declining in size.

While natural increase has been the main reason for population growth in the past, it is now projected that slightly over half the increase up to 2031 will come from net migration.

The dependency ratio

The effect of migration on the dependency ratio is complex. On the one hand, the fact that migrants are mainly of working age reduces the dependency ratio.

On the other hand, immigrant women tend to have higher fertility rates, which in the short term contributes to a higher dependency ratio by adding more children to the population.

However, this also reduces the average age of the population and in due course produces more workers, thereby lowering the dependency ratio as these children grow up and reach working age.

Finally, to complicate matters further, evidence suggests that the longer an immigrant group is settled in the country, the closer their fertility rate comes to the national average.

Internal migration

While most media attention focuses on international migration, we should note the importance of internal migration within the UK.

During the industrial revolution of the 19th century, which was based geographically in the North of England, South Wales and West Scotland, there was a population shift from the largely agricultural South to the industrial North to take up jobs in textiles, mining, shipbuilding and iron and steel.

This produced a corresponding shift from rural to urban living; in 1851, Britain was the first country to see more than half its population living in towns and cities.

During the 20th century, as these industries began to decline and newer ones such as motor cars, electrical engineering and chemicals began to develop in the South and Midlands, there began a population shift in the opposite direction in search of economic opportunities.

More recently, London and the South East have exerted an important pull because of the growth of the finance and service industries located there.

A corresponding trend has been suburbanisation, with the growth of large residential areas surrounding the major cities. However, in recent years, there has been a reversal of the outflow of population from inner city areas.

For more activities on Demography...

Go to www.sociology.uk.net

Summary

Population size is influenced by **natural change** (births and deaths) and **net migration** (immigration and emigration).

Since 1900, the **birth rate** and **total fertility rate** have **declined**, producing smaller family sizes. Reasons include **lower infant mortality** and changes in the **position of children**.

The **death rate declined** and **life expectancy increased** because of better **nutrition, public health** measures and other **social changes** and, to a lesser extent, medical advances. The UK has an **ageing population**. Effects of this may include greater need for expenditure on health care and **pensions**, ageism, and an increase in the **dependency ratio**.

Until the 1980s, more people left the UK than arrived to settle. **Migration** has implications for age structure and fertility rates. Reasons for migration can involve both **'push'** and **'pull'** factors.

QuickCheck Questions

1 Identify two public health measures that helped to produce the decline in the death rate.

2 Suggest two reasons for the decline in the birth rate in the 20th Century.

3 Suggest two reasons for class differences in infant mortality.

4 How might population trends in the UK be related to the increase in the proportion of married women working?

5 Suggest two reasons for the decline in maternal mortality.

6 Identify three reasons why many women today are having their children at a later age than earlier generations.

7 What is the typical effect of immigration on fertility rates?

8 Identify two effects migration may have on the dependency ratio.

 Check your answers at www.sociology.uk.net

Examining demography

Item A The main factors determining the overall size of a population are natural increase (or decrease) and net migration. Between 1900 and the present day, there were major changes in the size of the United Kingdom's population. During this period, the total population increased from about 38 million to about 61 million people.

The structure of a population refers to features such as the sex balance and the age structure of its members. The age structure is affected by the birth rate and the total fertility rate, and by average life expectancy. In the UK, life expectancy increased enormously during the 20th century, in part due to the huge fall in the infant mortality rate and, to a lesser extent, the reduction of the death rate among adults. For example, a baby born in 1900 had an 85% chance of surviving until their first birthday, whereas a baby born today has the same chance of living until their 65th birthday.   5

(a) Explain the difference between the birth rate and the total fertility rate (**Item A**, line 5).   (4 marks)

(b) Explain the difference between natural change and net migration (**Item A**, line 1).   (4 marks)

(c) Explain the difference between the infant mortality rate and the death rate (**Item A**, line 6).   (4 marks)

Essay Examine the main trends in births and deaths in the United Kingdom since 1900.   (24 marks)

The examiner's advice

The essay carries 14 AO1 marks (knowledge and understanding) and 10 AO2 marks (interpretation, application, analysis and evaluation). The emphasis is on showing a sound, detailed sociological knowledge, but to score high marks you must also demonstrate AO2 skills.

You need to describe the main trends in both births and deaths since 1900. For births, you should note the overall fall in both birth rates and total fertility rates (or family sizes), as well as the main 'baby booms'. Likewise, for deaths, you should describe the trend since 1900 – a fairly steady number, but a falling *rate* as population grew. As well as describing these trends, you should examine some of their causes. Causes of falls in the death rate and infant mortality rate include better nutrition, improved housing and environmental health (e.g. clean drinking water, better sewage systems) and immunisation. Causes of changes in the birth rate include changes in the position of women, availability of contraception and abortion, reduced infant mortality, children becoming an economic liability etc. You should also consider some of the consequences of population trends, such as the effect of an ageing population on the dependency ratio.

Topic 5 Changing family patterns

In the past 30 or 40 years there have been some major changes in family and household patterns. For example:

- The number of traditional nuclear family households – a married couple with their dependent children – has fallen.
- Divorce rates have increased.
- There are fewer first marriages, but more re-marriages. People are marrying later in life.
- More couples are cohabiting.
- Same-sex relationships can be legally recognised through civil partnerships.
- Women are having fewer children and having them later.
- There are more births outside marriage.
- There are more lone-parent families.
- More people live alone.
- There are more stepfamilies, and more couples without children.

In this Topic, we examine the changes in patterns of family life in Britain and the reasons for them. These changes include marriage, cohabitation and divorce. Such changes are contributing to greater family diversity, and we examine how sociologists have interpreted them.

Learning objectives

When you have studied this Topic, you should:

- Know the main changes in partnerships, including marriage, divorce, cohabitation and civil partnerships, as well as one-person and extended family households.
- Know the main changes in childbearing and childrearing, including births outside marriage, lone-parent families and stepfamilies.
- Understand how these changes have contributed to greater family diversity.
- Be able to analyse and evaluate the reasons for these changes in families and households.

Divorce

We look first at divorce because divorce is a major cause of changing family patterns and greater family diversity. For example, most re-marriages involve a divorcee, and divorce creates both lone-parent families and one-person households.

Changing patterns of divorce

Since the 1960s, there has been a great increase in the number of divorces in the United Kingdom, as Figure 2.6 shows. The number of divorces doubled between 1961 and 1969, and doubled again by 1972. The upward trend continued, peaking in 1993 at 180,000.

Since then, numbers have fallen somewhat, but still stood at 157,000 in 2001 – about six times higher than in 1961. This rate means that about 40% of all marriages will end in divorce.

About 7 out of every 10 petitions (applications) for divorce now come from women. This is in sharp contrast to the situation in the past. For example, in 1946, only 37% of petitions came from women – barely half today's figure. The commonest reason for a woman to be granted a divorce is the unreasonable behaviour of her husband.

Some couples are more likely than others to divorce. Couples whose marriages are at greatest risk include those who marry young, have a child before they marry or cohabit before marriage, and those where one or both partners have been married before.

Explanations of the increase in divorce

Sociologists have identified the following reasons for the increase in divorce:

1 changes in the law

2 declining stigma and changing attitudes

3 secularisation

4 rising expectations of marriage

5 changes in the position of women.

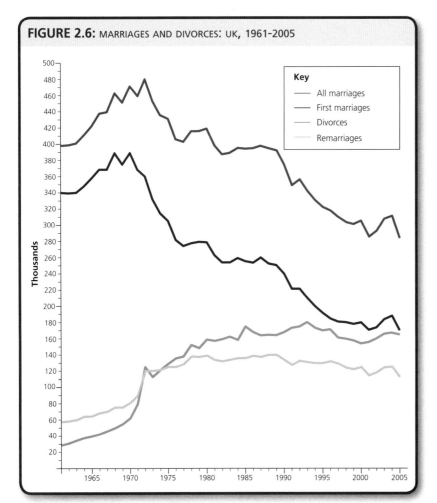

FIGURE 2.6: MARRIAGES AND DIVORCES: UK, 1961-2005

Key
— All marriages
— First marriages
— Divorces
— Remarriages

1 Study Figure 2.6 and answer the following questions:

(a) Roughly how many divorces were there in 1971?

(b) Roughly how many marriages were there in 2001?

(c) Describe the trends in the number of first marriages, re-marriages and divorces over the period shown.

(d) Suggest three reasons why the total number of marriages has been declining.

2 Between 1981 and 2005, the proportion of marriages conducted with civil rather than religious ceremonies rose from 40% to 65%. Where both partners had been married before, the figure was around 90%. Suggest reasons why:

(a) there has been such a decline in church marriages.

(b) re-marriages are much less likely than first marriages to take place in church.

Box 6	A brief history of divorce law

Before 1857, divorce was virtually non-existent and only obtainable by a special and costly Act of Parliament.

1857   Men could divorce unfaithful wives, but women also had to prove husbands' cruelty or another matrimonial offence in addition to adultery. Divorce still very costly.

1921   3,000 divorces.

1923   Grounds for divorce equalised for men and women.

1937   Grounds widened to include desertion and cruelty.

1949   Legal aid available, making divorce more affordable.

1961   27,000 divorces – nine times higher than in 1921.

1969   Divorce Law Reform Act passed (came into effect in 1971). This made 'irretrievable breakdown' of marriage the sole ground for divorce, established by proving unreasonable behaviour, adultery, desertion, or separation either with or without consent. Divorce available after two years' agreed separation, or five years if only one spouse wants divorce.

1984   The minimum period after marriage before a divorce petition could be filed was reduced from three years to one.

1996   Family Law Act encourages couples to seek mediation but allows divorce by agreement after a 'period of reflection'.

2004   Civil Partnership Act allows for legal dissolution of a civil partnership on the same grounds as for a marriage – irretrievable breakdown.

2007   Appeal Court ruling: in divorce settlements, the principle of equality applies, so the starting point is a 50-50 split of all assets, including salaries and pension rights.

1 Changes in the law

Divorce was very difficult to obtain in 19th-century Britain, especially for women. Gradually, changes in the law have made divorce easier. There have been three kinds of change in the law:

- Equalising the grounds (the legal reasons) for divorce between the sexes
- Widening the grounds for divorce
- Making divorce cheaper.

When the grounds were equalised for men and women in 1923, this was followed by a sharp rise in the number of divorce petitions from women. Similarly, the widening of the grounds in 1971 to 'irretrievable breakdown' made divorce easier to obtain and produced a doubling of the divorce rate almost overnight. The introduction of legal aid for divorce cases in 1949 lowered the cost of divorcing. Divorce rates have risen with each change in the law.

Although divorce is the legal termination of a marriage, couples can and do find other solutions to the problem of an unhappy marriage. These include:

- **Desertion**, where one partner leaves the other but the couple remain legally married
- **Legal separation**, where a court separates the financial and legal affairs of the couple but where they remain married and are not free to re-marry
- **'Empty shell'** marriage, where the couple continue to live under the same roof but remain married in name only.

However, as divorce has become more easily available, these solutions have become less popular.

Yet although changes in the law have given people the freedom to divorce more easily, this does not in itself explain why more people should choose to take advantage of this freedom. To explain the rise in divorce rates we must therefore look at other changes too. These include changes in public attitudes towards divorce.

2 Declining stigma and changing attitudes

Stigma refers to the negative label, social disapproval or shame attached to a person, action or relationship. In the past, divorce and divorcees have been stigmatised. For example, churches tended to condemn divorce and often refused to conduct marriage services involving divorcees. Juliet Mitchell and Jack Goody (1997) note that an important change since the 1960s has been the rapid decline in the stigma attached to divorce.

As stigma declines and divorce becomes more socially acceptable, couples become more willing to resort to divorce as a means of solving their marital problems. In turn, the fact that divorce is now more common begins to 'normalise' it and reduces the stigma attached to it. Rather than being seen as shameful, today it is more likely to be regarded simply as a misfortune.

3 Secularisation

Secularisation refers to the decline in the influence of religion in society. Many sociologists argue that religious institutions and ideas are losing their influence and society is becoming more secular. For example, church attendance rates continue to decline.

As a result of secularisation, the traditional opposition of the churches to divorce carries less weight in society and people are less likely to be influenced by religious teachings when making decisions. For example, according to 2001 Census data, 43% of young people with no religion were cohabiting, as against only 34% of Christians, 17% of Muslims, 11% of Hindus and 10% of Sikhs.

At the same time, many churches have also begun to soften their views on divorce and divorcees, perhaps because they fear losing credibility with large sections of the public and with their own members.

Activity

Which religions now allow divorce and re-marriage and under what circumstances?

Try to find out about a range of churches, e.g. Church of England, Catholic, Baptist, Jehovah's Witnesses, Pentecostalist. Also find out about the attitudes of non-Christian religions.

4 Rising expectations of marriage

Functionalist sociologists such as Ronald Fletcher (1966) argue that the higher expectations people place on marriage today are a major cause of rising divorce rates. Higher expectations make couples nowadays less willing to tolerate an unhappy marriage.

This is linked to the ideology of romantic love – an idea that has become dominant over the last couple of centuries. This is the belief that marriage should be based solely on love, and that for each individual there is a Mr or Miss Right out there. It follows that if love dies, there is no longer any justification for remaining married and every reason to divorce so as to be able to renew the search for one's true soulmate.

In the past, by contrast, individuals often had little choice in whom they married, and at a time when the family was also a unit of production, marriages were often contracted largely for economic reasons or out of duty to one's family.

Under these circumstances, individuals were unlikely to have the high expectations about marriage as a romantic union of two souls that many couples have today. Entering marriage with lower expectations, they were less likely to be dissatisfied by the absence of romance and intimacy.

Today, on the other hand, marriage is increasingly viewed not as a binding contract, but as a relationship in which individuals seek personal fulfilment, and this encourages couples to divorce if they do not find it. As Graham Allan and Graham Crow (2001) put it:

> 'Love, personal commitment and intrinsic satisfaction are now seen as the cornerstones of marriage. The absence of these feelings is itself justification for ending the relationship.'

However, despite today's high divorce rates, functionalists such as Fletcher take an optimistic view. They point to the continuing popularity of marriage. Most adults marry, and the high rate of re-marriage after divorce shows that although divorcees may have become dissatisfied with a particular partner, they have not rejected marriage as an institution.

However, critics argue that this is too rosy a view. Feminists argue that the oppression of women within the family is the main cause of marital conflict and divorce, but functionalists ignore this. Although functionalists offer an explanation of rising divorce rates, they fail to explain why it is mainly women rather than men who seek divorce.

5 Changes in the position of women

One reason for women's increased willingness to seek divorce is that improvements in their economic position have made them less financially dependent on their husband and therefore freer to end an unsatisfactory marriage.

- Women today are much more likely to be in paid work. The proportion of women working rose from 47% in 1959 to 70% in 2005.
- Although women generally still earn less than men, equal pay and anti-discrimination laws have helped to narrow the pay gap.
- Girls' greater success in education now helps them achieve better-paid jobs than previous generations.
- The availability of welfare benefits means that women no longer have to remain financially dependent on their husbands.

These developments mean that women are more likely to be able to support themselves in the event of divorce.

Allan and Crow put forward a similar view. They argue that "marriage is less embedded within the economic system" now. There are fewer family firms and the family is no longer a unit of production, so spouses are not so economically interdependent – each has their own separate source of income from paid work. Not having to rely on each other financially, they do not have to tolerate conflict or the absence of love, and in such circumstances they are more willing to seek divorce.

Many feminists also argue that the fact that women are now wage earners as well as homemakers has itself created a new source of conflict between husbands and wives and this is leading to more divorces.

While there have been big improvements in women's position in the public sphere of employment, education, politics and so on, feminists argue that in the private sphere of family and personal relationships, change has been slow. They argue that marriage remains patriarchal, with men benefiting from their wives' 'triple shift' of paid work, domestic work and emotion work (see page 23).

Similarly, Arlie Hochschild (1997) argues that for many women, the home compares unfavourably with work. At work, women feel valued. At home, men's continuing resistance to doing housework is a source of frustration and makes marriage less stable. In addition, the fact that both partners now go out to work leaves less time and energy for the emotion work needed to address the problems that arise. Both these factors contribute to the rising divorce rate.

According to Wendy Sigle-Rushton (ESRC, 2007), working mothers are more likely to divorce than women in relationships with a traditional division of labour between male breadwinner and female homemaker. However, where the husband of a working wife is actively involved in housework, the likelihood of divorce falls to the same level as that of couples with a traditional division of labour.

▲ *Divorced fathers campaigning for rights of custody and access. Why do the courts usually give custody to mothers?*

Radical feminists such as Jessie Bernard (1976) observe that many women feel a growing dissatisfaction with patriarchal marriage. She sees the rising divorce rate, and the fact that most petitions come from women, as evidence of their growing acceptance of feminist ideas: women are becoming conscious of patriarchal oppression and more confident about rejecting it.

The meaning of high divorce rates

Sociologists disagree as to what today's high divorce rate tells us about the state of marriage and the family.

- **The New Right** see a high divorce rate as undesirable because it undermines the traditional nuclear family. In their view, divorce creates an underclass of welfare-dependent female lone parents and leaves boys without the adult male role model they need.

- **Feminists** disagree. They see a high divorce rate as desirable because it shows that women are breaking free from the oppression of the patriarchal nuclear family.

- **Postmodernists** see a high divorce rate as giving individuals the freedom to choose to end a relationship when it no longer meets their needs. They see it as a cause of greater family diversity.

- **Functionalists** argue that a high divorce rate does not necessarily prove that marriage as a social institution is under threat. It is simply the result of people's higher expectations of marriage today. The high rate of re-marriage shows people's continuing commitment to the idea of marriage.

- **Interactionists** aim to understand what divorce means to the individual. David Morgan (1996) argues that we cannot generalise about the meaning of divorce because every individual's interpretation of it is different. Mitchell and Goody provide an example of this. One of their interviewees described the day her father left as the best day of her life, whereas another said she had never recovered from her father deserting the family.

Partnerships

Marriage

There have been a number of important changes in the pattern of marriage in recent years:

- Fewer people are marrying: marriage rates are at their lowest since the 1920s. In 2005, there were 170,800 first marriages – less than half the number for 1970.
- However, there are more re-marriages (marriages where one or both partners have been married before). In 2005, 4 out of every 10 marriages were re-marriages. For many people, this is leading to 'serial monogamy': a pattern of marriage – divorce – re-marriage.
- People are marrying later: the average age of first marriage rose by seven years between 1971 and 2005, when it reached 32 years for men and 30 for women.
- Couples are less likely to marry in church. In 1981, 60% of weddings were conducted with religious ceremonies, but by 2005 this had fallen to 35%.

Reasons for changing patterns of marriage

Many of the reasons for a fall in the number of first marriages are similar to the reasons for the increase in divorce examined earlier. They include the following:

- Changing attitudes to marriage. There is less pressure to marry and more freedom for individuals to choose the type of relationship they want. There is now a widespread belief that the quality of a couple's relationship is more important than its legal status. The norm that everyone ought to get married has greatly weakened.
- This may be linked to secularisation. The churches are in favour of marriage, but as their influence declines, people feel freer to choose not to marry. For example, according to the 2001 Census, only 3% of young people with no religion were married, as against up to 17% of those with a religion.
- Declining stigma attached to alternatives to marriage. Cohabitation, remaining single, and having children outside marriage are all now widely regarded as acceptable, so that pregnancy no longer automatically leads to a 'shotgun wedding'. Of those interviewed for the British Social Attitudes survey in 1989, 70% believed that couples who want children should get married; but by 2000 only 54% thought so.

- Changes in the position of women. With better educational and career prospects, many women are now less economically dependent on men. This gives them greater freedom not to marry. The growing impact of the feminist view that marriage is an oppressive patriarchal institution may also dissuade some women from marrying.
- Fear of divorce. With the rising divorce rate, some may be put off marrying as they see the increased likelihood of marriage ending in divorce.

1 What is meant by a 'pre-nuptial agreement'?

2 What does the rise of pre-nuptial agreements tell us about attitudes to marriage today?

▲ *One estimate puts the total cost of a white wedding at over £17,000*

The main reason for the increase in re-marriages is the rise in the number of divorces. As Figure 2.6 shows, the two have grown together, so that the rising number of divorcees provides a supply of people available to re-marry.

The age at which couples marry is rising because young people are postponing marriage in order to spend longer in full-time education, and perhaps to establish themselves in a career first. Another reason is that more couples are now cohabiting for a period before they marry.

Couples nowadays are less likely to marry in church for two main reasons:

- Secularisation: fewer people see the relevance of a religious ceremony.
- Many churches refuse to marry divorcees (who make up a growing proportion of those marrying) and divorcees may in any case have less desire to marry in church.

However, despite a fall in the numbers marrying for the first time, the institution of marriage remains popular, at least as an ideal to aspire to. For example, the British Social Attitudes (2000) survey found that only 9% agreed with the view that 'there is no point in getting married – it is only a piece of paper', while 74% disagreed.

Cohabitation

Cohabitation involves an unmarried couple in a sexual relationship living together. While the number of marriages has been falling, the number of couples cohabiting continues to increase and is the fastest growing family type in the UK:

- There are over two million cohabiting couples in Britain. About a quarter of all unmarried adults under 60 are now cohabiting – double the number in 1986.
- The number of cohabiting couples is expected to double again by 2021.

Reasons for the increase in cohabitation

- Increased cohabitation rates reflect the decline in stigma attached to sex outside marriage. In 1989, only 44% of people agreed that 'premarital sex is not wrong at all', but by 2000, 62% took this view (British Social Attitudes, 2000).
- The young are more likely to accept cohabitation: 88% of 18-24 year olds thought 'it is alright for a couple to live together without intending to get married', but only 40% of those over 65 agreed (Social Trends 34, 2004).
- Increased career opportunities for women may also mean that they have less need for the financial security of marriage and are freer to opt for cohabitation.
- Secularisation: according to the 2001 Census, young people with no religion were more likely to cohabit than those with a religion.

The relationship between cohabitation and marriage

Although cohabitation is increasing as marriage decreases, the relationship between the two is not clear-cut. For some couples, cohabitation is just a step on the way to getting married, whereas for others it is a permanent alternative to marriage.

Robert Chester (1985) argues that for most people, cohabitation is part of the process of getting married. For example, according to Ernestina Coast (2006), 75% of cohabiting couples say they expect to marry each other. Many see cohabitation as a trial marriage and intend to marry if it goes well. Most cohabiting couples decide to marry if they have children. In some cases, cohabitation is a temporary phase before marriage because one or both partners are awaiting a divorce.

On the other hand, some couples see cohabitation as a permanent alternative to marriage. André Bejin (1985) argues that cohabitation among some young people represents a conscious attempt to create a more personally negotiated and equal relationship than conventional patriarchal marriage. For example, Shelton and John (1993) found that women who cohabit do less housework than their married counterparts.

Clearly, then, cohabitation does not mean the same thing to every couple. Eleanor Macklin (1980) argues that the term covers a diverse range of partnerships, and that the relationship between marriage and cohabitation is a complex and variable one.

Activity

Group discussion: Cohabitation is becoming 'marriage by another name'.

You might like to consider issues such as the following: whether cohabitation is just a temporary phase before marriage; same sex couples; why some couples choose to cohabit permanently rather than marry; similarities and differences in the rights and obligations of married versus cohabiting couples; the significance of high divorce rates.

Same-sex relationships

Stonewall (2008), the campaign for lesbian, gay and bisexual rights, estimates that about 5-7% of the adult population today have same-sex relationships. It is impossible to judge whether this represents an increase because in the past, stigma and illegality meant that such relationships were more likely to be hidden.

There is evidence of increased social acceptance of same-sex relationships in recent years. Male homosexual acts were decriminalised in 1967 for consenting adults over 21. More recently the age of consent has been equalised with heterosexuals. Opinion polls show more tolerance of homosexuality.

Social policy is now beginning to treat all couples more equally, whether homosexual or heterosexual, cohabiting or married. For example, since 2002, cohabiting couples have had the same right to adopt as married couples. Since 2004, the Civil Partnership Act has given same-sex couples similar legal rights to married couples in respect of pensions, inheritance, tenancies and property.

Jeffrey Weeks (1999) argues that increased social acceptance may explain a trend in recent years towards same-sex cohabitation and stable relationships that resemble those found among heterosexuals. Weeks sees gays as creating families based on the idea of 'friendship as kinship', where friendships become a type of kinship network. He describes these as 'chosen families' and argues that they offer the same security and stability as heterosexual families.

Similarly, Kath Weston (1992) describes same-sex cohabitation as 'quasi-marriage' and notes that many gay couples are now deciding to cohabit as stable partners. She contrasts this with the gay lifestyle of the 1970s, which largely rejected monogamy and family life in favour of casual relationships.

Others sociologists have noted the effect on same-sex relationships of a legal framework such as civil partnerships. For example, Allan and Crow argue that, because of the absence of such a framework until recently, same-sex partners have had to negotiate their commitment and responsibilities more than married couples. This may have made same-sex relationships both more flexible and less stable than heterosexual relationships.

Similarly, David Cheal (2002) notes that, while many gays and lesbians welcome the opportunity to have their partnerships legally recognised, others fear that it may limit the flexibility and negotiability of relationships. Rather than adopt what they see as heterosexual relationship norms, they wish to retain a status of 'difference'.

One-person households

Fewer people today are living in couples:

- There has been a big rise in the number of people living alone. In 2006, almost three in ten households (6.8 million people) contained only one person – nearly three times the figure for 1961.

- Half of all one-person households are people of pensionable age. Pensioner one-person households have doubled since 1961, while those of non-pensioners tripled. Men under 65 were the group most likely to live alone, with a particularly large increase in the number of young men living alone.

Reasons for the changes

The increase in separation and divorce has created more one-person households, especially among men under 65. This is because, following divorce, any children are more likely to live with their mother; their father is more likely to leave the family home.

The decline in the numbers marrying, and the trend towards people marrying later, mean that more people are remaining single. The proportion of adults who are single has risen by about half since 1971.

Many of these are living alone. Peter Stein (1976) argues that a growing number of people are opting for 'creative singlehood' – the deliberate choice to live alone.

However, while many of these choose to remain single and live alone, some are alone because there are too few partners available in their age group. These are mainly older widows.

'Living apart together'

It is often assumed that those not living with a partner do not have one, whether from choice or not. However, research by Simon Duncan and Miranda Phillips for the British Social Attitudes survey (Thomson et al, 2008) found that about one in 10 adults are 'living apart together' or 'LATs' – that is, in a significant relationship, but not married or cohabiting. It has been suggested that this may reflect a trend towards less formalised relationships and 'families of choice'.

However, Duncan and Phillips found that both choice and constraint play a part in whether couples live together. For example, some said they could not afford to. However, a minority actively chose to live apart, for example because they wanted to keep their own home.

Public attitudes towards LATs are favourable. A majority believe that 'a couple do not need to live together to have a strong relationship', while 20% saw LATs as their 'ideal relationship' (more than the number who preferred cohabitation).

Duncan and Phillips conclude that, while being a LAT is no longer seen as abnormal, it probably does not amount to a rejection of more traditional relationships.

Parents and children

Childbearing

- Over four in every ten children are now born outside marriage: five times more than in 1971. However, nearly all these births are jointly registered by both parents. In most cases, the parents are cohabiting.

- Women are having children later: between 1971 and 2005, their average age at the birth of their first child rose by more than three years to 27.3 years.

- Women are having fewer children than in the 20th century, though the number increased slightly in the early 21st century. The average number of children per woman fell from a peak of 2.95 in 1964 to a record low of 1.63 in 2001, rising somewhat to 1.84 by 2006.

- More women are remaining childless: it is predicted that a quarter of those born in 1973 will be childless when they reach the age of 45.

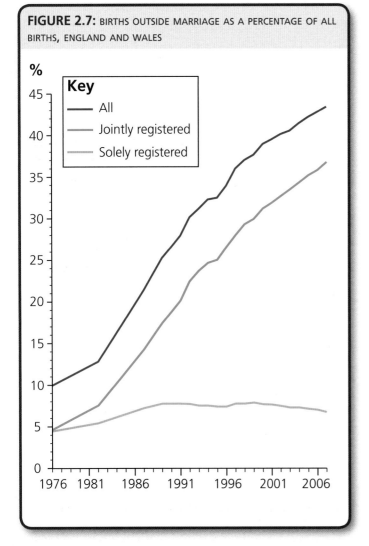

FIGURE 2.7: BIRTHS OUTSIDE MARRIAGE AS A PERCENTAGE OF ALL BIRTHS, ENGLAND AND WALES

Key
— All
— Jointly registered
— Solely registered

Reasons for the changes

- Reasons for the increase in births outside marriage include a decline in stigma and increase in cohabitation. For example, only one-third of 18-24 year olds now think marriage should come before parenthood. The rise is largely the result of an increase in births to cohabiting couples rather than to women living alone.

- The later age at which women are having children, smaller family sizes and the fact that more women are remaining childless, all reflect the fact that women now have more options than just motherhood. Many are seeking to establish themselves in a career before starting a family, or instead of having children at all.

> 1 By how many percentage points did the births that were solely registered by the mother alone increase between 1976 and 2007?
>
> 2 By how many percentage points did the births that were jointly registered by both parents increase during this period?

Lone-parent families

Lone-parent families now make up 24% of all families. One child in four lives in a lone-parent family.

- Over 90% of these families are headed by lone mothers.
- Until the early 1990s, divorced women were the biggest group of lone mothers. From the early 1990s, single (never married) women became the biggest group of lone mothers.
- A child living with a lone parent is more than twice as likely to be in poverty as a child living with two parents.

Reasons for the patterns

The number of lone-parent families has increased due to the increase in divorce and separation and more recently, the increase in the number of never-married women having children. This is linked to the decline in stigma attached to births outside marriage. In the past, the death of one parent was a common cause of lone-parent families, but this is no longer very significant.

Lone-parent families tend to be female-headed for several reasons. These include the widespread belief that women are by nature suited to an 'expressive' or nurturing role; the fact that divorce courts usually give custody of children to mothers and the fact that men may be less willing than women to give up work to care for children.

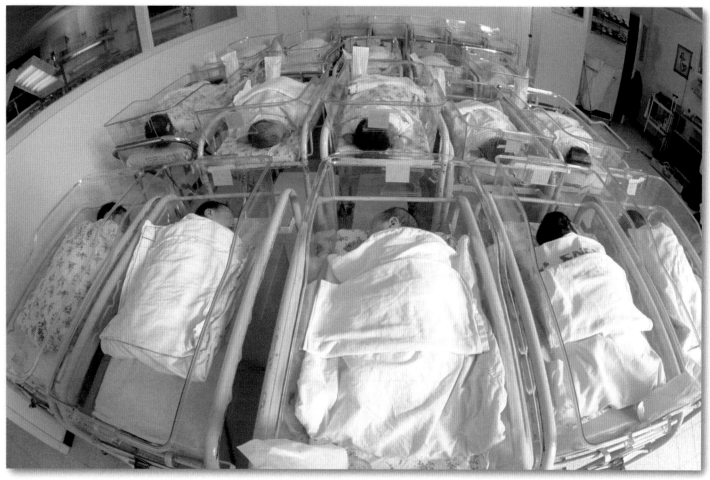

▲ *There were 275,000 fewer births in 2006 than in 1961.*

Many lone-parent families are female-headed because the mothers are single by choice. They may not wish to cohabit or marry, or they may wish to limit the father's involvement with the child. Jean Renvoize (1985) found that professional women were able to support their child without the father's involvement.

Equally, as Ellis Cashmore (1985) found, some working-class mothers with less earning power chose to live on welfare benefits without a partner, often because they had experienced abuse. Feminist ideas, and greater opportunities for women, may also have encouraged an increase in the number of never-married lone mothers.

Lone parenthood, the welfare state and poverty

The New Right thinker Charles Murray (1984) sees the growth of lone-parent families as resulting from an over-generous welfare state providing benefits for unmarried mothers and their children.

Murray argues that this has created a 'perverse incentive'; that is, it rewards irresponsible behaviour, such as having children without being able to provide for them. The

welfare state creates a 'dependency culture' in which people assume that the state will support them and their children.

For Murray, the solution is to abolish welfare benefits. This would reduce the dependency culture that encourages births outside marriage.

However, critics of New Right views argue that welfare benefits are far from generous and lone-parent families are much more likely to be in poverty. Reasons for this include:

- Lack of affordable childcare prevents lone parents from working: 60% of them are unemployed.
- Inadequate welfare benefits.
- Most lone parents are women, who generally earn less than men.
- Failure of fathers to pay maintenance, especially if they have formed a second family that they have to support.

1 Suggest two reasons for the increased number of lone-parent families today.

2 Suggest two reasons why so few lone-parent families are headed by fathers.

3 Why is it easier for women today to choose to have a child without marrying?

Stepfamilies

- Stepfamilies (often called reconstituted families) account for over 10% of all families with dependent children in Britain.
- In 86% of stepfamilies, at least one child is from the woman's previous relationship, while in 11% there is at least one child from the man's previous relationship. In 3% of stepfamilies there are children from both partners' previous relationships.
- Elsa Ferri and Kate Smith (1998) found that stepfamilies are very similar to first families in all major respects, and that the involvement of stepparents in childcare and childrearing is a positive one. However, they found that in general stepfamilies are at greater risk of poverty.
- However, according to Graham Allan and Graham Crow (2001), stepfamilies may face particular problems of divided loyalties and issues such as contact with the non-resident parent can cause tensions.
- Jane Ribbens McCarthy et al (2003) conclude that there is diversity among these families and so we should speak

of 'stepfamilies' plural rather than 'the stepfamily'. Some have few tensions, while for those that do, the tensions are not so different from those in 'intact' families.

Reasons for the patterns

- Stepfamilies are formed when lone parents form new partnerships. Thus the factors causing an increase in the number of lone parents, such as divorce and separation, are also responsible for the creation of stepfamilies.
- More children in stepfamilies are from the woman's previous relationship than the man's because, when marriages and cohabitations break up, children are more likely to remain with their mother.
- Stepparents are at greater risk of poverty because there are often more children and because the stepfather may also have to support children from a previous relationship.
- Some of the tensions faced by stepfamilies may be the result of a lack of clear social norms about how individuals should behave in such families.

Ethnic differences in family patterns

Immigration into Britain over the last 60 years has helped to create greater ethnic diversity. Analysis of the 2001 Census shows that 92.1% of the UK population (54 million people) were White. Of the 7.9% belonging to an ethnic minority, the main groups were Indian, Pakistani or Bangladeshi (3.6%); mixed ethnicity (1.2%); Black Caribbean (1%); Black African (0.8%) and Chinese (0.4%). Greater ethnic diversity has contributed to changing family patterns in the UK.

Black families

Black Caribbean and Black African people have a higher proportion of lone-parent households. In 2002, just over half of families with dependent children headed by a black person were lone-parent families (see Table 2B). This compared with one in 11 Indian families and just under a quarter for the population as a whole.

The high rate of female-headed, lone-parent black families has sometimes been seen as evidence of family disorganisation that can be traced back to slavery or, more recently, to high rates of unemployment among black males.

Table 2B — Families with dependent children: by ethnic group, 2002

United Kingdom	Couples	Lone parents
White	77	23
Mixed	39	61
Asian or Asian British		
Indian	91	9
Pakistani	85	15
Bangladeshi	89	11
Other Asian	90	10
All Asian groups	89	11
Black or Black British		
Black Caribbean	46	54
Black African	54	46
All Black groups	49	51
Chinese	79	21
Other ethnic group	80	20
All families	77	23

Source: Office for National Statistics

Under slavery, when couples were sold separately, children stayed with the mother. It is argued that this established a pattern of family life that persists today. It is also argued that male unemployment and poverty have meant that black men are less able to provide for their family, resulting in higher rates of desertion or marital breakdown.

However, Heidi Safia Mirza (1997) argues that the higher rate of lone-parent families among blacks is not the result of disorganisation, but rather reflects the high value that black women place on independence. Tracey Reynolds (1997) argues that the statistics are misleading, in that many apparently 'lone' parents are in fact in stable, supportive but non-cohabiting relationships.

Asian families

Bangladeshi, Pakistani and Indian households tend to be larger than those of other ethnic groups, at 4.5, 4.1 and 3.3 persons per household respectively, compared with 2.3 for both Black Caribbean and White British households, and 2.4 for the population as a whole.

Such households sometimes contain three generations, but most are in fact nuclear rather than extended. Larger household sizes are partly a result of the younger age profile of British Asians, since a higher proportion are in the childbearing age groups compared with the population as a whole.

Larger Asian households also to some extent reflect the value placed on the extended family in Asian cultures. However, practical considerations, such as the need for assistance when migrating to Britain, are also important. For example, Roger Ballard (1982) found that extended family ties provided an important source of support among Asian migrants during the 1950s and 1960s.

In this early period of migration, houses were often shared by extended families. Later, although most Asian households were now nuclear, relatives often lived nearby. There was frequent visiting, and kinship networks continued to be a source of support. Today, Sikhs, Muslims and Hindus are still more likely than other ethnic or religious groups to live in extended family units.

The extended family today

The existence of the extended family among minority ethnic groups raises the question of how widespread this kind of family is in the UK today. As we saw in Topic 3, according to functionalists such as Parsons, the extended family is the dominant family type in pre-industrial society, but in modern industrial society it is replaced by the nuclear family.

For example, as Nickie Charles' (2005) study of Swansea found, the classic three-generation family all living together under one roof is now "all but extinct". The only significant exceptions she found were among the city's Bangladeshi community.

However, while the extended family may have declined, it has not entirely disappeared. Instead, as Peter Willmott (1988) argues, it continues to exist as a 'dispersed extended family', where relatives are geographically separated but maintain frequent contact through visits and phone calls.

Similarly, Mary Chamberlain's (1999) study of Caribbean families in Britain found that, despite being geographically dispersed, they continue to provide support. She describes them as 'multiple nuclear families' with close and frequent contact between siblings, uncles, aunts and cousins, who often make a big contribution to childrearing.

Activity **The extended family today**

Go to www.sociology.uk.net

▲ *Three generations celebrate a wedding, Bethnal Green, 1952. Is the extended family now 'all but extinct'?*

As Chamberlain suggests, the extended family survives because it performs important functions for its members. For example, Colin Bell's (1968) earlier research in Swansea found that both working-class and middle-class families had emotional bonds with kin and relied on them for support:

- Among the middle class, there was more financial help from father to son.
- Working-class families had more frequent contact (they lived closer) and there was more domestic help from mothers to daughters.

Similarly, four decades later, Charles found that contact remains high between mothers and daughters. However, in the case of brothers and sisters, there had been a sharp decline in both support and contact. This affected who counts as 'family'- those who don't keep in touch or provide support may cease to be defined as family. Conversely, friends may become 'family' if they are seen often and help one another.

As Charles shows, there is some variability in what can be expected of different relatives. For example, Janet Finch and Jennifer Mason (1993) found that more is expected of females than males. However, people do continue to feel some obligation towards their extended kin – in Finch and Mason's study, over 90% had given or received financial help, and about half had cared for a sick relative. They also found that the principle of reciprocity or balance was important – people felt that help given should be returned to avoid any feelings of indebtedness.

Overall, evidence suggests that the extended family continues to play an important role for many people today, providing both practical and emotional support when called upon. However, this is very different from Parsons' classic extended family, whose members lived and worked together and were bound by strong mutual obligations. Nevertheless, some sense of obligation does remain, at least to some kin and as a last resort in times of crisis.

Activity

Test your knowledge of the changes in family patterns with this quiz. When you have finished, check the text to see how many you got right.

1 What proportion of children lives in a lone-parent family?
(a) 1 in 4   (b) 1 in 5   (c) l in 10

2 What proportion of households contains one person living alone?
(a) 1 in 10   (b) 2 in 10   (c) 3 in 10

3 What proportion of unmarried adults under 60 is cohabiting?
a) a tenth   (b) a quarter (c) a half

4 In 2002, the average age of women at the birth of their first child was:
(a) 24   (b) 27   (c) 30

5 What percentage of families with dependent children are stepfamilies?
(a) 10   (b) 15   (c) 20

6 Out of every 10 petitions for divorce, how many are filed by women?
(a) 5   (b) 6   (c) 7

7 What percentage of marriages are religious ceremonies?
(a) 35%   (b) 45%   (c) 55%

8 What percentage of adults have same-sex relationships?
(a) 1-3%   (b) 5-7%   (c) 10-12%

9 Out of every 10 marriages, how many are likely to end in divorce?
(a) 2   (b) 3   (c) 4

For more activities on Changing family patterns...

Go to www.sociology.uk.net

Summary

Recent decades have seen some major changes in family patterns. Changes in partnerships include **fewer first marriages, more divorces, re-marriages** and **cohabitations**. Changing patterns of parenting include **more births outside marriage, lone parents** and **stepfamilies**. There are more **one-person** households and **same-sex** families. There are also **ethnic** differences in household composition. The **extended** family survives mainly in dispersed form.

Reasons for these changes include greater **individualism, secularisation**, reduced **stigma** and changes in **attitudes**, changes in the **law** (e.g. regarding divorce and homosexuality) and in the **position of women**.

QuickCheck Questions

1 Identify three changes in family patterns where decline in stigma may be partly responsible for the changes.

2 True or false? There are now more re-marriages than first marriages.

3 What is the sole ground for divorce in the UK today?

4 Explain what is meant by secularisation.

5 Identify two changes in patterns of childbearing in recent years.

6 Suggest two reasons why lone-parent families tend to be poorer than couple families.

7 Suggest two reasons why Asian households tend to be larger than the national average size.

 Check your answers at www.sociology.uk.net

Examining changing family patterns

Item A Along with the trend towards people getting married later in life, there has been an increase in the proportion of marriages ending in divorce. In 1961, there were only 27,000 divorces in the United Kingdom. The number doubled between 1961 and 1969, and more than doubled again by 1972. Although there was a drop in the number of divorces in 1973, the number increased again in 1974 and peaked in 1993 at 180,000. By 2000, the annual number of divorces had declined to 155,000 and it has remained fairly steady at around this number ever since – about six times as many as in 1961. 5

The UK is not alone in experiencing a high divorce rate – average rates across the European Union have more than trebled since 1961. One effect of higher divorce rates is to contribute to greater family diversity, including a trend towards 'serial monogamy'.

Source: adapted from Social Trends, volume 37 (2007)

(a) Explain what is meant by 'serial monogamy' (**Item A**, line 7). (2 marks)

(b) Identify **two** reasons for the trend towards getting married later in life (**Item A**, line 1). (4 marks)

(c) Suggest **three** reasons for the increase in the number of divorces (**Item A**). (6 marks)

Essay Examine changes in the patterns of childbearing and childrearing in the United Kingdom since the 1970s. (24 marks)

The examiner's advice

The essay carries 14 AO1 marks (knowledge and understanding) and 10 AO2 marks (interpretation, application, analysis and evaluation). The emphasis is on showing a sound, detailed sociological knowledge, but to score high marks you must also demonstrate AO2 skills.

You need to identify and describe the main patterns of both childbearing and childrearing and the changes in these since the 1970s. You should examine issues such as the numbers of children born to unmarried mothers (both lone and cohabiting), reconstituted families, later births, declining fertility and smaller family sizes and lone-parent families. A few statistics to illustrate some of these changes would be a good idea.

You also need to explain the changes that you have described. Consider the role of factors such as reasons for the decline in stigma attached to premarital sex, cohabitation and births outside marriage; the impact of high divorce rates (e.g. on the creation of lone-parent and reconstituted families); increased career opportunities for women; the availability of contraception and abortion etc. Write a separate conclusion.

Women's liberation march, 1971. Are women now liberated?

Topic 6 Family diversity and the life course

The changing family patterns that we examined in Topic 5 are bringing about increased family diversity in the UK today. For example, there are now fewer households containing a nuclear family and more lone-parent families and one-person households than there were in the 1970s. More couples, both straight and gay, now cohabit, many more children are born outside marriage than previously, and many more marriages end in divorce.

In this Topic, we now turn our attention to the ways in which sociologists have classified the different types of family diversity and how they have tried to understand the meaning and significance of increased diversity today.

For example, does family diversity mean the breakdown of the family – or a new era of choice and personal fulfilment? Will individuals and society benefit from increased diversity, or is the decline of the traditional family likely to damage us?

Learning objectives

When you have studied this Topic, you should:

- Know a range of different sociological views of family diversity.
- Understand the difference between modernist and postmodernist approaches to family diversity.
- Be able to analyse and evaluate sociological explanations of family diversity.

Modernism and the nuclear family

Perspectives such as functionalism and the New Right have been described as 'modernist'. That is, they see modern society as having a fairly fixed, clear-cut and predictable structure. They see one 'best' family type – the nuclear family – as slotting into this structure and helping to maintain it by performing certain essential functions.

For example, according to Talcott Parsons, there is a 'functional fit' between the nuclear family and modern society. As we saw in Topic 3, Parsons sees the nuclear family as uniquely suited to meeting the needs of modern society for a geographically and socially mobile workforce, and as performing two 'irreducible functions' – the primary socialisation of children and the stabilisation of adult personalities. These contribute to the overall stability and effectiveness of society.

In the functionalist view, therefore, because of its ability to perform these essential functions, we can generalise about the type of family that we will find in modern society – namely, a nuclear family with a division of labour between husband and wife. Hence, other family types can be considered as abnormal, inadequate or even deviant, since they are less able to perform the functions required of the family.

The New Right

The New Right have a conservative and anti-feminist perspective on the family. They are firmly opposed to family diversity.

Like functionalists, the New Right hold the view that there is only one correct or normal family type. This is the traditional or conventional patriarchal nuclear family consisting of a married couple and their dependent children, with a clear-cut division of labour between the breadwinner-husband and homemaker-wife. This is the same as the functionalist distinction between the 'instrumental' and 'expressive' roles performed by husband and wife respectively (see Topic 1, page 19).

The New Right see this family as 'natural' and based upon fundamental biological differences between men and women. In their view, this family is the cornerstone of society; a place of refuge, contentment and harmony.

The New Right argue that the decline of the traditional nuclear family and the growth of family diversity are the cause of many social problems, such as higher crime rates and educational failure. They oppose most of the changes in family patterns that we examined in Topic 5:

- They see lone-parent families as both unnatural and harmful, especially to children. They argue that lone mothers cannot discipline their children properly, they are a burden on the welfare state and they leave boys without an adult male role model, resulting in higher rates of delinquency and threatening social stability.
- They disapprove of mothers going out to work because they believe women should make caring for their family their first priority. As the Conservative politician, Patrick Jenkin, said:

'Quite frankly, I don't think that mothers have the same right to go out to work as fathers do. If the good Lord had intended us to have equal rights to go out to work, he would not have created men and women. These are biological facts.'

- They see marriage as the essential basis for creating a stable environment in which to bring up children. They regard both cohabitation and divorce as creating family instability by making it easier for adults to avoid commitment and responsibility. This then has negative effects on children.

For example, Harry Benson's (2006) analysis of data on the parents of over 15,000 babies born in 2000-01 found that nearly 3,000 of the mothers had become lone parents during the first three years of their child's life. However, the rate of family breakdown was much lower among married couples – only 6%, compared with 20% of cohabiting couples and 74% of those "closely involved" but not living together.

The New Right argue that family breakdown increases the risks to children. For example, according to Amato (2000), children in these families face greater risks of poverty, educational failure, crime and health problems, as well as an increased chance of future family breakdown when they become adults themselves.

Conservative politicians and New Right thinkers have used such evidence to support the view that both the family and society at large are 'broken'. They argue that a return to 'traditional values', including the value of marriage, is necessary to prevent social disintegration and damage to children.

However, critics argue that it may not be marriage as such that provides protection against family breakdown, but simply the degree of commitment – those who are more committed to one another to begin with may be both more likely to marry, *and* more likely to stay together afterwards.

The New Right oppose many of the recent trends in family life on economic and political grounds. As conservatives, they are strongly opposed to high levels of taxation and government spending. They argue that family breakdown and the increase in numbers of lone-parent families has led to more spending on welfare benefits. As this has to be paid for out of public funds, it places a bigger tax burden on the working population.

These high levels of taxation and benefits act as 'perverse incentives' – that is, they punish responsible behaviour and reward irresponsible behaviour:

- They undermine the traditional family by discouraging men from working to support their families.
- They encourage a 'dependency culture' of living off welfare benefits.

The New Right therefore favour cutting welfare benefits or even abolishing them entirely to reduce the dependency culture and encourage the conventional family. (See Topic 7, *Families and social policy*, for further discussion of New Right views on welfare policy.)

However, the New Right view has been criticised:

- The feminist Ann Oakley (1997) argues that the New Right wrongly assume that husbands and wives' roles are fixed by biology. In fact, cross-cultural studies show great variation in the roles men and women perform within the family. Oakley believes that the New Right view of the family is a negative reaction against the feminist campaign for women's equality.
- Feminists also argue that the traditional nuclear family favoured by the New Right is based on the patriarchal oppression of women and is a fundamental cause of gender inequality. In their view, it prevents women working, keeps them financially dependent on men, and denies them an equal say in decision-making.
- Critics argue that there is little or no evidence that lone-parent families are part of a 'dependency culture', nor that their children are more likely to be delinquent than those brought up in a two-parent family of the same social class.

Chester: the neo-conventional family

Robert Chester (1985) recognises that there has been some increased family diversity in recent years. However, unlike the New Right, he does not regard this as very significant, nor does he see it in a negative light. Chester argues that the only important change is a move from the dominance of the traditional or conventional nuclear family, to what he describes as the 'neo-conventional family'.

By the conventional family, Chester means the type of nuclear family described by the New Right and Parsons, with its division of labour between a male breadwinner and a female homemaker.

By contrast, Chester defines the neo-conventional family as a dual-earner family in which both spouses go out to work.

This is similar to the symmetrical family described by Young and Willmott (see Topic 1, page 19).

Apart from this, Chester does not see any other evidence of major change. He argues that most people are not choosing to live in alternatives to the nuclear family (such as lone-parent families) on a long-term basis, and the nuclear family remains the ideal to which most people aspire.

Although many people are not part of a nuclear family at any one time, Chester argues that this is largely due to the life cycle. Many of the people who are currently living in a one-person household, such as elderly widows, divorced men or young people who have not yet married, were either part of a nuclear family in the past or will be in the future.

Statistics on household composition are thus a misleading snapshot of where everyone is living at a single moment in time; they don't show us the fact that most people will spend a major part of their lives in a nuclear family.

As evidence of his view that little has changed, Chester identifies a number of patterns:

- Most people live in a household headed by a married couple.
- Most adults still marry and have children. Most children are reared by their two natural parents.
- Most marriages continue until death. Divorce has increased, but most divorcees remarry.
- Cohabitation has increased, but for most couples it is a temporary phase before marrying. Most couples get married if they have children.
- Although births outside marriage have increased, most are jointly registered, indicating that the parents are committed to bringing up children as a couple.

For Chester, then, the extent and importance of family diversity has been exaggerated. Like the functionalists, Chester sees the nuclear family as dominant. The only important difference between his view and that of the functionalists is that Chester sees a change from a conventional to a neo-conventional nuclear family where both spouses play an 'instrumental' or breadwinner role.

Activity

1 Either as a whole class or in groups of four, devise a set of questions that you will use to ask a sample of people of different generations about their attitudes to family and personal relationships. You will need to include questions about divorce, cohabitation, homosexuality, births outside marriage, lone-parent families and abortion.

2 Each of you should interview at least two people. Try to ensure that as a group you have a good spread of ages (e.g. from under 20s to over 60s).

3 When you have completed the interviews, get back together to collate and discuss your results. How far did attitudes vary according to age? How would you account for any differences?

The Rapoports: five types of family diversity

Unlike Chester, Rhona and Robert Rapoport (1982) argue that diversity is of central importance in understanding family life today. They believe that we have moved away from the traditional nuclear family as the dominant family type, to a range of different types. Families in Britain have adapted to a pluralistic society – that is, one in which cultures and lifestyles are more diverse.

In their view, family diversity represents greater freedom of choice and the widespread acceptance of different cultures and ways of life. Unlike the New Right, the Rapoports see diversity as a response to people's different needs and wishes, and not as abnormal or a deviation from the assumed norm of the nuclear family.

They identify five different types of family diversity in Britain today:

- **Organisational diversity:** this refers to differences in the ways family roles are organised. For example, some couples have joint conjugal roles and two wage-earners, while others have segregated conjugal roles and one wage-earner.

- **Cultural diversity:** different cultural, religious and ethnic groups have different family structures. For example, there is a higher proportion of female-headed families among African-Caribbean households.

- **Social class diversity:** differences in family structure are partly the result of income differences between households of different classes. Likewise, there are class differences in child-rearing practices.

- **Life-stage diversity:** family structures differ according to the stage reached in the life cycle – for example, newlyweds, couples with children, retired couples whose children have left home, and widows or widowers who are living alone.

- **Generational diversity:** older and younger generations have different attitudes and experiences that reflect the historical periods in which they have lived. For example, they may have different views about the morality of divorce or cohabitation (see Topic 5, page 62).

1 Suggest two reasons why there might be differences in child-rearing practices between middle-class and working-class families.

2 Suggest two ways in which cultural or religious factors may affect family structures or relationships.

▲ *Most Asian households in Britain are nuclear, but the extended family remains a source of support and identity.*

Postmodernity and the life course

Modernist approaches to the family, such as functionalism and the New Right, emphasise the dominance of one family type – the nuclear family – in modern society. These approaches take a structural or 'top down' view – that is, they see the family as a structure that shapes the behaviour of its members so that they perform the functions society requires.

However, other sociologists reject the modernist idea that there is one 'best' family type or that the family's structure shapes its members' behaviour. Sociologists influenced by social action and postmodernist views argue that structural or modernist approaches ignore two key facts:

- As individual social actors, we make choices about our family life and relationships. Structural approaches wrongly assume that our actions are shaped and dictated by the 'needs of society'.
- We now have much greater choice about our personal relationships, and this has increased family diversity so much that we can no longer talk about a single 'best' or dominant type, or even a set of types (such as those that the Rapoports identify, for example).

Life course analysis

In this view, therefore, if we want to understand family life, we need to focus on individual family members and how they make their choices.

To do this, sociologists such as Tamara Hareven (1978) use the approach known as life course analysis. This starts from the idea that there is flexibility and variation in people's family lives – in the choices and decisions they make, and in the timing and sequence of the events and turning points in their lives. For example, these might include the decision to have a baby, come out as gay, or move into sheltered accommodation.

Similarly, Clare Holdsworth and David Morgan (2005) examine how young people experience leaving home, for example in relation to what it means to be independent or 'adult' and in terms of how others such as parents and friends influence their decisions.

Life course analysis therefore focuses on the meanings people give to these life events and choices. Hareven favours the use of unstructured in-depth interviews with family members as the best way to uncover these meanings and understand their choices about family life and relationships.

In the view of its supporters, life course analysis has two major strengths:

1 It focuses on what family members themselves consider important, rather than what sociologists may regard as important. It looks at how families and households change from the viewpoint of the people involved and the meanings they give to their lives, relationships and choices.

2 It is particularly suitable for studying families in today's society, where there is more choice about personal relationships and more family diversity. Family structures are increasingly just the result of the choices made by their members.

Family practices

Life course analysis focuses on the meanings people give to events, choices and decisions in order to understand how they construct their family life. Similarly, David Morgan (1996) uses the concept of 'family practices' to describe the routine actions through which we create our sense of 'being a family member', such as feeding the children or doing the DIY.

Our family practices are influenced by the beliefs we have about our rights and obligations within the family. For example, some men may see feeding the children as the wife's job, not theirs.

The concept of family practices thus allows us to see why conflict may exist within families – because different members may hold different beliefs or expectations about each other's responsibilities.

▲ *Does having your own place mean you are an adult?*

Morgan prefers the concept of family practices, rather than family structure, as a way of describing how we construct our life course and relationships. In his view, families are not concrete 'things' or structures – they are simply what people actually *do*.

Morgan argues that the idea of family practices gets us "closer to the realities of everyday experience" of family life than structural approaches such as functionalism – particularly in today's society, where individuals are much freer to choose how they organise their relationships.

Functionalism sees 'the family' as a clear-cut, distinct structure separate from other aspects of society. However, Morgan (2007) argues that as today's society becomes more fragmented, networks such as family, friendship and other kinds of relationships become less clear-cut and boundaries between them become blurred.

Similarly, Weeks' idea of 'chosen families' and 'friendship as kinship' among gays suggests that the distinction between 'family' and 'non-family' may be becoming less clear. (See Topic 5, page 63).

However, Morgan does not reject structural theories altogether. Although life courses and family practices are the actions of individuals, they take place in the context of wider social structures and norms. These may still exert an influence over family members' expectations and actions. For example, gender norms and differences in job opportunities in wider society may dictate that males must be the breadwinners and women the homemakers, and this will influence individuals' expectations of each other within the family.

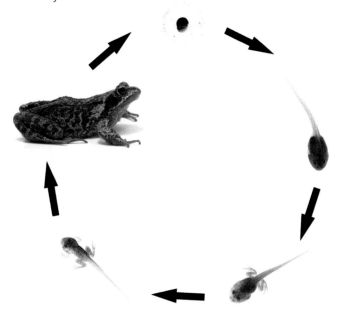

▲ Unlike frogs or butterflies, people don't go through fixed stages in a life cycle. Instead we follow a life course involving many points where we must choose which path to take.

Activity

In pairs, list at least ten points during the course of a lifetime when choices might have to be made about families, households or relationships (e.g. the decision whether to move into sheltered accommodation).

Postmodernism and family diversity

While the Rapoports identify a range of types of family diversity (see page 73), postmodernists such as David Cheal (1993) go much further. Postmodernists argue that we no longer live in the 'modern' world, with its predictable, orderly structures such as the nuclear family. Instead, society has entered a new, chaotic *postmodern* stage. In postmodern society, family structures are fragmented and individuals have much more choice in their lifestyles, personal relationships and family arrangements (see Box 7).

As a result, family life has become more diverse than even the Rapoports recognise. In today's postmodern society, there is no longer one single type of family that is dominant (such as the nuclear family) – only families *plural*.

Some writers argue that this greater diversity and choice brings with it both advantages and disadvantages:

- It gives individuals greater freedom to plot their own life course – to choose the kind of family and personal relationships that meet their needs.
- But greater freedom of choice in relationships means a greater risk of instability, since these relationships are more likely to break up.

While not accepting everything postmodernism says about the nature of society today, a number of sociologists have been influenced by postmodernist ideas about family life. We shall now examine their views on family diversity.

Giddens: choice and equality

Anthony Giddens (1992) argues that in recent decades the family and marriage have been transformed by greater choice and a more equal relationship between men and women. This transformation has occurred because:

- Contraception has allowed sex and intimacy rather than reproduction to become the main reason for the relationship's existence.
- Women have gained independence as a result of feminism and because of greater opportunities in education and work.

As a result, the basis of marriage and the family has changed into one in which the couple are free to define their relationship themselves, rather than simply acting out roles that have been defined in advance by law or tradition. For example, a couple nowadays can choose to cohabit rather than marry.

Giddens describes this kind of relationship as the 'pure relationship'. It exists solely to meet each partner's needs and is likely to continue only so long as it succeeds in doing so. Couples stay together because of love, happiness or sexual attraction, rather than because of tradition, a sense of duty or for the sake of the children. Relationships become part of the process of self-discovery or self-identity: trying different relationships becomes a way of establishing 'who we are'.

However, Giddens notes that with more choice, personal relationships inevitably become less stable. Relationships can be ended more or less at will by either partner.

Beck: 'risk society' and the negotiated family

Ulrich Beck (1992) puts forward a similar view. He argues that we now live in a 'risk society' where tradition has less influence and people have more choice. As a result, we are more aware of risks. This is because making choices involves calculating the risks and rewards of the different courses of action available.

Today's risk society contrasts with an earlier time when roles were more fixed and people had much less choice in how they lived their lives. For example, people were expected to marry. Once married, men were expected to play the role of breadwinner and disciplinarian and to make the important financial decisions, while women took responsibility for the housework and childcare.

Although this traditional patriarchal family was unequal and oppressive, it did provide a stable and predictable basis for family life by defining each member's role and responsibilities. However, the patriarchal family has been undermined by two trends:

- **Greater gender equality**, which has challenged male domination in all spheres of life. Women now expect equality both at work and in marriage.
- **Greater individualism**, where people's actions are influenced more by calculations of their own self-interest than by a sense of obligation to others.

These trends have led to a new type of family replacing the patriarchal family. Ulrich Beck and Elisabeth Beck-Gernsheim (1995) call this the 'negotiated family'. Negotiated families do not conform to the traditional family norm, but vary according to the wishes and expectations of their members, who decide what is best for themselves by negotiation. They enter the relationship on an equal basis.

However, although the negotiated family is more equal than the patriarchal family, it is less stable. This is because individuals are free to leave if their needs are not met.

Thus although in today's uncertain risk society, people turn to the family as a haven of security, the irony is that family relationships are themselves now subject to greater risk than ever.

> Suggest three reasons why there is now greater gender equality in the family and society.

| Box 7 | Postmodern society and the family |

Postmodernists argue that since the late 20th century, society has entered a new 'postmodern' phase. Postmodern society has two key characteristics:

- **Diversity and fragmentation:** Society today is increasingly fragmented, with an ever greater diversity of cultures and lifestyles — more a collection of subcultures than a single culture shared by all. People can 'pick and mix', creating their identities and lifestyles from a wide range of choices. For example, different ethnic and youth subcultures, sexual preferences, and social movements such as environmentalism, all offer sources of identity.
- **Rapid social change:** New technology and the electronic media have dissolved old barriers of time and space, transformed our patterns of work and leisure, and accelerated the pace of change. One effect of this rapid change is to make life less predictable.

Not surprisingly, family life in postmodern society is therefore less stable, but at the same time it gives individuals more choice about their personal relationships. As a result, family life is now much more diverse than previously. This means it is no longer possible to generalise about it in the way that modernist sociologists such as Parsons have done in the past.

Stacey: the divorce-extended family

Judith Stacey (1998) argues that greater choice has benefited women. It has enabled them to free themselves from patriarchal oppression and to shape their family arrangements to meet their needs.

Stacey used life history interviews to construct a series of case studies of postmodern families in Silicon Valley, California. She found that women rather than men have been the main agents of changes in the family. Many of the women she interviewed had rejected the traditional housewife-mother role. They had worked, returned to education as adults, improved their job prospects, divorced and re-married. These women had often created new types of family that better suited their needs.

One of these new family structures Stacey calls the 'divorce-extended family', whose members are connected by divorce rather than marriage. The key members are usually female and may include former in-laws, such as mother- and daughter-in-law, or a man's ex-wife and his new partner.

For example, Stacey describes in one of her case studies how Pam Gamma created a divorce-extended family. Pam married young in the 1950s, then divorced and cohabited for several years before re-marrying. Her second husband had also been married before. By the mid-1980s the children of Pam's first marriage were in their twenties and she had formed a divorce-extended family with Shirley, the woman cohabiting with her first husband. They helped each other financially and domestically, for example by exchanging lodgers in response to the changing needs of their households.

Such cases illustrate the idea that postmodern families are diverse and that their shape depends on the active choices people make about how to live their lives – for example, whether to get divorced, cohabit, come out as gay etc.

Thus, as Morgan (1996) argues, it is pointless trying to make large-scale generalisations about 'the family' as if it were a single thing, as functionalists do. Instead, sociologists ought to give more attention to how people create their own diverse family lives and practices.

Weeks: the growing acceptance of diversity

Jeffrey Weeks (2000) identifies a long-term shift in attitudes since the 1950s. Over this period, sexual morality has become largely a matter of personal choice. At the same time, the church and state have lost much of their power to influence individual morality.

There is growing acceptance of sexual and family diversity, especially by the under-35s. Attitudes have become more favourable towards issues such as cohabitation and homosexuality.

However, Weeks observes that despite these changing attitudes, family patterns continue to be fairly traditional. Most people still live in a family; most children are brought up by couples; most couples marry and many divorcees re-marry.

Nevertheless, Weeks argues that sexual and family diversity are now an undeniable and widely accepted fact. Although the New Right continue to oppose diversity, Weeks sees them as fighting a losing battle.

Two views of family diversity

From the different contributions made by sociologists to our understanding of family diversity we can identify two broad views – one against diversity and the other in favour of it.

▼ *Lesbian couple and their daughter*

Against diversity

The first view opposes greater family diversity. It is held by functionalists and the New Right. It is based on the belief that there is only one 'best' or normal type of family. This is the traditional patriarchal nuclear family, consisting of a married couple and their dependent children, with a division of labour between an 'instrumental' male breadwinner role and an 'expressive' female housewife role.

Its supporters see the nuclear family as 'natural' – based on biological differences between men and women that suit them to their different roles. As such, they see the nuclear family as best equipped to meet the needs of society and its members. By contrast, other family types are seen as unnatural and dysfunctional. For example, the New Right see lone-parent families as causing juvenile delinquency.

In favour of diversity

The second view is held by postmodernists and feminists. It rejects the New Right's view that only the nuclear family is a 'proper' family. Instead, writers such as Weeks take the view that a family is simply whatever arrangements those involved choose to call a family. In this view, the family is not 'natural', but rather socially constructed by its members.

Postmodernists and feminists are in favour of greater family diversity. Writers such as Stacey see diversity as desirable because it brings people the freedom to choose the personal relationships and ways of living that meet their needs. In particular, it enables women to liberate themselves from the oppression of the traditional patriarchal family.

However, while many sociologists recognise the trend to greater diversity and choice, they also see the continuing importance of factors such as patriarchy and class inequality in restricting people's choices and shaping family life.

Activity

Fill in the gaps in the table below.

Against diversity	In favour of diversity
	Different family types are equally valid.
	Postmodernism and feminism
Gender roles in the family are fixed, based on biological differences between men and women.	
	Diversity is good because it gives people more freedom of choice of lifestyle.

For more activities on Diversity and the life course...

Go to www.sociology.uk.net

Summary

Modernists such as **functionalists** and the **New Right** see only the conventional **nuclear family as normal** and other family types as deviant. **Chester** sees only one major change – the **neo-conventional** family – whereas the **Rapoports** identify **five types** of diversity.

Sociologists influenced by **postmodernism** and **social action theories** reject structural views. They belive individuals today have more **choice** in their relationships and **family practices**, and use **life course analysis** to uncover their meaning.

Gender equality and increased choice are producing both **diversity** and **risk and instability**, since people can now leave unsatisfying relationships. Couples now seek the **pure relationship,** based solely on satisfying their own needs.

While the New Right and functionalism oppose diversity, postmodernists and **feminists** welcome it since it represents freedom, especially from patriarchal oppression.

QuickCheck Questions

1 True or false? The New Right favour greater welfare spending to meet the needs of lone-parent families.

2 True or false? In Chester's view, the only important change in the family has been a move from the dominance of the conventional nuclear family, to the neo-conventional family.

3 Complete the list of Rapoport and Rapoport's five types of family diversity: cultural, social class...

4 True or false? Functionalism is a modernist perspective.

5 Identify two factors that Giddens believes have led to greater choice and more equal relationships between men and women.

6 Why do Beck and Beck-Gernsheim see the negotiated family as less stable than the patriarchal family?

7 What does Stacey mean by the divorce-extended family?

Check your answers at www.sociology.uk.net

Examining family diversity and the life course

Item A Sociologists are divided over both the extent of family diversity and its importance. For example, functionalists and the New Right view increased diversity as a serious threat. They argue that many forms of diversity today undermine the division between expressive and instrumental roles that they view as essential for the well being of individuals and the maintenance of social stability. By contrast, Robert Chester argues that the only real change in family life in recent times has been a shift from the conventional to the neo-conventional family.   5

However, others believe that there has been a major change in family life in recent years and that we are now faced with a much greater diversity of family forms. For example, Rapoport and Rapoport identify five different types of diversity among Britain's families. Sociologists influenced by postmodernist and social action approaches go much further in their claims about the extent of change in family life today.

(a) Explain what is meant by the 'neo-conventional family' (**Item A**, line 5). (2 marks)

(b) Explain the difference between 'expressive' and 'instrumental' roles (**Item A**, line 3). (4 marks)

(c) Identify **three** of the types of family diversity described by Rapoport and Rapoport (**Item A**, line 7). (6 marks)

Essay Using material from **Item A** and elsewhere, assess sociological explanations of the nature and extent of family diversity today.
(24 marks)

The examiner's advice

The essay carries 10 AO1 marks (knowledge and understanding) and 14 AO2 marks (interpretation, application, analysis and evaluation). The emphasis is on showing well-developed AO2 skills, but to score high marks you must also show a good sociological knowledge. You must also make sure you use the Item.

Start by outlining the nature and extent of diversity in terms of the range of different family types today and which ones have increased in recent years. (A few statistics on this from Topic 5 would be useful here.) Then go on to discuss a range of different explanations – use the Item to get you started on some of those it refers to. You should give an account of the reasons why the New Right oppose family diversity.

You need to evaluate their view, which you can do by using Chester, but you should also examine in detail some of the social action and postmodernist-influenced approaches, such as Cheal, Morgan, Giddens, Beck, Stacey or Weeks. What factors do they see as responsible for increased choice in relationships and for greater family instability? You can show analysis and evaluation by contrasting such approaches with functionalism and the New Right, and ideas such as life course analysis and family practices with the idea of family structure.

为国分忧，为国奉献
——请自觉实行计划生育

Poster promoting China's one-child policy.

Topic 7 Families and social policy

Social policy refers to the plans and actions of government agencies, such as the health and social services, the welfare benefits system, schools and other public bodies.

Policies are usually based on laws that provide the framework within which these agencies operate. For example, laws lay down who is entitled to each specific welfare benefit.

Most social policies affect families in some way or other. Some are aimed directly at families, such as laws governing marriage and divorce, abortion and contraception, child protection, adoption and so on.

Other policies, although not necessarily aimed directly at families, still have an effect on them. For example:

- The policy of compulsory education enables parents to go out to work while schools provide a free 'childminding' service.
- The policy of 'care in the community' often means that it is family members rather than hospitals or nursing homes who have to care for the sick or elderly.
- Taxation policies affect how much money is taken from families and how much is made available to pay for the services provided for families.

Learning objectives

When you have studied this Topic, you should:

- Know some of the ways in which social policies may affect families.
- Understand the different sociological perspectives on families and social policy.
- Be able to analyse these perspectives and evaluate their usefulness in understanding the relationship between families and social policy.

A comparative view of family policy

The actions and policies of governments can sometimes have profound effects on families and their members.

Cross-cultural examples from different societies and historical periods can show us some of the more extreme ways in which the state's policies can affect family life. This can help us to see the relationship between families and social policies in a new light.

Abolishing the family

One particularly striking attempt by the state to shape family life was the policy followed after the Russian Revolution of 1917.

The government of the newly formed Soviet Union sought to destroy the old pre-revolutionary patriarchal family structure, which it regarded as an obstacle to the creation of a socialist society based on equality.

Consequently, the Soviet government in the 1920s changed the laws to make divorce and abortion easy to obtain, the constitution guaranteed equality between the sexes, women entered paid employment on a vast scale, and the state began to provide workplace and other communal nurseries.

In keeping with the Marxist perspective on the family, it was expected that the abolition of capitalist ownership of the means of production would lead to the traditional family 'withering away'. (See Topic 3, page 41 on the Marxist perspective.)

However, the new Soviet state was beset by many difficulties, including civil war, famine and, after Hitler's rise to power in 1933, the threat of war with Nazi Germany. The need to industrialise rapidly and to prepare for war meant a change of policy.

Divorce laws were tightened, abortion made illegal, and parents encouraged to have more children and rewarded with bigger family allowances. The state and media glorified parenthood, and highly fertile women were given the title of 'Hero Mother of the Soviet Union'.

China's one-child policy

By contrast with the former Soviet Union's attempts to encourage population growth through its family policies, in China the government's population control policy has discouraged couples from having more than one child.

According to Adrian Wilson (1985), the policy is supervised by workplace family planning committees; women must seek their permission to try to become pregnant, and there is often both a waiting list and a quota for each factory.

Couples who comply with the policy get extra benefits, such as free child healthcare and higher tax allowances. An only child will also get priority in education and housing later in life.

Couples who break their agreement to have only one child must repay the allowances and pay a fine. Women face pressure to undergo sterilisation after their first child.

At the other extreme, the former communist government of Romania in the 1980s introduced a series of policies to try to drive up the birth rate, which had been falling as living standards declined.

It restricted contraception and abortion, set up infertility treatment centres, made divorce more difficult, lowered the legal age of marriage to 15, and made unmarried adults and childless couples pay an extra 5% income tax.

Nazi family policy

In Nazi Germany in the 1930s, the state pursued a twofold policy. On the one hand, it encouraged the healthy and supposedly 'racially pure' to breed a 'master race' (e.g. by restricting abortion and contraception).

Official policy sought to keep women out of the workforce and confine them to 'children, kitchen and church', the better to perform their biological role.

On the other hand, the state compulsorily sterilised 375,000 disabled people that it deemed unfit to breed on grounds of 'physical malformation, mental retardation, epilepsy, imbecility, deafness or blindness'. Many of these people were later murdered in Nazi concentration camps.

By contrast with these extreme examples, some people argue that in democratic societies such as Britain, the family is a private sphere of life in which the government does not intervene, except perhaps when things 'go wrong', for example in cases of child abuse.

However, sociologists argue that in fact, even in democratic societies, the state's social policies play a very important role in shaping family life. In this Topic we shall examine a range of ways in which this occurs.

Perspectives on families and social policy

Although sociologists agree that social policy can have an important influence on family life, they hold different views about what kinds of effects it has and whether these are desirable. We shall examine a range of different sociological views or perspectives on the impact of social policy on families.

Functionalism

Functionalists see society as built on harmony and consensus (shared values), and free from major conflicts. They see the state as acting in the interests of society as a whole and its social policies as being for the good of all. Functionalists see policies as helping families to perform their functions more effectively and make life better for their members.

For example, Ronald Fletcher (1966) argues that the introduction of health, education and housing policies in the years since the industrial revolution has gradually led to the development of a welfare state that supports the family in performing its functions more effectively. For example, the existence of the National Health Service means that with the help of doctors, nurses, hospitals and medicines, the family today is better able to take care of its members when they are sick.

> 1 Identify two functions that families perform for their members apart from healthcare.
>
> 2 Suggest ways in which welfare policies may help families to carry out each of these two functions more effectively.

The functionalist view has been criticised on two main counts:

- It assumes that all members of the family benefit from social policies, whereas feminists argue that policies often benefit men at the expense of women.
- It assumes that there is a 'march of progress', with social policies steadily making family life better and better, whereas Marxists argue that policies can also turn the clock back and reverse progress previously made, for example by cutting welfare benefits to poor families.

The New Right

The New Right have had considerable influence on government thinking about social policy and its effects on the family. They see the traditional nuclear family, with its division of labour between a male provider and a female home-maker, as self-reliant and capable of caring for its members. In their view, social policies should therefore avoid doing anything that might undermine this 'natural', self-reliant family.

Activity

Much of the New Right perspective arose as a criticism of the welfare state that had been introduced following the 1942 Beveridge Report. Using the library or the Internet, find out about the Beveridge Report and the setting up of the welfare state.

1 Who was Beveridge?

2 What were the main parts of the welfare state set up at the end of the Second World War and what 'giant evils' were these meant to combat?

3 What is meant by the phrase 'welfare from the cradle to the grave'? What principles underlie this phrase?

The New Right criticise many existing government policies for undermining the family. In particular, they argue that governments often weaken the family's self-reliance by providing generous welfare benefits. These include providing council housing for unmarried teenage mothers and cash payments to support lone-parent families.

Charles Murray (1984) argues that these benefits offer 'perverse incentives' – that is, they reward irresponsible or anti-social behaviour. For example:

- If fathers see that the state will maintain their children, some of them will abandon their responsibilities towards their families.
- Providing council housing for unmarried teenage mothers encourages young girls to become pregnant.
- The growth of lone-parent families encouraged by generous benefits means more boys grow up without a male role model and authority figure. This lack of paternal authority is responsible for a rising crime rate among young males.

Thus for the New Right, social policy can have a major impact on family roles and relationships. It can encourage a dependency culture, where individuals come to depend on the state to support them and their children rather than being self-reliant.

The New Right's solution to these problems is simple. They argue that the policy must be changed, with cuts in welfare spending and tighter restrictions on who is eligible for benefits.

In their view, this would have several advantages. For example, cutting benefits would mean that taxes could also be reduced, and both these changes would give fathers more incentive to work and provide for their families. Similarly, denying council housing to unmarried teenage mothers would remove at least one incentive to become pregnant when very young.

The New Right also advocate policies to support the traditional nuclear family, such as taxes that favour married rather than cohabiting couples, and the Child Support Agency, whose main role is to make absent fathers financially responsible for their children.

Whereas functionalists take the view that state welfare policies can benefit the family and make it better able to meet its members' needs, the New Right disagree. In their view, the less the state 'interferes' in families, the better family life will be. Greater self-reliance, and not reliance on the state, is what will enable the family to meet its members' needs most effectively.

The New Right view has been criticised on several counts:

- Feminists argue that it is an attempt to justify a return to the traditional patriarchal family that subordinated women to men and confined them to a domestic role.
- It wrongly assumes that the patriarchal nuclear family is 'natural' rather than socially constructed.
- Cutting benefits would simply drive many poor families into even greater poverty.

Activity

Divide into groups of 3 or 4. Each group is allocated the role of either supporters or critics of New Right ideas.

Note down your arguments, then get together with an opposing group to debate the ideas. Each group should put forward their ideas and then give the other group a chance to criticise them. Try to be polite!

New Labour

Although the New Right's ideas are usually associated with the Conservative Party, many commentators have noted similarities between these ideas and New Labour views on the family and social policy. Both before and after being elected to government in 1997, New Labour politicians have made statements supporting the traditional family.

For example, New Labour favours strengthening the institution of marriage and regards a family headed by a married couple as normally the best place in which to bring up children. New Labour has also cut benefits to some lone parents.

On the other hand, New Labour takes a more positive view of the role of social policy than the New Right and believes that certain kinds of state intervention can improve life for families. New Labour has introduced a number of policies that are at odds with a New Right view. For example:

- New Labour changed the law on adoption to give unmarried cohabiting couples, including gay couples, the right to adopt on the same basis as married couples.

- New Labour's welfare, taxation and minimum wage policies have been partly aimed at lifting children out of poverty by re-distributing income to the poor through higher benefits, whereas the New Right disapprove of income re-distribution through increased benefits.

However, in keeping with New Right thinking, many of New Labour's main anti-poverty benefits, such as Working Families Tax Credit, are means-tested (only available to those on a low income) rather than being universal benefits available to everyone, like child benefit, for example.

Identify two other means-tested benefits that are only available to families on a low income.

Feminism

Feminists take a conflict view (see Box 8). They see society as patriarchal (male-dominated), benefiting men at women's expense. They argue that all social institutions, including the state and its policies, help to maintain women's subordinate position and the unequal gender division of labour in the family.

In the case of social policy, the way this often works is that policies are based on assumptions about what the 'normal' family is like. In turn, the effect of the policies is often to reinforce that type of family at the expense of other types.

For example, if the state assumes that 'normal' families are based on marriage and offers benefits and tax incentives to married couples that are not available to cohabiting couples, these policies may encourage marriage and discourage cohabitation. In effect, this creates a 'self-fulfilling prophecy', making it more difficult for people to live in other family types than the one that policy-makers assume they live in.

Feminists such as Hilary Land (1978) argue that social policies often assume that the ideal family is the patriarchal nuclear family with a male provider and female homemaker, along with their dependent children. This is the family type that Edmund Leach (1967) calls the 'cereal packet norm' because it is the kind of family that often appears in advertisements for breakfast cereals.

This norm of what the family should be like affects the kind of policies governing family life. In turn, these policies reinforce existing patriarchal roles and relationships. For example:

- Tax and benefits policies may assume that husbands are the main wage-earners and that wives are their financial dependants. This can make it impossible for wives to claim social security benefits in their own right, since it is expected that their husbands will provide. This then reinforces women's dependence on their husbands.

- Courts may assume that women should have custody of children in divorce cases because they are seen as the 'natural' carers.

Diana Leonard (1978) argues that even where policies appear to support women, they may still reinforce the patriarchal family and act as a form of social control over women.

For example, although maternity leave policies benefit women, they also reinforce patriarchy in the family. Maternity leave entitlement is much more generous than that for paternity leave and this encourages the assumption that the care of infants is the responsibility of mothers rather than fathers.

Similarly, child benefit is normally paid to the mother and, although this gives her a source of income that does not depend on the father, it also assumes that the child's welfare is primarily her responsibility.

Box 8	Conflict theories

Conflict theories do not share the functionalist view that society is built on harmony and consensus. Conflict theories of the family and social policy have two key features:

- They see society as based on a conflict of interest between social groups with unequal power – for example, rich and poor, or men and women.
- They see the state and its policies as serving the interests of powerful groups in society. State policies shape family life and define what counts as a 'normal' family in ways that benefit the powerful.

Conflict theories of the family and social policy include feminism, Marxism and Jacques Donzelot's surveillance theory.

Examples like these show the importance of social policies in the social construction of family roles and relationships. By making it easier for women to take responsibility for the care of infants or by assuming that men are the main economic providers, social policies help to create and maintain the patriarchal roles and relationships that they assume to be the norm.

The feminist view of social policy has been criticised. Not all policies are directed at maintaining patriarchy. For example, equal pay and sex discrimination laws, benefits for lone parents, refuges for women escaping domestic violence and equal rights to divorce could all be said to challenge the patriarchal family.

Activity

Find out about maternity and paternity leave provision. How do the two differ? What effects might it have on family life if they were the same?

Gender regimes

As we have seen, feminists argue that social policy reinforces the patriarchal family. By examining policy from a comparative perspective across different societies, we can see whether this is inevitable, or whether different policies can encourage more equal family relationships.

For example, a country's policies on taxation, childcare, welfare services and equal opportunities will affect whether women can work full-time, or whether they have to forego paid work to care for children or elderly relatives.

Eileen Drew (1995) uses the concept of 'gender regimes' to describe how social policies in different countries can either encourage or discourage gender equality in the family and at work. She identifies two types of gender regime following different types of family policies:

- Traditional 'familistic' gender regimes
- More equal 'individualistic' gender regimes.

familistic gender regimes

These base their family policies on the assumption that the husband works to support the family while his wife stays at home and is responsible for domestic work, childrearing and the care of family members.

In Greece, for example, there is little state welfare or publicly funded childcare. Women have to rely heavily on support from their extended kin and there is a traditional division of labour.

individualistic gender regimes

These base their family policies on the belief that husbands and wives should be treated the same. Wives are not assumed to be financially dependent on their husbands. This means that each partner has a separate entitlement to state benefits.

In Sweden, for example, policies treat husbands and wives as equally responsible both for breadwinning and domestic tasks. Equal opportunities policies, state provision of childcare, parental leave and good quality welfare services mean that women are less dependent on their husbands and have more opportunities to work.

Drew argues that most European Union countries are now moving away from familistic gender regimes and towards individualistic ones. This is likely to bring a move away from the traditional patriarchal family and towards greater gender equality in family roles.

However, policies such as publicly funded childcare do not come cheap, and they involve major conflicts about who should benefit from social policies and who should pay for them. It would therefore be naive to assume that there is an inevitable 'march of progress' towards gender equality.

▲ ▼ *Familistic or individualistic gender regimes? Support from extended kin versus state provision of childcare.*

Nevertheless, the differences between European countries show that social policies can play an important role in promoting or preventing gender equality in the family.

Marxism

Marxists are conflict theorists (see Box 8). They see society as based on class conflict. Capitalist society contains two classes – capitalists and workers. The dominant capitalist class owns the means of production, such as factories,

machinery and raw materials, while the working class owns nothing but its labour power.

To survive, therefore, the workers must sell their labour to the capitalists in return for wages. This enables the capitalists to exploit the workers, making profits by paying them less than the value of what they produce. This produces conflict between the classes.

In capitalist society, all institutions – such as education, the media and religion – help to maintain class inequality and exploitation. The family too serves the interests of capitalism, for example by reproducing the labour power of the workforce.

Unlike functionalists, Marxists do not see social policies as benefiting all members of society equally. They see the state and its policies as serving capitalism. For example, they see the low level of state pensions as evidence that once workers are too old to produce profits, they are 'maintained' at the lowest possible cost.

Similarly, Marxists do not accept that there is a steady march of progress towards ever better welfare policies producing ever happier families. They argue that improvements for working-class families, such as pensions or free healthcare, have often only been won through class struggle to extract concessions from the capitalist ruling class. Furthermore, these improvements can easily be lost again, as when Mrs Thatcher's government made major cuts to public services in the 1980s.

Activity **Evaluation of the Marxist perspective**

Go to www.sociology.uk.net

Marxists also argue that some policies affecting families have come about because of the needs of capitalism. For example, during the Second World War, when large numbers of male workers were conscripted into the armed

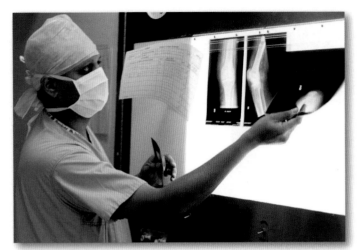

▲ *Free healthcare – a concession won through class struggle?*

forces, women were needed as a reserve army of labour to fill the jobs the men had left vacant in the factories. According to Wilson, the government quickly set up 1,450 full-time nurseries for the children of working mothers.

However, at the end of the war, when the men had returned and women were no longer needed in the labour force, the nurseries were closed down. This prevented many women from working, making them financially dependent on their husbands and weakening their bargaining power within the family. This example illustrates how social policies simultaneously serve the needs of capitalism and affect family relationships.

Donzelot: the policing of families

Like Marxists and feminists, Jacques Donzelot (1977) sees policy as a form of state power over families. He uses Michel Foucault's (1976) concept of surveillance. Foucault sees power not just as something held by the government or state, but as diffused (spread) throughout society and found within all relationships. In particular, Foucault sees professionals such as doctors and social workers as exercising power over their clients by using their expert knowledge.

Donzelot applies these ideas to the family. He is interested in how professionals carry out surveillance (observing and monitoring) of families. He argues that social workers, health visitors and doctors use their knowledge to control and change families. Donzelot calls this 'the policing of families'.

Surveillance is not targeted equally on all social classes. Poor families are more likely to be seen as 'problem' families and as the cause of crime and anti-social behaviour. These are the families that professionals target for 'improvement'.

For example, as Rachel Condry (2007) notes, the state may seek to control and regulate family life by imposing compulsory parenting orders through the courts. Parents of young offenders, truants or badly behaved children may be forced to attend parenting classes to learn the 'correct' way to bring up their children.

Donzelot rejects the 'march of progress' view that social policy and the professionals who carry it out have created a better, freer or more humane society. Instead he agrees with other conflict theorists that social policy is a form of state control of the family.

By focusing on the micro level of how the 'caring professions' act as agents of social control through their surveillance of families, Donzelot shows the importance of professional knowledge as a form of power and control.

However, Marxists and feminists criticise Donzelot for failing to identify clearly who benefits from such policies of surveillance. Marxists argue that social policies generally operate in the interests of the capitalist class, while feminists argue that men are the main beneficiaries.

Activity

Research any three areas of government policy for their effects on family roles and relationships. For example you could look at policies on areas such as immigration and asylum, adoption and fostering, taxation, the social security system, child support etc.

1   What assumptions are made about 'normal' family life?

2   Have the policies been changed in any way recently?

Which other professionals might be engaged in surveillance of 'problem' families apart from those mentioned above?

For more activities on Families and social policy...

Go to www.sociology.uk.net

Summary

Social policies may work to undermine or support different kinds of family. The **New Right** argue that over-generous **welfare benefits** to unmarried mothers encourage a **dependency culture**. **Feminists** disagree, arguing that government policies **legitimate** the heterosexual **patriarchal nuclear family** and make other family types seem less valid.

Countries with **individualistic gender regimes** follow policies promoting women's equality. **Familistic** regimes perpetuate women's patriarchal dependence. **Marxists** see policies on the family as serving the needs of **capitalism**. **Donzelot** argues that state professionals exercise control and **surveillance**, intervening to regulate family life.

QuickCheck Questions

1 True or false? Functionalists see social policy as benefiting men at the expense of women.

2 Why do the New Right believe that welfare benefits are a 'perverse incentive'?

3 Identify one social policy that may reinforce gender roles.

4 Explain the difference between familistic and individualistic gender regimes.

5 Which of the two gender regimes would feminists favour?

6 True or false? Marxism and functionalism are both consensus views of the family and social policy.

 Check your answers at www.sociology.uk.net

Examining families and social policy

Item A   The declared aim of New Labour governments from 1997 onwards has been to pursue policies to strengthen the family and marriage. The term 'family' here means two co-resident parents of opposite sexes.

New Labour sees marriage and the family as vital to the moral stability of society, while divorce and single parenthood are viewed as potentially disruptive and damaging both to children and to society as a whole. Critics argue that New Labour has mainly advocated the traditional nuclear family and paid only lip service to other forms of family and household. Subsequent policy statements, including the party's election manifestos, have tended to continue this trend.

   5

Roger Sapsford (1995) argues that even though the family is seen as a 'private' space, it often gets the blame for social problems that occur in the public sphere of wider society. Equally, although families are often seen as a place where we can be 'free', they are in fact massively policed and regulated by the state – for example by welfare, medical and educational professionals.

Sources: adapted from Liz Steel and Warren Kidd (2001); the Labour Party manifesto (2005)

(a)   Suggest **two** social problems that the family 'often gets the blame for' (**Item A**, line 7).   (4 marks)

(b)   Suggest **two** examples of ways in which professionals police and regulate families (**Item A**, line 9).   (4 marks)

(c)   Identify **one** similarity and **one** difference between New Labour and New Right views on family policy.   (4 marks)

Essay   Examine the ways in which laws and social policies affect family life.   (24 marks)

The examiner's advice

The essay carries 14 AO1 marks (knowledge and understanding) and 10 AO2 marks (interpretation, application, analysis and evaluation). The emphasis is on showing a sound, detailed sociological knowledge, but to score high marks you must also demonstrate AO2 skills.

Look at a range of laws and policies. These can be policies directly about family life (e.g. on marriage, divorce, abortion, homosexuality, child support, child protection, benefits etc), as well as policies in other areas that affect family life (e.g. compulsory schooling, child labour laws, immigration restrictions). How might policies affect the rights, duties or positions of different family members – e.g. couples, parents, children or other relatives? How far do different policies support or undermine different kinds of family (e.g. nuclear, lone-parent, gay, extended)? You could also look at policies from different countries and times (Nazi Germany, the Soviet Union, China, Romania, gender regimes in Europe today). You can develop analysis and evaluation by comparing and contrasting different perspectives (e.g. functionalist, New Right, feminism, Donzelot). Which policies provide evidence for or against any of these perspectives? Write a separate conclusion.

Exam question and student answer

Examining families and households

Item A Most sociologists agree that the many legal changes of the last hundred years have had a major effect on the position of children. For example, the introduction of various laws and social policies concerned with children has altered their status and helped to shape our ideas of what childhood should be like.

However, demographic trends may also have had some effect on the position of children. For example, the fall in the infant mortality rate from 1900 is thought to have played a part in reducing the birth rate, since couples could be more certain that the children they had would survive. In turn, this may have resulted in parents investing more in their children, both emotionally and financially.   5

Item B Marriage, and the roles and relationships within it, continue to be an unequal 'partnership'. The domestic division of labour may not be as clear-cut as it once was, but it is still a highly gendered division in most marriages. Just as the employment structure continues to discriminate against women in the opportunities available for well-paid work, so too the tasks of childcare and housework remain defined predominantly as female ones.

Current high levels of divorce also highlight the gap between the ideology and the reality of marriage, as does the prevalence of domestic violence.   5

Source: adapted from Graham Allan (1996)

(a) Explain what is meant by the 'infant mortality rate' (**Item A**, line 4).   (2 marks)

(b) Identify **two** demographic trends in the United Kingdom since 1900, **apart from** those referred to in **Item A**.   (4 marks)

(c) Identify **three** laws or social policies that have affected the status of children (**Item A**, line 2).   (6 marks)

(d) Examine the reasons for changes in the divorce rate since 1970.   (24 marks)

(e) Using material from **Item B** and elsewhere, assess the view that roles and relationships among couples are becoming more equal. (24 marks)

The examiner's advice

Part (d) carries 14 AO1 marks (knowledge and understanding) and 10 AO2 marks (interpretation, application, analysis and evaluation). The emphasis is on showing a sound, detailed sociological knowledge, but to score high marks you must also demonstrate AO2 skills.

You need to know the general pattern of changes in the divorce rate: very big increases until the 1990s, then a smaller fall followed by a levelling off at a high rate. Avoid going back to the period before 1970 in your answer. You should examine a range of reasons: the changes in the law, decline in stigma attached to divorce, secularisation, changes in women's position, higher expectations of marriage etc. Write at least a paragraph on each – by explaining clearly and logically how each factor might affect the rates, you can gain marks both for understanding and for analysis. Link different perspectives (e.g. feminist, New Right, functionalist, postmodernist) to these reasons where possible. Write a separate conclusion.

Part (e) carries 10 AO1 marks (knowledge and understanding) and 14 AO2 marks (interpretation, application, analysis and evaluation). The emphasis is on showing well-developed AO2 skills, but to score high marks you must also show a good sociological knowledge. You must also make sure you use the Item.

You need to deal with both roles and relationships. 'Roles' refers to both domestic labour and breadwinning roles. 'Relationships' involves power and control, so look at who controls the family's resources, makes the decisions, uses violence. To score high marks, you must use Item B, so build on the references to gendered housework and childcare, paid work and domestic violence. Are cohabiting couples (heterosexual and same-sex) more equal than married couples? Evaluate the view through a debate: e.g. 'march of progress' or functionalists versus feminists on domestic labour; radical feminists and their critics on domestic violence. Consider whether women doing paid work makes roles and relationships more equal. Use a range of studies and explanations. Write a separate conclusion.

Activity

Here are two things you can do to practise your exam skills:

1   Attempt the whole question on the page opposite. You could try doing it under timed conditions. If so, allow yourself one hour to answer all five parts – plus an extra 10 minutes to study the examiner's advice on parts (d) and (e).

2   Read the student answer to part (e) below, together with Item B. Study the examiner's advice and comments. Then write an improved version of it that takes on board the advice and comments. (You can copy any bits of the original that you want to keep.)

In both cases, make a brief plan. Try swopping your answer with a friend and marking each other's work, using the examiner's advice to help you.

For further exam practice, see Chapter 5, pages 242-4, where you will find mock exam papers for both AS units.

Answer by Elaine

(e) Whether the conjugal roles of husband and wife are becoming more equal or symmetrical is one that has been much studied by sociologists. Young and Willmott argue that the division of labour between couples has now become more or less equal and they now have joint conjugal roles (JCRs).

> Some relevant concepts introduced on the division of labour.

They base this claim on their study in which they questioned couples on the roles that husbands and wives took in the domestic division of labour in relation to childcare and housework. They found that just under three-quarters of the men contributed to household chores.

> Shows knowledge of a relevant study.

However, this figure has been criticised because of the question on which it was based – "do you contribute at least once a week to household tasks?" This means that if the man irons his own shirt once a week, that couple could be defined as having joint conjugal roles. Also, it ignores the fact that even if men help with housework, it is still seen as the woman's responsibility, not the man's.

> Two appropriate evaluation points, effectively made.

Other sociologists have undertaken research that contradicts Young and Willmott. For example, Ann Oakley conducted a study in London with 40 young women (20 middle-class and 20 working-class) who had one child under 5. She found that 25% of their husbands helped with childcare and 15% with housework. They also tended to choose the more 'fun' aspects, such as playing with the children rather than changing nappies. More recent research by Ferri and Smith and by Boulton backs up Oakley's findings.

> Applies relevant knowledge to evaluate Young and Willmott.

Edgell studied professional couples and concluded that none of them had JCRs as far as housework was concerned, and less than half as far as childcare was concerned. He also found that important decisions were more likely to be taken by the husband alone, and the least important ones by the wife alone.

> More evidence against JCRs – plus a good point about decision-making.

To conclude, there does seem to be some move towards greater equality in roles and relationships, though they are still a long way from being truly equal. Perhaps as women go out to work more, this will speed up the move to equality.

> Relevant conclusion, but not fully supported by the essay. Good point about women working – but undeveloped.

The examiner's comments

Overall, this is quite a good answer as far as domestic roles are concerned. Elaine looks at the findings of several studies of housework and she takes an evaluative approach to the issue. However, it would be better to spend a little less time on the Young and Willmott versus Oakley debate. Instead, she could refer to studies looking at the effects of women's paid employment on the domestic division of labour, e.g. Kan, Gershuny, Sullivan or Crompton. This would allow her to develop the important point she makes at the very end.

Apart from a brief mention of Edgell's findings about decision-making, Elaine doesn't really get to grips with the 'relationships' side of the question. She should look at reasons why men make the important decisions. She should also consider other aspects of relationships in terms of power and control – for example, over the family's resources, and domestic violence against women. The question requires you to use Item B, which gives several pointers to these issues. Very importantly, Elaine also needs some theory (e.g. 'march of progress', functionalism, different types of feminism), as well as more concepts – such as patriarchy, dual burden, triple shift, expressive and instrumental roles. Lastly, she shouldn't leave it until the final sentence to introduce a new important idea. $\frac{15}{24}$

Education
with special links to research methods

CHAPTER 3

Key questions about education

Sociologists are interested in four main questions about education.

Firstly, why do some pupils achieve more than others? On average, middle-class pupils do better in education than working-class pupils and girls do better than boys, while there are also differences in the achievements of pupils from different ethnic groups.

To explain these differences, sociologists have studied the impact of processes within schools such as the ways teachers label pupils, as well as factors outside school such as children's home background.

Secondly, sociologists have examined the role of education in society and who benefits from it. For example, functionalists claim that education acts as a way of allocating people to jobs on the basis of ability. By contrast, Marxists see it as a means of providing capitalism with an obedient workforce.

Thirdly, sociologists are interested in how pupils experience schooling. For example, girls and boys often study different subjects, while pupils from minority ethnic groups may face racism in school and girls may experience sexism. Such experiences may affect not only pupils' achievement, but also their identity and self-esteem.

Fourthly, the government makes laws and policies that affect education. Sociologists are interested in their impact. For example, do they produce equal opportunity for all pupils? Do they produce the kind of labour force the economy needs?

The AQA Specification

The specification is the syllabus produced by the exam board, telling you what you have to study. The AQA specification for Education requires you to examine the following:

- The role and purpose of education, including vocational education and training, in contemporary society.

- Differential educational achievement of social groups by social class, gender and ethnicity in contemporary society.

- Relationships and processes within schools, with particular reference to teacher/pupil relationships, pupil subcultures, the hidden curriculum, and the organisation of teaching and learning.

- The significance of educational policies, including selection, comprehensivisation and marketisation, for an understanding of the structure, role, impact and experience of education.

- The application of sociological research methods to the study of education.

For full details of the specification, visit: www.aqa.org.uk

Methods Link: researching education

In the exam, you have to answer a question that requires you to apply sociological research methods to a particular issue in education.

Look out for Methods Link boxes like this one throughout this chapter. These deal with the way sociologists apply different research methods to particular educational issues.

The Methods Link boxes also give you a link into the Sociological Methods chapter, where you will find special **Methods in Context** sections. These show you how each method can be applied to a range of different topics in education.

Read more about researching education in Chapter 4, Topic 2 on pages 168-71.

Topic 1 Class differences in achievement (1) external factors

Learning objectives

After studying this Topic, you should:

- Be able to describe the pattern of class differences in educational achievement.
- Understand the difference between internal and external factors affecting achievement.
- Understand and be able to evaluate the role of different external factors, including cultural deprivation, material deprivation and cultural capital.

One of the most striking features of education in Britain is the difference in achievement between pupils from different social classes. Despite great improvements in the educational level of the nation as a whole since state education began in 1870, social class differences continue. In this Topic we shall look at the evidence of these differences and at how sociologists have explained them.

When examining social class differences in achievement, the main comparison sociologists make is between working-class and middle-class pupils. Most sociologists use parental occupation to determine a pupil's social class. For example:

- **Middle-class** or non-manual occupations traditionally include professionals such as doctors or teachers, together with managers and other 'white collar' office workers and owners of businesses.
- **Working-class** or manual occupations traditionally include skilled workers such as plumbers and electricians, together with semi-skilled workers such as waitresses or lorry drivers, and unskilled or routine workers such as cleaners and labourers.

Explaining class differences

Social class background has a powerful influence on a child's chances of success in the education system. Children from middle-class families on average perform better than working-class children, and the class gap in achievement grows wider as children get older. Children of the middle class do better at GCSE (see Figure 3.1), stay longer in full-time education and take the great majority of university places (see Table 3A on page 98).

One popular explanation of class differences in achievement is that better-off parents can afford to send their children to private schools, which many believe provide a higher standard of education. For example, average class sizes are less than half those in state schools. Although these schools educate only 7% of Britain's children, nearly all these pupils (over 90%) go on to university and they account for nearly half of all students entering the elite universities of Oxford and Cambridge. Andrew Adonis and Stephen Pollard (1998) see private education as a major way in which class privileges are transmitted from generation to generation.

Activity   Private schools

Go to www.sociology.uk.net

However, the existence of private education does not account for class differences within *state* education, and most sociological research has focused on why middle-class pupils do better than working-class pupils within the state sector itself.

Internal and external factors

Sociologists are interested in why these class differences in educational achievement exist and have put forward a number of explanations. We can group these into 'internal' and 'external' explanations or factors – though in reality, of course, these factors are very often linked:

- **Internal factors** – these are factors within schools and the education system, such as interactions between pupils and teachers, and inequalities between schools.
- **External factors** – these are factors outside the education system, such as the influence of home and family background and wider society.

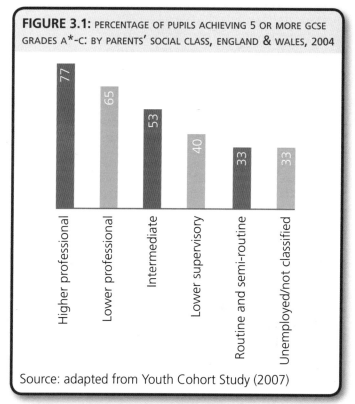

FIGURE 3.1: PERCENTAGE OF PUPILS ACHIEVING 5 OR MORE GCSE GRADES A*-C: BY PARENTS' SOCIAL CLASS, ENGLAND & WALES, 2004

- Higher professional: 77
- Lower professional: 65
- Intermediate: 53
- Lower supervisory: 40
- Routine and semi-routine: 33
- Unemployed/not classified: 33

Source: adapted from Youth Cohort Study (2007)

We shall focus first on the following external factors that affect pupils' educational achievement:

1. **cultural deprivation**
2. **material deprivation**
3. **cultural capital**

Cultural deprivation

Cultural deprivation theorists argue that most of us begin to acquire the basic values, attitudes and skills that are needed for educational success through primary socialisation in the family. This basic 'cultural equipment' includes things such as language, self-discipline and reasoning skills.

However, according to cultural deprivation theorists, many working-class families fail to socialise their children adequately. These children grow up 'culturally deprived'. That is, they lack the cultural equipment needed to do well at school and so they under-achieve. There are three main aspects of cultural deprivation:

- intellectual development
- language
- attitudes and values.

Intellectual development

This refers to the development of thinking and reasoning skills, such as the ability to solve problems and use ideas and concepts.

Cultural deprivation theorists argue that many working-class homes lack the books, educational toys and activities that would stimulate a child's intellectual development. Thus children from such homes start school without having developed the intellectual skills needed to progress.

For example, J.W.B. Douglas (1964) found that working-class pupils scored lower on tests of ability than middle-class pupils. He argues that this is because working-class parents are less likely to support their children's intellectual development through reading with them or other educational activities in the home.

Basil Bernstein and Douglas Young (1967) reached similar conclusions. They found that the way mothers think about and choose toys has an influence on their children's intellectual development. Middle-class mothers are more likely to choose toys that encourage thinking and reasoning skills and prepare children for school.

▲ *In what ways do middle-class parents give their children a head start?*

Language

The importance of language for educational achievement is highlighted by Carl Bereiter and Siegfried Engelmann (1966). They claim that the language used in lower-class homes is deficient. They describe lower-class families as communicating by gestures, single words or disjointed phrases.

As a result, their children fail to develop the necessary language skills. They grow up incapable of abstract thinking and unable to use language to explain, describe, enquire or compare. Because of this, they are unable to take advantage of the opportunities that school offers.

Like Bereiter and Engelmann, Basil Bernstein (1975) also identifies differences between working-class and middle-class language that influence achievement. He distinguishes between two types of speech code:

- **The restricted code** is the speech code typically used by the working class. It has a limited vocabulary and is based on the use of short, often unfinished, grammatically simple sentences. Speech is predictable and may involve only a single word, or even just a gesture instead. It is descriptive not analytic. The restricted code is context-bound: that is, the speaker assumes that the listener shares the same set of experiences.
- **The elaborated code** is typically used by the middle class. It has a wider vocabulary and is based on longer, grammatically more complex sentences. Speech is more varied and communicates abstract ideas. The elaborated code is context-free: the speaker does not assume that the listener shares the same experiences, and so s/he uses language to spell out his or her meanings explicitly for the listener. Box 9 gives examples of the two codes.

These differences in speech code give middle-class children an advantage at school and put working-class children at a disadvantage. This is because the elaborated code is the language used by teachers, textbooks and exams. Not only is it taken as the 'correct' way to speak and write, but in Bernstein's view it is also a more effective tool for analysing and reasoning and for expressing thoughts clearly and effectively – essential skills in education.

Early socialisation into the elaborated code means that middle-class children are already fluent users of the code when they start school. Thus they feel 'at home' in school and are more likely to succeed. By contrast, working-class children, lacking the code in which schooling takes place, are likely to feel excluded and to be less successful.

Critics argue that Bernstein is a cultural deprivation theorist because he describes working-class speech as inadequate. However, unlike most cultural deprivation theorists, Bernstein recognises that the school – and not just the home – influences children's achievement. He argues that working-class pupils fail not because they are culturally deprived, but because schools fail to teach them how to use the elaborated code.

Box 9	Restricted and elaborated codes: an illustration

The difference between speech codes is illustrated by these descriptions given by two five-year-old children, one working-class, the other middle-class, who were each shown the same set of pictures and asked to tell the story:

'They're playing football and he kicks it and it goes through there it breaks the window and they're looking at it and he comes out and shouts at them because they've broken it so they run away and then she looks out and she tells them off.'

'Three boys are playing football and one boy kicks the ball and it goes through the window the ball breaks the window and the boys are looking at it and a man comes out and shouts at them because they've broken the window so they run away and then the lady looks out of her window and she tells the boys off.'

The first child uses the restricted code, where the speech is context-bound. The second child is using the elaborated code, where the speech is context-free.

Source: adapted from Bernstein (1976), *Education cannot compensate for society*

1 Explain why the first example is context-bound speech and the second is context-free.

2 In what ways might the context-free elaborated code be more useful when writing in an exam or answering questions at an interview for university?

Attitudes and values

Cultural deprivation theorists argue that parents' attitudes and values are a key factor affecting educational achievement. For example, Douglas found that working-class parents placed less value on education, were less ambitious for their children, gave them less encouragement and took less interest in their education. They visited schools less often and were less likely to discuss their children's progress with teachers. As a result, their children had lower levels of achievement motivation.

Similarly, Leon Feinstein (1998) found that working-class parents' lack of interest was the main reason for their children's under-achievement and was even more important than financial hardship or factors within school. Feinstein argues that middle-class children are more successful because their parents provide them with the necessary motivation, discipline and support.

Cultural deprivation theorists argue that lack of parental interest in their children's education reflects the subcultural values of the working class. A subculture is a group whose attitudes and values differ from those of the mainstream culture. According to cultural deprivation theorists, large sections of the working class have different goals, beliefs, attitudes and values from the rest of society and this is why their children fail at school.

Herbert Hyman (1967) takes this view. He argues that the values and beliefs of lower-class subculture are a 'self-imposed barrier' to educational and career success. The lower class believe that they have less opportunity for individual advancement and place little value on achieving high status jobs, so they see no point in education. They are less willing to make the sacrifices involved in staying on at school and leave early to take manual work. Their subcultural beliefs and values ensure that they neither want educational success, nor know how to get it.

Similarly, Barry Sugarman (1970) argues that working-class subculture has four key features that act as a barrier to educational achievement:

- **Fatalism**: a belief in fate – that 'whatever will be, will be' and there is nothing you can do to change your status. This contrasts with middle-class values, which emphasise that you can change your position through your own efforts.
- **Collectivism**: valuing being part of a group more than succeeding as an individual. This contrasts with the middle-class view that an individual should not be held back by group loyalties.
- **Immediate gratification**: seeking pleasure now rather than making sacrifices in order to get rewards in the future. By contrast, middle-class values emphasise deferred gratification, making sacrifices now for greater rewards later.
- **Present-time orientation**: seeing the present as more important than the future and so not having long-term goals or plans. By contrast, middle-class culture has a future-time orientation that sees planning for the future as important.

Working-class children internalise the beliefs and values of their subculture through the socialisation process and this results in them under-achieving at school.

Why do these differences in values exist? Sugarman argues that they stem from the fact that middle-class jobs are secure careers offering prospects for continuous individual advancement. This encourages ambition, long-term planning and a willingness to invest time and effort in gaining qualifications. By contrast, working-class jobs are less secure and have no career structure through which individuals can advance. There are few promotion opportunities and earnings peak at an early age.

Cultural deprivation theorists argue that parents pass on the values of their class to their children through primary socialisation. Middle-class values equip children for success, whereas working-class values fail to do so.

Activity Working-class subculture

 *Go to www.sociology.uk.net*

Explain why:

1 working-class job insecurity may lead to an attitude of fatalism

2 lack of a clear career ladder for manual workers may encourage a present-time orientation

3 an attitude of fatalism and present-time orientation may lead to educational failure.

Compensatory education

Compensatory education is a policy designed to tackle the problem of cultural deprivation by providing extra resources to schools and communities in deprived areas. Compensatory education programmes attempt to intervene early in the socialisation process to compensate children for the deprivation they experience at home.

The best known example of such programmes is Operation Head Start in the United States, a multi-billion dollar scheme of pre-school education in poorer areas introduced in the 1960s. Its aim was 'planned enrichment' of the deprived child's environment to develop learning skills and instil achievement motivation. It included improving parenting skills, setting up nursery classes, home visits by health visitors and educational psychologists, and the creation of intensive learning programmes for deprived children.

The well known television programme Sesame Street was initially conceived as part of Head Start, providing a means of reaching young children and transmitting – in this case literally – values and attitudes needed for educational success. These included the importance of punctuality, numeracy, literacy and general knowledge.

In Britain, there have been several compensatory education programmes. Educational Priority Areas were created in the 1960s. More recently, Education Action Zones were introduced in the late 1990s, while Sure Start, a nationwide programme aimed at pre-school children and their parents, was launched in 2000. Although it also has non-educational goals such as improving children's health, Sure Start has similarities to earlier compensatory education programmes (see Box 10).

The myth of cultural deprivation?

Although it draws our attention to the role of the child's social background, cultural deprivation theory has been widely criticised as an explanation of class differences in achievement.

Nell Keddie (1973) describes cultural deprivation as a 'myth' and sees it as a victim- blaming explanation. She dismisses the idea that failure at school can be blamed on a culturally deprived home background. She points out that a child cannot be deprived of its own culture and argues that working-class children are simply culturally different, not culturally deprived. They fail because they are put at a disadvantage by an education system that is dominated by middle-class values.

Keddie argues that rather than seeing working-class culture as deficient, schools should recognise and build on its strengths and should challenge teachers' anti-working class prejudices.

Likewise, Barry Troyna and Jenny Williams (1986) argue that the problem is not the child's language but the school's attitude towards it. Teachers have a 'speech hierarchy': they label middle-class speech highest, followed by working-class speech and finally black speech.

Other critics reject the view that working-class parents are not interested in their children's education. According to Tessa Blackstone and Jo Mortimore (1994), they attend fewer parents' evenings, not because of a lack of interest, but because they work longer or less regular hours or are put off by the school's middle-class atmosphere. They may want to help their child progress but they lack the knowledge and education to do so. There is also evidence that schools with mainly working-class pupils have less effective systems of parent-school contacts. This makes it harder for parents to keep in touch about their children's progress.

Finally, some critics argue that compensatory education schemes act as a smokescreen concealing the real cause of under-achievement, namely social inequality and poverty. They argue that the real problem is not cultural deprivation, but poverty and material deprivation.

Explain briefly Keddie's arguments that:

1 'a child cannot be deprived of its own culture'.

2 cultural deprivation theory 'blames the victims'.

3 it is the education system that is at fault.

Box 10	Sure Start

Sure Start is a major element in the British government's policies to tackle poverty and social exclusion. By 2008, there were around 2,500 local Sure Start Children's Centres, rising to 3,500 by 2010, with all young children in the most disadvantaged areas having access to one. The centres provide integrated education, care, family support, health services and support with parental employment.

The aim of Sure Start is to work with parents to promote the physical, intellectual and social development of babies and young children, particularly those who are disadvantaged, so that they can flourish at home and when they go to school, and thereby break the cycle of disadvantage.

One objective of Sure Start is to improve children's ability to learn, by encouraging high quality environments that promote early learning, provide stimulating and enjoyable play, improve language skills and ensure early identification and support of children with special needs.

Source: adapted from www.surestart.gov.uk

What similarities can you see between Sure Start and Operation Head Start?

Material deprivation

▲ *Material factors such as inadequate housing can have a powerful effect on children's achievement.*

Unlike cultural deprivation theorists, who blame educational failure on the inadequacy of working-class subculture, many other sociologists see material deprivation as the main cause of under-achievement. The term 'material deprivation' refers to poverty and a lack of material necessities such as adequate housing and income.

Poverty is closely linked to educational under-achievement. For example:

- In 2006, only 33% of children receiving free school meals (a widely used measure of child poverty) gained five or more GCSEs at A*-C, as against 61% of pupils not receiving free school meals.
- According to Jan Flaherty (2004), money problems in the family were a significant factor in younger children's non-attendance at school.
- Exclusion and truancy are more likely for children from poorer families. Children excluded from school are unlikely to return to mainstream education, while a third of all persistent truants leave school with no qualifications.
- Nearly 90% of 'failing' schools are located in deprived areas.

There is a close link between poverty and social class. Working-class families are much more likely to have low incomes or inadequate housing. Factors such as these can affect their children's education in several ways.

Methods Link: using official statistics

The government collects official statistics on education, so using them can save sociologists time and money. Sociologists use official statistics to establish correlations (links) between social factors. For example, statistics on the exam results of children eligible for free school meals (FSM) show a correlation between material deprivation and achievement.

However, statistical correlations in themselves cannot prove that deprivation is the cause of under-achievement. Also, the government does not always collect statistics that might be of interest to sociologists. For example, the 87% of children who do not receive FSM are all lumped together, even though they range from the super-rich to those just above the poverty line.

Read more about official statistics and researching education in **Methods in Context** on page 226-7.

Housing

Poor housing can affect pupils' achievement both directly and indirectly. For example, overcrowding can have a direct effect by making it harder for the child to study. Overcrowding means less room for educational activities, nowhere to do homework, disturbed sleep from sharing beds or bedrooms and so on.

For young children especially, development can be impaired through lack of space for safe play and exploration. Families living in temporary (bed and breakfast) accommodation may find themselves having to move frequently, resulting in constant changes of school and disrupted education.

Poor housing can also have indirect effects, notably on the child's health and welfare. For example, children in crowded homes run a greater risk of accidents. Cold or damp housing can also cause ill health, especially respiratory illnesses. Families in temporary accommodation suffer more psychological distress, infections and accidents. Such health problems mean more absences from school.

Diet and health

Marilyn Howard (2001) notes that young people from poorer homes have lower intakes of energy, vitamins and minerals. Poor nutrition affects health, for example by weakening the immune system and lowering children's energy levels. This may result in more absences from school due to illness, and difficulties concentrating in class.

Children from poorer homes are also more likely to have emotional or behavioural problems. According to Richard Wilkinson (1996), among ten year olds, the lower the social class, the higher the rate of hyperactivity, anxiety and conduct disorders, all of which are likely to have a negative effect on the child's education.

Financial support and the costs of education

Lack of financial support means that children from poor families have to do without equipment and miss out on experiences that would enhance their educational achievement. David Bull (1980) refers to this as 'the costs of free schooling'. A study in the Oxford area by Emily Tanner et al (2003) found that the cost of items such as transport, uniforms, books, computers, calculators, and sports, music and art equipment, places a heavy burden on poor families.

As a result, poor children may have to make do with hand-me-downs and cheaper but unfashionable equipment, and this may result in being stigmatised or bullied by peers. Yet, for many children, suitable clothes are essential for self-esteem and 'fitting in'. For example, Tess Ridge (2002), in her study examining poverty from the child's perspective, quotes 12-year-old Bella:

"I just want to fit in the group, 'cos it's like… people take the mick out of me because I can't afford things. Like my trainers are messy… and I need new trainers and clothes… I can't get decent clothes like everyone else does."

According to Flaherty, fear of stigmatisation may also help to explain why 20% of those eligible for free school meals do not take up their entitlement:

"I realised when I was in year 7 that the people who got free school meals were teased… I couldn't handle that as I was already getting teased enough, so I don't get free school meals." (Quoted in Ridge 2002)

Lack of funds also means that children from low-income families often need to work. Ridge found that children in poverty take on jobs such as baby sitting, cleaning and paper rounds, and that this often had a negative impact on their schoolwork.

These financial restrictions help to explain why many working-class pupils leave school at 16 and why relatively few go on to university, as Table 3A shows. There is

evidence that fear of debt deters poor students from applying. Students from poorer families starting university can expect to leave with substantial debts as a result of the introduction of fees for higher education.

Dropout rates are also higher for universities with a large proportion of poor students: for example, 13% at Sunderland, a university with a large working-class intake, but only 1.4% at Oxford, where over four students out of 10 come from private schools. The National Audit Office (2002) found that working-class students spent twice as much time in paid work to reduce their debts as middle-class students.

Table 3A	Percentage of young people (under 21) participating in higher education, by social class

Social class	2003
I Professional	79
II Intermediate	50
IIIN Skilled non-manual	33
IIIM Skilled manual	21
IV Semi-skilled manual	18
V Unskilled manual	15
All social classes	35

Source: DfES

Roughly how many times greater was the participation rate in higher education for young people from the professional class than for those from the unskilled manual class?

Cultural or material factors?

While material factors clearly play a part in achievement, the fact that some children from poor families do succeed suggests that material deprivation is only part of the explanation.

For example, the cultural, religious or political values of the family may play a part in creating and sustaining the child's motivation, even despite poverty. Similarly, the quality of the school may play an important part in enabling some poor children to achieve.

Nevertheless, Peter Mortimore and Geoff Whitty (1997) argue that material inequalities have a greater effect on achievement than school factors. For this reason, Peter Robinson (1997) argues that tackling child poverty would be the most effective way to boost achievement.

Cultural capital

Bourdieu: three types of capital

Pierre Bourdieu (1984) argues that both cultural and material factors contribute to educational achievement and are not separate but interrelated. He uses the concept of 'capital' to explain why the middle class are more successful.

The term capital usually refers to wealth but in addition to this economic capital, Bourdieu identifies two further types. These are 'educational capital' or qualifications, and 'cultural capital'. He argues that the middle class generally possess more of all three types of capital.

cultural capital

Bourdieu uses the term cultural capital to refer to the knowledge, attitudes, values, language, tastes and abilities of the middle class. He sees middle-class culture as a type of capital because, like wealth, it gives an advantage to those who possess it. Like Bernstein, he argues that through their socialisation, middle-class children acquire the ability to grasp, analyse and express abstract ideas. They are more likely to develop intellectual interests and an understanding of what the education system requires for success.

This gives middle-class children an advantage in school, where such abilities and interests are highly valued and rewarded with qualifications. This is because the education system is not neutral, but favours and transmits the dominant middle-class culture.

By contrast, working-class children find that school devalues their culture as 'rough' and inferior. Their lack of cultural capital leads to exam failure. Many working-class pupils also 'get the message' that education is not meant for them and respond by truanting, early leaving or just not trying.

educational and economic capital

Bourdieu argues that educational, economic and cultural capital can be converted into one another.

For example, middle-class children with cultural capital are better equipped to meet the demands of the school curriculum and gain qualifications. Similarly, wealthier parents can convert their economic capital into educational capital by sending their children to private schools and paying for extra tuition. As Dennis Leech and Erick Campos' (2003) study of Coventry shows, middle-class parents are also more likely to be able to afford a house in the catchment area of a school that is highly placed in the exam league tables. This has become known as 'selection by mortgage' because it drives up demand for houses near to successful schools and excludes working-class families.

a test of Bourdieu's ideas

Alice Sullivan (2001) used questionnaires to conduct a survey of 465 pupils in four schools. To assess their cultural capital, she asked them about a range of activities, such as reading and TV viewing habits, and whether they visited art galleries, museums and theatres. She also tested their vocabulary and knowledge of cultural figures.

She found that those who read complex fiction and watched serious TV documentaries developed a wider vocabulary and greater cultural knowledge, indicating greater cultural capital. The pupils with the greatest cultural capital were children of graduates. These pupils were more likely to be successful at GCSE.

However, although successful pupils with greater cultural capital were more likely to be middle-class, Sullivan found that cultural capital only accounted for part of the class difference in achievement. Where pupils of different classes had the same level of cultural capital, middle-class pupils still did better. Sullivan concludes that the greater resources and aspirations of middle-class families explain the remainder of the class gap in achievement.

Activity

Cultural capital includes aspects such as taste (e.g. in music, art and literature), language, experiences, knowledge and manners. Choose three of these and explain how each one might give a middle-class child an advantage in school.

Gewirtz: marketisation and parental choice

One example of how cultural and economic capital can lead to differences in educational achievement is via the impact of marketisation and parental choice. Since the creation of an 'education market' by the 1988 Education Reform Act (see page 152), sociologists have been interested in the effect of increased parental choice that the Act introduced. Has greater parental choice of school benefited one social class more than the other?

Sharon Gewirtz (1995) examines this question in a study of class differences in parental choice of secondary school. Her study of 14 London schools is based on interviews with teachers and parents, and on secondary data such as school documents. She uses Bourdieu's ideas to explain her findings.

Gewirtz found that differences in economic and cultural capital lead to class differences in how far parents can exercise choice of secondary school. She identifies three main types of parents, whom she calls privileged-skilled choosers, disconnected-local choosers and semi-skilled choosers.

Methods Link: using documents

Gewirtz studied the ways in which schools responded to being part of an 'education market'. She collected a range of school documents including brochures, prospectuses and planning reports. These gave her an insight into the increasing amount of resources schools were now devoting to 'selling' themselves to potential 'customers', i.e. parents.

However, such documents need to be treated with caution. They are part of a school's public relations effort and their content may give a selective and distorted picture.

Read more about documents and researching education in **Methods in Context** on pages 227-8.

privileged-skilled choosers

These were mainly professional middle-class parents who used their economic and cultural capital to gain educational capital for their children. Being prosperous, confident and well educated, they were able to take full advantage of the choices open to them.

These parents possessed cultural capital. They knew how school admissions systems work, 'how to approach schools, present and mount a case, maintain pressure, make an impact and be remembered'. They understood the importance of putting a particular school as first choice, meeting deadlines, and using appeals procedures and waiting lists to get what they wanted. They saw choosing a school as part of the process of planning their child's future, and they had the time to visit schools and the skills to research the options available.

Their economic capital also meant they could afford to move their children around the education system to get the best deal out of it, for example by paying extra travel costs so that their children could attend 'better' schools out of their area.

disconnected-local choosers

These were working-class parents whose choices were restricted by their lack of economic and cultural capital.

They found it difficult to understand school admissions procedures. They were less confident in their dealings with schools, less aware of the choices open to them, and less able to manipulate the system to their own advantage. Many of them attached more importance to safety and the quality of school facilities than to league tables or long-term ambitions.

Distance and cost of travel were major restrictions on their choice of school. Their funds were limited and a place at the local comprehensive was often the only realistic option for their children.

semi-skilled choosers

These parents were also mainly working-class, but unlike the disconnected-local choosers, they were ambitious for their children. However, they too lacked cultural capital and found it difficult to make sense of the education market, often having to rely on other people's opinions about schools. They were often frustrated at their inability to get their children into the schools they wanted.

Gewirtz concludes that middle-class families with cultural and economic capital are better placed to take advantage of the available opportunities for a good education. Although in theory the education market gives everyone greater choice, in practice those who possess cultural and economic capital have more choice than others.

As Geoff Whitty (1998) notes, marketisation has not led to more opportunities for working-class children. Instead, it has allowed the middle class to use their wealth and knowledge even more effectively than before.

▲ Cultural capital includes developing a taste for fine art, classical music and other 'high culture'. What difference might this make to educational achievement?

For more activities on Class differences in achievement (1) external factors...

Go to www.sociology.uk.net

Summary

Middle-class pupils tend to achieve more than working-class pupils. Some explanations focus on external factors outside school. These include **cultural deprivation** – working-class pupils are seen as lacking the right attitudes, values, language and knowledge for educational success (e.g. they lack deferred gratification). **Material deprivation** means working-class children are more likely to have poorer diets, health and housing, and parents who are less able to meet the hidden costs of schooling. The middle class have more **cultural capital**. They are better placed to take advantage of the choices offered in a marketised education system.

QuickCheck Questions

1   What advantages in terms of intellectual development might a middle-class child have before s/he starts school?

2   Explain the difference between deferred and immediate gratification.

3   Identify three characteristics of the elaborated code.

4   What is meant by 'compensatory education'?

5   Suggest three ways in which poverty may affect achievement.

6   What is the difference between cultural and economic capital?

7   What are 'disconnected-local choosers'?

Check your answers at www.sociology.uk.net

Examining class differences in achievement (1) external factors

Item A   J.W.B. Douglas' study, *The Home and the School*, explained working-class failure as the result of a lack of parental interest and stimulation in the home. Two of the measures of parental interest he used were the number of times parents visited their child's school, and what teachers said about parents. Douglas proposed an improvement in primary school teaching and an increase in nursery schools to give working-class children the stimulus lacking in their homes. This picture of the culturally deprived child was given further weight by the publication of several official reports into child development.

5

These reports and studies like Douglas' led to the setting up of Educational Priority Areas (EPAs) in a number of inner-city areas. An area acquired its EPA status, which brought extra funds, by virtue of its measurable indices of poverty, such as the proportion of children receiving free school dinners. Educational factors included pupils' average reading ages and truancy rates. A major aim of the EPAs was to increase the involvement of parents in their children's education.

Source: adapted from Karen Chapman (1986), *The Sociology of Schools*

(a) Explain briefly what is meant by the term 'elaborated speech code'. (2 marks)

(b) Identify **three** policies that governments have introduced to compensate for material and cultural disadvantage, **apart from** Educational Priority Areas. (6 marks)

(c) Outline some of the ways in which material deprivation may affect educational achievement. (12 marks)

(d) Using material from **Item A** and elsewhere, assess the view that working-class children under-achieve because they are culturally deprived. (20 marks)

The examiner's advice

Part (c) carries 8 AO1 marks (knowledge and understanding) and 4 AO2 marks (interpretation, application, analysis and evaluation). You should explain what is meant by material deprivation and identify the forms it can take, e.g. low income, poor housing, diet and health etc. Explain how each of these may affect the educational achievement of children from poor families. Analyse the ways in which material and cultural deprivation may be linked.

Part (d) carries 8 AO1 marks and 12 AO2 marks. Explain what is meant by cultural deprivation and how it may affect achievement, e.g. in terms of lack of parental interest, inadequate language skills and values such as immediate gratification. Use evidence from studies and Item A to do so. You need to evaluate the view that cultural deprivation (CD) is the cause of working-class failure. A good focus is that CD theory, by 'blaming the victim' for failure, lets both social inequality (poverty) and teachers/the education system off the hook. Use Keddie's claim that CD is a myth, as well as criticisms from other explanations, e.g. Blackstone and Mortimore, material deprivation, Bourdieu, Gewirtz, and internal factors such as labelling, pupil subcultures and selection processes (internal factors are explained in Topic 2). Make reference to policies to overcome cultural deprivation. Write a separate conclusion.

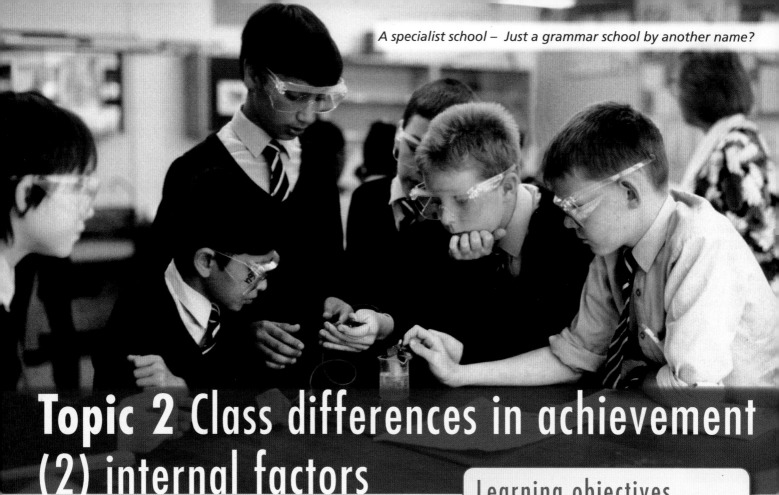

Topic 2 Class differences in achievement (2) internal factors

Learning objectives

After studying this Topic, you should:

- Understand the effect on social class differences in educational achievement of the following internal factors: labelling, the self-fulfilling prophecy, streaming, pupil subcultures and marketisation and selection.

- Be able to evaluate the relative importance of internal and external factors in causing social class differences in educational achievement.

As we saw in Topic 1, external factors (that is, those factors outside the education system) such as cultural deprivation, material deprivation and cultural capital, may play an important part in creating social class differences in educational achievement.

However, we also need to examine the part that is played by internal factors and processes *within* schools and the education system in causing these class differences in achievement. These internal factors include:

1 **Labelling**

2 **The self-fulfilling prophecy**

3 **Pupil subcultures**

4 **Marketisation and selection policies**

Topic 2 explores these factors and their effects upon the educational achievement of pupils from different social class backgrounds.

Labelling

To label someone is to attach a meaning or definition to them. For example, teachers may label a pupil as bright or thick, trouble maker or hardworking.

Studies show that teachers often attach such labels regardless of the pupil's actual ability or attitude. Instead, they label pupils on the basis of stereotyped assumptions about their class background, labelling working-class pupils negatively and middle-class pupils positively.

A number of studies of labelling have been carried out by interactionist sociologists. Interactionists study small-scale, face-to-face interactions between individuals, such as in the classroom or playground. They are interested in how people attach labels to one another, and the effects that this has on those who are labelled.

Labelling in secondary schools

Howard Becker (1971) carried out an important interactionist study of labelling. Based on interviews with 60 Chicago high school teachers, he found that they judged pupils according to how closely they fitted an image of the 'ideal pupil'.

Pupils' work, conduct and appearance were key factors influencing teachers' judgements. The teachers saw children from middle-class backgrounds as the closest to the ideal, and lower working-class children as furthest away from it because they regarded them as badly behaved.

Aaron Cicourel and John Kitsuse's (1963) study of educational counsellors in an American high school shows how such labelling can disadvantage working-class students. Counsellors play an important role in deciding which students will get on to courses that prepare them for higher education.

Cicourel and Kitsuse found inconsistencies in the way the counsellors assessed students' suitability for courses. Although they claimed to judge students according to their ability, in practice they judged them largely on the basis of their social class and/or race. Where students had similar grades, counsellors were more likely to label middle-class students as having college potential and to place them on higher-level courses.

Labelling in primary schools

Labelling occurs from the outset of a child's educational career, as Ray Rist's (1970) study of an American kindergarten shows. He found that the teacher used information about children's home background and appearance to place them in separate groups, seating each group at a different table. Those she decided were fast learners, whom she labelled the 'tigers', tended to be middle-class and of neat and clean appearance. She seated these at the table nearest to her and showed them greatest encouragement.

The other two groups – whom she labelled the 'cardinals' and the 'clowns' – were seated further away. These groups were more likely to be working-class. They were given lower-level books to read and fewer opportunities to demonstrate their abilities. For example, they had to read as a group, not as individuals.

Activity

Working in pairs and drawing on your own experiences:

1 List the characteristics you think teachers see as making up the 'ideal pupil'.

2 Teachers gradually build up a picture of the 'type' of child they are dealing with. Make a list of all the facts, influences etc that might determine how a particular child is labelled by a teacher.

British studies show similar patterns. Rachel Sharp and Tony Green (1975) studied Mapledene, a 'child-centred' primary school where children were allowed to choose activities for themselves and develop at their own pace. The teachers felt that when a child was ready to learn they would seek help, for example with reading.

▲ Do teachers label some children as 'ready to learn' and give them more attention?

On the other hand, the teachers believed that children who were not yet ready to learn should be allowed to engage in 'compensatory play' in the Wendy House until they too were ready. In practice, however, this meant that middle-class children, who started reading earlier, gained the help they needed, while working-class children were ignored.

Sharp and Green's findings support the interactionist view that children of different class backgrounds are labelled differently. However, their explanation goes beyond the level of small-scale, face-to-face interactions. They argue that the negative labelling of working-class children is also the result of inequalities between the social classes in wider society, not just classroom interactions.

High and low status knowledge

These studies show how the labelling of working-class pupils puts them at a disadvantage. Other studies show that labelling can be applied not just to pupils, but also to the knowledge they are taught. As Nell Keddie (1971) found, both pupils and knowledge can be labelled as high or low status.

The comprehensive school classes she observed were streamed by ability, but all streams followed the same humanities course and covered the same course content. However, Keddie found that although teachers believed they were teaching all pupils in the same way, in practice when they taught the A stream, they gave them abstract, theoretical, high status knowledge.

The 'less able' C stream pupils, on the other hand, were given descriptive, commonsense, low status knowledge, related more to everyday experience. As lower streams generally contain more working-class pupils, this withholding of high status knowledge from the C stream is likely to increase class differences in achievement.

A more recent study by David Gillborn and Deborah Youdell (2001) shows how schools use teachers' notions of 'ability' to decide which pupils have the potential to achieve five A*-C grade GCSEs. They found that working-class and black pupils are less likely to be perceived as having ability, and more likely to be placed in lower sets and entered for lower-tier GCSEs. This denies them the knowledge and opportunity needed to gain good grades and so widens the class gap in achievement.

The self-fulfilling prophecy

A self-fulfilling prophecy is a prediction that comes true simply by virtue of it having been made. Interactionists argue that labelling can affect pupils' achievement by creating a self-fulfilling prophecy, as the following example illustrates:

Step 1: The teacher labels a pupil (e.g. as being very intelligent) and on the basis of this label, makes predictions about him (e.g. he will make outstanding academic progress).

Step 2: The teacher treats the pupil accordingly, acting as if the prediction is already true (e.g. by giving him more attention and expecting a higher standard of work from him).

Step 3: The pupil internalises the teacher's expectation, which becomes part of his self-concept or self-image, so that he now actually becomes the kind of pupil the teacher believed him to be in the first place. He gains confidence, tries harder and is successful. The prediction is fulfilled.

Teachers' expectations

In their study of Oak community school, a California primary school, Robert Rosenthal and Leonora Jacobson (1968) show the self-fulfilling prophecy at work. They told the school that they had a new test specially designed to identify those pupils who would 'spurt' ahead. This was untrue, because the test was in fact simply a standard IQ test. Importantly, however, the teachers believed what they had been told.

The researchers tested all the pupils, but then picked 20% of them purely at random and told the school, again falsely, that the test had identified these children as 'spurters'. On returning to the school a year later, they found that almost half (47%) of those identified as spurters had indeed made significant progress. The effect was greater on younger children.

Why do you think the effect was greater on younger children?

Rosenthal and Jacobson suggest that the teachers' beliefs about the pupils had been influenced by the supposed test results. The teachers had then conveyed these beliefs to the pupils through the way they interacted with them – for example, through their body language and the amount of attention and encouragement they gave them.

This demonstrates the self-fulfilling prophecy: simply by accepting the prediction that some children would spurt ahead, the teachers brought it about. The fact that the children were selected at random strongly suggests that if teachers believe a pupil to be of a certain type, they can actually make him or her into that type. The study's findings illustrate an important interactionist principle: that what people believe to be true will have real effects – even if the belief was not true originally.

The self-fulfilling prophecy can also produce under-achievement. If teachers have low expectations of certain children and communicate these expectations in their interaction, these children may develop a negative self-concept. They may come to see themselves as failures and give up trying, thereby fulfilling the original prophecy.

Activity

Rosenthal and Jacobson's study is entitled *Pygmalion in the Classroom* – from George Bernard Shaw's play *Pygmalion* (later made into the film *My Fair Lady*). Find out the plot of the play or film and see why Rosenthal and Jacobson borrowed from it.

Methods link: using experiments

Rosenthal and Jacobson used a method known as the field experiment. Sociologists occasionally use field experiments because they allow the researchers to manipulate a real, naturally occurring social situation to discover cause-and-effect relationships. Rosenthal and Jacobson were able to manipulate classroom interaction by labelling some pupils as 'spurters' to see whether this would cause a self-fulfilling prophecy.

However, the researchers cannot control all the possible factors that might have led to the pupils 'spurting', so they cannot be certain that they have in fact discovered the real cause of their improved performance.

Read more about experiments and researching education in **Methods in Context** on pages 177-9.

Streaming and the self-fulfilling prophecy

Streaming involves separating children into different ability groups or classes called 'streams'. Each ability group is then taught separately from the others for all subjects. Studies show that the self-fulfilling prophecy is particularly likely to occur when children are streamed.

As Becker shows, teachers do not usually see working-class children as ideal pupils. They tend to see them as lacking ability and have low expectations of them. As a result, working-class children are more likely to find themselves put in a lower stream.

Once streamed, it is usually difficult to move up to a higher stream; children are more or less locked into their teachers' low expectations of them. Children in the lower streams 'get the message' that their teachers have written them off as no-hopers.

This creates a self-fulfilling prophecy in which the pupils live up to their teachers' low expectations by under-achieving. For example, Douglas found that children placed in a lower stream at age 8 had suffered a decline in their IQ score by age 11.

By contrast, middle-class pupils tend to benefit from streaming. They are likely to be placed in higher streams, reflecting teachers' view of them as ideal pupils. As a result, they develop a more positive self-concept, gain confidence, work harder and improve their grades. For example, Douglas found that children placed in a higher stream at age 8 had improved their IQ score by age 11.

Pupil subcultures

A pupil subculture is a group of pupils who share similar values and behaviour patterns. Pupil subcultures often emerge as a response to the way pupils have been labelled, and in particular as a reaction to streaming.

A number of studies have shown how pupil subcultures may play a part in creating class differences in achievement. We can use Colin Lacey's (1970) concepts of differentiation and polarisation to explain how pupil subcultures develop:

- **Differentiation** is the process of teachers categorising pupils according to how they perceive their ability, attitude and/or behaviour. Streaming is a form of differentiation, since it categorises pupils into separate classes. Those that the school deems 'more able' are given high status by being placed in a high stream, whereas those deemed 'less able' and placed in low streams are given an inferior status.

- **Polarisation**, on the other hand, is the process in which pupils respond to streaming by moving towards one of two opposite 'poles' or extremes.

In his study of Hightown boys' grammar school, Lacey found that streaming polarised boys into a pro-school and an anti-school subculture.

the pro-school subculture

Pupils placed in high streams (who are largely middle-class) tend to remain committed to the values of the school. They gain their status in the approved manner, through academic success. Their values are those of the school: they tend to form a pro-school subculture.

the anti-school subculture

Lacey found that those placed in low streams (who tend to be working-class) suffer a loss of self-esteem: the school has undermined their self-worth by placing them in a position of inferior status.

This label of failure pushes them to search for alternative ways of gaining status. Usually this involves inverting (turning upside down) the school's values of hard work, obedience and punctuality As Lacey says, 'a boy who does badly academically is predisposed to criticise, reject or even sabotage the system where he can, since it places him in an inferior position'.

Such pupils form an anti-school subculture as a means of gaining status among their peers, for example by cheeking a teacher, truanting, not doing homework, smoking, drinking or stealing.

Unfortunately, however, although joining an anti-school subculture may solve the problem of lack of status, it creates further problems for the pupils who become involved in it. As Lacey says,

'the boy who takes refuge in such a group because his work is poor finds that the group commits him to a behaviour pattern which means that his work will stay poor — and in fact often gets progressively worse'.

In other words, joining an anti-school subculture is likely to become a self-fulfilling prophecy of educational failure.

Lacey's study is a striking example of the power of labelling and streaming to actually create failure. The boys had all been successful at primary school and were among an elite of about 15% of the town's pupils who had passed the eleven plus (11+) exam to get into grammar school.

Once there, however, the competitive atmosphere and streaming meant that many boys were soon labelled as failures, and many showed extreme physical reactions such as bed-wetting and insomnia. By their second year, many boys had become distinctly anti-school as they adjusted to their status as failures.

David Hargreaves (1967) found a similar response to labelling and streaming in a secondary modern school. From the point of view of the education system, boys in the lower streams were triple failures: they had failed their 11+ exam; they had been placed in low streams; and they had been labelled as 'worthless louts'.

One solution to this status problem was for pupils to seek each other out and form a group within which high status went to those who flouted the school's rules. In this way, they formed a delinquent subculture that helped to guarantee their educational failure.

Activity

Working alone or in pairs, use the concepts of labelling, the self-fulfilling prophecy and pupil subcultures to write an explanation of as many of the differences between the two bands as you can.

Box 11	Banding and polarisation

Comparison of top band and middle band year 8 pupils at Beachside Comprehensive

	Top band	Middle band
Teachers' stereotypes of each band	Academic potential	Not up to much
	Neat workers	Rowdy and lazy
	Bright, alert and enthusiastic	Cannot take part in discussions
	Wanting to get on	Not interested
	Rewarding	Unrewarding
Percentage of pupils from working-class homes	36	78
Percentage of teachers' time in class devoted to maintaining order	1.5	12.5
Average number of detentions, per pupil per year	0.4	3.8
Average number of absences per pupil in term 1	8.1	12.6
Average number of minutes spent on homework per pupil	47	16
Percentage of end-of-year subject tests graded at 50% or higher	58	11
Number of extra-curricular activities or club memberships, per class	43	10
Percentage of pupils who dislike school	13	48
Views held about each band by pupils in the other band	Brainy	Thick
	Unfriendly	Rough
	Stuck-up	Boring
	Arrogant	Simple

Source: adapted from Bilton et al (1987), compiled from Ball (1981), *Beachside Comprehensive*

abolishing streaming

Stephen Ball (1981) takes the analysis a step further in his study of Beachside, a comprehensive that was in the process of abolishing banding (a type of streaming) in favour of teaching mixed-ability groups. As Box 11 shows, banding had produced the kind of polarisation described by Lacey.

Ball found that when the school abolished banding, the basis for pupils to polarise into subcultures was largely removed and the influence of the anti-school subculture declined.

Nevertheless, although pupil polarisation all but disappeared, differentiation continued. Teachers continued to categorise pupils differently and were more likely to label middle-class pupils as cooperative and able.

This positive labelling was reflected in their better exam results, suggesting that a self-fulfilling prophecy had occurred. Ball's study shows that class inequalities can continue as a result of teachers' labelling, even without the effect of subcultures or streaming.

Since Ball's study, and especially since the Education Reform Act (1988), there has been a trend towards more streaming and towards a variety of types of school, some of which have a more academic curriculum than others.

This has created new opportunities for schools and teachers to differentiate between pupils on the basis of their class, ethnicity or gender and treat them unequally, as studies such as Gillborn and Youdell (2001) show. (See pages 104 and 108).

the variety of pupil responses

Pro- and anti-school subcultures are two possible responses to labelling and streaming. However, as Peter Woods (1979) argues, other responses are also possible. These include:

- **ingratiation:** being the 'teacher's pet'
- **ritualism:** going through the motions and staying out of trouble
- **retreatism:** daydreaming and mucking about
- **rebellion:** outright rejection of everything the school stands for.

Moreover, as John Furlong (1984) observes, pupils are not committed permanently to any one response, but may move between different types of response, acting differently in lessons with different teachers.

The theme of pupil subcultures is an important one in several areas of education, and elsewhere in this chapter there are further examples in relation to ethnicity and gender as well as class, including studies by Fuller, Sewell, Mac an Ghaill and Willis (see pages 118, 119-20 and 146-7).

The limitations of labelling theory

The approaches we have examined start from the idea that under-achievement is the result of pupils being negatively labelled. This results in a self-fulfilling prophecy, with pupils often joining anti-school subcultures that help to guarantee their failure.

These studies are useful in showing how the interactions within schools actively create class inequalities. Schools are not neutral institutions, as cultural deprivation theorists assume.

Nevertheless, labelling theory has been accused of determinism. That is, it assumes that pupils who are labelled have no choice but to fulfil the prophecy and will inevitably fail. However, studies such as Mary Fuller's (1984) show that this is not always true. (See page 118.)

Marxists also criticise labelling theory for ignoring the wider structures of power within which labelling takes place. Labelling theory tends to blame teachers for labelling pupils, but fails to explain why they do so.

Marxists argue that labels are not merely the result of teachers' individual prejudices, but stem from the fact that teachers work in a system that reproduces class divisions. (See Topic 6 for a discussion of Marxist views of education.)

Marketisation and selection policies

So far, we have focused on small scale, 'micro' level processes within classrooms and schools, such as labelling, the self-fulfilling prophecy and streaming. However, schools operate within a wider education system, whose policies directly affect these micro level processes to produce class differences in achievement. Such policies include marketisation and selection. Marketisation brought in:

- **A funding formula** that gives a school the same amount of funds for each pupil.
- **Exam league tables** that rank each school according to its exam performance and make no allowance for the level of ability of its pupils. For example, secondary schools are ranked in terms of what percentage of their pupils succeed in gaining five or more GCSE grades A*-C.
- **Competition** among schools to attract pupils.

The A-to-C economy and educational triage

These changes explain why schools are under pressure to stream and select pupils. For example, schools need to achieve a good league table position if they are to attract pupils and funding. However, this can widen the class gap in achievement within a school, as Gillborn and Youdell's study of two London secondary schools shows (see also page 104).

The policy of publishing league tables creates what Gillborn and Youdell call the 'A-to-C economy'. This is a system in which schools ration their time, effort and resources, concentrating them on those pupils they perceive as having the potential to get five grade Cs at GCSE and so boost the school's league table position.

Gillborn and Youdell call this process 'educational triage'. Triage literally means 'sorting'. The term is normally used to describe the process on battlefields or in major disasters whereby medical staff decide who is to be given scarce medical resources. Medics have to sort casualties into three categories: (1) the 'walking wounded', who can be ignored because they will survive; (2) those who will die anyway, who will also be ignored, and (3) those with a chance of survival, who are given treatment in the hope of saving them.

The authors argue that the A-to-C economy produces educational triage. Schools categorise pupils into 'those who will pass anyway', 'those with potential' and 'hopeless cases'. Teachers do this using notions of 'ability' in which working-class and black pupils are labelled as lacking ability. As a result, they are likely to be classified as 'hopeless cases' and ignored. This produces a self-fulfilling prophecy and failure.

Gillborn and Youdell's notion of 'triage' or sorting is very similar to Lacey's idea of differentiation (see page 105), since both involve labelling and treating pupils differently. Both ideas are closely linked to the process of streaming, where teachers' beliefs about pupils' ability are used to segregate them into different classes, offer them different curricula and exams, and thus produce different levels of achievement.

However, Gillborn and Youdell put the labelling and streaming process into a wider context than simply individual teachers or schools. Instead, they link triage to marketisation policies within the education system as a whole (such as league tables) and show how these, when combined with teachers' stereotypical ideas about pupils' ability, lead to differences in achievement.

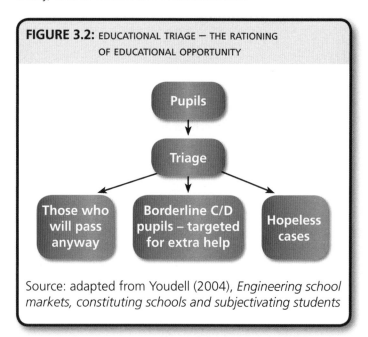

FIGURE 3.2: EDUCATIONAL TRIAGE – THE RATIONING OF EDUCATIONAL OPPORTUNITY

Source: adapted from Youdell (2004), *Engineering school markets, constituting schools and subjectivating students*

Competition and selection

Marketisation also explains why schools are under pressure to select more able, largely middle-class pupils who will gain the school a higher ranking in the league tables. Those schools with a good league table position will then be better placed to attract other able/middle-class pupils. This will further improve the school's results and make it more popular still, thus increasing its funding. Increased popularity will enable it to select from a larger number of applicants and recruit the most able, thereby improving its results once again, and so on.

However, while popular schools can afford to screen out less able or more 'difficult' pupils from disadvantaged backgrounds, unpopular schools are obliged to take them, get worse results, become less popular still and see their funding further reduced.

These pressures have resulted in increased social class segregation between schools. Will Bartlett (1993) argues that marketisation leads to popular schools:

- **cream-skimming**: selecting higher ability pupils, who gain the best results and cost less to teach
- **silt-shifting**: off-loading pupils with learning difficulties, who are expensive to teach and get poor results.

One example of how this can disadvantage working-class children is through the use of home/school contracts. Selective schools often require parents to sign demanding home/school contracts before being offered a place. Gewirtz describes one school where the contract required parents to:

'ensure attendance and punctuality, encourage and support their daughter with her work, supervise her homework, attend parents' evenings and school functions in which their daughter is involved, keep her in the correct uniform, provide her with a well-stocked pencil-case, a calculator, dictionary and recorder, pay for the replacement of damaged or lost books, and support the policies of the school.'

She quotes a school governor as saying that having the contracts 'will really be influential in bringing the right sort of parents into this school'.

An image to attract middle-class parents

Some schools have responded to marketisation by creating a 'traditional' image to attract middle-class parents and this too has reinforced class divisions. Studies of grant maintained (GM) schools (now known as foundation schools) and city technology colleges (CTCs) show how this has occurred.

Geoffrey Walford's (1991) research on CTCs found that although they were intended to provide vocational education in partnership with employers and to recruit pupils from all social backgrounds, in practice they have come to be just another route to elite education. They became attractive to middle-class parents not because of a hi-tech image,

▲ *Why might marketisation discourage schools from taking pupils with special educational needs?*

1 In what ways might working-class parents find it more difficult to meet the requirements of such a contract?

2 Explain in your own words what advantages attracting 'the right sort of parents' might have for a school.

FIGURE 3.3: MARKETISATION – HOW SUCCESS BREEDS SUCCESS

School gets better results

Can 'cream skim' more able pupils

Increased funding and more facilities

School becomes more popular

Can 'silt-shift' less able pupils to less successful schools but because they were seen as the next best thing to a traditional grammar school.

Similarly, John Fitz's (1997) study of GM schools, which were allowed to opt out of local education authority control, found them 're-inventing tradition'. One school had spent £10,000 on a new pipe organ for assemblies and had re-named its canteen the 'dining hall'. The organ was in fact newer than the school's computer suite. Fitz concludes that the reason most schools adopt a traditional image is to attract middle-class parents. According to Stephen Ball et al (1994), schools have had to spend more on marketing themselves to parents, often at the expense of spending on special needs or other areas.

Activity

Use websites and your local press to find examples of the ways in which local schools or colleges market themselves. For example, what sorts of things do their adverts for open evenings tell you? What kinds of photographs do they use? Do different schools use different 'selling points'? If so, why?

▲ Exam success means a school is likely to get plenty of high-ability applicants – and further success in the future.

There is evidence, then, that marketisation and selection processes have created a polarised education system: popular, successful, well-resourced schools with a more able, largely middle-class intake at one extreme and unpopular, 'failing', under-resourced schools with mainly low-achieving working-class pupils at the other. Gewirtz describes this as a 'blurred hierarchy' of schools.

Sheila Macrae (1997) sees a similar pattern in post-16 education. At the top are highly selective sixth form colleges attracting middle-class students and providing academic courses leading to university and professional careers. Then come general further education colleges catering for mainly working-class students and providing largely vocational courses. At the bottom are government-funded training organisations providing low-level courses leading to low-paid jobs.

For more activities on Class differences in achievement (2) internal factors...

 Go to www.sociology.uk.net

Summary

Some explanations of class differences in achievement focus on internal factors within school and the education system. **Interactionists** argue that schools actively create inequality through **labelling** and the **self-fulfilling prophecy**, **streaming** and polarisation into pro- and **anti-school subcultures**.

Marketisation and selection policies increase streaming within schools and inequalities between schools, through processes such as **educational triage** and cream skimming, and this disadvantages working-class pupils.

QuickCheck Questions

1 Explain the difference between labelling and the self-fulfilling prophecy.

2 State two criticisms of labelling theory.

3 Identify two characteristics of a pro-school subculture.

4 Suggest one reason why anti-school subcultures develop.

5 Explain what is meant by 'marketisation'.

6 Name one policy that has helped to create an education market.

7 Which pupils are likely to benefit most from educational triage? Give reasons for your answer.

Check your answers at www.sociology.uk.net

Examining class differences in achievement (2) internal factors

Item A   Some sociologists explain social class differences in achievement in terms of school processes such as labelling. Interactionists such as Becker have found that teachers judged pupils according to how well they fitted an image of the 'ideal pupil'. As middle-class pupils were more likely to fit this image, teachers treated them more favourably. By contrast, working-class pupils were negatively labelled as non-academic and often as 'difficult'.

Other sociologists have taken this approach further. They have examined the way in which labelling is linked to other processes within schools that result in class differences in achievement. These processes include the self-fulfilling prophecy, streaming and the formation of pupil subcultures.   5

More recently, Gillborn and Youdell (2001) have examined the role of educational policies in creating the context for such school processes to take place.

(a) Explain what is meant by 'educational triage'. (2 marks)

(b) Suggest **three** types of pupil subcultures that might be found in schools. (6 marks)

(c) Outline some of the ways in which marketisation and selection policies may produce social class differences in educational achievement. (12 marks)

(d) Using material from **Item A** and elsewhere, assess the view that social class differences in educational achievement are the result of school processes such as labelling. (20 marks)

The examiner's advice

Part (c) carries 8 AO1 marks (knowledge and understanding) and 4 AO2 marks (interpretation, application, analysis and evaluation). You should explain what is meant by marketisation, e.g. funding formula, league tables and competition between schools. Explain how this leads to schools being selective in the pupils they take (e.g. cream-skimming; strategies for attracting middle-class parents) and treating them differently once they are in school (e.g. the A-to-C economy; educational triage). Explain how each of these may produce class differences in achievement.

Part (d) carries 8 AO1 marks and 12 AO2 marks. Explain what is meant by labelling and other school processes, e.g. the self-fulfilling prophecy, streaming and pupil subcultures. Explain how these may create class differences in achievement. Use evidence from Item A and studies (e.g. Becker, Rist, Sharp and Green, Gillborn and Youdell, Lacey, Hargreaves, Ball) to do so.

You need to evaluate the view in the question – e.g. by considering the relative importance of external factors such as cultural and material deprivation and cultural capital, or by criticising labelling theory (e.g. for its determinism, or for not explaining why only certain groups get negatively labelled). Write a separate conclusion.

Topic 3 Ethnic differences in achievement

In Topics 1 and 2, we saw that social class plays an important part in educational achievement. Just as we can think of everyone as 'belonging to' a class, so too we can see individuals as being part of an ethnic group – whether a minority or a majority group.

Tony Lawson and Joan Garrod (2000) define ethnic groups as 'people who share common history, customs and identity, as well as, in most cases, language and religion, and who see themselves as a distinct unit'. When we use terms such as customs, language and religion, we are talking about culture – that is, about all those things that are learned, shared and valued by a social group.

One difficulty in studying ethnicity and education is the problem of deciding who to include in an ethnic group. For example, should all 'Asians' be classified together – when this would include people of many different nationalities, religions and languages?

It is a mistake to think of ethnic groups as always being defined by physical features such as skin colour. Although many ethnic minority groups in Britain are non-white, this is not true of all groups. However, it happens that the largest minority groups in Britain are non-white: mainly of African, Caribbean or South Asian origin. There are, however, many other minority groups. According to David Crystal (2003), well over 100 languages are in routine use in the UK. Today, children from minority ethnic backgrounds make up about 21% of the pupils in English schools.

Learning objectives

After studying this Topic, you should:

- Be able to describe the patterns of ethnic differences in educational achievement.

- Understand and be able to evaluate the role of different external factors, including cultural deprivation, material deprivation and racism in wider society.

- Understand and be able to evaluate the role of different internal factors, including labelling, pupil subcultures, the curriculum, institutional racism, and selection and segregation.

Evidence of ethnic differences in achievement

We can see from Figure 3.4 that there are inequalities in the educational achievements of different ethnic groups. For example, whites and Asians on average do better than blacks. However, as Figure 3.4 also shows, there are significant variations among Asians. For example, Indians do better than Pakistanis and Bangladeshis.

There are also important gender and class differences within and between ethnic groups. Among all groups other than Gypsy/Roma and Traveller children, girls do better than boys. Similarly, within each ethnic group, middle-class children do better than working-class children.

White pupils' achievements are very close to the national average – not surprisingly, since whites are by far the largest group, accounting for about four fifths of all pupils. However, when we look more closely, we find major class differences in their performance, with many working-class white pupils performing at a lower level than that of other ethnic groups.

For example, according to a DfES (2007) study, in 2006 only 24% of white boys on free school meals – a common measure of low income – gained five A*-C grades at GCSE. According to Steven Hastings (2006), white pupils make less progress between 11 and 16 than black or Asian pupils, and it is possible that whites may soon become the worst performing ethnic group in the country, because minority groups are improving more rapidly.

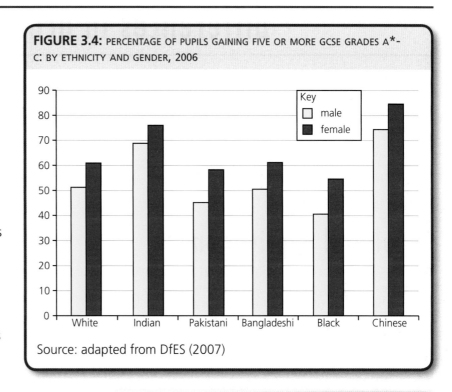

FIGURE 3.4: PERCENTAGE OF PUPILS GAINING FIVE OR MORE GCSE GRADES A*-C: BY ETHNICITY AND GENDER, 2006

Key: male / female

Source: adapted from DfES (2007)

> What relationships between ethnicity, gender and achievement can you identify from this chart? Note the differences both within and between groups.

Methods Link: using official statistics

Governments collect a vast amount of statistical data on the educational achievements of different ethnic groups. Given that there are millions of pupils in schools, sociologists would not be able to collect all this data themselves, so official statistics save them time and money. This data allows sociologists to identify the patterns of differences in achievement between ethnic groups.

However, simply knowing the patterns of ethnic differences in achievement does not in itself explain them. A further problem is that the government's definition of ethnicity may be different from that of the sociologist and so the way that official data is categorised may not be useful to the researcher.

Read more about official statistics and researching education in **Methods in Context** on pages 226-7.

Sociologists are interested in the reasons for these differences in achievement and have put forward a number of explanations. Some of these are similar to the explanations of social class differences in achievement we examined in Topics 1 and 2.

As with class differences, we can separate them into internal and external factors, though in reality, these two factors are very often linked.

- **Internal factors** – factors within schools and the education system, such as interactions between pupils and teachers, and inequalities between schools.
- **External factors** – factors outside the education system, such as the influence of home and family background and wider society.

External factors and ethnic differences in achievement

Many sociologists argue that ethnic differences in achievement can best be explained by looking at factors outside the school – in the home, family and culture of the child and the impact of wider society. The main explanations of this kind are:

1 Cultural deprivation

2 Material deprivation and class

3 Racism in wider society

1 Cultural deprivation

As with explanations of class differences in achievement (see pages 93-6), cultural deprivation theory sees the under-achievement of some ethnic groups as the result of inadequate socialisation in the home. The explanation has three main aspects:

■ intellectual and linguistic skills

■ attitudes and values

■ family structure.

Intellectual and linguistic skills

Cultural deprivation theorists see the lack of intellectual and linguistic skills as a major cause of under-achievement for many minority children. They argue that many children from low-income black families lack intellectual stimulation and enriching experiences. This leaves them poorly equipped for school because they have not been able to develop reasoning and problem-solving skills.

Similarly, Bereiter and Engelmann (see page 94) consider the language spoken by low-income black American families as inadequate for educational success. They see it as ungrammatical, disjointed and incapable of expressing abstract ideas. Likewise, Gordon Bowker (1968) identifies their lack of Standard English as a major barrier to progress in education and integration into wider society.

There has also been concern that children who do not speak English at home may be held back educationally. However, the Swann Report (1985) found that language was not a major factor in under-achievement, while David Gillborn and Heidi Safia Mirza (2000) note that Indian pupils do very well despite often not having English as their home language.

Attitudes and values

Cultural deprivation theorists see lack of motivation as a major cause of the failure of many black children. Most

> What term might sociologists use to describe a 'live for today' attitude?

other children are socialised into the mainstream culture, which instils ambition, competitiveness and willingness to make the sacrifices necessary to achieve long-term goals. This equips them for success in education. By contrast, cultural deprivation theorists argue, some black children are socialised into a subculture that instils a fatalistic, 'live for today' attitude that does not value education and leaves them unequipped for success.

Family structure and parental support

Cultural deprivation theorists argue that this failure to socialise children adequately is the result of a dysfunctional family structure. For example, Daniel Moynihan (1965) argues that because many black families are headed by a lone mother, their children are deprived of adequate care because she has to struggle financially in the absence of a male breadwinner. The father's absence also means that boys lack an adequate role model of male achievement. Moynihan sees cultural deprivation as a cycle where inadequately socialised children from unstable families go on to fail at school and become inadequate parents themselves.

The New Right put forward similar explanations. For example, Charles Murray (1984) argues that a high rate of lone parenthood and a lack of positive male role models lead to the under-achievement of some minorities. Similarly, Anthony Flew (1984) believes that ethnic differences in achievement stem from cultural differences outside the education system, not discrimination within it. Roger Scruton (1986) sees the low achievement levels of some ethnic minorities as resulting from a failure to embrace mainstream British culture.

Ken Pryce (1979) also sees family structure as contributing to the under-achievement of black Caribbean pupils in Britain. From a comparison of black and Asian pupils, he claims that Asians are higher achievers because their culture is more resistant to racism and gives them a greater sense of self-worth. By contrast, he argues, black Caribbean culture is less cohesive and less resistant to racism. As a result, many black pupils have low self-esteem and under-achieve.

Pryce argues that the difference is the result of the differing impact of colonialism on the two groups. He argues that the experience of slavery was culturally devastating for blacks. Being transported and sold into slavery meant that

▲ *Is motivation the key to success in school?*

they lost their language, religion and entire family system. By contrast, Asian family structures, languages and religions were not destroyed by colonial rule.

Asian families

Driver and Ballard (1981) also argue that Asian family structures bring educational benefits. Asian parents have more positive attitudes towards education, and higher aspirations for their children's future, and as a result are more supportive.

In a more recent study, Ruth Lupton (2004) argues that adult authority in Asian families is similar to the model that operates in schools. She found that respectful behaviour towards adults was expected from children. This had a knock-on effect in school, since parents were more likely to be supportive of school behaviour policies.

However, some sociologists see the Asian family as an obstacle to success, despite the high levels of achievement of some Asian minorities. For example, Verity Khan (1979) describes Asian families as 'stress ridden', bound by tradition and with a controlling attitude towards children, especially girls.

white working-class families

Most research has focused on black and Asian family structures as possible causes of under-achievement. However, as we saw earlier, white working-class pupils under-achieve and have lower aspirations. For example, a survey of state schools for the Sutton Trust (MORI, 2004) found that 80% of 11-16 year old ethnic minority pupils aspired to go to university, as against only 68% of white pupils.

This lower level of aspiration and achievement may be the result of a lack of parental support. For example, Lupton studied four mainly working-class schools – two predominantly white, one serving a largely Pakistani community and the fourth drawing pupils from an ethnically mixed community.

She found that teachers reported poorer levels of behaviour and discipline in the white working-class schools – despite the fact that they had fewer children on free school meals (a common measure of poverty among pupils). Teachers blamed this on lower levels of parental support and the negative attitude that white working-class parents had towards education. By contrast, ethnic minority parents were more likely to see education as "a way up in society".

Similarly, Gillian Evans (2006) argues that street culture in white working-class areas can be brutal and so young people have to learn how to withstand intimidation and intimidate others. In this context, school can become a place where the power games that young people engage in on the street are played out again, bringing disruption and making it hard for pupils to succeed.

compensatory education

The main policy that has been adopted to tackle cultural deprivation is compensatory education. For example, the aim of Operation Head Start (see page 96) was to compensate children for the cultural deficit they are said to suffer because of deprived backgrounds.

Criticisms of cultural deprivation

Geoffrey Driver (1977) criticises cultural deprivation theory for ignoring the positive effects of ethnicity on achievement. He shows that the black Caribbean family, far from being dysfunctional, provides girls with positive role models of strong independent women. Driver argues that this is why black girls tend to be more successful in education than black boys.

Errol Lawrence (1982) challenges Pryce's view that black pupils fail because their culture is weak and they lack self-esteem. He argues that black pupils under-achieve not because of low self-esteem, but because of racism.

Keddie sees cultural deprivation as a victim-blaming explanation (see page 96). She argues that ethnic minority children are culturally different, not culturally deprived. They under-achieve because schools are ethnocentric: biased in favour of white culture and against minorities.

Critics oppose compensatory education because they see it as an attempt to impose the dominant white culture on children who already have a coherent culture of their own.

They propose two main alternatives:

- multicultural education: a policy that recognises and values minority cultures and includes them in the curriculum
- anti-racist education: a policy that challenges the prejudice and discrimination that exists in schools and wider society.

Some sociologists argue that material deprivation rather than cultural deprivation is the main cause of under-achievement. We examine their view next.

2 Material deprivation and class

Material deprivation means a lack of those physical necessities that are seen as essential or normal for life in today's society. In general, working-class people are more likely to face poverty and material deprivation.

Material deprivation explanations see educational failure as resulting from factors such as substandard housing and low income. Ethnic minorities are more likely to face these problems. For example, according to Flaherty (2004):

- Pakistanis and Bangladeshis are over three times more likely than whites to be in the poorest fifth of the population.
- Unemployment is three times higher for African and Bangladeshi/Pakistani people than for whites.
- 15% of ethnic minority households live in overcrowded conditions, compared with only 2% of white households.
- Pakistanis are nearly twice as likely to be in unskilled or semi-skilled jobs compared to whites. Ethnic minority workers are more likely to be engaged in shift work.
- Bangladeshi and Pakistani women are more likely to be engaged in low-paid homeworking, sometimes for as little as £1.50 per hour.

How might having (a) parents working shifts and (b) parents engaged in low-paid homeworking affect their children's education?

Such inequalities reflect differences in the proportion of children from different ethnic groups who are eligible for free school meals, as Figure 3.5 shows.

These inequalities parallel those seen in educational achievement. For example, Indians and whites generally have a higher social class position than Bangladeshis and Pakistanis, who often face high levels of poverty. The material deprivation explanation argues that such class differences explain why Bangladeshi and Pakistani pupils tend to do worse than Indian and white pupils.

Evidence for this view comes from the Swann Report (1985), which estimated that social class accounts for at least 50% of the difference in achievement between ethnic groups. If we fail to take the different class positions of ethnic groups into account when we compare their educational achievements, there is a danger that we may over-estimate the effect of cultural deprivation and under-estimate the effect of poverty and material deprivation.

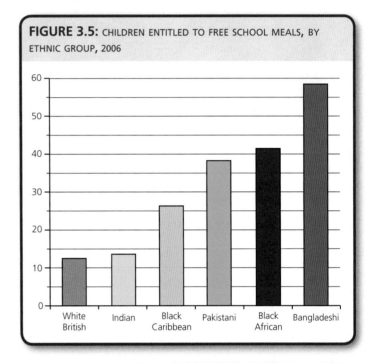

FIGURE 3.5: CHILDREN ENTITLED TO FREE SCHOOL MEALS, BY ETHNIC GROUP, 2006

▲ *Hindu temple, Reading: does learning about minority cultures promote equal opportunity?*

However, Gillborn and Mirza argue that social class factors do not override the influence of ethnicity. When we compare pupils of the same social class but different ethnic origins, we still find differences in achievement. This is particularly the case for black children, since even middle-class black pupils do comparatively poorly at GCSE.

3 Racism in wider society

While material deprivation and poverty has an impact on the educational achievement of some ethnic minority children, some sociologists argue that poverty is itself the product of another factor – namely, racism. As David Mason (1995) puts it, 'discrimination is a continuing and persistent feature of the experience of Britain's citizens of minority ethnic origin'.

John Rex (1986) shows how racial discrimination leads to social exclusion and how this worsens the poverty faced by ethnic minorities. In housing, for instance, discrimination means that minorities are more likely to be forced into substandard accommodation than white people of the same class.

In employment, too, there is evidence of direct and deliberate discrimination. For example, Mike Noon (1993) sent identical pairs of letters of enquiry about future employment opportunities to the top 100 UK companies, signed by fictitious applicants called 'Evans' and 'Patel' with the same qualifications and experience. In terms of both the number and the helpfulness of replies, the companies were more encouraging to the 'white' candidate.

This helps to explain why members of ethnic minorities are more likely to face unemployment and low pay, and this in turn has a negative effect on their children's educational prospects.

Internal factors and ethnic differences in achievement

According to Gillborn and Youdell (2000), in one local education authority African Caribbean children were the highest achievers on entry to primary school, yet by the time it came to GCSE, they had the worst results of any ethnic group.

If a group can begin their compulsory schooling as the highest achievers and yet finish it as the lowest achievers, this suggests that factors internal to the education system itself may be playing a major part in producing ethnic differences in achievement. These internal factors include:

1 Labelling and teacher racism

2 Pupil responses and subcultures

3 The ethnocentric curriculum

4 Institutional racism

5 Selection and segregation.

1 Labelling and teacher racism

To label someone is to attach a meaning or definition to them. For example, teachers may label a pupil as a troublemaker or cooperative, bright or stupid. Interactionist sociologists study the face-to-face interactions in which such labelling occurs.

When looking at ethnic differences in achievement, interactionists focus on the different labels teachers give to children from different ethnic backgrounds. Their studies show that teachers often see black and Asian pupils as being far from the 'ideal pupil' (see page 103). For example, black pupils are often seen as disruptive and Asians as passive. Negative labels may lead teachers to treat ethnic minority pupils differently. This disadvantages them and may result in their failure.

Black pupils

A good illustration of the impact of labelling on black pupils comes from studies by Gillborn (1990) and Gillborn and Youdell (2000). Gillborn found that teachers were quicker to discipline black pupils than others for the same behaviour.

Gillborn and Youdell argue that this is the result of teachers' 'racialised expectations'. They found that teachers expected black pupils to present more discipline problems and misinterpreted their behaviour as threatening or as a challenge to authority. When teachers acted on this misperception, the pupils responded negatively and further conflict resulted. In turn, black pupils felt teachers underestimated their ability and picked on them. Gillborn and Youdell conclude that much of the conflict between white teachers and black pupils stems from the racial stereotypes teachers hold, rather than the pupils' actual behaviour.

This may explain the higher level of exclusions from school of black boys (see Figure 3.6). As Jenny Bourne (1994) found, schools tend to see black boys as a threat and to label them negatively, leading eventually to exclusion.

Similarly, Peter Foster (1990) found that teachers' stereotypes of black pupils as badly behaved could result in them being placed in lower sets than other pupils of similar ability. Both exclusions and allocation to lower sets are likely to lead to lower levels of achievement.

Asian pupils

Cecile Wright's (1992) study of a multi-ethnic primary school shows that Asian pupils can also be the victims of teachers' labelling. She found that despite the school's apparent commitment to equal opportunities, teachers held ethnocentric views: that is, they took for granted that British culture and Standard English were superior.

This affected how they related to Asian pupils. For example, teachers assumed they would have a poor grasp of English and left them out of class discussions or used simplistic, childish language when speaking to them.

Asian pupils also felt isolated when teachers expressed disapproval of their customs or mispronounced their names. In general, teachers saw them not as a threat (unlike black pupils), but as a problem they could ignore. The effect was that Asian pupils, especially the girls, were marginalised – pushed to the edges and prevented from participating fully.

Methods Link: using observation

Wright observed the classroom interactions of over 1,000 pupils and teachers. This enabled her to see how teachers actually behaved towards their pupils – rather than how they *claimed* they behaved. As a result, she witnessed how teachers sometimes labelled Asian pupils negatively.

However, with this method, the researcher cannot hide their presence in the classroom and this may change the teacher's behaviour. If so, then Wright would not see their 'real' behaviour, thereby reducing the validity of the results.

Read more about observation and researching education in **Methods in Context** on pages 214-7

1 What is meant by 'stereotyping'?

2 What stereotypes do you think teachers hold of pupils of different ethnic backgrounds? How far does this affect the way pupils are streamed?

2 Pupil responses and subcultures

As we have seen, there is evidence of teacher racism and negative labelling. However, research shows that pupils can respond to this in a variety of ways. For example, they may respond by becoming disruptive or withdrawn. Alternatively, pupils may refuse to accept the label and even decide to prove it wrong by working extra hard. Negative labels do not automatically turn into self-fulfilling prophecies.

Fuller and Mac an Ghaill: rejecting negative labels

A good example of pupils responding by rejecting negative labels is Mary Fuller's (1984) study of a group of black girls in year 11 of a London comprehensive school. The girls were untypical because they were high achievers in a school where most black girls were placed in low streams.

Fuller describes how, instead of accepting negative stereotypes of themselves, the girls channelled their anger about being labelled into the pursuit of educational success. However, unlike other successful pupils, they did not seek the approval of teachers, many of whom they regarded as racist. Nor did they limit their choice of friends to other academic achievers. Instead, they were friends with other black girls from lower streams.

Also unlike other successful pupils, they conformed only as far as the schoolwork itself was concerned. They worked conscientiously, but gave the appearance of not doing so, and they showed a deliberate lack of concern about school routines. They had a positive attitude to academic success but, rather than seeking the approval of teachers, they preferred to rely on their own efforts and the impartiality of external exams.

Fuller sees the girls' behaviour as a way of dealing with the contradictory demands of succeeding at school while remaining friends with black girls in lower streams and avoiding the ridicule of black boys, many of whom were anti-school. They were able to maintain a positive self-image by relying on their own efforts rather than accepting the teachers' negative stereotype of them.

The study highlights two important points. Firstly, pupils may still succeed even when they refuse to conform. Secondly, negative labelling does not always lead to failure. These girls were able to reject the labels placed on them and they remained determined to succeed. There was no self-fulfilling prophecy.

Mairtin Mac an Ghaill's (1992) study of black and Asian 'A' level students at a sixth form college reached similar conclusions. Students who believed teachers had labelled them negatively did not necessarily accept the label. How they responded depended on factors such as their ethnic group and gender and the nature of their former schools. For example, some girls felt that their experience of having attended an all-girls school gave them a greater academic commitment that helped them to overcome negative labels at college. As with Fuller's study, this research shows that a label does not inevitably produce a self-fulfilling prophecy.

Mirza: failed strategies for avoiding racism

Like Fuller, Heidi Safia Mirza (1992) studied ambitious black girls who faced teacher racism. However, the girls in Mirza's study failed to achieve their ambitions because their coping strategies restricted their opportunities and resulted in under-achievement.

Mirza found that racist teachers discouraged black pupils from being ambitious through the kind of advice they gave them about careers and option choices. For example, teachers discouraged them from aspiring to professional careers.

▲ *A positive attitude to academic success.*

A large majority of teachers in the study held racist attitudes. Mirza identifies three main types of teacher racism:

- **The colour-blind**: teachers who believe all pupils are equal but in practice allow racism to go unchallenged.

- **The liberal chauvinists**: teachers who believe black pupils are culturally deprived and who have low expectations of them.
- **The overt racists**: teachers who believe blacks are inferior and actively discriminate against them.

Much of the girls' time at school was spent trying to avoid the effects of teachers' negative attitudes. The strategies they employed to do this included being selective about which staff to ask for help; getting on with their own work in lessons without taking part and not choosing certain options so as to avoid teachers with racist attitudes.

However, although the girls had high self-esteem, these strategies put them at a disadvantage by restricting their opportunities. Unlike the girls in Fuller's study, their strategies were unsuccessful.

Sewell: the variety of boys' responses

Like Mirza, Tony Sewell (1998) examines the responses and strategies black pupils adopt to cope with racism. In his study of a boys' secondary school, he found that many teachers had a stereotype of 'black machismo', which sees all black boys as rebellious, anti-authority and anti-school. One effect of this stereotyping is that black boys are more likely to be excluded from school.

Using Robert Merton's (1949) classification of conformity and deviance, Sewell identifies four ways in which the boys responded to racist stereotyping.

the rebels

The rebels were the most visible and influential group, but they were only a small minority of black pupils. They were often excluded from school. They rejected both the goals and the rules of the school and expressed their opposition through peer group membership, conforming to the stereotype of the 'black macho lad'. The rebels believed in their own superiority based on the idea that black masculinity equates with sexual experience and virility. They were contemptuous of white boys, who they saw as effeminate, and dismissive of conformist black boys.

the conformists

The conformists were the largest group. These boys were keen to succeed, accepted the school's goals and had friends from different ethnic groups. They were not part of a subculture and were anxious to avoid being stereotyped either by teachers or their peers.

the retreatists

The retreatists were a tiny minority of isolated individuals who were disconnected from both school and black subcultures, and were despised by the rebels.

the innovators

The innovators were the second largest group. Like Fuller's girls, they were pro-education but anti-school. They valued success, but did not seek the approval of teachers and conformed only as far as schoolwork itself was concerned. This distanced them from the conformists and allowed them to maintain credibility with the rebels while remaining positive about academic achievement.

Sewell shows that only a small minority fit the stereotype of the 'black macho lad'. Nevertheless, teachers tend to see them all in this way and this contributes to the under-achievement of many boys, whatever their attitude to school. Furthermore, many of the boys' negative attitudes are themselves a response to this racism.

In addition to teacher stereotyping, however, Sewell recognises that other factors outside school also contribute to the under-achievement of black boys. These include low aspirations and the absence of fathers as role models in some black families. He also blames a media inspired role model of anti-school black masculinity, whose ideal Chris Arnot (2004) describes as 'the ultra-tough ghetto superstar, an image constantly reinforced through rap lyrics and MTV videos'.

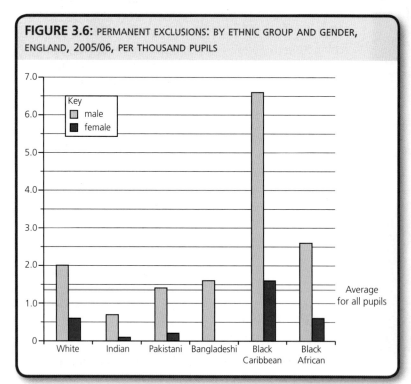

FIGURE 3.6: PERMANENT EXCLUSIONS: BY ETHNIC GROUP AND GENDER, ENGLAND, 2005/06, PER THOUSAND PUPILS

Activity

In pairs, discuss what sort of behaviour and attitudes you would expect to find from pupils responding as: (i) conformists; (ii) retreatists; (iii) innovators; (iv) rebels?

Evaluation of labelling and pupil responses

Rather than blaming the child's home background, as cultural deprivation theory does, labelling theory shows how teachers' stereotypes can be a cause of failure.

However, there is a danger of seeing these as simply the product of individual teachers' prejudices, rather than of racism in wider society. Factors outside the classroom or individual school, such as the influence of role models in the family and media, also play a part, as may government and school educational policies. As we saw in Topic 2, page 108, Gillborn and Youdell argue that the policy of publishing league tables creates an 'A-to-C economy' and leads to large numbers of black and working-class pupils being placed in lower streams or entered for lower-tier exams.

There is also a danger of assuming that once labelled, pupils automatically fall victim to the self-fulfilling prophecy and fail. Nevertheless, as Mirza shows, although pupils may devise strategies to try to avoid teachers' racism, these too can limit their opportunities.

3 The ethnocentric curriculum

The term 'ethnocentric' describes an attitude or policy that gives priority to the culture and viewpoint of one particular ethnic group while disregarding others.

Troyna and Williams (1986) describe the curriculum in British schools as ethnocentric because it gives priority to white culture and the English language. Similarly, Miriam David (1993) describes the National Curriculum as a 'specifically British' curriculum that teaches the culture of the 'host community', while largely ignoring non-European languages, literature and music.

Equally, Stephen Ball (1994) criticises the National Curriculum for ignoring cultural and ethnic diversity and for promoting an attitude of 'little Englandism'. For example, the history curriculum tries to recreate a 'mythical age of empire and past glories', while ignoring the history of black and Asian people.

Bernard Coard (1971; 2005) explains how the ethnocentric curriculum may produce under-achievement. For example, in history the British are presented as bringing civilisation to the 'primitive' peoples they colonised. This image of black people as inferior undermines black children's self-esteem and leads to their failure.

However, it is not clear what impact the ethnocentric curriculum has. For example, while it may ignore Asian culture, Indian and Chinese pupils' achievement is above the national average. Similarly, Maureen Stone (1981) argues that black children do not in fact suffer from low self-esteem.

Heb. 3. 13.

PHŒBE.

Jamaica Royal Gazette, Oct. 7, 1826.

35—42   Spanish-Town Workhouse.

Notice is hereby given, that unless the undermentioned Slave is taken out of this Workhouse, prior to Monday the 30th day of October next, she will on that day, between the hours of 10 and 12 o'Clock in the forenoon, be put up to Public Sale, and sold to the highest and best bidder, at the Cross-Keys Tavern, in this Town, agreeably to the Workhouse Law now in force, for payment of her fees.

▲ *Poster advertising the sale of a black female slave, Jamaica, 1826. How does the history curriculum portray black people?*

Activity

In small groups, discuss the following questions.

1   How ethnocentric was the curriculum you followed in school? How much non-European history, geography, literature, music etc did you study? Did you study any non-European languages or non-Christian religions?

2   How far do your experiences support Troyna and Williams' view?

4 Institutional racism

Troyna and Williams argue that explanations of ethnic differences in achievement need to go beyond simply examining individual teacher racism to look at how schools and colleges routinely discriminate against ethnic minorities. They therefore make a distinction between:

- **individual racism** that results from the prejudiced views of individuals
- **institutional racism** – discrimination that is built into the way institutions such as schools and colleges operate.

From this point of view, the ethnocentric curriculum is a prime example of institutional racism. Troyna and Williams see the meagre provision for teaching Asian languages as institutional racism because it is an example of racial bias being built into the everyday workings of schools and colleges.

Studies of school governing bodies provide further examples of institutional racism. Richard Hatcher (1996) found that they gave low priority to race issues and failed to deal with pupils' racist behaviour. In the schools he studied, there were no formal channels of communication between school governors and ethnic minority parents. This meant, for example, that nothing was done about parents' concerns over lack of language support.

These examples show that institutional racism may create an environment in which ethnic minority pupils are routinely disadvantaged by a system that disregards their needs.

5 Selection and segregation

David Gillborn (1997) argues that marketisation has given schools greater scope to select pupils and this puts some ethnic minority pupils at a disadvantage. This is because selection gives more scope for negative stereotypes to influence decisions about school admissions.

Gillborn's view is supported by Donald Moore and Susan Davenport's (1990) American research. Their study focuses on how selection procedures lead to ethnic segregation, with minority pupils failing to get into better schools. They found that these schools discriminated against 'problem students'. For example, they used primary school reports to screen out pupils with language or learning difficulties, while the application process was difficult for less educated or non-English speaking parents to understand.

These procedures favoured white, middle-class pupils and put those from low-income and ethnic minority backgrounds at a disadvantage. Moore and Davenport thus conclude that selection leads to an ethnically stratified education system.

The Commission for Racial Equality (1993) has identified similar biases in British education. Their report notes that racism in school admissions procedures means that ethnic minority children are more likely to end up in unpopular schools. The report identifies the following reasons:

- reports from primary schools that stereotype minority pupils
- racist bias in interviews for school places
- lack of information and application forms in minority languages
- ethnic minority parents are often unaware of how the waiting list system works and the importance of deadlines.

However, schools' selection policies are not the only cause of segregation. It can also be the result of an active choice by parents, as Gewirtz's study of 'Gorse' and 'Flightpath' schools shows. Gorse attracted a mainly Asian intake. Many white parents refused to consider it because of this, opting instead for Flightpath. By contrast, Asian parents saw Gorse as 'safe' and having an academic orientation and firm discipline. They viewed Flightpath as 'a bit rough', with a reputation for racism.

Activity

Some minorities have set up their own schools. For example, black communities have set up Saturday or supplementary schools for their children, while Muslims and Seventh Day Adventists have set up their own faith schools. Alone or in small groups:

1 Research the different reasons for setting up such schools.

2 List the arguments for and against having schools for a single ethnic or religious group.

Ethnicity, class and gender

Gillian Evans (2006) argues that, to understand the relationship between ethnicity and achievement, we need to look at how ethnicity interacts with gender and class. She claims that in examining black children's achievement, sociologists tend to look at their culture and ethnicity, but rarely at their class. By contrast, when they examine white children's achievement, the focus is on their class rather than their culture and ethnicity. Evans concludes that, "we need to look at all of those things for every child".

One example of the ways in which ethnicity intersects with gender to affect achievement is Paul Connolly's (1998) study of five and six year olds in a multi-ethnic inner-city primary school. He shows how pupils and teachers construct masculinity differently depending on a child's ethnicity.

On the one hand, Connolly found that teachers saw black boys as disruptive under-achievers and controlled them by punishing them more and by channelling their energies into sport. The boys, in turn, responded by seeking status in non-academic ways, such as playing kiss-chase and football.

On the other hand, teachers saw Asian pupils as passive and conformist. They regarded the boys as keen and academic; when they misbehaved, they were seen as silly or immature rather than threatening. Other boys picked on them to assert their own masculinity and excluded them from playing football. Both teachers and pupils saw Asian boys as more 'feminine', vulnerable and in need of protection from bullying.

Studies such as those by Evans and Connolly show that we cannot consider ethnicity in isolation from gender and class when explaining differences in achievement.

For more activities on Ethnic differences in achievement...

 Go to www.sociology.uk.net

Summary

There are achievement **differences between ethnic groups**. For example, Indian pupils tend to do better than average, while Bangladeshi and black pupils do worse. There are class and gender **differences within groups**: e.g. black females do better than black males.

Some explanations focus on **external factors** (outside school), such as **cultural deprivation** due to unstable family structures or inadequate socialisation. Others argue that the lower **class position** of many minorities, along with **racism in wider society**, leads to material deprivation and lower achievement.

Other explanations focus on **internal factors. Teachers' racist labelling** may create a **self-fulfilling prophecy** and **anti-school subcultures**. The **ethnocentric curriculum** and **institutional racism** disadvantage ethnic minorities. Increased **selection** in schools resulting from marketisation is producing racial segregation.

QuickCheck Questions

1 List the following groups in order of achievement at GCSE, highest first: whites, blacks, Bangladeshis, Chinese, Indians.

2 State one criticism of cultural deprivation theory as an explanation of ethnic differences in achievement.

3 Name three sociologists who have studied the labelling of ethnic minority pupils.

4 List three ways in which pupils may respond to negative labels.

5 What is meant by the ethnocentric curriculum?

6 Suggest two reasons why marketisation might result in increased ethnic segregation in education.

 Check your answers at www.sociology.uk.net

Examining ethnic differences in achievement

Item A According to a report produced by the Cabinet Office in summer 2002, 'Bangladeshi, black and Pakistani pupils achieve less well than other pupils at all stages of education. Black Caribbean children have equal, if not higher, ability than white children on entrance to school, but Black Caribbean boys make the least progress through school.'

Some sociologists explain these differences in achievement as the result of teacher racism and the responses of pupils to this. For example, Gillborn and Youdell (2000) found that teachers have racialised expectations of black pupils. Although these were rarely openly stated or conscious, teachers often interpreted black pupils' behaviour as a threat or a challenge to their authority. Pupils then felt teachers picked on them unfairly and responded accordingly.

5

There are also important gender differences between ethnic groups. On average, boys and girls have similar staying-on rates, but among blacks and Chinese the rate is higher for females, while among Indians, Bangladeshis and Pakistanis males have the higher rate.

(a) Explain what is meant by the term 'ethnic group'. (2 marks)

(b) Suggest **three ways** in which the education system may encourage separation between children of different ethnic backgrounds. (6 marks)

(c) Outline the ways in which factors in children's home background may lead to differences in achievement levels between ethnic groups. (12 marks)

(d) Assess the importance of school factors such as racism and pupils' responses to racism in creating ethnic differences in educational achievement. (20 marks)

The examiner's advice

Part (c) carries 8 AO1 marks (knowledge and understanding) and 4 AO2 marks (interpretation, application, analysis and evaluation). You should briefly identify ethnic patterns of achievement. Explain factors such as intellectual and linguistic skills, attitudes and values, and the role of family structure and parental support. In your account, differentiate between white, black and Asian family backgrounds. Include some analysis and/or evaluation, such as criticisms of these explanations.

Part (d) carries 8 AO1 marks and 12 AO2 marks. You should identify the patterns of ethnic achievement – both between and within ethnic groups. Explain the range of school factors – teacher labelling and institutional racism, pupil subcultures, the ethnocentric curriculum, and selection and segregation. Use material from Item A, such as teachers' racialised expectations, as well as studies of teacher racism/ stereotyping of pupils and the different ways pupils respond to this (e.g. Wright, Sewell, Mirza, Fuller). Evaluate these explanations by referring to external, non-school factors or by showing the way gender and class interact with ethnicity to create ethnic differences in achievement.

Topic 4 Gender differences in education

Along with social class and ethnicity, gender has a major impact on people's experience of education. In recent years, there have been some important changes in this area. In particular, while both sexes have raised their level of achievement, girls have now overtaken boys.

On the other hand, one area where gender patterns have been slower to change is in subject choice, with boys and girls often opting to study traditional 'sex-typed' subjects and courses. Similarly, there is also evidence that schooling continues to reinforce differences in gender identity between boys and girls.

The main questions that interest sociologists in the study of gender differences in education are:

- Why do girls now generally achieve better results than boys?
- Why do girls and boys opt to study different subjects?
- How does schooling help to reinforce gender identities?

This Topic examines some of the answers that sociologists have given to these questions.

Learning objectives

After studying this Topic, you should:

- Be able to describe the patterns of gender differences in educational achievement.
- Understand and be able to evaluate the explanations for these differences.
- Understand and be able to evaluate the explanations for gender differences in subject choice.
- Understand the effect of school experiences in shaping gender identities.

The gender gap in achievement

Official statistics provide evidence of differences in the achievements of girls and boys at several important stages of their education:

- **On starting school**, children are given baseline assessments, where the teacher assesses what each child knows, understands and can do. A national survey of 6,953 children by the Qualifications and Curriculum Authority found that girls scored higher in all tests. While 62% of girls could concentrate without supervision for 10 minutes, only 49% of boys could do this. Similarly, 56% of girls could write their own name and spell it correctly, but only 42% of boys could do so. According to a DfES (2007) study, 70% of children with identified special educational needs are boys.
- **At Key Stages 1 to 3,** girls do consistently better than boys. This is especially so in English, where the gender gap steadily widens with age. In science and maths the gap is much narrower, but girls still do better.
- **At GCSE**, as Figure 3.7 shows, the gender gap stands at around 10 percentage points.
- **At AS and A level**, girls are more likely to pass, and to get higher grades, though the gap is narrower than at GCSE. In 2006, for example, 95.8% of girls passed two or more A levels, as against 94% of boys. At both AS and A level, girls were more likely to gain A, B and C grades, even in so-called 'boys" subjects such as maths and physics. The average A level points score in state schools was 274 for boys, but 295 for girls.
- **On vocational courses** preparing students for a career, results show a similar pattern. A larger proportion of girls achieve distinctions in every subject, including those such as engineering and construction where girls are a tiny minority of the students.

Although results for both sexes have improved at all levels over the years, the girls' rate of improvement has been more rapid and a significant gap has opened up, particularly at GCSE.

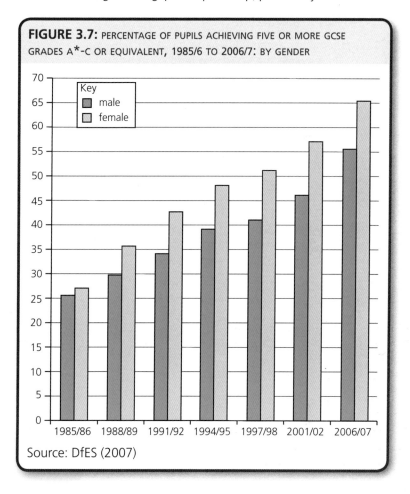

FIGURE 3.7: PERCENTAGE OF PUPILS ACHIEVING FIVE OR MORE GCSE GRADES A*-C OR EQUIVALENT, 1985/6 TO 2006/7: BY GENDER

Key
- male
- female

Source: DfES (2007)

External factors and gender differences in achievement

There are a number of reasons for gender differences in achievement. As with explanations of class and ethnic differences in achievement, we can divide them into external and internal factors:

- **External factors** – factors outside the education system, such as home and family background and wider society
- **Internal factors** – factors within schools and the education system, such as the effect of schools' equal opportunities policies.

Many sociologists argue that gender differences in achievement, and especially the more rapid improvement in girls' results, can best be explained by changes that have occurred in factors outside the school, such as the following:

1 The impact of feminism

2 Changes in the family

3 Changes in women's employment

4 Girls' changing perceptions and ambitions.

1 The impact of feminism

Feminism is a social movement that strives for equal rights for women in all areas of life. Since the 1960s, the feminist movement has challenged the traditional stereotype of a woman's role as solely that of mother and housewife, subordinate to her breadwinner husband in a patriarchal nuclear family and inferior to men outside the home, in work, education and the law.

Although feminists argue that we have not yet achieved full equality between the sexes, the feminist movement has had considerable success in improving women's rights and opportunities through changes in the law. More broadly, feminism has raised women's expectations and self-esteem.

These changes are partly reflected in media images and messages. A good illustration of this comes from Angela McRobbie's (1994) comparison of girls' magazines in the 1970s and the 1990s. In the 1970s, girls' magazines such as Jackie emphasised the importance of getting married and not being 'left on the shelf', whereas nowadays, they contain images of assertive, independent women. Similarly, current affairs programmes and soap operas now highlight the importance of self-esteem and personal choice for young women.

As we shall see, the changes encouraged by feminism may affect girls' self-image and ambitions with regard to the family and careers. In turn, this may explain improvements in their educational achievement.

Activity

Carry out an analysis of girls' magazines. Get a range of magazines and analyse them to find any evidence (a) supporting and (b) contradicting McRobbie's views. Are there any differences between the magazines?

2 Changes in the family

There have been major changes in the family since the 1970s. These include:

- an increase in the divorce rate
- an increase in cohabitation and a decrease in the number of first marriages
- an increase in the number of lone-parent families (mainly female-headed)
- smaller families.

These changes are affecting girls' attitudes towards education in a number of ways. For example, increased numbers of female-headed lone-parent families may mean more women need to take on a breadwinner role. This in turn creates a new adult role model for girls – the financially independent

woman. To achieve this independence, of course, women need well-paid jobs and therefore good qualifications. Likewise, increases in the divorce rate may suggest to girls that it is unwise to rely on a husband to be their provider. Again, this may encourage girls to look to themselves and their own qualifications to make a living.

3 Changes in women's employment

There have been important changes in women's employment in recent decades. These include the following:

- The 1970 Equal Pay Act makes it illegal to pay women less than men for work of equal value, and the 1975 Sex Discrimination Act outlaws sex discrimination in employment.
- The proportion of women in employment has risen from 47% in 1959 to over 70% in 2007. The growth of the service sector and flexible part-time work has offered opportunities for women, while traditional 'men's' jobs have declined.
- Since 1975, the pay gap between men and women has fallen from 30% to 17%.
- Some women are now breaking through the 'glass ceiling' – the invisible barrier that keeps them out of high-level professional and managerial jobs.

As Margaret Prosser (2006) puts it:

"In the 30 years since the Equal Pay Act there have been many changes in women's economic participation and achievement. More women are working than ever before …and accessing training and jobs which previous generations would not have considered open to women."

▲ *What policies might encourage more girls to pursue a career in construction?*

These changes have encouraged girls to see their future in terms of paid work rather than as housewives. Greater career opportunities and better pay for women, and the role models that successful career women offer, provide an incentive for girls to gain qualifications.

4 Girls' changing ambitions

The view that changes in the family and employment are producing changes in girls' ambitions is supported by evidence from sociological research. For example, Sue Sharpe (1994) compared the results of interviews she conducted with girls in the 1970s and the 1990s. Her findings show a major shift in the way girls see themselves and their future.

In 1974, the girls Sharpe interviewed had low aspirations; they felt educational success was unfeminine and believed that if they appeared to be ambitious and intelligent they would be considered unattractive. They gave their priorities as 'love, marriage, husbands, children, jobs and careers, more or less in that order'.

By the 1990s, girls' ambitions had changed and they had a different order of priorities – careers and being able to support themselves. Sharpe found that girls were now more likely to see their future as an independent woman with a career rather than as dependent on their husband and his income. Similarly, when Becky Francis (2001) asked girls about their career ambitions, most had high aspirations and very few saw their future in traditional female jobs. Clearly, these aspirations require educational qualifications, whereas those of the 1970s girls did not.

Methods Link: using unstructured interviews

Sharpe's study included using unstructured interviews to study girls' attitudes to education, family and work. By asking open-ended questions and allowing the girls to respond in their own words, she was able to obtain rich qualitative data that gave her a valid picture of their feelings, aspirations and views.

However, open-ended questions do not usually produce data that can be easily categorised or counted to establish correlations. There is also a danger that the interviewer will unintentionally influence the interviewees' answers. This may be even more of a risk where the interviewees are much younger than the researcher.

Read more about interviews and researching education in **Methods in Context** on pages 202-5.

Internal factors and gender differences in achievement

While factors outside school may play an important part in explaining gender differences in achievement, factors within the education system itself are also important. These include:

1 Equal opportunities policies

2 Positive role models in schools

3 GCSE and coursework

4 Teacher attention and classroom interaction

5 Challenging stereotypes in the curriculum

6 Selection and league tables.

1 Equal opportunities policies

Many sociologists argue that feminist ideas have had a major impact on the education system. Those who run the system are now much more aware of gender issues and teachers are more sensitive to the need to avoid gender stereotyping. The belief that boys and girls are equally capable and entitled to the same opportunities is now part of mainstream thinking in education and it influences educational policies.

For example, policies such as GIST (Girls into science and technology) and WISE (Women into science and engineering) encourage girls to pursue careers in these non-traditional areas. Female scientists have visited schools, acting as role models; efforts have been made to raise science teachers' awareness of gender issues; non-sexist careers advice has been provided and learning materials in science reflecting girls' interests have been developed.

Similarly, the introduction of the National Curriculum in 1988 removed one source of gender inequality by making girls and boys study mostly the same subjects, which was often not the case previously. Alison Kelly (1987) argues that making science part of the compulsory core curriculum for all pupils helps to equalise opportunities.

Jo Boaler (1998) sees the impact of equal opportunities policies as a key reason for the changes in girls' achievement. Many of the barriers have been removed and schooling has become more meritocratic (based on equal opportunities) – so that girls, who generally work harder than boys, achieve more.

2 Positive role models in schools

As Table 3B shows, in recent years there has been an increase in the proportion of female teachers and head teachers. These women in positions of authority and seniority may act as role models for girls, showing them women can achieve positions of importance and giving them non-traditional goals to aim for.

Women teachers are likely to be particularly important role models as far as girls' educational achievement is concerned since, to become a teacher, the individual must undertake a lengthy and successful education herself. It could be argued that primary schools in particular have become 'feminised', with a virtually all-female staff. This may have an impact on how far each gender sees schooling as part of their 'gender domain' or territory (see pages 133-4).

Table 3B	Percentage of teachers and head teachers who are women, 1992 and 2005			
	Nursery and primary schools		Secondary schools	
	1992	2005	1992	2005
Head teachers	50	66	22	35
Teachers	81	84	49	56

Source: adapted from DfES (2007)

1 Approximately how many times more male than female secondary head teachers were there in 2005?

2 Suggest reasons why there are bigger proportions of female teachers and female heads in primary schools than in secondary schools.

3 GCSE and coursework

Some sociologists argue that changes in the way pupils are assessed have favoured girls and disadvantaged boys. For example, Stephen Gorard (2005) found that the gender gap in achievement was fairly constant from 1975 until 1988-9, when it increased sharply. This was the year in which GCSE was introduced, bringing with it coursework as a major part of nearly all subjects. Gorard concludes that the gender gap in achievement is a "product of the changed system of assessment rather than any more general failing of boys".

Eirene Mitsos and Ken Browne (1998) support this view. They conclude that girls are more successful in coursework because they are more conscientious and better organised than boys. Girls:

- spend more time on their work
- take more care with the way it is presented
- are better at meeting deadlines
- bring the right equipment and materials to lessons.

Mitsos and Browne argue that these factors have helped girls to benefit from the introduction of coursework in GCSE, AS and A level. They also note that girls gain from maturing earlier than boys and from their ability to concentrate for longer.

Along with GCSE has come the greater use of oral exams. This is also said to benefit girls because of their generally better developed language skills.

Sociologists argue that these characteristics and skills are the result of early gender role socialisation in the family. For example, girls are more likely than boys to be encouraged to be neat, tidy and patient. These qualities become an advantage in today's assessment system, helping girls achieve greater success than boys. The New Right thinker, Madsen Pirie, makes a similar point (see page 137, Item A.)

However, Jannette Elwood (2005) argues that although coursework has some influence, it is unlikely to be the only cause of the gender gap. Analysing the weighting of coursework and written exams, she concludes that exams have more influence on final grades.

Activity

As a group, design and carry out a survey on gender differences in how conscientious and organised students are and in their attitudes to coursework. Ask about time spent on homework, meeting deadlines, how much revision they did for GCSE, whether they prefer coursework or exams etc. Do your results support Mitsos and Browne's views?

4 Teacher attention

The way in which teachers interact with boys and girls differs. Dale Spender (1983) found that teachers spend more time interacting with boys than with girls. However, when Jane and Peter French (1993) analysed classroom interaction, they found that the amount of attention teachers paid to boys and girls for academic reasons was similar. Boys only received more attention because they attracted more reprimands. Becky Francis (2001) also found that while boys got more attention, they were disciplined more harshly and felt picked on by teachers, who tended to have lower expectations of them.

Similarly, Joan Swann and David Graddol (1994) found that boys are generally more boisterous and attract the teacher's gaze more often than girls, and so get more opportunity to speak. However, they found that the way teachers interacted with girls was more positive because it focused on schoolwork rather than behaviour.

Swann (1998) also found gender differences in communication styles. Boys dominate in whole-class discussion, whereas girls prefer pair-work and group-work and are better at listening and cooperating. When working in groups, girls' speech involves turn taking, and not the hostile interruptions that often characterise boys' speech.

This may explain why teachers respond more positively to girls, whom they see as cooperative, than to boys, whom they see as potentially disruptive. This may lead to a self-fulfilling prophecy in which successful interactions with teachers promote girls' self-esteem and raise their achievement levels.

5 Challenging stereotypes in the curriculum

Some sociologists argue that the removal of gender stereotypes from textbooks, reading schemes and other learning materials in recent years has removed a barrier to girls' achievement. Research in the 1970s and 80s found that reading schemes portrayed women mainly as housewives and mothers, that physics books showed them as frightened or amazed by science, and that maths books depicted boys as more inventive than girls.

Gaby Weiner (1995) argues that since the 1980s, teachers have challenged such stereotypes. Also, in general, sexist images have been removed from learning materials. This may have helped to raise girls' achievement by presenting them with more positive images of what women can do.

Methods Link: using documents

Sociologists have analysed the contents of educational documents such as reading schemes and textbooks for evidence of gender stereotyping. Glenys Lobban (1974) examined 179 stories in six reading schemes used in primary schools and found that females were nearly always presented in traditional domestic roles.

Quantitative content analysis of schoolbooks can reveal statistical patterns of gender images in learning materials. It is easily replicated to show trends over time in stereotyping. For example, Lesley Best's (1993) analysis of reading schemes found little had changed. However, content analysis merely tells us how often an image appears in a document; it tells us nothing about its meaning to those who see it.

Read more about documents and researching education in *Methods in Context* on pages 227-8.

6 Selection and league tables

Marketisation policies (see pages 152-3) have created a more competitive climate in which schools see girls as desirable recruits because they achieve better exam results.

David Jackson (1998) notes that the introduction of exam league tables, which place a high value on academic achievement, has improved opportunities for girls: high-achieving girls are attractive to schools, whereas low-

achieving boys are not. This tends to create a self-fulfilling prophecy – because girls are more likely to be recruited by good schools, they are more likely to do well.

Roger Slee (1998) argues that boys are less attractive to schools because they are more likely to suffer from behavioural difficulties and are four times more likely to be excluded.

As a result, boys may be seen as 'liability students' – obstacles to the school improving its league table scores. They give the school a 'rough, tough' image that deters high-achieving girls from applying.

Activity

Investigate what steps your school or college has taken to encourage girls or boys to opt for non-traditional subjects and courses. What further steps could be taken?

Two views of girls' achievement

While there have clearly been changes in gender and educational achievement, sociologists differ in their interpretation of the importance of these changes.

liberal feminists

Liberal feminists celebrate the progress made so far in improving achievement. They believe that further progress will be made by the continuing development of equal opportunities policies, encouraging positive role models and overcoming sexist attitudes and stereotypes.

This is similar to the functionalist view that education is a *meritocracy* where all individuals, regardless of gender, ethnicity or class, are given an equal opportunity to achieve (see page 139).

radical feminists

Radical feminists take a more critical view. While they recognise that girls are achieving more, they emphasise that the system remains patriarchal (male-dominated) and conveys the clear message that it is still a man's world. For example:

- Sexual harassment of girls continues at school.
- Education still limits their subject choices and career options (see pages 132-3).
- Although there are now more female head teachers, male teachers are still more likely to become heads of secondary schools.
- Women are under-represented in many areas of the curriculum. For example, their contribution to history is largely ignored. Weiner (1993) describes the secondary school history curriculum as a 'woman-free zone'.

Boys and achievement

We have focused so far on the thing that appears to have changed most – girls' performance. Recently, however, the gender gap in achievement has given rise to concern about boys falling behind.

Several possible factors may be responsible for this. These include external factors (outside the education system) such as boys' poorer literacy skills and the decline of traditional 'men's jobs', as well as internal factors (within the education system), such as the feminisation of education, the shortage of male primary school teachers and 'laddish' subcultures.

Boys and literacy

According to the DCSF (2007), the gender gap is mainly the result of boys' poorer literacy and language skills. One reason for this may be that parents spend less time reading to their sons. Another may be that it is mothers who do most of the reading to young children, who thus come to see it as a feminine activity.

In addition, boys' leisure pursuits, such as football and computer games, do little to help develop their language and communication skills. By contrast, girls tend to have a 'bedroom culture' centred on staying in and talking with friends.

Poor language and literacy skills are likely to affect boys' performance across a wide range of subjects. In response to this problem, government has introduced a range of policies to improve boys' skills. (See Box 12.)

Activity

Carry out a brief survey of male and female students. Ask them the following questions:

1 Who mostly read to you when you were a child?

2 How many books other than schoolbooks have you read in the last three months?

3 List your top three leisure pursuits in order of time spent on them.

Pool your results with the rest of the class. What gender patterns do you find?

Globalisation and the decline of traditional men's jobs

Since the 1980s, there has been a significant decline in heavy industries such as iron and steel, shipbuilding, mining, engineering and other manufacturing. This has been partly the result of the globalisation of the economy, which has led to much manufacturing industry relocating to developing countries such as China to take advantage of cheap labour.

Traditionally, these sectors of the economy employed mainly men. Mitsos and Browne claim that this decline in male employment opportunities has led to an 'identity crisis for men'. Many boys now believe that they have little prospect of getting a proper job. This undermines their motivation and self-esteem and so they give up trying to get qualifications.

While there may be some truth in this claim, we should note that the decline has largely been in traditional manual working-class jobs, many of them unskilled or semi-skilled. Traditionally, most of these jobs would have been filled by working-class boys with few if any qualifications – largely because qualifications were (and are) unnecessary for this kind of work. Thus it seems unlikely that the disappearance of such jobs would have much impact on boys' motivation to obtain qualifications.

Feminisation of education

Tony Sewell is reported as claiming that boys fall behind because education has become 'feminised' (BBC, 2006). That is, schools do not nurture 'masculine' traits such as competitiveness and leadership. Instead, they celebrate qualities more closely associated with girls, such as methodical working and attentiveness in class.

Like Gorard (see page 128), Sewell sees coursework as a major cause of gender differences in achievement. He argues that some coursework should be replaced with final exams and a greater emphasis placed on outdoor adventure in the curriculum. He argues: "We have challenged the 1950s patriarchy and rightly said this is not a man's world. But we have thrown the boy out with the bath water."

Shortage of male primary school teachers

The increasing lack of strong positive male role models both at home and at school is said to be a cause of boys' under-achievement. For example, large numbers of boys are being brought up in the 1.5 million female-headed lone parent families in the UK.

Similarly, according to the DfES (2007), men now make up only 16% of primary school teachers. As a result, according to a Yougov (2007) poll, 39% of 8-11 year old boys have no lessons whatsoever with a male teacher. Yet the majority of boys surveyed said the presence of a male teacher made them behave better and 42% said it made them work harder.

However, recent research suggests that this approach is too simplistic and that the absence of male teachers may not be a major factor in explaining boys' under-achievement. For example, Becky Francis (2006) found that two-thirds of 7-8 year olds believed that the gender of teachers does not matter. Similarly, Myhill and Jones (2006) found that 13-15 year olds felt male teachers treated boys more harshly.

'Laddish' subcultures

Some sociologists argue that the growth of 'laddish' subcultures has contributed to boys' under-achievement. Debbie Epstein (1998) examined the way masculinity is constructed within school. She found that working-class boys are likely to be harassed, labelled as sissies and subjected to homophobic (anti-gay) verbal abuse if they appear to be 'swots'.

This supports Francis' (2001) finding that boys were more concerned than girls about being labelled by peers as swots, because this label is more of a threat to their masculinity than it is to girls' femininity.

This is because in working-class culture, masculinity is equated with being tough and doing manual work. Non-manual work, and by extension schoolwork, is seen as effeminate and inferior. As a result, working-class boys tend to reject schoolwork to avoid being called 'gay'. As Epstein observes, 'real boys don't work' – and if they do they get bullied. She notes that:

'The main demand on boys within their peer group, but also sometimes from teachers, is to appear to do little or no work, to be heavily competitive at sports and hetero-sex, to be rough, tough and dangerous to know.'

Epstein's findings on working-class masculinity and schooling parallel those of Mac an Ghaill and Willis (see pages 135 and 146).

According to Francis, laddish culture is becoming increasingly widespread. She argues that this is because, as girls move into traditional masculine areas such as careers, boys respond by "becoming increasingly laddish in their effort to construct themselves as non-feminine".

Suggest two reasons why boys are more likely to be seen as disruptive in school.

Box 12	Policies to raise boys' achievement

Government has introduced a range of policies to improve boys' achievement:

- The *Raising Boys Achievement* project involves a range of teaching strategies, including single-sex teaching
- The *National Literacy Strategy* includes a focus on improving boys' reading.
- The *Reading Champions* scheme uses male role models celebrating their own reading interests.
- *Playing for Success* uses football and other sports to boost learning skills and motivation among boys.
- The *Dads and Sons* campaign encourages fathers to be more involved with their sons' education.
- Recruitment campaigns aim to attract more men into primary school teaching.

Gender, class and ethnicity

However, it would be wrong to conclude that boys are a 'lost cause'. In fact, as Figure 3.7 shows, the performance of both sexes has actually improved considerably in recent years. Boys may now be lagging behind girls, but boys today are achieving more than they did in the past.

Furthermore, as Tracey McVeigh (2001) notes, the similarities in girls and boys' achievement are far greater than the differences, especially when compared with class or ethnic patterns of achievement. For example, a DfES (2007) study found that the class gap in achievement at GCSE is three times wider than the gender gap.

As a result, girls and boys of the same social class tend to achieve fairly similar results. For example, at GCSE in 2006, the gender gap within any given social class was never greater than 12 percentage points. By contrast, pupils of the same gender but different social classes achieved widely different results. For example, girls from the highest social class were 44 points ahead of girls from the lowest class. These figures show that class is a more important influence on a pupil's achievement than gender.

▲ *Ninety-four per cent of all hairdressing apprentices are girls.*

Nonetheless, this Topic has shown us that girls generally do better than boys – so gender clearly does influence achievement. However, the extent of this influence itself varies depending on a pupil's class and ethnic group. This may be because pupils define their gender differently according to their class or ethnicity.

For example, the gender gap among black Caribbean pupils is greater than among other ethnic groups. As Fuller shows, many black girls are successful at school because they define their femininity in terms of educational achievement and independence. By contrast, as Sewell found, some black boys fail at school because they define their masculinity in opposition to education, which they see as effeminate. Similarly, as Willis shows (page 147), working-class boys' definitions of masculinity are often hostile to schooling and contribute to their under-achievement.

These examples show that we need to take the interplay of class, gender and ethnicity into account in order to achieve a better understanding of differences in educational achievement. As Connolly (2006) suggests, there may be an 'interactions effect' – so that certain combinations of gender, class and ethnicity have more effect than others. For example, being female raises performance more when 'added to' being black Caribbean than it does when 'added to' being white. By contrast, class differences have more effect in producing performance differences among white pupils than among black pupils.

Subject choice and gender identity

In the previous section, we looked at how sociologists have explained the growing gender gap in achievement. In this section, we examine two closely related issues: subject choice and gender identity.

Firstly, despite the improvement in girls' achievement relative to boys', there continues to be a fairly traditional pattern of 'boys' subjects' and 'girls' subjects'. Boys still tend to opt for subjects such as maths and physics, while girls are more likely to choose modern languages, for example.

Secondly, schooling reinforces gender identity in various ways, both through the curriculum and in the interactions between teachers and pupils and among pupils themselves.

Subject choice

The introduction of the National Curriculum reduced pupils' freedom to choose or drop subjects by making most subjects compulsory until 16.

However, where choice is possible, both in the National Curriculum and much more so after 16, boys and girls tend to follow different 'gender routes' through the education system and there are some clear gender differences in subject choices. This is shown in National Curriculum options, AS and A levels, and vocational courses.

National Curriculum options

Andrew Stables and Felicity Wikeley (1996) found that where there is a choice in the National Curriculum, girls and boys choose differently. For example, although design and technology is a compulsory subject, girls tend to choose the food technology option whereas boys choose graphics and resistant materials.

AS and A levels

Gendered subject choices become more noticeable after the National Curriculum, when students have greater freedom of choice. For example, there are big gender differences in entries for different A level subjects (see Table 3C), with boys opting for maths and physics and girls choosing subjects such as sociology, English and foreign languages. These differences are mirrored in subject choices at university.

vocational courses

Vocational courses prepare students for particular careers. Evidence shows a similar but more exaggerated pattern to that for A levels. As Table 3D shows, gender segregation is a very noticeable feature of vocational training. For example, only one in 100 construction apprentices is a girl.

> Suggest two reasons why so few females choose engineering courses.

Table 3C	Candidates sitting GCE A level exams: by gender and subject, UK, 2007	
	% male	% female
Computing	90	10
Physics	78	22
Further Maths	71	29
Mathematics	60	40
History	50	50
Biology	41	59
English	31	69
French	31	69
Drama	29	71
Sociology	24	76
All subjects	48	52

Source: adapted from Joint Council for Qualifications (2007)

Table 3D	Young people aged 16-24 in work based learning: by sex and area of learning, England, 2005/06		
		% male	% female
Construction, planning and the built environment		99	1
Engineering and manufacturing technologies		97	3
Information and communication technology		81	19
Leisure, travel and tourism		54	46
Agriculture, horticulture and animal care		51	49
Retail and commercial enterprise		35	65
Business, administration and law		28	72
Health, public services and care		9	91
All areas of learning		58	42

Source: adapted from LSC; DfES (2007)

Explanations of gender differences in subject choice

Why do boys and girls tend to choose different subjects? Sociologists have put forward a number of explanations:

1 Early socialisation

2 Gendered subject images

3 Peer pressure

4 Gendered career opportunities.

1 Early socialisation

According to Ann Oakley (1973), 'sex' refers to inborn physical differences between males and females, whereas 'gender' refers to the learned cultural differences between them. Gender role socialisation is the process of learning the behaviour expected of males and females in society.

Early socialisation shapes children's gender identity. As Fiona Norman (1988) notes, from an early age, boys and girls are dressed differently, given different toys and encouraged to take part in different activities. Parents tend to reward boys for being active and girls for being passive.

Schools also play an important part. Eileen Byrne (1979) shows that teachers encourage boys to be tough and show initiative and not be weak or behave like sissies. Girls on the other hand are expected to be quiet, helpful, clean and tidy, not rough or noisy.

As a result of differences in socialisation, boys and girls develop different tastes in reading. Patricia Murphy and Jannette Elwood (1998) show how these lead to different subject choices. Boys read hobby books and information texts, while girls are more likely to read stories about people. This helps to explain why boys prefer science subjects and why girls prefer subjects such as English.

gender domains

Naima Browne and Carol Ross (1991) argue that children's beliefs about 'gender domains' are shaped by their early experiences and the expectations of adults. By gender domains, they mean the tasks and activities that boys and girls see as male or female 'territory' and therefore as relevant to themselves. For example, mending a car is seen as falling within the male gender domain, but looking after a sick child is not.

Children are more confident when engaging in tasks that they see as part of their own gender domain. For example, when they are set the same mathematical task, girls are more confident in tackling it when it is presented as being about food and nutrition, whereas boys are more confident if it is about cars.

Boys and girls also interpret tasks differently. Patricia Murphy (1991) set primary and lower secondary pupils open-ended tasks where they were asked to design boats and vehicles and to write estate agents' adverts for a house.

▲ Sex-typing of jobs influences boys' and girls' choice of vocational courses.

- Boys designed powerboats and battleships with elaborate weaponry and little living accommodation, whereas girls designed cruise ships, paying attention to social and domestic details.
- Boys designed sports cars and army vehicles, whereas girls designed family cars.
- When writing an estate agent's advert, boys focused on 'masculine' spheres such as garage space, whereas girls focused on 'feminine' ones such as decor and kitchen design.

This study shows that boys and girls pay attention to different details even when tackling the same task. In general, girls focus more on how people feel, whereas boys focus on how things are made and work. This helps to explain why girls choose humanities and arts subjects, while boys choose science.

> Suggest six interests or activities that are seen as part of the masculine gender domain and six that are seen as part of the feminine gender domain.

2 Gendered subject images

The gender image that a subject 'gives off' affects who will want to choose it. Sociologists have tried to explain why some subjects are seen as boys' or girls' subjects in the first place. For example, Kelly argues that science is seen as a boys' subject for several reasons:

- Science teachers are more likely to be men.
- The examples that teachers use, and those found in textbooks, often draw on boys' rather than girls' interests and experiences.
- In science lessons, boys monopolise the apparatus and dominate the laboratory, acting as if it is 'theirs'.

Similarly, Anne Colley (1998) notes that computer studies is seen as a masculine subject for two reasons:

- It involves working with machines – part of the male gender domain.
- The way it is taught is off-putting to females. Tasks tend to be abstract and teaching styles formal, with few opportunities for group work which, as we saw earlier, girls tend to favour.

Interestingly, according to a DfES (2007) study, pupils who attend single-sex schools tend to hold less stereotyped subject images. For example, they are less likely to see science as a boys' subject. As Diana Leonard (2006) found, this may result in them making less traditional subject choices. Analysing data on 13,000 individuals, she found that, compared to pupils in mixed schools, girls in girls' schools were more likely to take maths and science A levels, while boys in boys' schools were more likely to take English and modern languages. Girls from single-sex schools were also more likely to study male-dominated subjects at university and to earn higher salaries.

3 Peer pressure

Subject choice can be influenced by peer pressure. Other boys and girls may apply pressure to an individual if they disapprove of his or her choice. For example, boys tend to opt out of music and dance because such activities fall outside their gender domain and so are likely to attract a negative response from peers.

Carrie Paetcher (1998) found that because pupils see sport as mainly within the male gender domain, girls who are 'sporty' have to cope with an image that contradicts the conventional female stereotype. This may explain why girls are more likely than boys to opt out of sport.

Similarly, a study of American college students by Alison Dewar (1990) found that male students would call girls 'lesbian' or 'butch' if they appeared to be more interested in sport than in boys.

▲ How do peer groups reinforce gender identity?

By contrast, an absence of peer pressure from the opposite sex may explain why girls in single-sex schools are more likely to choose traditional boys' subjects. The absence of boys may mean there is less pressure on the girls to conform to restrictive stereotypes of what subjects they can or cannot study.

4 Gendered career opportunities

An important reason for differences in subject choice is the fact that employment is highly gendered: jobs tend to be sex-typed as 'men's' or 'women's'. Women's jobs often involve work similar to that performed by housewives, such as childcare and nursing. Women are concentrated in a narrow range of occupations. Over half of all women's employment falls within four categories: clerical, secretarial, personal services and occupations such as cleaning. By contrast, only a sixth of male workers work in these jobs.

This sex-typing of occupations affects boys' and girls' ideas about what kinds of job are possible or acceptable. Thus for example, if boys get the message that nursery nurses are women, they will be less likely to opt for a career in childcare. In turn, this affects what subjects and courses they will choose.

This also helps to explain why vocational courses are much more gender-specific than academic courses, since vocational studies are by definition more closely linked to students' career plans.

Gender identity

We have seen how early socialisation into a gender identity strongly influences pupils' subject preferences. Here we examine how pupils' experiences in school reinforce their gender and sexual identities. These experiences include:

1 verbal abuse

2 male peer groups

3 teachers and discipline

4 the male gaze

5 double standards.

These experiences may all contribute to reinforcing what Bob Connell (1995) calls 'hegemonic masculinity' – the dominance of heterosexual masculine identity and the subordination of female and gay identities.

1 Verbal abuse

What Connell calls "a rich vocabulary of abuse" is one of the ways in which dominant gender and sexual identities are reinforced. For example, boys use name-calling to put girls down if they behave or dress in certain ways. Sue Lees

(1986) found that boys called girls 'slags' if they appeared to be sexually available – and 'drags' if they didn't.

Similarly, Paetcher sees name-calling as helping to shape gender identity and maintain male power. The use of negative labels such as 'gay', 'queer' and 'lezzie' are ways in which pupils 'police' each other's sexual identities. For example, Andrew Parker (1996) found that boys were labelled 'gay' simply for being friendly with girls or female teachers. Both Lees and Paetcher note that these labels often bear no relation to pupils' actual sexual behaviour. Their function is simply to reinforce gender norms.

2 Male peer groups

Male peer groups also use verbal abuse to reinforce their definitions of masculinity. For example, as studies by Epstein and Willis show, boys in anti-school subcultures often accuse boys who want to do well of being gay or effeminate (see pages 131 and 146-7).

Similarly, Mairtin Mac an Ghaill's (1994) study of Parnell School examines how peer groups reproduce a range of different class-based masculine identities. For example, the working-class 'macho lads' were dismissive of other working-class boys who worked hard and aspired to middle-class careers, referring to them as the 'dickhead achievers'. By contrast, the middle-class 'real Englishmen' tried to project an image of 'effortless achievement' – of succeeding without really trying (though in some cases actually working hard 'on the quiet').

Interestingly, Redman and Mac an Ghaill (1997) found that the dominant definition of masculine identity changes from that of the macho lads in the lower school to that of the real Englishmen by the sixth form. This represents a shift away from a working-class definition based on toughness to a middle-class one based on intellectual ability. This in turn reflects the more middle-class composition and atmosphere of the sixth form.

3 Teachers and discipline

Research shows that teachers also play a part in reinforcing dominant definitions of gender identity. Chris Haywood and Mairtin Mac an Ghaill (1996) found that male teachers told boys off for 'behaving like girls' and teased them when they gained lower marks in tests than girls. Teachers tended to ignore boys' verbal abuse of girls and even blamed girls for attracting it.

Sue Askew and Carol Ross (1988) show how male teachers' behaviour can subtly reinforce messages about gender. For example, male teachers often have a protective attitude towards female colleagues, coming into their classes to 'rescue' them by threatening pupils who are being disruptive. However, this reinforces the idea that women cannot cope alone.

4 The male gaze

There is also a visual aspect to the way pupils control each other's identities. Mac an Ghaill refers to this as the 'male gaze': the way male pupils and teachers look girls up and down, seeing them as sexual objects and making judgements about their appearance.

Mac an Ghaill sees the male gaze as a form of surveillance through which dominant heterosexual masculinity is reinforced and femininity devalued. It is one of the ways boys prove their masculinity to their friends and is often combined with constant telling and retelling of stories about sexual conquests. Boys who do not display their heterosexuality in this way run the risk of being labelled gay.

5 Double standards

A double standard exists when we apply one set of moral standards to one group but a different set to another group. In the case of gender identity, Sue Lees (1993) identifies a double standard of sexual morality in which boys boast about their own sexual exploits, but call a girl a 'slag' if she doesn't have a steady boyfriend or if she dresses and speaks in a certain way. Sexual conquest is approved of and given status by male peers and ignored by male teachers, but 'promiscuity' among girls attracts negative labels.

Feminists see double standards as an example of a patriarchal ideology that justifies male power and devalues women. Along with verbal abuse, the male gaze and school discipline, double standards can be seen as a form of social control that reinforces gender inequality by keeping females subordinate to males.

Activity

Working alone or in pairs, review Topic 4 on *Gender differences in education* and decide:

1   Which of the factors you have read about contribute to the continuation of patriarchy (male dominance) in society?

2   Which factors are leading to greater gender equality in society?

For more activities on Gender differences in education...

Go to www.sociology.uk.net

Summary

Girls now do better than boys at all stages of education. Some explanations focus on **external factors** outside the education system – changes in the family, more employment opportunities for women, the impact of feminist ideas and changes in girls' ambitions.

Others focus on **changes within education**, such as the influence of feminist ideas via equal opportunities policies and challenges to stereotyping in the curriculum, more female teachers, coursework and exam league tables.

There are gender differences in **subject choice**. Choices are influenced by early socialisation into gender identities, the image subjects have, peer pressure and career opportunities.

Education also **reinforces gender identities** and hierarchies e.g. through verbal abuse, male peer groups, the male gaze, school discipline and double standards of sexual morality.

QuickCheck Questions

1   Identify two changes in wider society that may have contributed to girls' improved achievement.

2   Identify three changes within the education system that may have improved girls' achievement.

3   Suggest three reasons for boys' lower achievement levels.

4   Suggest two reasons why science is seen as a boys' subject.

5   Suggest two reasons for gender differences in choice of vocational courses.

6   Suggest one way in which male teachers may reinforce pupils' gender identities.

Check your answers at www.sociology.uk.net

Examining gender differences in education

Item A According to Madsen Pirie of the New Right Adam Smith Institute, the modular courses and continuous assessment found in education today favour the systematic approach of girls as against the risk-taking approach of boys. Pirie argues that the old O level exam (replaced by GCSE in 1988), 'with its high risk, swot it all up for the final throw... was a boys' exam'. By contrast, GCSE, AS and A levels emphasise preparation and modules that can be worked on over time. This favours what Pirie calls the 'more systematic, consistent, attention-to-detail qualities' of girls. In his view, it is not laddish anti-school subcultures that explains why girls have now overtaken boys, but the examination system.

5

(a) Explain what is meant by the term 'secondary socialisation'. (2 marks)

(b) Suggest **three** ways in which features of school life may help to shape pupils' gender identities. (6 marks)

(c) Outline the reasons for gender differences in subject choice. (12 marks)

(d) Using material from **Item A** and elsewhere, assess the view that gender differences in achievement are largely the result of changes in the education system. (20 marks)

The examiner's advice

Part (c) carries 8 AO1 marks (knowledge and understanding) and 4 AO2 marks (application, interpretation, analysis and evaluation). You need to stay focused on differences in subject choice and avoid discussing differences in achievement here. Start by briefly outlining the main gender differences in both academic and vocational subjects and courses.

Then consider a range of possible reasons, such as differences in early socialisation and gender domains, gendered subject images, peer pressure and gendered career opportunities. Use evidence and arguments from studies such as Murphy and Elwood, Kelly, Colley and Paetcher in explaining these reasons.

Part (d) carries 8 AO1 marks and 12 AO2 marks. First, briefly describe gender differences in achievement; then go on to consider different explanations for them. You could organise your answer in terms of internal and external factors. You should therefore explain the changes in the education system – the internal factors – such as changes in assessment (use Item A for this), feminisation of teaching, equal opportunities policies, changes in learning materials etc.

You can develop evaluation by looking at explanations that focus on factors external to the education system (e.g. changes in the family, employment, girls' aspirations etc). Although you can focus mainly on girls, you should also look at possible reasons for boys' relative under-achievement, such as laddish subcultures (Item A), lack of role models etc.

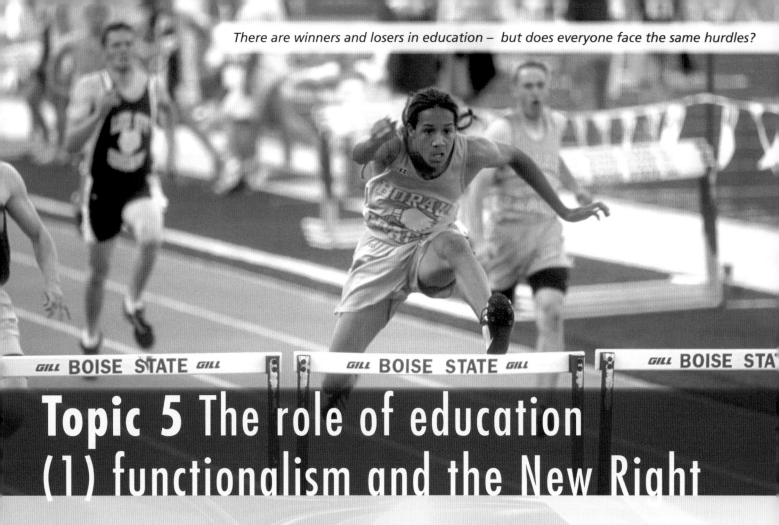

There are winners and losers in education – but does everyone face the same hurdles?

Topic 5 The role of education (1) functionalism and the New Right

When studying the role of education in society, sociologists are interested in questions such as:

- How far does education provide all individuals with equal opportunities for achievement?
- How far does education recreate existing social inequalities?
- In what ways does education serve the needs of the economy?
- What kind of knowledge, skills, attitudes and values does education transmit?

As we shall see, sociologists hold different and conflicting views on these questions. Often, this is because they have different sociological perspectives or viewpoints that see society differently. In this Topic and Topic 6, we focus on the following perspectives or theories of the role of education in society:

- **Functionalism** – a consensus approach
- **The New Right** – a conservative approach

In Topic 6, we look at a further perspective on the role of education: Marxism – a class conflict approach. In addition, Topic 6 also examines the more recent ideas of postmodernism, post-Fordism and critical modernism.

Learning objectives

After studying this Topic, you should:

- Know the questions sociologists ask about the role of education.
- Know the functions of education that functionalists identify.
- Understand the New Right view of the role of the market in education.
- Be able to evaluate the functionalist and New Right views of education.
- Be able to evaluate explanations of vocational education and training.

The functionalist perspective on education

Functionalism is based on the view that society is a system of interdependent parts held together by a shared culture or value consensus – an agreement among society's members about what values are important. Each part of society, such as the family, economy or education system, performs functions that help to maintain society as a whole. When studying education, functionalists seek to discover what functions it performs – that is, what does it do to help meet society's needs?

Durkheim: solidarity and skills

The French sociologist Emile Durkheim (1903), the founder of functionalist sociology, identified two main functions of education:

- creating social solidarity
- teaching specialist skills.

Social solidarity

Durkheim argues that society needs a sense of solidarity; that is, its individual members must feel themselves to be part of a single 'body' or community. He argues that without social solidarity, social life and cooperation would be impossible because each individual would pursue their own selfish desires.

The education system helps to create social solidarity by transmitting society's culture – its shared beliefs and values – from one generation to the next. For example, Durkheim argues that the teaching of a country's history instils in children a sense of a shared heritage and a commitment to the wider social group.

School also acts as a 'society in miniature', preparing us for life in wider society. For example, both in school and at work we have to cooperate with people who are neither family nor friends – teachers and pupils at school, colleagues and customers at work. Similarly, both in school and at work we have to interact with others according to a set of impersonal rules that apply to everyone.

Specialist skills

Modern industrial economies have a complex division of labour, where the production of even a single item usually involves the cooperation of many different specialists. This cooperation promotes social solidarity but, for it to be successful, each person must have the necessary specialist knowledge and skills to perform their role. Durkheim

argues that education teaches individuals the specialist knowledge and skills that they need to play their part in the social division of labour. For further discussion of the role of education and training in equipping young people with specialist skills, see Box 13.

Parsons: meritocracy

The American functionalist Talcott Parsons (1961) draws on many of Durkheim's ideas. Parsons sees the school as the 'focal socialising agency' in modern society, acting as a bridge between the family and wider society. This bridge is needed because family and society operate on different principles, so children need to learn a new way of living if they are to cope with the wider world.

Within the family, the child is judged by particularistic standards; that is, rules that apply only to that particular child. Similarly, in the family, the child's status is ascribed; that is, fixed by birth. For example, an elder son and a younger daughter may be given different rights or duties because of differences of age and sex.

By contrast, both school and wider society judge us all by the same universalistic and impersonal standards. For example, in society, the same laws apply to everyone. Similarly, in school each pupil is judged against the same standards (for example, they all sit the same exam and the pass mark is the same for everyone).

Likewise, in both school and wider society, a person's status is largely achieved, not ascribed. For example, at work we gain promotion or get the sack on the strength of how good we are at our job, while at school we pass or fail through our own individual efforts.

Parsons sees school as preparing us to move from the family to wider society because school and society are both based on meritocratic principles. In a meritocracy, everyone is given an equal opportunity, and individuals achieve rewards through their own effort and ability.

Activity

Explain in your own words what functionalists mean by the following terms:

(a) social solidarity
(b) complex division of labour
(c) universalistic standards
(d) a set of impersonal rules (in school)
(e) meritocracy

Davis and Moore: role allocation

Parsons argues that schools also perform a second function: that of selecting and allocating pupils to their future work roles. By assessing individuals' aptitudes and abilities, schools help to match them to the job they are best suited to.

Like Parsons, Kingsley Davis and Wilbert Moore (1945) also see education as a device for selection and role allocation, but they focus on the relationship between education and social inequality.

They argue that inequality is necessary to ensure that the most important roles in society are filled by the most talented people. For example, it would be inefficient and dangerous to have less able people performing roles such as surgeon or airline pilot. Not everyone is equally talented, so society has to offer higher rewards for these jobs. This will encourage everyone to compete for them and society can then select the most talented individuals to fill these positions.

Education plays a key part in this process, since it acts as a proving ground for ability. Put simply, education is where individuals show what they can do. It 'sifts and sorts' us according to our ability. The most able gain the highest qualifications, which then gives them entry to the most important and highly rewarded positions.

Similarly, Peter Blau and Otis Duncan (1978) argue that a modern economy depends for its prosperity on using its 'human capital' – its workers' skills. They argue that a meritocratic education system does this best, since it enables each person to be allocated to the job best suited to their abilities. This will make most effective use of their talents and maximise their productivity.

1 Name three functions that functionalists see education as performing.

2 In what ways can school be seen as a 'society in miniature'?

3 In your own words, explain why a meritocratic education system might enable society to make best use of people's talents.

| Box 13 | Vocational education and training (VET) |

Vocational education involves work-related study, mostly in school or college. In vocational training, learners acquire job-specific knowledge and skills mainly on the job or in work-like situations. From a functionalist perspective, VET teaches individuals the specialist skills they need to perform their role in the division of labour and meet society's economic needs.

However, there has long been concern that the British education system has lost touch with the economy. For example, in 1976, Labour Prime Minister Jim Callaghan initiated a 'Great Debate' on the role of education. He argued that Britain faced a 'skills crisis': pupils were leaving school unemployable, lacking the knowledge and skills needed for Britain to compete in the global economy.

In this view – known as 'new vocationalism' – the main function of education is to provide the economy with a skilled workforce. The result has been a variety of schemes and courses, including the Youth Training Scheme (YTS), apprenticeships, and NVQ and GNVQ courses, all designed to prepare young people for work. New Labour governments have also introduced other VET initiatives such as vocational A levels.

Criticisms of the new vocationalism

Marxists criticise new vocationalism. They argue that its true function is to serve the needs of capitalism at the expense of young people by reproducing existing inequalities.

For example, Phil Cohen (1984) argues that YTS serves capitalism by teaching young workers not genuine job skills, but the attitudes and values needed in a subordinate labour force. It lowers their aspirations so that they will accept low paid work. (See also Topic 6, pages 145-6 on Bowles and Gintis).

Similarly, Dan Finn (1987) argues that YTS provides cheap labour for employers, undermines trade union power, keeps the unemployment statistics down and reduces social unrest by taking youth off the streets.

Rob Strathdee (2003) concludes that New Labour's VET policy has not delivered a 'high-wage/high-skill society'. Rather, it continues to reproduce inequality by forcing working-class and ethnic minority students onto courses that lead to low paid, low status jobs. Meanwhile, middle-class students largely opt for academic courses.

Similarly, Carol Buswell (1987) found that YTS channels girls into traditional low paid women's employment such as retail work.

Evaluation of the functionalist perspective

- As Topics 1-4 show, there is evidence that equal opportunity in education does not exist. For example, achievement is greatly influenced by class background rather than ability.
- Melvin Tumin (1953) criticises Davis and Moore for putting forward a circular argument, as follows: How do we know that a job is important? Answer: because it's highly rewarded. Why are some jobs more highly rewarded than others? Answer: because they are more important!
- Functionalists see education as a process that instils the shared values of society as a whole, but Marxists argue that education in capitalist society only transmits the ideology of a minority – the ruling class.

- The interactionist Dennis Wrong (1961) argues that functionalists have an 'over-socialised view' of people as mere puppets of society. Functionalists wrongly imply that pupils passively accept all they are taught and never reject the school's values.
- Unlike Davis and Moore, the New Right argue that the state education system fails to prepare young people adequately for work. This is because state control of education discourages efficiency, competition and choice.

Activity

Critics argue that education is not meritocratic. Alone or in pairs, using your knowledge of class and ethnic differences in achievement (Topics 1-3), list some of the evidence in support of the critics' view.

The New Right perspective on education

The New Right is a conservative political perspective. However, its ideas have influenced both Labour and Conservative policies (see Box 14). A central principle of New Right thinking is the belief that the state cannot meet people's needs and that people are best left to meet their own needs through the free market. For this reason, the New Right favour the marketisation of education (see Topic 7, pages 152-3).

The New Right are similar in many ways to functionalists:

- They believe that some people are naturally more talented than others.
- They broadly favour an education system run on meritocratic principles of open competition, and one that serves the needs of the economy by preparing young people for work.
- They believe that education should socialise pupils into shared values, such as competition, and instil a sense of national identity.

However, a key difference with functionalism is that the New Right do not believe that the current education system is achieving these goals. The reason for its failure, in their view, is that it is run by the state.

The New Right argue that in all state education systems, politicians and educational bureaucrats use the power of the state to impose their view of what kind of schools we should have. The state takes a 'one size fits all' approach, imposing uniformity and disregarding local needs. The local consumers who use the schools – pupils, parents and employers – have no say. State education systems are therefore unresponsive and breed inefficiency. Schools that waste money or get poor results are not answerable to their consumers. This means

lower standards of achievement for pupils, a less qualified workforce and a less prosperous economy.

Box 14	Conservative party policy: education vouchers

In a speech in 2006, David Willetts MP, Conservative party spokesperson on education, outlined the case for education vouchers of the kind proposed by Chubb and Moe (page 142).

'Every MP must have had the experience of a parent turning up saying that they had chosen the best school for their child but then being told that the school wasn't able to let the child in. There is another approach, which appears to have great appeal because it trusts parents – introduce school vouchers. The idea is to empower parents to choose the good schools by giving them direct spending power.'

1. How would the introduction of a voucher system in the state sector make the state and private sectors more similar?

2. Critics argue that in reality those in deprived areas are unlikely to benefit from education vouchers. Suggest reasons why the well-off might benefit more.

The New Right's solution to these problems is the marketisation of education – creating an 'education market'. They believe that competition between schools and the laws of supply and demand will empower the consumers, bringing greater diversity, choice and efficiency to schools and increasing their ability to meet the needs of pupils, parents and employers.

Chubb and Moe: consumer choice

A good example of the New Right perspective on education comes from the work of the Americans, John Chubb and Terry Moe (1990). They argue that American state education has failed and they make the case for opening it up to market forces of supply and demand. They make a number of claims:

- Disadvantaged groups – the lower classes, ethnic and religious minorities and rural communities – have been badly served by state education. State education has failed to create equal opportunity.
- State education is inefficient because it fails to produce pupils with the skills needed by the economy.
- Private schools deliver higher quality education because, unlike state schools, they are answerable to paying consumers – the parents.

Chubb and Moe base their arguments on a comparison of the achievements of 60,000 pupils from low-income families in 1,015 state and private high schools, together with the findings of a parent survey and case studies of 'failing' schools apparently being 'turned around'. Their evidence shows that pupils from low-income families consistently do about 5% better in private schools.

Based on these findings, Chubb and Moe call for the introduction of a market system in state education that would put control in the hands of the consumers (parents and local communities). They argue that this would allow consumers to shape schools to meet their own needs and would improve quality and efficiency.

Methods Link: using surveys

Chubb and Moe carried out a survey of parental attitudes to schooling. Surveys involve asking people a fixed list of questions either through interviews or written questionnaires. This is a very quick way of collecting data from a large sample of people. Chubb and Moe chose this method so as to make generalisations about parents' views on the way schools should be run and on how much choice parents should have.

However, interpretivist sociologists argue that using a fixed list of questions imposes the researcher's meanings on respondents by limiting what answers they can give. Chubb and Moe's survey may thus have produced results that suited their New Right perspective.

Read more about surveys and researching education in *Methods in Context* on pages 191-3 and 202-5.

To introduce a market into state education, Chubb and Moe propose an end to the system where schools automatically receive guaranteed funding, regardless of how good or bad they are. Instead, they propose a system in which each family would be given a voucher to spend on buying education from a school of their choice. This would force schools to become more responsive to parents' wishes, since the vouchers would be the school's main source of income. Like private businesses, schools would have to compete to attract 'customers' by improving their 'product'.

These principles are already at work in the private education sector. In Chubb and Moe's view, educational standards would be greatly improved by introducing the same market forces into the state sector.

Two roles for the state

However, while the New Right stress the importance of market forces in education, this does not mean they see no role at all for the state. In the New Right view, there remain two important roles for the state.

- Firstly, the state imposes a framework on schools within which they have to compete. For example, by publishing Ofsted inspection reports and league tables of schools' exam results, the state gives parents information with which to make a more informed choice between schools.
- Secondly, the state ensures that schools transmit a shared culture. By imposing a single National Curriculum, it seeks to guarantee that schools socialise pupils into a single cultural heritage.

The New Right believe that education should affirm the national identity. For example, the curriculum should emphasise Britain's positive role in world history and teach British literature, and there should be a Christian act of worship in school each day because Christianity is Britain's main religion. The aim is to integrate pupils into a single set of traditions and cultural values. For this reason, the New Right also oppose multi-cultural education that reflects the cultures of the different minority groups in Britain.

Evaluation of the New Right perspective

- Gewirtz and Ball both argue that competition between schools benefits the middle class, who can use their cultural and economic capital to gain access to more desirable schools.
- Critics argue that the real cause of low educational standards is not state control but social inequality and inadequate funding of state schools.
- There is a contradiction between the New Right's support for parental choice on the one hand and the state imposing a compulsory national curriculum on all its schools on the other.
- Marxists argue that education does not impose a shared national culture, as the New Right argue, but imposes the culture of a dominant minority ruling class.

For more activities on The role of education (1) functionalism and the New Right...

Go to www.sociology.uk.net

Summary

Functionalists take a **consensus** view of the role of education. They see it as performing three important functions – **socialisation into the shared culture**, equipping individuals with **work skills** for the division of labour, and **selection for work roles**. Education is organised on **meritocratic** principles and rewards pupils' ability, not their social background.

The **New Right** take a **conservative** view. They believe education can only perform its role effectively if it is organised on market principles rather than run by the state. In their view, **marketisation** will increase **competition**, ensure **choice** and raise **standards**.

QuickCheck Questions

1 Explain the difference between ascribed status and achieved status.

2 Which type of status is found in meritocratic education systems?

3 Explain what is meant by 'particularistic standards'.

4 According to functionalists, how might pupils be 'sifted and sorted'?

5 What is 'new vocationalism'?

6 What was the 'Great Debate'?

7 Identify two ways in which New Right ideas are similar to those of functionalists.

8 Why do Chubb and Moe believe private education can deliver better quality and greater efficiency than state education?

Check your answers at www.sociology.uk.net

Examining the role of education (1) functionalism and the New Right

Item A   Functionalists take a very positive view of education. They see it as a form of secondary socialisation essential to the maintenance of society. It performs vital social functions, including transmitting shared norms and values and equipping pupils with the knowledge, skills and habits needed for work. School also acts as a bridge between the family and the world of work, reflecting the values of equal opportunity and individual achievement found in wider society. It gives everyone an equal chance of discovering and developing their talents. Education also sifts and sorts individuals, allocating them their future occupational roles on the basis of their ability   5 and effort and enabling the talented to become upwardly mobile.

(a) Explain what is meant by 'upwardly mobile' (**Item A**, line 6).   (2 marks)

(b) Suggest **three** criticisms of 'new vocationalism'.   (6 marks)

(c) Outline the New Right view of the role of education.   (12 marks)

(d) Using material from **Item A** and elsewhere, assess the contribution of functionalism to our understanding of the role of education.
     (20 marks)

The examiner's advice

Part (c) carries 8 AO1 marks (knowledge and understanding) and 4 AO2 marks (interpretation, application, analysis and evaluation). You should briefly identify the New Right's key ideas (e.g. reduced role of the state, marketisation, parental choice, raising standards through competition) and note their influence on government policy. Make reference to studies such as Chubb and Moe. You can evaluate New Right ideas by using studies such as Gewirtz and Ball, and the concept of cultural capital. You could compare the New Right view with functionalism.

Part (d) carries 8 AO1 marks and 12 AO2 marks. For this essay, you need to explain what functionalists have said about education and so you should look at a range of functions. Use Item A for clues about the different functions you could write about. 'Assess' means you need to evaluate, e g. by using criticisms from Tumin, Wrong, and especially Marxism (e.g. see Topic 6 dealing with Bowles and Gintis on the myth of meritocracy). Mentioning studies that show inequality of opportunity/under-achievement (e.g. from Topics 1 and 2 on class and achievement) is relevant if linked to meritocracy, but don't write long descriptions of these studies, as this will take you away from the question. Write a separate conclusion.

Topic 6 The role of education (2) Marxism

Where functionalists see society and education as based on value consensus, Marxists see it as based on class division and capitalist exploitation. Karl Marx (1818-83) described capitalism as a two-class system:

- **The capitalist class** or bourgeoisie are the minority class. They are the employers who own the means of production (land, factories, machinery, offices etc). They make their profits by exploiting the labour of the majority – the proletariat or working class.

- **The working class** are forced to sell their labour power to the capitalists since they own no means of production of their own and so have no other source of income. As a result, work under capitalism is poorly paid, alienating, unsatisfying, and something over which workers have no real control.

This creates the potential for class conflict. For example, if workers realise they are being exploited, they may demand higher wages, better working conditions or even the abolition of capitalism itself. Marx believed that ultimately the proletariat would unite to overthrow the capitalist system and create a classless, equal society.

However, despite this potential for revolution that capitalism contains, it is able to continue because the bourgeoisie also control the state. A key component of the state is the education system, and Marxists see education as functioning to prevent revolution and maintain capitalism.

Learning objectives

After studying this Topic, you should:

- Understand different Marxist views of the role of education, particularly the reproduction and legitimation of inequality.
- Be able to evaluate Marxist views of education.
- Understand the impact of the post-Fordist economy on the role of education.

Althusser: the ideological state apparatus

Marxists see the state as the means by which the capitalist ruling class maintain their dominant position. According to Louis Althusser (1971), the state consists of two elements or 'apparatuses', both of which serve to keep the bourgeoisie in power:

- **The repressive state apparatuses** (RSAs), which maintain the rule of the bourgeoisie by force or the threat of it. The RSAs include the police, courts and army. When necessary, they use physical coercion (force) to repress the working class.
- **The ideological state apparatuses** (ISAs), which maintain the rule of the bourgeoisie by controlling people's ideas, values and beliefs. The ISAs include religion, the mass media and the education system.

In Althusser's view, the education system is an important ISA. He argues that it performs two functions:

- Education **reproduces** class inequality by transmitting it from generation to generation, by failing each successive generation of working-class pupils in turn.
- Education **legitimates** (justifies) class inequality by producing ideologies (sets of ideas and beliefs) that disguise its true cause. The function of ideology is to persuade workers to accept that inequality is inevitable and that they deserve their subordinate position in society. If they accept these ideas, they are less likely to challenge or threaten capitalism.

Activity

In pairs, explain in your own words the following Marxist terms: (i) capitalism; (ii) means of production; (iii) reproduction of class inequality; (iv) ideology; (v) exploitation; (vi) ideological state apparatuses; (vii) proletariat; (viii) bourgeoisie; (ix) legitimation of class inequality.

Bowles and Gintis: schooling in capitalist America

The American Marxists Samuel Bowles and Herbert Gintis (1976) develop these ideas further. They argue that capitalism requires a workforce with the kind of attitudes, behaviour and personality-type suited to their role as alienated and exploited workers willing to accept hard work, low pay and orders from above. In the view of Bowles and Gintis, this is the role of the education system in capitalist society – to reproduce an obedient workforce that will accept inequality as inevitable.

From their own study of 237 New York high school students and the findings of other studies, Bowles and Gintis conclude that schools reward precisely the kind of personality traits that make for a submissive, compliant worker. For instance, they found that students who showed independence and creativity tended to gain low grades, while those who showed characteristics linked to obedience and discipline (such as punctuality) tended to gain high grades.

Bowles and Gintis conclude from this evidence that schooling helps to produce the obedient workers that capitalism needs. They do not believe that education fosters personal development. Rather, it stunts and distorts students' development.

Methods Link: using questionnaires

Bowles and Gintis measured students' personality traits using a questionnaire similar to those used to reveal the traits valued by employers. Bowles and Gintis compared their questionnaire results with students' school grade averages and exam scores. They found a correlation between personality traits valued by employers, such as docility, passivity and obedience, and high scores at school.

The questionnaire allowed Bowles and Gintis to study a large sample and to establish a correlation that supported their hypothesis (the existence of the correspondence principle). However, questionnaires about attitudes and personality traits may lack depth, and students who complete them may misunderstand the questions or not take them seriously.

Read more about questionnaires and researching education in **Methods in Context** on pages 191-3.

The correspondence principle and the hidden curriculum

Bowles and Gintis argue that there are close parallels between schooling and work in capitalist society. Both schools and workplaces are hierarchies, with head teachers or bosses at the top making decisions and giving orders, and workers or pupils at the bottom obeying. Box 15 shows some other ways in which school mirrors the workplace. As Bowles and Gintis put it, schooling takes place in 'the long shadow of work'.

Bowles and Gintis refer to these parallels between school and workplace as examples of the 'correspondence principle'. The relationships and structures found in education mirror or correspond to those of work.

Bowles and Gintis argue that the correspondence principle operates through the hidden curriculum – that is, all the 'lessons' that are learnt in school without being directly taught. For example, simply through the everyday workings of the school, pupils become accustomed to accepting hierarchy and competition, working for extrinsic rewards and so on.

In this way, schooling prepares working-class pupils for their role as the exploited workers of the future, reproducing the workforce capitalism needs and perpetuating class inequality from generation to generation. However, as Box 16 explains, postmodernist sociologists reject the idea of the correspondence principle.

The myth of meritocracy: the legitimation of class inequality

Because capitalist society is based on inequality, there is always a danger that the poor will feel that this inequality is undeserved and unfair, and that they will rebel against the system responsible for it. In Bowles and Gintis' view, the education system helps to prevent this from happening, by legitimating class inequalities. It does this by producing ideologies that explain and justify why inequality is fair, natural and inevitable.

Bowles and Gintis describe the education system as 'a giant myth-making machine'. A key myth that education promotes is the 'myth of meritocracy'. Meritocracy means that everyone has an equal opportunity to achieve, that rewards are based on ability and effort, and that those who gain the highest rewards deserve them because they are the most able and hardworking.

Unlike functionalists such as Parsons (see page 139), Bowles and Gintis argue that meritocracy does not in fact exist.

Evidence shows that the main factor determining whether or not someone has a high income is their family and class background, not their ability or educational achievement.

By disguising this fact, the myth of meritocracy serves to justify the privileges of the higher classes, making it seem that they gained them through open and fair competition at school. This helps persuade the working class to accept inequality as legitimate, and makes it less likely that they will seek to overthrow capitalism.

The education system also justifies poverty, through what Bowles and Gintis describe as the 'poor-are-dumb' theory of failure. It does so by blaming poverty on the individual ('I'm poor because I wasn't clever enough/didn't work hard enough at school'), rather than blaming capitalism. It therefore plays an important part in reconciling workers to their exploited position, making them less likely to rebel against the system.

Willis: learning to labour

All Marxists agree that capitalism cannot function without a workforce that is willing to accept exploitation. Likewise, all Marxists see education as reproducing and legitimating class inequality. That is, it ensures that working-class pupils are slotted into and learn to accept jobs that are poorly paid and alienating.

Box 15	The correspondence principle		
School in capitalist society	**reflects**	**work in capitalist society**	
Hierarchy of authority among teachers (e.g. head – deputy – classroom teacher) and between teachers and students	reflects	hierarchy of authority in the workplace (e.g. managers – supervisors – workers).	
Alienation through students' lack of control over education (e.g. over what to study, timetabling)	reflects	alienation through workers' lack of control over production (e.g. managers decide what, how, when and where to produce).	
Extrinsic satisfaction (rewards external to the work itself), e.g. from grades, rather than from interest in the subjects studied	reflects	extrinsic satisfaction, e.g. from pay, rather than from doing the job itself.	
Fragmentation and compartmentalisation of knowledge into unconnected subjects	reflects	fragmentation of work through the division of labour into small, meaningless tasks.	
Competition and divisions among students, e.g. to come top of class; to be in a higher stream	reflects	competition and divisions among the workforce, e.g. through differences in status and pay.	
Levels of education (streams, year groups) ■ lower levels: few choices; close supervision ■ higher levels: trusted to get on with work; self-directed learning	reflects	levels of the occupational structure ■ lower levels: workers closely supervised; given orders. ■ higher levels: workers internalise company's goals; self-supervision.	

Suggest ways in which lower ability and younger pupils are given fewer choices and supervised more closely.

Box 16 | **Post-Fordism and postmodernism**

Bowles and Gintis' correspondence principle states that school mirrors the workplace. Capitalism requires large numbers of low-skilled workers willing to put up with alienating, repetitive work on mass production assembly lines. This system is often called **Fordism** because the Ford Motor Company was the first to introduce it. Bowles and Gintis see the mass education system as preparing pupils to accept this kind of work.

However, postmodernists argue that the Marxist view is outdated. They claim that society has entered a new, postmodern, phase and is now fundamentally different from the modern society that both Marxists and functionalists have written about. Postmodernists reject the Marxist idea that we still live in a two-class society and the claim that education reproduces class inequality. They argue that class divisions are no longer important and that society is now much more diverse and fragmented.

Postmodernists argue that the economy has shifted away from assembly-line mass production and is now based on 'flexible specialisation', where production is customised for small specialist markets. This **post-Fordist** system requires a skilled, adaptable workforce able to use advanced technology and transfer their skills rapidly from one specialised task to another.

Post-Fordism calls for a different kind of education system. Instead of preparing pupils to be low-skilled, low-paid, obedient workers, education must encourage self-motivation, self-supervision and creativity. It must also provide lifelong retraining, because rapid technological change and intensified competition in the globalised economy constantly make existing skills obsolete. As a result, postmodernists argue, education has become more diverse and responsive to the needs of different individuals and groups. In their view, the correspondence principle no longer operates. Unlike Marxists, postmodernists argue that education reproduces diversity, not inequality.

1. Explain the difference between Fordist and post-Fordist production systems.

2. Why do postmodernists argue that post-Fordism needs a different type of education system from that described by the correspondence principle?

However, whereas Bowles and Gintis see education as a fairly straightforward process of indoctrination into the myth of meritocracy, Paul Willis' (1977) study shows that working-class pupils can resist such attempts to indoctrinate them.

As a Marxist, Willis is interested in the way schooling serves capitalism. However, he combines this with an interactionist approach that focuses on the meanings pupils give to their situation and how these enable them to resist indoctrination.

Using qualitative methods including participant observation and unstructured interviews, Willis studied the counter-school culture of 'the lads' – a group of 12 working-class boys – as they make the transition from school to work.

The lads form a distinct counter-culture opposed to the school. They are scornful of the conformist boys who they call the 'ear'oles' (so called because, unlike the lads, they listen to what the teachers tell them). The lads have their own brand of intimidatory humour, 'taking the piss' out of the ear'oles and girls.

The lads find school boring and meaningless and they flout its rules and values, for example by smoking and drinking, disrupting classes and playing truant. For the lads, such acts of defiance are ways of resisting the school. They reject as a 'con' the school's meritocratic ideology that working-class pupils can achieve middle-class jobs through hard work.

Willis notes the similarity between this anti-school counter-culture and the shopfloor culture of male manual workers. Both cultures see manual work as superior and intellectual work as inferior and effeminate. The lads identify strongly with male manual work and this explains why they see themselves as superior both to girls and to the 'effeminate' ear'oles who aspire to non-manual jobs.

However, it also explains why the lads' counter-culture of resistance to school helps them to slot into the very jobs – inferior in terms of skill, pay and conditions – that capitalism needs someone to perform. For example:

- Having been accustomed to boredom and to finding ways of amusing themselves in school, they don't expect satisfaction from work and are good at finding diversions to cope with the tedium of unskilled labour.
- Their acts of rebellion guarantee that they will end up in unskilled jobs, by ensuring their failure to gain worthwhile qualifications.

For Willis, the irony is that by helping them resist the school's ideology, the lads' counter-culture ensures that they are destined for the unskilled work that capitalism needs someone to perform.

Methods Link: group interviews

Willis carried out unstructured group interviews to uncover the counter-school culture of the 'lads'. These interviews allowed the lads to talk freely in their own words about the way they viewed school, teachers and work. The interviews gave Willis an insight into their world.

However, critics argue that unstructured group interviews are an unreliable method – they cannot be repeated in exactly the same way with other groups. Also, the meaning of what is said in a group interview is so open to the researcher's own biased interpretation that the results may be of little value.

Read more about interviews and researching education in *Methods in Context* on pages 202-5.

Evaluation of Marxist approaches

Marxist approaches are useful in exposing the 'myth of meritocracy'. They show the role that education plays as an ideological state apparatus, serving the interests of capitalism by reproducing and legitimating class inequality.

However, as Box 16 shows, postmodernists criticise Bowles and Gintis' correspondence principle on the grounds that today's post-Fordist economy requires schools to produce a very different kind of labour force from the one described by Marxists. Postmodernists argue that education now reproduces diversity, not inequality.

Marxists disagree with one another as to how reproduction and legitimation take place. Bowles and Gintis take a deterministic view. That is, they assume that pupils have no free will and passively accept indoctrination. This approach fails to explain why pupils ever reject the school's values.

By contrast, Willis rejects the view that school simply 'brainwashes' pupils into passively accepting their fate. By combining Marxist and interactionist approaches, he shows how pupils may resist the school and yet how this still leads them into working-class jobs.

However, critics argue that Willis' account of the 'lads' romanticises them, portraying them as working-class heroes despite their anti-social behaviour and sexist attitudes. His small-scale study of only 12 boys in one school is also unlikely to be representative of other pupils' experience and it would be risky to generalise his findings.

Critical modernists such as Raymond Morrow and Carlos Torres (1998) criticise Marxists for taking a 'class first' approach that sees class as the key inequality and ignores all other kinds. Instead, like postmodernists, Morrow and Torres argue that society is now more diverse. They see non-class inequalities, such as ethnicity, gender and sexuality, as equally important. They argue that sociologists must explain how education reproduces and legitimates all forms of inequality, not just class, and how the different forms of inequality are inter-related.

Feminists make a similar point. For example, as Madeleine MacDonald (1980) argues, Bowles and Gintis ignore the fact that schools reproduce not only capitalism, but patriarchy too. Similarly, as Angela McRobbie (1978) points out, females are largely absent from Willis' study.

However, Willis' work has stimulated a great deal of research into how education reproduces and legitimates other inequalities. For example, Paul Connolly (1998) explores how education reproduces both ethnic and gender inequalities. Other studies of the inter-relationships between different forms of inequality include Sewell, Evans and Mac an Ghaill (see pages 119-20, 122 and 135).

▲ *Fordism: assembly line mass production at the Ford plant in Detroit, Michigan, 1940. How typical is this of industry today?*

Activity

1 Write a short paragraph explaining in your own words:

   a how the counter-school culture enables the lads to resist the school's ideology

   b how the counter-school culture helps to reproduce class inequality.

2 Look back at the accounts of Epstein, Mac an Ghaill and Connolly (pages 122, 131 and 135) as well as Willis. Make a list of the different groups or types of boys referred to in these studies. What similarities can you see? Try to categorise them into two main sorts and make a list of the characteristics of each category.

Summary

Marxists take a **class conflict** approach. They see education as serving the **needs of capitalism. Althusser** sees education as an **ideological state apparatus** that **reproduces** and **legitimates class inequality**, ensuring working-class pupils end up in working-class jobs, and that they accept their exploited role. According to **Bowles and Gintis**, this is achieved through the **correspondence principle** and the **myth of meritocracy. Willis** combines Marxist and **interactionist** approaches to argue that, although pupils may **resist** indoctrination, their counter-school culture actually prepares them for unskilled labour.

Postmodernists take a **diversity** approach. They argue class is no longer important – society has become more diverse and **fragmented** and the economy has become **post-Fordist**. Education reflects these changes and is becoming more diverse and **flexible**.

QuickCheck Questions

1 Give two examples each of repressive and ideological state apparatuses.

2 Explain the difference between the reproduction of class inequality and the legitimation of class inequality.

3 Explain what Bowles and Gintis mean by the correspondence principle and give two examples of it.

4 How do Bowles and Gintis see education legitimating inequality?

5 Explain what is meant by 'post-Fordism'.

6 How does the critical modernist view of education differ from the Marxist view?

 Check your answers at www.sociology.uk.net

Examining the role of education (2) Marxism

Item A   Marxists take a critical view of the role of education. Capitalist society is essentially a two-class system, with a ruling class exploiting the working class. Marxists see education as being run in the interests of the ruling class.

For example, Althusser argues that education is an important ideological state apparatus that helps to control people's ideas and beliefs. He suggests education has two purposes. It reproduces class inequalities through the generations by ensuring that most working-class pupils experience educational failure. Education also legitimates this inequality, persuading the working class to accept educational and social inequalities. Other Marxists have also pointed to the existence of a hidden curriculum in schools.

5

(a) Explain what is meant by 'hidden curriculum' (**Item A**, line 6). (2 marks)

(b) Suggest **three** other institutions in society that might 'control people's ideas and beliefs' **apart from** education (**Item A**, line 3). (6 marks)

(c) Outline the postmodernist view of the role of education. (12 marks)

(d) Using material from **Item A** and elsewhere, assess the contribution of Marxism to our understanding of the role of education. (20 marks)

The examiner's advice

Part (c) carries 8 AO1 marks (knowledge and understanding) and 4 AO2 marks (interpretation, application, analysis and evaluation). You should briefly identify the key ideas of postmodernism (e.g. rejection of the Marxist correspondence principle, the post-Fordist economy, the view that education produces diversity rather than inequality). You can also note their influence on government policy, e.g. on diversity and choice (see Topic 7). You can evaluate postmodernism by comparing it with Bowles and Gintis or even the New Right.

Part (d) carries 8 AO1 marks and 12 AO2 marks. You need to show what different Marxists say about education. Use Item A for clues – e.g. about important concepts such as ideological state apparatuses and the reproduction and legitimation of inequality. Explain the differences between Marxists such as Althusser, Bowles and Gintis, and Willis. 'Assess' means you need to evaluate, e g. by using criticisms from postmodernists, critical modernists, feminists and functionalists. Using studies of inequality of opportunity and achievement from Topics 1 and 2 is relevant if linked to the reproduction of inequality, but don't write long descriptions of these studies, because this will take you away from the question. Write a separate conclusion.

Working-class pupils, Walsgrove Colliery School, Coventry, 1952

Topic 7 Educational policy and inequality

'Educational policy' refers to the plans and strategies for education introduced by government, for example through Acts of Parliament, together with instructions and recommendations to schools and local education authorities (LEAs).

Before the industrial revolution in the late 18th and early 19th centuries, there was no government educational policy or provision of state schools. Education was available only to a minority of the population. It was provided either by private tutors or fee-paying schools for the well off, or by the churches and charities for a few of the poor. Before 1833, the state spent no public money on education.

Since then, the state has become increasingly involved in education and its policies now have a major impact on pupils' opportunities and achievements.

Some educational policies have helped to reduce inequality of achievement. However, other policies have helped to maintain and justify class, gender and ethnic inequalities. This Topic examines the relationship between inequality and educational policy.

Learning objectives

After studying this Topic, you should:

- Know the main features of important educational policies, including the tripartite system, comprehensivisation and marketisation, and those relating to gender and ethnicity.

- Understand and be able to apply sociological perspectives to educational policies.

- Be able to evaluate the impact of educational policies on inequality of achievement.

The main phases of educational policy in Britain

Industrialisation increased the need for an educated workforce, and from the late 19th century the state began to become more involved in education. In this period, the type of education children received depended on their class background. Schooling did little to change pupils' ascribed status (the position they were born into). Middle-class pupils were given an academic curriculum to prepare them for careers in the professions or office work.

By contrast, working-class pupils were given a schooling to equip them with the basic numeracy and literacy skills needed for routine factory work and to instil in them an obedient attitude to their superiors. Reflecting the growing importance of education, the state made schooling compulsory from the ages of 5 to 13 in 1880 (rising to 16 by 1973).

Selection: the tripartite system

From 1944, education began to be shaped by the idea of meritocracy – that individuals should achieve their status in life through their own efforts and abilities, rather than it being ascribed at birth by their class background.

The 1944 Education Act brought in the tripartite system, so called because children were to be selected and allocated to one of three different types of secondary school, supposedly according to their aptitudes and abilities. These were to be identified by the eleven plus (11+) exam, which was taken by every child at age 11.

- **Grammar schools** offered an academic curriculum and access to non-manual jobs and higher education. They were for pupils with academic ability who passed the 11+. These pupils were mainly middle-class.
- **Secondary modern schools** offered a non-academic, 'practical' curriculum and access to manual work for pupils who failed the 11+. These pupils were mainly working-class.

(The third type, technical schools, existed in a few areas only, so in practice it was more a bipartite than a tripartite system.)

Thus, rather than promoting meritocracy, the tripartite system and 11+ *reproduced* class inequality by channelling the two social classes into two different types of school that offered unequal opportunities. The system also reproduced gender inequality by discriminating against girls, often requiring them to gain higher marks than boys in the 11+ to obtain a grammar school place.

The tripartite system also *legitimated* (justified) inequality through the ideology that ability is inborn rather than the product of the child's upbringing and environment. It was thus argued that ability could be identified early on in life, through the 11+. However, as we saw in Topics 1 and 2,

in reality children's class background greatly affects their chances of success at school.

Activity

Go to www.elevenplusadvice.co.uk

1 Which is the area nearest to you that still has the 11+?

2 What types of exams must be taken?

3 Try answering some of the sample questions provided on this website (click on 'eleven plus free sample questions', then on 'sample pages')

 Go to www.elevenplusadvice.co.uk

The comprehensive system

The comprehensive system was introduced in many areas from 1965 onwards. It aimed to overcome the class divide of the tripartite system and make education more meritocratic. The 11+ was abolished along with grammars and secondary moderns, to be replaced by comprehensive schools that all pupils within the area would attend.

However, although there is evidence that comprehensives helped to reduce the class gap in achievement, the system continued to reproduce class inequality, for two reasons.

- **Streaming:** many comprehensives were streamed into ability groups, with middle-class pupils placed in higher streams and working-class pupils in lower streams. As Douglas shows (see page 105), streaming may lead to a self-fulfilling prophecy in which the achievements of pupils in lower streams deteriorate and those in higher streams improve.
- **Labelling:** as Ball shows (see page 107), even where streaming is not present, teachers may continue to label working-class pupils negatively and restrict their opportunities.

Comprehensives also *legitimated* inequality, especially through the 'myth of meritocracy'. Because all pupils now went to the same kind of school, it made it appear that they all had an equal opportunity regardless of class background, when as we have seen, in reality this is not the case.

Because it was left to local education authorities (LEAs) to decide whether to 'go comprehensive' after 1965, not all did so, particularly where they were Conservative-controlled. As a result, the grammar-secondary modern divide still exists in many areas, and there are still 164 grammar schools remaining in England.

Many sociologists see educational policy as playing an important part in reproducing and legitimating inequality.

'Reproduction' means the way in which education recreates and maintains inequality from one generation to the next. Policies may do this by structuring the education system in ways that give some groups greater opportunities than others.

'Legitimation' means the way in which education justifies inequality. Educational policies may do this by making the education system and the inequality it produces appear fair and just, for example by making failure appear to be the fault of the individual rather than the system.

Marketisation and parentocracy

The 1988 Education Reform Act (ERA), introduced by the then Conservative government of Margaret Thatcher, established the principle of marketisation in education favoured by the New Right. From 1997, the New Labour governments of Tony Blair and Gordon Brown followed similar policies, emphasising standards, diversity and choice.

Marketisation refers to the process of introducing market forces of consumer choice and competition between suppliers into areas run by the state, such as education or the NHS. ERA created an 'education market' by:

- reducing direct state control over education
- increasing both competition between schools and parental choice of school.

As we saw in Topic 5, the New Right favour marketisation. They argue that state control leads to low standards, inefficiency and lack of choice for parents. By contrast, marketisation means that schools are run more like businesses that have to attract customers (parents) by competing with each other in the market. Schools that provide customers with what they want – such as success in exams – will thrive, and those that don't will 'go out of business'.

Miriam David (1993) describes this phase as a 'parentocracy' (literally, 'rule by parents'). This is because supporters of marketisation argue that in an education market, power shifts away from the producers (teachers and schools) to the consumers (parents). They claim that this encourages diversity among schools and gives parents more choice, meets the needs of different pupils, and raises standards.

▲ *Selection by mortgage? Not all parents can afford to move into the catchment area of a popular school.*

Policies to promote marketisation include:

- Publication of exam league tables and Ofsted inspection reports to give parents the information they need to choose the right school
- Business sponsorship of schools, e.g. city technology colleges
- Open enrolment, allowing successful schools to recruit more pupils
- Formula funding, where schools receive the same amount of funding for each pupil
- Schools being allowed to opt out of LEA control
- Schools having to compete to attract pupils.
- Some politicians have proposed educational vouchers (see Box 14 on page 141).

The reproduction of inequality

However, despite the claimed benefits of marketisation, its critics argue that it has increased inequalities between pupils, for example because middle-class parents are better placed to take advantage of the available choices.

Similarly, Stephen Ball (1994) and Geoff Whitty (1998) examine how marketisation *reproduces* and legitimates inequality. They argue that it reproduces inequality through:

- exam league tables
- the funding formula.

exam league tables

The policy of publishing each school's exam results in a league table ensures that schools which achieve good results are more in demand, because parents are attracted to those with good league table rankings. This allows these schools to be more selective and to recruit high achieving, mainly middle-class pupils. As a result, middle-class pupils get the best education.

For schools with poor league table positions, the opposite applies: they cannot afford to be selective and have to take less able, mainly working-class pupils, so their results are poorer and they remain unattractive to middle-class parents. The overall effect of league tables is thus to produce unequal schools that reproduce social class inequalities.

the funding formula

Schools are allocated funds by a formula based on how many pupils they attract. As a result, popular schools get more funds and so can afford better-qualified teachers and better facilities. Again, their popularity allows them to be more selective and attracts more able or ambitious, generally middle-class applicants.

On the other hand, unpopular schools lose income and find it difficult to match the teacher skills and facilities of their more successful rivals. Thus, popular schools with good

results and middle-class pupils thrive; unpopular schools fail to attract pupils and their funding is further reduced.

Methods Link: using documents

Educational policies are usually set out in official documents such as Acts of Parliament or government regulations and guidance issued to schools. This makes such documents a useful source of information about policies. Other documents include parliamentary debates and speeches by politicians. These can give us insight into the reasons for educational policies as well as criticisms of them.

However, documents do not tell the whole story about educational policies. Politicians try to present their policies in as favourable a way as possible, so documents need to be treated with care and not simply taken at face value. Furthermore, schools do not always carry out policies in the way government expects them to.

Read more about documents and researching education in *Methods in Context* on pages 227-8.

The myth of parentocracy

Not only does marketisation reproduce inequality; it also *legitimates* it by concealing its true causes and by justifying its existence.

Ball believes that marketisation gives the appearance of creating a 'parentocracy'. That is, the education system seems as if it is based on parents having a free choice of school. However, Ball argues that parentocracy is a myth, not a reality. It makes it appear that all parents have the same freedom to choose which school to send their children to.

In reality, however, as Gewirtz shows, middle-class parents have more economic and cultural capital and so are better able to take advantage of the choices available. For example, as Leech and Campos show, they can afford to move into the catchment areas of more desirable schools (see page 99).

By disguising the fact that schooling continues to reproduce class inequality in this way, the 'myth of parentocracy' makes inequality in education appear to be fair and inevitable.

---

1 Explain the difference between the 'myth of parentocracy' and Bowles and Gintis' 'myth of meritocracy'.

2 What similarity is there between these two 'myths'?

Activity

There are several other examples of educational policies elsewhere in this chapter. In small groups, re-read the sections on compensatory education (page 96), selection and segregation (page 121-2), equal opportunities and gender (page 127), and vocational education (page 140). How far does each policy reproduce and/or legitimate existing inequalities?

New Labour policies since 1997

Labour governments since 1997 have sought both to reduce inequality of achievement and promote greater diversity, choice and competition. They believed that achieving these goals would also make Britain more competitive in the global economy by turning the nation into a high skill, high wage society.

Reducing inequality

The Labour Party has traditionally had a strong focus on promoting equality. After 1997, Labour governments introduced several policies aimed specifically at reducing inequality in achievement by targeting support on disadvantaged groups. These include:

- Designating some deprived areas as Education Action Zones and providing them with additional resources.
- The Aim Higher programme to raise the aspirations of groups who are under-represented in higher education.
- Educational Maintenance Allowances (EMAs): payments to students from low-income backgrounds to encourage them to stay on after 16 to gain better qualifications.
- A proposal to raise the school leaving age to 18 by 2015, so that there would no longer be any 16-17 year old 'Neets' (those 'not in education, employment or training'). This group is largely working-class and unqualified.

Labour also introduced policies to raise achievement and standards more generally, such as the National Literacy Strategy, literacy and numeracy hours, and reducing primary school class sizes. It is claimed that these policies are of greater benefit to disadvantaged groups and so help reduce inequality.

Promoting diversity and choice

Labour governments since 1997 have also aimed to promote greater diversity and choice. For example, as the then Prime Minister Tony Blair said in 2002, education needs to move into the 'post-comprehensive' era. The existing 'one size fits all, mass production' education system run by bureaucrats from the centre would be scrapped. In its place would be a new system built around the aptitudes and needs of the individual child and where power is in the hands of the parents.

To promote diversity and choice, Labour introduced a number of policies. For example, secondary schools were encouraged to apply for specialist school status in particular curriculum areas. By 2007, about 85% of all secondary schools had become specialist schools. It is argued that this offers parents a greater choice and raises standards of achievement by enabling schools to build on their strengths.

There is some evidence that this has raised standards. Results in specialist schools have outstripped those in non-specialist schools. For example, in 2006, 59.5% of their pupils gained five GCSE grades A*-C, compared to only 47.6% in non-specialist schools. However, it is unclear whether this has reduced inequality between different social groups.

Labour has also promoted academies as a policy for raising achievement and plans to have 200 academies by 2010. Many of these are former comprehensives with poor results and mainly working-class pupils, and it is claimed that creating academies will raise their achievements. However, results have been mixed: in some academies, they have improved, but in others they have worsened.

Activity

Go to the website of the Specialist Schools and Academies Trust. Follow the icon links to Academies and CTCs.

1   Find out exactly what these are and why they were set up.

2   Follow a link to find out about the Academy and/or CTC nearest to your home.

Go to www.schoolsnetwork.org.uk

What similarities are there between the New Labour view of education and that of the New Right (see pages 141-2)?

Postmodernism and New Labour policies

Labour's policies to promote diversity and choice in part reflect ideas put forward by postmodernists. For example, Kenneth Thompson (1992) argues that in postmodern society, schools can break free from the 'oppressive uniformity' of the old centralised 'one size fits all' mass education system, where all schools were expected to be the same.

Instead, Thompson argues, education becomes 'customised' to meet the differing needs of diverse communities – for example, the growth of 'faith schools' for different religious groups and the growing demand for specialist schools in technology, languages and so on. Robin Usher (1997) puts forward a similar view in his comparison of modern and postmodern education systems (see Box 18).

However, critics of postmodernism argue that it exaggerates the extent of diversity in education. For example, the National Curriculum is a 'one size fits all', state-controlled curriculum that gives little scope for expressing minority ethnic cultures (see page 120). Critics also argue that postmodernism neglects the continuing importance of inequality in education.

Criticisms of New Labour policies

Critics such as Whitty (2002) see a contradiction between Labour's policies to tackle inequality and its commitment to marketisation. For example, while EMAs may encourage working-class students to stay on until they are 18, tuition fees for higher education may deter them from going to university. Whitty thus concludes that Labour's anti-inequality policies are merely 'cosmetic' – they present a positive image without actually reducing class inequalities.

Other critics point to the continued existence of both selective grammar schools and fee-paying private schools. Despite the Labour Party's long-standing opposition to private schools as bastions of middle- and upper-class privilege, Labour governments have neither abolished them nor removed the charitable status that reduces the amount of tax they have to pay. Polly Curtis (2007) estimates this to be worth £100 million per year. Similarly, while not allowing any new grammar schools, New Labour have not abolished existing ones.

However, while Whitty and others argue that Labour governments' commitment to marketisation has prevented them from tackling class inequalities, others disagree. For example, Paul Trowler (2003) points to policies such as increased funding of state education, raising standards and a focus on a 'learning society' as evidence of Labour's commitment to reducing educational inequality.

Policies relating to gender and ethnicity

So far we have focused largely on policies affecting class differences in achievement. However, policies can also have an impact on other differences in achievement, such as gender and ethnicity.

Gender

In the 19th century, females were largely excluded from higher education. More recently, under the tripartite system, girls often had to achieve a higher mark than boys in the 11+ in order to obtain a grammar school place.

Since the 1970s, however, policies such as Girls into Science and Technology have been introduced to reduce gender differences in subject choice. Further discussion of policies in relation to gender and achievement can be found in Topic 4, pages 127-9.

Ethnicity

There have also been policies aimed at raising the achievements of children from minority ethnic backgrounds. These policies have gone through several phases:

1 **Assimilation** policies in the 1960s and 70s focused on the need for pupils from minority ethnic groups to assimilate into mainstream British culture as a way of raising their achievement, especially by helping those for whom English was not their first language. A related policy is that of compensatory education (see page 96).

   However, critics argue that some minority groups who are at risk of under-achieving, such as African Caribbean pupils, already speak English and that the real cause of their under-achievement lies in poverty or racism.

2 **Multicultural education** (MCE) policies through the 1980s and into the 1990s aimed to promote the achievements of children from minority ethnic groups by valuing all cultures in the school curriculum, thereby raising minority pupils' self-esteem and achievements.

Box 18	Modern versus postmodern education systems

Robin Usher (1997) contrasts modern and postmodern education.

Education in modern society

- 'One size fits all' mass education
- Controlled centrally by the state
- Fixed in time and place, e.g. on school premises following a fixed timetable
- Only takes place during a fixed period of the individual's life
- Teacher-led – the learner passively absorbs knowledge from the teacher.

Education in postmodern society

- Diverse and customised to individual learners' needs
- Controlled locally by communities
- Flexible, e.g. distance learning via the Internet
- Lifelong learning – individuals constantly update their skills in response to the changing needs of the economy
- The learner is active and learns through their own experience.

Postmodernists relate these changes in education to changes in the economy and wider society – especially the trend towards 'post-Fordism' (see Box 16).

However, MCE has been criticised on several grounds:

- Maureen Stone (1981) argues that black pupils do not fail for lack of self-esteem, so MCE is misguided.

- Others argue that MCE is mere tokenism – 'saris, samosas and steel bands'. It picks out stereotypical features of minority cultures for inclusion in the curriculum, but fails to tackle institutional racism, which some see as the real cause of under-achievement.

- The New Right criticise MCE for perpetuating cultural divisions. They take the assimilationist view that education should teach a shared national culture and identity into which minorities should be assimilated.

3 Social inclusion of pupils from minority ethnic groups, and policies to raise their achievement, have been the focus since the late 1990s. Policies include:

- Detailed monitoring of exam results by ethnicity

- Amending the Race Relations Act to place a legal duty on schools to promote racial equality

- Help for voluntary 'Saturday schools' in the black community

- Continued funding of English as an Additional Language programmes.

However, Heidi Safia Mirza (2005) sees little genuine change in policy. She argues that, instead of tackling the structural causes of ethnic inequality such as poverty and racism, educational policy still takes a 'soft' approach that focuses on culture, behaviour and the home.

For example, 'there are schemes for motivational and personal development, projects on parenting skills, homework and breakfast clubs, writers' clubs' and so on. Mirza argues that, while these might make a small difference, they are short-term policies unlikely to have any lasting impact.

Activity

Government policies may have a number of aims. In pairs, decide which aim(s) each of the policies below has. Some may have more than one aim.

Policies: (a) parental choice; (b) Education Action Zones; (c) applied A levels; (d) specialist schools; (e) Aim Higher; (f) academies; (g) comprehensive schools; (h) YTS; (i) EMA; (j) league tables.

Aims: policies aimed at (1) reducing inequality; (2) improving achievement; (3) providing more choice; (4) improving vocational training.

For more activities on The role of education (2) Marxism...

Go to www.sociology.uk.net

Summary

Policies can have important effects on **inequalities** within the education system. Educational policy has gone through three main phases since 1944.

The first was the **tripartite system,** with selection at 11+ (based on the idea of innate ability) for either grammar or secondary modern school.

Comprehensivisation from 1965 abolished the 11+; all children went to comprehensive schools, but **streaming** continued.

Marketisation since 1988 aimed to create an education market, with parental choice and competition between schools.

New Labour policies after 1997 have largely maintained the policy of marketisation, while seeking to reduce educational disadvantage.

Some sociologists see all of these policies as **reproducing and legitimating inequality**. Some policies have aimed to deal with **gender** and **ethnic** differences in achievement.

QuickCheck Questions

1 In what way did the tripartite system reproduce class inequality?

2 Identify two reasons why comprehensivisation did not end educational inequality.

3 Explain how the idea that there is a 'parentocracy' legitimates inequality.

4 Explain why an 'education market' might raise educational standards.

5 Identify two policies that have helped to create an 'education market'.

6 Explain why New Labour policies to help disadvantaged groups and those to raise standards for all might be contradictory.

7 Explain what is meant by 'assimilation' policies in relation to ethnicity and education.

8 Suggest two criticisms of multicultural education policies.

Check your answers at www.sociology.uk.net

Examining educational policy and inequality

Item A Since the 1980s, both Conservative and Labour governments have developed marketisation policies in education. Marketisation is the process of introducing market forces of consumer choice and competition into the state education system. It is claimed that increasing both competition between schools and parental choice of school will drive up educational standards. Polices designed to create an education market in the UK include publishing exam league tables, open enrolment, formula funding and business sponsorship of schools.

5

However, critics of these polices argue that marketisation has increased class and ethnic inequalities in educational opportunity and achievement. In an education market, middle-class parents have the economic and cultural capital to secure educational advantages for their children.

(a) Explain what is meant by 'comprehensive education'. (2 marks)

(b) Suggest **three** policies that governments could introduce to improve the educational achievement of boys. (6 marks)

(c) Outline some of the policies that governments have introduced to reduce ethnic inequalities in educational achievement. (12 marks)

(d) Using material from **Item A** and elsewhere, assess the effects of policies 'designed to create an education market' in the United Kingdom. (20 marks)

The examiner's advice

Part (c) carries 8 AO1 marks (knowledge and understanding) and 4 AO2 marks (interpretation, application, analysis and evaluation). You should briefly identify the patterns and causes of ethnic differences in achievement (see Topic 3) and outline policies intended to deal with these, such as assimilation, multicultural education (MCE), compensatory education, ethnic monitoring, anti-racist legislation and additional funding. Include some analysis and/or evaluation, such as criticisms of MCE.

Part (d) carries 8 AO1 marks and 12 AO2 marks. You should explain the meaning of an 'education market'. Identify the aims of marketisation, linking them to New Right ideas about the role of the market versus the state. Use examples of policies from Item A and elsewhere (e.g. parental choice, education vouchers, specialist schools).

Evaluate their effects, for example in terms of the myth of parentocracy, the increased use of selection, the widening of class and ethnic differences in achievement, economic and cultural capital, the legitimation and reproduction of inequalities, raising standards, increasing diversity etc.

Exam question and student answer

Examining education

Item A Bowles and Gintis put forward a Marxist explanation of the role of education. They argue that its primary purpose is to reproduce a labour force for capitalism. It does this largely by virtue of the 'correspondence principle' – the idea that there is a close correspondence between the school and the workplace. For example, in schools there is a hierarchy of authority with the head teacher at the top and the youngest pupils at the bottom. In work, there is a similar hierarchy of bosses, managers and supervisors down through the different grades of workers. School accustoms pupils to the kinds of authority relationships, rewards and so on that they will have to accept in   5
work. This is achieved largely through the hidden curriculum rather than the official curriculum.

As Bowles and Gintis recognise, though, education not only performs a reproduction role. It can also legitimate the class inequality that it helps to reproduce. However, critics argue that Bowles and Gintis neglect the role of education in reproducing other, non-class inequalities.

(a) Explain what sociologists mean by 'deferred gratification'. (2 marks)

(b) Identify **three** factors that may explain the educational under-achievement of boys. (6 marks)

(c) Outline some of the ways in which processes within the education system may lead to differences in achievement between ethnic groups. (12 marks)

(d) Using material from **Item A** and elsewhere, assess the view that the role of education is "to reproduce a labour force for capitalism". (20 marks)

The examiner's advice

Part (c) carries 8 AO1 marks (knowledge and understanding) and 4 AO2 marks (interpretation, application, analysis and evaluation). Look at a range of processes that may cause differences in achievement, including some of the following: labelling, streaming, the self-fulfilling prophecy, anti-school subcultures, the ethnocentric curriculum, selection and segregation. Refer to some relevant studies, and distinguish between different ethnic groups. You could gain analysis and evaluation marks by noting the importance of class or gender differences within ethnic groups, or the role of home factors in causing differences in achievement.

Part (d) carries 8 AO1 marks and 12 AO2 marks. The view in the question is a Marxist one. Use Item A to help you summarise it – an outline of the correspondence principle would make a good start to your answer. You also need to evaluate, and you should use Item A here too – for example, you can develop the idea that education may legitimate as well as reproduce class inequalities (e.g. the myth of meritocracy). Develop evaluation further by using Willis to contrast with Bowles and Gintis, and by using non-Marxists to criticise the Marxist view. These include functionalist views of the role of education, as well as postmodernist views on the effects on education of the move to a post-Fordist economy. Write a separate conclusion reflecting on the view in the question, based on what you have written in your answer.

Activity

Here are two things you can do to practise your exam skills:

1   Attempt the whole question above. You could try doing it under timed conditions. If so, allow yourself 50 minutes to answer all four parts – plus an extra 10 minutes to study the examiner's advice on parts (c) and (d).

2   Read the student answer to part (d) below, together with Item A. Study the examiner's advice and comments. As you will see, this is a good answer – but it can be improved. Write a better version of it that takes on board the advice and comments. (You can copy any bits of the original that you want to keep.)

In both cases, make a brief plan. Try swopping your answer with a friend and marking each other's work, using the examiner's advice to help you.

For further exam practice, see Chapter 5, pages 242-4, where you will find mock exam papers for both AS units.

Answer by Laura

(d) As Item A states, Marxists argue that education functions to reproduce a labour force for capitalism. This is very different to functionalists, who see education as performing a beneficial role both for society and individuals.

> Linking the question's claim to a perspective is a good way to show a little analysis right from the start. The second sentence brings in some analysis too.

According to Bowles and Gintis, this involves two elements. One is the way education reproduces a labour force and the other is the way the resulting inequality is legitimated (justified). They argue that capitalism requires a workforce prepared to accept hard work, low pay and orders from above. Workers also need to believe the system is fair.

> Some analysis through showing two elements to the Marxist claim.

Bowles and Gintis claim that education performs these roles through the 'correspondence principle', where school mirrors capitalist work. There are important similarities between school and work. As Item A states, both are hierarchies, with heads or bosses at the top and workers/pupils below obeying. Schools are also like work because pupils/workers have no control over what they do, leading to alienation. The hidden curriculum also plays an important part in teaching pupils to accept the capitalist 'rules of the game'.

> The correspondence principle is a key concept and is explained clearly, which gains analysis marks – but the hidden curriculum and its role needs proper explanation.

For Bowles and Gintis, the education system also helps capitalism by legitimating inequality – producing ideologies to explain and justify it. Education is 'a giant myth-making machine' and the most important is the 'myth of meritocracy'. It claims to be meritocratic – people get rewarded on the basis of their ability and effort. However, they argue that meritocracy doesn't exist – the main factor determining whether someone succeeds is class background, not ability or educational achievement.

> More concepts and this time they are explained clearly.

Other Marxists note how educational policies reproduce and legitimate inequality. For example, the tripartite system resulted in working-class pupils having an inferior education that directed them into low-paid work, while middle-class pupils got an education preparing them for well-paid jobs. The system legitimated this inequality by making it seem that being in a secondary modern was the fault of the individual's own low ability, not the system.

> Good links into a Marxist analysis of the role of educational policy in reproducing and legitimating inequality.

However, not everyone agrees with Bowles and Gintis' views. Willis argues that working-class 'lads' see through the smokescreen of ideas that try to legitimate inequality. They create a counter-culture that challenges the school's dominant ideas. However, Willis accepts that the outcome is similar, as their anti-school behaviour guarantees they will end up in dead-end jobs.

> Appropriate use of Willis to evaluate Bowles and Gintis here.

Others reject the Marxist view almost entirely. Functionalists see education as genuinely meritocratic. Postmodernists reject the correspondence principle because in a post-Fordist economy, schools have to produce a very different kind of labour force from the one Marxists describe. They argue that education reproduces diversity. Marxists, however, counter by pointing out that diversity is code for inequality.

> Functionalist views could be more developed, but postmodernist views explained clearly.

Feminists criticise Marxists for over-emphasising class. Critical modernists such as Morrow and Torres criticise Marxists for taking a 'class first' approach and argue that education reproduces inequalities of gender, ethnicity and sexuality as well as class. These are also often inter-related.

> Further relevant criticism from other perspectives.

The examiner's comments

Laura's answer displays a good range of accurate and detailed knowledge. This includes different kinds of Marxism (Bowles and Gintis as well as Willis – though she should identify the latter as a Marxist view), as well as a range of other approaches (although she is quite brief on functionalism). She also makes an interesting link to the role of educational policy. She starts well, uses material appropriately from Item A – as instructed by the question – and her answer is conceptually and theoretically well developed. Most of the points she raises are explained rather than simply stated, as they would be in a weaker answer – showing good skills of analysis. However, some elements, such as the hidden curriculum, could be explained better. There is a lot of evaluation; however, this mainly comes in a section at the end of the answer. It would have been much more effective if she had introduced her evaluation at appropriate points throughout the answer. Although this is a very good response, she also needs to bring her answer together at the end in a meaningful conclusion.

Sociological Methods

with special application to education

CHAPTER 4

In the previous two chapters we looked at what sociologists have discovered in studying families and households, and education. But how exactly do sociologists study the topics they are interested in? In this chapter, we examine how sociologists go about investigating society.

The purpose of sociology is to answer questions about social life and the social world.

For example, why do middle-class children generally achieve better exam results than working-class children? What causes divorce? How far do the mass media influence people's behaviour?

To answer questions like these, sociologists develop **theories**. A theory is a general explanation of how or why social life follows the patterns it does.

A good theory is one that explains these patterns. That is, it explains all the available **evidence** that can be found about the topic being investigated. If a theory does not explain the evidence that we or others have gathered about the topic, we need to replace it with one that does.

Sociologists therefore try to ensure that their theories are based on sound evidence. To do otherwise would risk their work being discredited by other sociologists.

We thus need good, sound evidence to test our theories. But what **methods** can we use to obtain it? This chapter is concerned with the different methods sociologists use for collecting information about society, and with the issues we need to think about when deciding which methods to use.

The AQA Specification

The specification is the syllabus produced by the exam board, telling you what you have to study. The AQA specification for Sociological Methods requires you to examine the following:

- Quantitative and qualitative methods of research; their strengths and limitations; research design.

- Sources of data, including questionnaires, interviews, participant and non-participant observation, experiments, documents and official statistics; the strengths and limitations of these sources.

- The distinction between primary and secondary data, and between quantitative and qualitative data.

- The relationship between positivism, interpretivism and sociological methods; the nature of 'social facts'.

- The theoretical, practical and ethical considerations influencing choice of topic, choice of method(s) and the conduct of research.

For full details of the specification, visit: www.aqa.org.uk

What personal skills and characteristics might be useful for a researcher studying this group?

Topic 1 Choosing a research method

Sociologists use a range of different research methods and sources of data to collect information and test their theories. In this Topic, we shall identify the main methods and sources used in sociology. We shall also look at the different types of data that these methods produce.

We shall also examine the factors that influence sociologists' choice of what topic they research, and at some of the main practical, theoretical and ethical (moral) factors that affect their choice of which methods to employ.

Learning objectives

After studying this Topic, you should:

- Know what the main types of data are and what research methods sociologists use.

- Understand the practical, ethical and theoretical factors influencing choice of method and topic, and be able to assess their relative importance.

- Understand the difference between positivist and interpretivist approaches to research.

Types of data

Sociologists use a wide variety of different methods and sources to obtain data (information or evidence) about society. To make sense of this variety, we can classify them into:

- Primary and secondary sources of data.
- Quantitative and qualitative data.

Primary and secondary sources of data

Primary data is information collected by sociologists themselves for their own purposes. These purposes may be to obtain a first-hand 'picture' of a group or society, or to test a hypothesis (an untested theory).

Methods for gathering primary data include:

- **Social surveys**: these involve asking people questions in a written questionnaire or an interview.
- **Participant observation**: the sociologist joins in with the activities of the group he or she is studying.
- **Experiments**: sociologists rarely use laboratory experiments, but they sometimes use field experiments and the comparative method.

A big advantage of using primary data is that sociologists may be able to gather precisely the information they need to test their hypotheses. However, doing so can often be costly and time consuming.

Secondary data is information that has been collected or created by someone else for their own purposes, but which the sociologist can then use.

Sources of secondary data include:

- **Official statistics** produced by government on a wide range of issues, such as crime, divorce, health and unemployment, as well as other statistics produced by charities, businesses, churches and other organisations.
- **Documents** such as letters, diaries, photographs, official reports, novels, newspapers and television broadcasts.

Using secondary data can be a quick and cheap way of doing research, since someone else has already produced the information. However, those who produce it may not be interested in the same questions as sociologists, and so secondary sources may not provide exactly the information that sociologists need.

Quantitative and qualitative data

Quantitative data refers to information in a numerical form. Examples of quantitative data include official statistics on how many girls passed five or more GCSEs or on the percentage of marriages ending in divorce.

Similarly, information collected by opinion polls and market research surveys often comes in the form of quantitative data – for example, on the proportion of the electorate intending to vote for a particular party or how many people take holidays abroad.

Qualitative data, by contrast, gives a 'feel' for what something is like – for example, what it feels like to get good GCSE results, or for one's marriage to end in divorce. Evidence gathered by using participant observation aims to give us a sense of what it feels like to be a member of a particular group.

Similarly, in-depth interviews that probe deeply into a person's views can give us an insight into what it is like to be in that person's 'shoes'. These methods can provide rich descriptions of people's feelings and experiences.

Box 19	Some examples of types of data	
	Quantitative data	**Qualitative data**
Primary sources	Questionnaires	Participant observation
	Structured interviews	Unstructured interviews
Secondary sources	Official statistics	Letters, newspaper articles

Which of the four categories above does each of the following belong in?

(a) diaries   (c) opinion polls   (e) experiments

(b) websites   (d) photographs   (f) historical documents

Factors influencing choice of methods

Given the wide range of methods available, how do we select the right one for our research? Different methods and sources of data have different strengths and limitations and we need to be able to evaluate these when selecting which to use.

We can look at these strengths and limitations in terms of a number of practical, ethical (moral) and theoretical issues.

Practical issues

Different methods present different practical problems. These include:

time and money

Different methods require different amounts of time and money and this may influence the sociologist's choice.

For example, large-scale surveys may employ dozens of interviewers and data-inputting staff and cost a great deal of money. By contrast, a small-scale project involving a lone researcher using participant observation may be cheaper to carry out, but it can take several years to complete.

The researcher's access to resources can be a major factor in determining which methods they employ. A well-known professor will probably have access to more research funds than a young student, for example.

requirements of funding bodies

Research institutes, businesses and other organisations that provide the funding for research may require the results to be in a particular form.
For example, a government department funding research into educational achievement may have targets for pass rates and so require quantitative data to see whether these targets are being achieved. This means the sociologist will have to use a method capable of producing such data, such as questionnaires or structured interviews.

personal skills and characteristics

Each sociologist possesses different personal skills, and this may affect their ability to use different methods. For example, participant observation usually requires the ability to mix easily with others as well as good powers of observation and recall, while depth interviews call for an ability to establish a rapport (relationship of empathy and trust) with the interviewee. Not all sociologists have these qualities and so some may have difficulty using these methods.

subject matter

It may be much harder to study a particular group or subject by one method than by another. For example, it might prove difficult for a male sociologist to study an all-female group by means of participant observation, while written questionnaires may be useless for studying those who cannot read.

research opportunity

Sometimes the opportunity to carry out research occurs unexpectedly and this means that it may not be possible to use structured methods such as questionnaires, which take longer to prepare. For example, a Glasgow gang leader offered James Patrick (1973) the chance 'out of the blue' to spend time with his gang. With little time to prepare, Patrick had no option but to use participant observation. In other circumstances, the researcher might have been able to set up the research opportunity carefully beforehand and have plenty of time to select their methods.

▼ *Using secondary data from the Census saves sociologists time and money, but may not provide exactly the information they need.*

Ethical issues

Ethics refers to moral issues of right and wrong. Methods that sociologists use to study people may raise a range of ethical questions. The British Sociological Association sets out guidelines for the conduct of research, including the following principles.

informed consent

Research participants (the people being studied) should be offered the right to refuse. The researcher should also tell them about all relevant aspects of the research so that they can make a fully informed decision. Consent should be obtained before research begins and, if the study is lengthy, again at intervals throughout the process.

confidentiality and privacy

Researchers should keep the identity of research participants secret in order to help to prevent possible negative effects on them. Researchers should also respect the privacy of research participants. Personal information concerning research participants should be kept confidential.

effects on research participants

Researchers need to be aware of the possible effects of their work on those they study. These could include police intervention, harm to employment prospects, social exclusion and psychological damage. Wherever possible, researchers should try to anticipate and prevent such harmful effects.

vulnerable groups

Special care should be taken where research participants are particularly vulnerable because of their age, disability, or physical or mental health.

For example, when studying children in schools, researchers should have regard for issues of child protection. They should obtain the consent of both the child and the parent, and they should provide information in language that the child can understand. (See page 169 for other ethical problems of studying children in schools.)

covert research

Covert research is when the researcher's identity and research purpose are hidden from the people being studied. This can create serious ethical problems, such as deceiving or lying to people in order to win their trust or obtain information. Clearly, it is impossible to gain informed consent while at the same time keeping the research or its purpose secret.

However, some sociologists argue that the use of covert methods may be justified in certain circumstances. These may include gaining access to areas of social life closed to investigation by secretive, deviant or powerful groups.

Activity

Go to the website of the British Sociological Association and follow the link to their Statement of Ethical Practice. In that statement, find examples of circumstances where it is acceptable to ignore any of the ethical principles listed above.

www.britsoc.co.uk

Theoretical issues

This refers to questions about what we think society is like and whether we can obtain an accurate, truthful picture of it. Our views on these issues will affect the kinds of methods we favour using.

validity

A valid method is one that produces a true or genuine picture of what something is really like. It allows the researcher to get closer to the truth.

Many sociologists argue that qualitative methods such as participant observation give us a more valid or truthful account of what it is like to be a member of a group than quantitative methods such as questionnaires can. This is because participant observation can give us a deeper insight through first hand experience.

reliability

Another word for reliability is replicability. A replica is an exact copy of something, so a reliable method is one which, when repeated by another researcher, gives the same results.

For example, in physics or chemistry, different researchers can repeat the same experiment and obtain the same results every time. In sociology, quantitative methods such as written questionnaires tend to produce more reliable results than qualitative methods such as unstructured interviews.

Which of the two statements below is an example of validity and which of reliability?

Give reasons for your answers.

1 A friend of mine was bullied at school recently. He told me in detail all about his feelings at the time and afterwards. Now I really understand what it must be like.

2 We were all given an intelligence test every day this week. Our results were very consistent. Each of us gained the same score every time we took the test.

representativeness

Representativeness refers to whether or not the people we study are a typical cross-section of the group we are interested in. Imagine for example that we want to know about the effects of divorce on children. It would take a great deal of time and money to study every child of divorced parents, and we might only be able to afford to study a sample of, say, 100 such children.

However, if we ensure that our sample is representative or typical of the wider population, we can then use our findings to make generalisations about all children of divorced parents, without actually having to study all of them.

Large-scale quantitative surveys that use sophisticated sampling techniques to select their sample (see pages 184-5) are more likely to produce representative data.

methodological perspective

Sociologists' choice of method is also influenced by their methodological perspective – their view of what society is like and how we should study it. There are two contrasting perspectives on the choice of methods: positivism and interpretivism.

Positivists

- Prefer quantitative data
- Seek to discover patterns of behaviour
- See sociology as a science.

Interpretivists

- Prefer qualitative data
- Seek to understand social actors' meanings
- Reject the view that sociology is a science

Box 20 explains more fully why positivists and interpretivists prefer different types of methods and data.

Functionalists and Marxists often take a positivist approach. They see society as a large-scale (macro-level) structure that shapes our behaviour. By contrast, interactionists favour an interpretivist approach. They take a micro-level view of society, focusing on small-scale, face-to-face interactions.

The sociologist's theoretical perspective is usually the most important factor when choosing which method to use. Whenever possible, they will want to obtain the type of data – quantitative or qualitative – that their perspective views as most appropriate.

However, practical and ethical factors usually limit the choice of method. Just because a sociologist prefers a particular kind of data, doesn't mean that they can simply go ahead and gather it. Time, resources, access, consent, privacy and so on are all constraints on their choice.

Finally, even sheer chance may determine the method used. For example, David Tuckett (2001) describes how one postgraduate sociology student found himself taken ill with tuberculosis and confined to a hospital ward, so he used this as an opportunity to conduct a participant observation study.

Box 20	Why do positivists and interpretivists prefer different types of data?

Positivists and interpretivists collect and use different types of data: positivists prefer quantitative data, while interpretivists prefer qualitative. This is because they make different assumptions about the nature of society and how we should study it.

- **Positivists** assume that society has an objective factual reality – it exists 'out there', just like the physical world.

  ↓

- Society exerts an influence over its members, systematically shaping their behaviour patterns.

  ↓

- Positivist research uses quantitative data to uncover and measure these patterns of behaviour.

  ↓

- By analysing quantitative data, positivists seek to discover the objective scientific laws of cause and effect that determine behaviour.

  ↓

- Positivists thus prefer questionnaires, structured interviews, experiments and official statistics. These produce data that is both reliable and representative.

- **Interpretivists** reject the idea of an objective social reality – we construct reality through the meanings we create in our interactions with others.

  ↓

- Our actions are based on the meanings we give to situations, not the product of external forces.

  ↓

- Interpretivist research uses qualitative data to uncover and describe the social actor's 'universe of meaning'.

  ↓

- By interpreting qualitative data, interpretivists seek to gain a subjective understanding of actors' meanings and 'life worlds'.

  ↓

- Interpretivists thus prefer participant observation, unstructured interviews, and personal documents. These produce data that is valid.

Choice of topic

Before choosing which method to use, sociologists need to decide what topic they wish to study. Several factors influence their choice.

theoretical perspective

The sociologist's theoretical perspective is a major influence upon their choice of research topic. For example, a New Right researcher may study the effects of welfare benefits on the growth of lone-parent families, since the idea of welfare dependency is central to their standpoint. By contrast, a feminist researcher is more likely to choose to study domestic violence, as opposition to gender oppression lies at the heart of feminist theory.

society's values

Sociologists themselves are part of the society they study and thus are influenced by its values. As these values change, so does the focus of research. The rise of feminism in the 1960s and 1970s led to a focus on gender inequality and the environmentalist concerns of the 21st century have generated interest in 'green crimes' such as serious pollution or the unlawful transport of nuclear material.

funding bodies

Most research requires funding from an external body. These bodies include government agencies, charitable organisations and businesses. As the funding body is paying for the research, it will determine the topic to be investigated. For example, one of the major social concerns of New Labour governments after 1997 was the 'social exclusion' of some disadvantaged groups. As a result, government departments were keen to fund research projects to investigate the causes and effects of social exclusion.

practical factors

Practical factors, such as the inaccessibility of certain situations to the researcher, may also restrict what topic they are able to study. For example, although sociologists may wish to study the ways in which global corporations make their decisions, this may not be possible because these are made in secrecy.

For more activities on Choosing a research method...

 Go to www.sociology.uk.net

Summary

Sociologists test their theories using **quantitative** or **qualitative** data. Sociologists obtain **primary** data themselves, using methods including questionnaires, interviews and observation. **Secondary** data are produced by others but used by sociologists.

In choosing a method, sociologists take several issues into account:

- **Practical** issues include time and funding.

- **Ethical** issues include whether the researcher deceives the subjects.

- **Theoretical** issues include **validity** (does the method give a truthful picture?), **reliability** (can it be replicated?) and **representativeness** (does it study a typical cross-section?).

Perspective also affects choice of method. **Positivists** prefer **quantitative** data; **interpretivists** favour **qualitative** data. Choice of **topic** is also affected by society's values and funding bodies.

QuickCheck Questions

1. Explain the difference between (a) quantitative and qualitative data (b) primary and secondary sources of data.

2. Give one example of (a) a primary method that produces quantitative data (b) a secondary source that gives qualitative data.

3. Identify two ethical issues that sociologists may face in studying people.

4. True or false? If a method is reliable then if another researcher uses it they should get the same results.

5. What does 'validity' mean?

6. Name two practical issues that might affect a researcher's choice of method.

7. True or false? Positivists (a) see sociology as a science (b) prefer qualitative data.

 Check your answers at www.sociology.uk.net

What differences are there between studying schoolchildren and adults?

Topic 2 Education: the research context

As we saw in Chapter 3, sociologists have studied many different issues in education, such as classroom interaction, pupil subcultures, teacher labelling, parental choice and so on.

In studying these and other educational issues, sociologists need to take account of the particular characteristics of education, since these will affect their choice of research method.

For example, in studying pupil subcultures, there might be problems using covert participant observation, simply because it would prove very difficult for a researcher to pass themselves off as a pupil. Similarly, in studying parental attitudes to schooling, there might be difficulties in using written questionnaires to discover the opinions of parents who are illiterate or whose first language is not English.

In this Topic, we examine some of the key characteristics of education as an area of research for sociologists, and we look at the kinds of opportunities and problems that these characteristics can present to the researcher. From this, you will be able to see the kinds of issues that you need to take account of when using different methods to research educational issues.

This will help you to prepare for the ***Methods in Context*** question in the AS Unit 2 exam. In this exam, you are required to apply a given research method to a particular issue in education, such as gender and subject choice, pupil subcultures, class and achievement and so on.

Throughout the rest of this chapter, we will be applying each of the different research methods we look at to the study of education. You will find this in the special ***Methods in Context*** sections at the end of each Topic.

Learning objectives

After studying this Topic, you should:

- Know the main characteristics of education as a context for sociological research.
- Understand some of the problems and opportunities that researching educational issues presents for sociologists.
- Be aware of some of the research strategies sociologists use to investigate education.

Researching education

We can identify the following five characteristics of education as an area for research.

1 Pupils

2 Teachers

3 Parents

4 Classrooms

5 Schools

Each of these presents particular problems and opportunities for the sociologist in choosing a suitable method to use. We shall examine each of these characteristics in turn.

1 Researching pupils

In education, many of the people sociologists study are children and young people – pupils and students. There are three major differences between studying young people and studying adults: power and status; ability, and vulnerability and ethical issues. We shall examine each of these in turn.

power and status

In school contexts, children and young people have less power and status than adults. This makes it more difficult for them to state their views openly, especially if these challenge adult opinions. This is further reinforced by the nature of schools as hierarchical institutions, which gives teachers status and power over pupils.

Researchers therefore have to consider ways in which they can overcome the power differences between adult researchers and young participants. For example, group interviews rather than formal one-to-one interviews may be a good way of doing this.

However, it is likely that whatever research methods are used, some power and status differences between researchers and pupils will remain.

ability

Pupils' vocabulary, powers of self-expression, thinking skills and confidence are likely to be more limited than those of adults – particularly when trying to express abstract ideas. Given that abstract concepts are a central part of sociological investigation, this poses problems for researchers. For example, the sociologist will need to take great care in how they word their questions to make sure they are understood clearly.

Limitations in pupils' understanding also make it more difficult to gain their informed consent. This is because the sociologist may not be able to explain the nature of the research in words that they can clearly understand.

vulnerability and ethical issues

As a result of their more limited power and ability, young people are often more vulnerable to physical and psychological harm than adults. This raises ethical issues for the researcher.

It is not enough simply to obtain the informed consent of parents or teachers. Most research guidelines emphasise that the young person too should be aware of what the research entails. However, it may be difficult to explain this to a child, and they may not yet be mature enough to make the moral choice to participate.

Given the vulnerability of school-age pupils, child protection issues are very important. For example, personal data should not be kept unless it is vital to the research.

The researcher should also consider the form that participation will take and any stress that may result. For example, questioning young children for long periods of time would be considered inappropriate.

Finally, the researcher must consider whether the participation of young people in the research is actually necessary and whether they stand to benefit from it.

As a result of these concerns, organisations such as UNICEF, Barnardo's and the National Children's Bureau have developed special codes of practice for researching young people. These take the British Sociological Association's research guidelines even further in terms of protecting the rights of children.

There are also practical issues involved in researching young people in education. They are likely to require more time than adults to understand questions. Given children's greater vulnerability, it is even more important to establish rapport and gain trust. It may also be important to match the gender and ethnicity of the young person and the researcher to help to achieve this.

1 If an outsider rather than a teacher carried out interviews with a class of 14-year-olds about their attitudes to school, how do you think their results might differ, and why?

2 Whose prior consent would you need to obtain if you wanted to observe the play and relationships of children in a playgroup or nursery? How much would you need to tell them about your research?

| Box 21 | The sociologist's own experience of education |

Everybody – including researchers – has had experience of education. Researchers can draw on their own experience of education in formulating hypotheses, interpreting data etc.

However, sociologists' personal experience and familiarity with classrooms and schools can dull their awareness of just how different these are to other social settings. Because sociologists have spent years in schools and colleges, these places may seem 'natural' to them. Thus, when carrying out research, we need to be aware of our taken-for-granted assumptions about schools and classrooms, teachers and pupils.

Likewise, the fact that the researcher has probably been quite successful in education may make it difficult for them to empathise with the experience or world-view of students in an under-achieving, anti-school subculture.

2 Researching teachers

Power relationships in the school are not equal. Teachers have more power and status because of their age, experience and responsibility within the school. They also have legal responsibilities and a duty of care towards the young people they teach.

The nature of the classroom reinforces the power of the teacher. Teachers often see it as 'my classroom', in which the researcher may be viewed as a trespasser. However, teachers are not fully independent, even in 'their' classroom. Heads, governors, parents and pupils all constrain what teachers may do.

Teachers are often over-worked and may be less than fully cooperative, even when they want to be helpful. This may mean that interviews and questionnaires need to be kept short, and this may restrict the amount of data that can be gathered.

Teachers are used to being inspected and scrutinised. They are experienced enough to be able to 'put on a show' for the researcher so as to create the best possible impression.

3 Researching classrooms

The classroom is unusual in being a closed, highly controlled social setting. It has clear boundaries, and restrictions on access and behaviour. Although not as closed as a prison or psychiatric ward, the classroom is less open than most settings such as leisure centres or shops. For example, the teacher and the school control time, behaviour, noise, dress, language and the layout of the classroom. Young people rarely experience this level of control in other areas of their lives.

In classroom interactions, teachers and pupils are very experienced at disguising their real thoughts and feelings from each other; they may conceal these from the researcher too.

Young people in school-based groups such as classes and friendship groups may be more sensitive to peer pressure and the need to conform, and this may affect the way they respond to being researched. It may therefore be important for example to supervise pupils when they are filling in questionnaires, especially if this is done in class.

4 Researching schools

Educational establishments are formal organisations with rules and hierarchies. Researchers may come to be seen as part of the hierarchy. For example, students may see them as teachers, while teachers may see them as inspectors. In schools where there is conflict, for example between students and teachers, researchers may even be seen as 'the enemy'.

Head teachers have a great deal of power, including the power to refuse the researcher access to the school. Heads and governors may refuse permission if they believe that the research will interfere with the work of the school. Roland Meighan (1981) found that heads sometimes viewed research negatively. Their reactions to a research project he wanted to carry out on consulting pupils about teaching included:

- 'It is dangerous to involve pupils in commenting on their teachers'.

◀ *A closed institution. What are the similarities and the differences between prisons and schools? How may these affect research?*

- 'Discipline would be adversely affected'.
- 'It would be bad for classroom relationships'.
- 'Children are not competent to judge teachers'.

Schools operate within a particular legal framework. For example, the law requires them to collect information on pupils' attendance, achievement and so on, and this may be useful to sociologists. On the other hand, the legal duty of care that schools have towards their pupils may mean that researchers' access to them is restricted.

Some situations and school settings may be 'off limits' to a researcher – for example, head teachers' interviews with parents. Beynon and Atkinson (1984) noted that gatekeepers such as heads often steer the researcher away from sensitive situations, such as classes where the teacher has poor classroom control.

Education is under close scrutiny by the media, parents and politicians. Partly as a result, there is a great deal of publicly available information about it. This includes exam results and league tables; figures on truancy, subject choices etc; Ofsted reports; government inquiries and school policy documents. Schools also produce large quantities of more personal documents such as students' reports.

Sociologists may be able to make use of all these secondary sources in their research. However, school records are confidential and researchers may not be able to gain access to them.

Unlike most other organisations in today's society, many schools are single-sex. This may pose problems where the researcher is of a different sex from the pupils.

Schools operate to a daily and yearly timetable. This may affect when and how research can be carried out.

The law requires young people to be educated, usually meaning they have to attend school. The only other major institution whose inmates have no choice about being there is the prison system. Having a 'captive population' to study has both advantages and disadvantages for the researcher.

5 Researching parents

Parents may influence what goes on in education, both by the way they bring up their children and by their involvement in school through parent-teacher contacts, parent governors, attendance at parents' evenings and so on. Marketisation policies also encourage parents to see themselves as consumers, for example in choice of school.

However, unlike most other important groups within education, parents are unusual in that they are for the most part physically outside the school. This may make them more difficult to contact and research. For example, while classroom interactions between teachers and pupils can often be observed easily, there are few opportunities to observe whether parents help children with their homework.

The social class and ethnicity of parents play a very important role within schooling. Unfortunately, however, class and ethnic differences between sociologists and some parents may be a barrier to researching this issue.

Some parents may be more willing to participate in research. For example, middle-class parents who are more pro-school may be more likely than working-class parents to return questionnaires about their children's education and this will make the research findings unrepresentative.

Activity

We can identify themes running through the Topic you have just read. These include:

1 legal issues (e.g. schools are legally responsible for pupils' welfare while in school)

2 ethics (e.g. the greater vulnerability of young people)

3 problems of access

4 power relationships

5 availability of secondary data.

In groups of three or four, draw up a chart using these five themes. Now go through the Topic and find as many examples of each theme as you can. Add any other examples from your own knowledge of education. Report back to the rest of the class.

For more activities on Education – the research context...

Go to www.sociology.uk.net

Summary

Education is a research context with many distinctive characteristics. For example, the need to protect **pupils** poses ethical problems. **Classrooms** are highly controlled settings and this may make it difficult to uncover real attitudes. **Teachers** are accustomed to being observed and may 'put on a show' when being studied. **Schools** are closed, hierarchical organisations and this may make access difficult. **Parents** may be difficult to contact without the school's cooperation.

QuickCheck Questions

1 Suggest two ways in which the classroom may be a closed social setting.

2 Identify three characteristics of young people that may make them more difficult to study.

3 Suggest two barriers that sociologists may face when seeking to carry out research in schools.

Check your answers at www.sociology.uk.net

Topic 3 Experiments

Learning objectives

After studying this Topic, you should:

- Know the similarities and differences between different types of experiments.
- Be able to evaluate the strengths and limitations of experiments.
- Be able to apply your understanding of experiments to the study of education.

In the natural sciences such as chemistry and biology, scientists set out to discover scientific laws of cause-and-effect. For example, physicists have discovered that an increase in the temperature of a gas will cause it to expand.

The method favoured by natural scientists for discovering these laws is the laboratory experiment. The laboratory is an artificial environment in which the scientist can control all the different variables (factors that can vary, such as temperature) to see what effect they have.

Sociologists have occasionally used the laboratory experiment as a way of studying human behaviour. In fact, however, this is just one of three different types of experimental method that sociologists have sometimes used in their research. These are:

- **Laboratory experiments**
- **Field experiments**
- **The comparative method**

In this Topic, we shall examine these different forms of experiment and their strengths and limitations as ways of investigating the social world.

Laboratory Experiments

An example will help to illustrate the basic principle of the experimental method. Suppose we want to discover what causes plants to grow. One way would be to take a set of identical plants and randomly divide them into two groups – an experimental group and a control group. We then treat them differently, as follows:

- **The experimental group:** with this group, we might vary the quantity of nutrients that they received, carefully measuring and recording any changes in the plants' size that we observe.
- **The control group:** with this group, we would keep the quantity of nutrients constant, also measuring and recording any changes in the size of the plants.

On comparing the results, we notice that the plants in the experimental group have grown more rapidly than the plants in the control group after receiving extra nutrients. In other words, we may have discovered a cause-and-effect relationship: nutrients cause growth.

In scientific terms, the nutrient is the independent variable (the causal factor) and the resulting growth is the effect or dependent variable (since it depends on the first variable, nutrition).

The logic of the experimental method is that the scientist manipulates (alters) the variables in which they are interested, in order to discover what effect they have. By following this method, the scientist can establish a cause-and-effect relationship. In turn, this will allow them to predict accurately what will happen in the future under specified conditions. In our example, the scientist will be able to predict what will happen when a certain quantity of nutrient is given to the plants.

Reliability

Once an experiment has been conducted, other scientists can then replicate it. That is, they can repeat it exactly in every detail. The laboratory experiment is therefore highly reliable, producing the same results each time, for two reasons:

- The original experimenter can specify precisely what steps were followed in the original experiment so other researchers can repeat these in future.
- It is a very detached method: the researcher merely manipulates the variables and records the results. The scientist's personal feelings and opinions have no effect on the conduct or outcome of the experiment.

The laboratory experiment therefore has major advantages as the method used to identify cause-and-effect relationships in the natural sciences. For this reason, we

might expect positivist sociologists to use laboratory experiments, since they favour a scientific approach. Despite this, however, there are several reasons why such experiments are rarely used in sociology, even by positivists.

Box 22 | **Positivism, interpretivism and experiments**

Positivists favour the *laboratory* experiment in principle because it achieves their main goal of reliability:

- Careful control over experimental conditions and experimenter detachment produce reliable data because other researchers can replicate the experiment.
- It allows the researcher to identify and measure behaviour patterns quantitatively and to manipulate variables to establish cause-and-effect relationships.

However, positivists recognise the shortcomings of laboratory experiments:

- It is often impossible or unethical to control the variables.
- Their small scale means that results may not be representative or generalisable.

For these reasons, positivists sometimes use the *comparative method* instead.

Interpretivists reject the laboratory experiment because it fails to achieve their main goal of validity. It is an artificial situation producing unnatural behaviour. Interpretivists favour more naturalistic field experiments, but positivists criticise this method for reducing control over variables.

See Box 20 on page 166 for more about positivism, interpretivism and research methods.

Practical problems

Society is a very complex phenomenon. In practice, it would be impossible to identify, let alone control, all the variables that might exert an influence on, say, a child's educational achievement or a worker's attitude to work.

Another practical problem is that the laboratory experiment cannot be used to study the past, since by definition it is impossible to control variables that were acting in the past rather than the present.

In addition, laboratory experiments usually only study small samples. This makes it very difficult to investigate large-scale social phenomena such as religions or voting patterns. The small-scale nature of laboratory experiments also reduces their representativeness.

Ethical problems

There are ethical (moral) objections to conducting experiments on human beings, at least under certain circumstances. As a general principle, the researcher needs the informed consent of the research participants.

However, this may be difficult to obtain from groups such as children or people with learning difficulties who may be unable to understand the nature and purpose of the experiment.

It is also generally considered wrong to mislead people as to the nature of the experiment, as Stanley Milgram (1974) did in his famous studies of obedience to authority.

Milgram lied to his subjects about the purpose of the research, telling them that they were assisting in an experiment on learning, in which they were told by the researcher to administer electric shocks when the learner failed to answer questions correctly.

In reality, however, the purpose of the experiment was to test people's willingness to obey orders to inflict pain. Unbeknown to Milgram's subjects, no electric shocks were actually used. Milgram found that 65 per cent of them were prepared to administer shocks of 450 volts.

The experiment may also cause harm to the participants. For example, in Milgram's experiments, many research participants were observed to "sweat, stutter, tremble, groan, bite their lips and dig their nails into their flesh. Full-blown, uncontrollable seizures were observed for three subjects."

However, supporters of Milgram argue that his experiments can be justified ethically because they alert us to the dangers of blindly obeying authority figures. Moreover, the great majority of his participants – 74 per cent – said afterwards that they had learned something of lasting value.

The Hawthorne Effect

A laboratory is not a normal or natural environment (except for scientists, maybe!). As a result, it is likely that any behaviour that occurs in these conditions is also unnatural or artificial. If people do not behave in true-to-life ways, the experiment will not produce valid results.

If people know they are being studied, they may behave differently; for example, by trying to second-guess what the researcher wants them to do and acting accordingly. This will ruin the experiment, which depends on the subjects responding to the variables that the researcher introduces into the situation, not to the fact that they are being observed.

This problem has become known as the 'Hawthorne Effect' or 'experimental effect'. In 1927, Elton Mayo began conducting research into factors affecting workers' productivity at the Western Electric Company's Hawthorne plant in Chicago.

Working with five female volunteer workers who knew he was conducting an experiment, Mayo altered different variables such as lighting, heating, rest breaks and so on to see what effect they had on the volunteers' output.

Surprisingly, not only did output go up when he improved their working conditions, but it continued to rise even when conditions were worsened. Mayo concluded that the workers were not responding to the changes he was making in the experimental variables (such as the lighting), but simply to the fact that they were being studied and wished to please the experimenter who was showing an interest in them.

Free will

Interpretivist sociologists, such as interactionists, argue that human beings are fundamentally different from plants, rocks and other natural phenomena studied by natural scientists. Unlike these objects, we have free will, consciousness and choice.

This means our behaviour cannot be explained in terms of cause and effect. Instead, it can only be understood in terms of the choices we freely make. In this view, the experimental method, with its search for causes, is therefore not an appropriate method for studying human beings.

Activity

Some sociologists and psychologists have used experiments to try to discover the effects of media violence on children. Write a short account of the difficulties they might face in doing this. Use the following ideas: the complexity of social life; long- and short-term effects; artificial environment; ethical problems; children's previous socialisation.

Two alternatives to the laboratory experiment

Given these problems, sociologists have developed two alternatives that follow the same logic as laboratory experiments, but which overcome some of the difficulties identified above. These are:

- Field experiments
- The comparative method or 'thought experiment'.

Field experiments

A field experiment has two features that distinguish it from a laboratory experiment:

- It takes place in the subject's natural surroundings, such as school or workplace, rather than in an artificial laboratory environment.
- Those involved are generally not aware that they are the subjects of an experiment, in which case there is no Hawthorne Effect.

The researcher manipulates one or more of the variables in the situation to see what effect it has on the unwitting subjects of the experiment. For example, Rosenthal and Jacobson manipulated teachers' expectations about children's abilities in order to discover what effects labelling has on achievement.

Similarly, in David Rosenhan's (1973) 'pseudopatient' experiment, a team of eight 'normal' researchers presented themselves at 12 California mental hospitals, complaining that they had been hearing voices. Each was admitted and diagnosed as schizophrenic solely on the basis of this claim, which obviously no-one else could prove. Once in hospital, they ceased to complain of hearing voices and acted normally throughout. Nevertheless, hospital staff treated them all as if they were mentally ill. None was found out (although some fellow patients were suspicious).

This suggests that it was not the patients' behaviour that led to them being treated as sick (since they didn't behave abnormally), but the label 'schizophrenic' itself that led staff to treat them in this way. For example, the pseudopatients kept notes of their experiences, but hospital staff interpreted this as a symptom of mental illness. On one pseudopatient's nursing notes was written 'patient exhibits writing behaviour' – writing apparently being a sign of illness!

Rosenhan's study shows the value of field experiments. They are more 'natural' and realistic, and they avoid the artificiality of laboratory experiments.

However, the more realistic we make the situation, the less control we have over the variables that might be operating. If so, we cannot be certain that the causes we have identified are the correct ones.

For example, while it might have been the label 'schizophrenic' that led doctors and nurses to treat the pseudopatients as mentally ill (as Rosenhan claims), it may in fact have been some other factor that the researchers had not controlled that led the hospital staff to behave in this way.

Some critics also argue that field experiments are unethical, since they involve carrying out an experiment on their subjects (in this case, the hospital staff) without their knowledge or consent.

The comparative method

Unlike both field experiments and laboratory experiments, the comparative method is carried out only in the mind of the sociologist. It is a 'thought experiment' and it does not involve the researcher actually experimenting on real people at all. However, it too is designed to discover cause-and-effect relationships. It works as follows:

- Identify two groups of people that are alike in all major respects except for the one variable we are interested in.
- Then compare the two groups to see if this one difference between them has any effect.

An example of the comparative method is Emile Durkheim's (1897) classic study of suicide. Durkheim's hypothesis was that low levels of integration of individuals into social groups caused high rates of suicide. He argued that different religions produced different levels of integration, with Catholicism producing higher levels than Protestantism. From this, he therefore predicted that Protestants would have a higher suicide rate than Catholics.

Durkheim then tested his prediction by comparing the suicide rates of Catholics and Protestants who were similar in all other important respects (for example, in terms of where they lived, whether they were married or single etc). His prediction was supported by the official statistics on suicide, which showed Catholics to have lower suicide rates than Protestants. Durkheim claimed from this that his hypothesis was correct.

In seeking to discover cause-and-effect relationships, the comparative method has three advantages over laboratory experiments:

- It avoids artificiality.
- It can be used to study past events.
- It poses no ethical problems, such as harming or deceiving subjects.

However, the comparative method gives the researcher even less control over variables than do field experiments, so we can be even less certain whether a thought experiment really has discovered the cause of something.

For more activities on Experiments...

Go to www.sociology.uk.net

Summary

In **laboratory** experiments, scientists manipulate variables to discover **laws** of cause and effect. Although they produce reliable data, experiments are rare in sociology. They suffer from **practical** problems (e.g. they cannot be used to study the past), **ethical** problems of experimenting on humans, and are prone to the **Hawthorne Effect**. **Field** experiments and the **comparative method** are used as alternatives to laboratory experiments.

QuickCheck Questions

1. Fill in the missing words: The laboratory experiment is an artificial ... in which the scientist is able to ... all the different ... to see what effect they have.

2. What are the similarities and differences between a laboratory experiment and the comparative method?

3. State (a) one practical problem and (b) one ethical problem of conducting laboratory experiments in sociology.

4. What is the Hawthorne Effect?

5. Explain what is meant by (a) an independent variable; (b) experimenter bias.

6. Suggest two advantages of using the comparative method.

Check your answers at www.sociology.uk.net

Examining Experiments

(a) Explain what is meant by a 'control group'. (2 marks)

(b) Explain the difference between the dependent variable and the independent variable in an experiment. (4 marks)

(c) Suggest **two** criticisms of field experiments. (4 marks)

(d) Examine the reasons why some sociologists choose not to use experiments when conducting research. (20 marks)

The examiner's advice

Part (d) is an 'Examine' question of the type you will see in the exam. It carries 10 AO1 marks (knowledge and understanding) and 10 AO2 marks (interpretation, application, analysis and evaluation).

Focus mainly on *laboratory* experiments, but remember to discuss *field* experiments and the *comparative method* too.

Most of the AO1 marks are for knowledge of practical, theoretical and ethical *limitations*. With *laboratory* experiments, practical problems include controlling all the possible variables, studying the past or large-scale social phenomena. Theoretical problems include representativeness, validity, artificiality and the Hawthorne Effect. You should relate these points to the positivist-interpretivist debate (see Box 22). Ethical limitations include deceiving and potentially harming participants.

For *field* experiments, the main limitations are deception and reduced control over variables. The *comparative method* also cannot control variables.

You can gain AO2 marks by referring briefly to the *strengths* of experiments by linking a strength to each limitation in turn (rather than listing all the strengths at the end). For example, an ethical problem is that experimenters may have to deceive participants, but in so doing they may overcome the Hawthorne Effect.

You can also gain AO2 marks by comparing experiments with other methods or contrasting different types of experiment, and by applying examples from studies such as Mayo, Milgram, Rosenthal and Jacobson, Rosenhan and Durkheim.

METHODS IN CONTEXT
using experiments to investigate education

Sociologists sometimes use experiments to study issues such as:

- Teacher expectations
- Classroom interaction
- Labelling
- Pupils' self-concepts

Before reading this section, re-visit Topic 2 to refresh your understanding of what is different about researching education.

We shall focus here on the use of experiments to study the nature and impact of teacher expectations. Many sociologists claim that teachers' expectations of different groups of pupils have important effects, leading to labelling, the self-fulfilling prophecy and unequal achievement. Both field and laboratory experiments can be used to investigate these 'expectancy effects'. These effects can be positive or negative.

Laboratory experiments and teacher expectations

Several researchers have used laboratory experiments to investigate teacher expectations. For example, Harvey and Slatin (1976) examined whether teachers had preconceived ideas about pupils of different social classes. They used a sample of 96 teachers. Each teacher was shown 18 photographs of children from different social class backgrounds. To control other variables, the photographs were equally divided in terms of gender and ethnicity. The teachers were asked to rate the children on their performance, parental attitudes to education, aspirations and so on.

Harvey and Slatin found that lower-class children were rated less favourably, especially by more experienced teachers. Teachers based their ratings on the similarities they perceived between the children in the photographs and pupils they had taught. This study indicates that teachers label pupils from different social classes and use these labels to pre-judge pupils' potential.

Such expectations may be passed on to pupils through non-verbal communication. Charkin et al (1975) used a sample of 48 university students who each taught a lesson to a ten-year-old boy.

- One third (the high expectancy group) were told that the boy was highly motivated and intelligent.
- One third were told that he was poorly motivated with a low IQ (the low expectancy group)
- One third were given no information.

Charkin et al videoed the lessons and found that the high expectancy group made more eye contact and gave out more encouraging body language than the low expectancy group.

Mason (1973) looked at whether negative or positive expectations had the greater effect. Teachers were given positive, negative or neutral reports on a pupil. The teachers then observed video recordings of the pupil taking a test, watching to see if any errors were made. Finally, they were asked to predict the pupil's end of year attainment. Mason found that the negative reports had a much greater impact than the positive ones on the teachers' expectations.

ethical problems

Laboratory experiments that do not involve real pupils have fewer ethical problems than those that do. Neither Mason nor Harvey and Slatin used real pupils, so no child suffered any negative effects.

However, others, such as Charkin et al, have used real pupils and this raises ethical concerns. Young people's vulnerability and their more limited ability to understand what is happening mean that there are greater problems of deception, lack of informed consent and psychological damage. These ethical concerns are the main reason why laboratory experiments play only a limited role in educational research.

narrow focus

Laboratory experiments usually only examine one specific aspect of teacher expectations, such as body language for example. This can be useful because it allows the researcher to isolate and examine this variable more thoroughly.

However, this means that teacher expectations are not seen within the wider process of labelling and the self-fulfilling prophecy. For example, although Charkin et al identified the existence of positive and negative body language, they did not examine how it might then affect pupils' performance.

practical problems

There are practical problems in conducting experiments on teachers' expectations in schools. Schools are large, complex institutions in which many variables may affect teacher expectations. For example, they may be influenced by a wide range of variables such as class size, streaming, type of school and so on. In practice, it is impossible even to identify, let alone control, all the variables that might exert an influence on teachers' expectations.

Sociologists are often interested in the role of large-scale social factors and processes such as the impact of government policies on educational achievement, which cannot be studied in small-scale laboratory settings.

artificiality

The artificiality of laboratory experiments may mean that they tell us little about the real world of education. For example, Charkin used university students rather than teachers, while Harvey and Slatin used photographs of pupils rather than real pupils. It is unlikely that university students behave in the same way as experienced teachers, and teachers' expectations are based on more than just pupils' appearance. For example, behaviour, accent and impressions of parents may all play a part.

Field experiments and teacher expectations

Concerns about laboratory experiments have led some sociologists to use field experiments located in real educational settings instead. However, these too have their limitations. Rosenthal and Jacobson's (1968) 'Pygmalion in the Classroom' illustrates the difficulties of using field experiments to study teacher expectations.

They carried out their research in a California primary school they called 'Oak School'. Pupils were given an IQ test and teachers were told that this had enabled the researchers to identify the 20 per cent of pupils who were likely to 'spurt' in the next year. In reality, the test did no such thing and the pupils were, in fact, selected at random.

Rosenthal and Jacobson's aims were, firstly, to plant in the minds of the teachers a particular set of expectations about their pupils and, secondly, to see if this had any effect on pupil performance. Because the 'spurters' were selected at random, there was no reason to expect their performance would be any different to others in the class unless teacher expectations had an influence. 'Teacher expectations' was therefore isolated as the independent variable in their experiment.

All the pupils were re-tested eight months later and then again after a further year. Over the first eight months, pupils gained on average eight IQ points, but the 'spurters' gained 12 points. When this was broken down by age, the greatest improvement in performance was found in the youngest children, those aged 6-8. However, after a further year, this 'expectancy advantage' only seemed to have an effect among 10-11 year olds.

ethical problems

Field experiments in educational settings pose major ethical problems. The potential impact of the Oak School experiment on pupils is substantial. For example, while the 'spurters'

benefited from the study, the remaining 80 per cent of pupils did not. Some may even have been held back educationally because they received less attention and encouragement from teachers. Children have more rights than in the 1960s and the legal duty of care that schools have today means that such an experiment is unlikely to be carried out now.

Field experiments work best when those involved are unaware that they are in an experiment. Yet this requires deception – in this case, of the teachers. Had they known the true nature of the IQ test and the purpose of the research, it would have been impossible to plant expectations in their minds and the experiment would have failed in its purpose.

Read the accounts of Rosenthal and Jacobson's field experiment here and in Chapter 3, page 104.

1. What were (a) the independent and (b) the dependent variables that they were studying?

2. How useful was the study in showing evidence of the self-fulfilling prophecy?

3. Did they control all the variables? Were there any other variables that could have affected the results?

4. Were some of the children given an advantage over the rest by Rosenthal and Jacobson? If so, was this ethical?

5. How might you feel if you were one of the pupils not identified as a 'spurter'?

reliability

Rosenthal and Jacobson's research design was relatively simple and therefore easy to repeat. Within five years of the original study, it had been repeated no less than 242 times. However, given all the many differences between school classes, for example in terms of the age of the pupils, teaching styles and so on, it is unlikely that the original could be replicated exactly.

validity

Rosenthal and Jacobson claimed that teachers' expectations were passed on through differences in the way they interacted with pupils. However, the researchers did not carry out any observation of classroom interaction, so they had no data to support this claim. Later studies that did use observation, such as Claiborn (1969), found no evidence of teacher expectations being passed on through classroom interaction.

broader focus

However, Rosenthal and Jacobson did look at the whole labelling process from teacher expectations through to their effect on pupils, rather than just examining single elements in isolation. Their study was also longitudinal, which allowed them to identify trends over time.

Examining experiments in context

Item A   Researching labelling in schools

Interactionist sociologists such as Becker claim that teachers label different groups of pupils and treat them unequally. This affects pupils' self-esteem and educational achievement.

Teachers are required to treat pupils fairly and so are unlikely to admit that they label them. If teachers are aware that they are being studied, they may avoid saying or doing anything that could be taken as 'labelling'.

Whether or not a particular action by a teacher is part of a labelling process is open to interpretation. For example, one researcher might   5
see telling off a pupil as 'labelling', while another might view it as 'justifiable classroom discipline'.

Researchers not only want to know whether labelling occurs. They also want to measure its effect on pupils' self-esteem and achievement.

Question

Using material from **Item A** and elsewhere, assess the strengths and limitations of experiments for the study of labelling in schools.

(20 marks)

The examiner's advice

This question carries 8 AO1 marks (knowledge and understanding) and 12 AO2 marks (interpretation, application, analysis and evaluation). It requires you to **apply** your knowledge and understanding of different types of experiments – laboratory, field and the comparative method – to the study of the **particular** issue of labelling in schools. It is not enough simply to discuss experiments in general.

For example, Item A suggests teachers are unlikely to admit that they label pupils and are likely to change their behaviour when researched. Covert field experiments overcome this 'Hawthorne Effect' because teachers and pupils, unaware of the research purpose, will act normally.

However, covert experiments mean that informed consent cannot be obtained and participants have no opportunity to withdraw from the research. Other ethical problems of experiments include risk of harm to vulnerable young people.

You should consider how useful laboratory experiments are in studying labelling in school. How likely are teachers and pupils to act as they normally would in class? Schools are large institutions – can their scale and complexity be reproduced in a laboratory?

You need to keep a reasonable balance between the strengths and limitations of different types of experiments. You can also refer to studies that have used this method (e.g. Rosenthal and Jacobson) and to any relevant research you have been involved in.

Social surveys are a good way of studying large numbers of people.

Topic 4 Social surveys

Learning objectives

After studying this Topic, you should:

- Be able to explain the main stages in conducting a survey.
- Understand the importance of sampling.
- Be able to describe the different sampling techniques.

The most obvious way of gathering data about people is simply to ask them questions. Social surveys involve gathering information by asking people questions about their lives, attitudes, opinions or behaviour.

Most of us are familiar with market research surveys of consumers' preferences and opinion polls on people's voting intentions, but sociologists also use social surveys to collect data and test hypotheses on subjects as varied as income, family patterns, crime, social mobility, sexual behaviour, attitudes to school or work, religious beliefs, and housework.

In fact, social surveys are probably the research method that sociologists use most often. This is partly because of the undoubted practical advantages that they offer to the researcher.

However, as we shall see in Topics 5 and 6, there are also a number of problems associated with surveys that sociologists need to consider when choosing a research method.

In this Topic, we consider the main stages in conducting a social survey, including the importance of obtaining a representative sample and the different types of sample that sociologists use.

Preparing to conduct a survey

Social surveys take two basic forms. Questions can be put to people via:

- **Written questionnaires**, which respondents are asked to complete and return by post or e-mail.
- **Interviews**, either face-to-face or by telephone.

Types of question

Whether we use questionnaires or interviews to carry out our survey, the questions we ask can be of two types:

- **Closed-ended questions:** the respondent (the person answering the questions) must choose their answer from a limited range of possible answers that the researcher has decided upon in advance, such as 'Yes', 'No' or 'Don't know', or like multiple-choice questions in an exam.

Activity

Working in pairs:

1   Choose a topic with which you are familiar (e.g. gender and education) and design:

    (a) three open-ended questions

    (b) three closed-ended questions: one with yes/no answers and two others.

2   Different types of question are suited to different research purposes. For each of the following, would you use closed-ended or open-ended questions? If you want:

    (a) to collect information quickly

    (b) respondents to answer in their own words

    (c) to discover the reasons behind the respondent's behaviour

    (d) the answers to be easily quantified

    (e) to maximise validity

    (f) to maximise reliability

Closed-ended questions are often pre-coded for ease of analysis later. Each possible answer to the question is given a code, and the interviewer or respondent rings the number corresponding to the answer chosen. The information can then be fed into a computer for processing, enabling the researchers to quantify (count) the number of respondents choosing each of the available answers.

- **Open-ended questions:** the person answering is free to give whatever answer they wish, in their own words, and without any pre-selected choices being offered by the researcher (see Box 23).

Survey research begins with the choice of a topic to investigate and with formulating an aim or hypothesis. Then, before the actual survey, a pilot study needs to be conducted and a sample selected for study. We examine each of these stages below.

Choosing a topic

The first stage is choosing a topic for investigation. Sociologists use surveys to study a wide variety of issues, but survey methods are not suitable for all subjects. For example, historical topics cannot be investigated, unless there are survivors we can question.

Once we have chosen a suitable topic for research, there are a number of stages we need to go through before we can start gathering data. The first of these is to formulate an aim or hypothesis for the research.

Formulating an aim or hypothesis

Most surveys either have a general aim or seek to test a specific hypothesis. An aim is a statement that identifies what

Box 23	**Open-ended and closed-ended questions**

The following example of a closed-ended question comes from John Goldthorpe and David Lockwood's (1969) study of 'affluent workers':

Here are some things often thought important about a job: which one would you look for first in a job?

- Interest and variety
- Pleasant working conditions
- A strong and active union
- Good pay and the chance of plenty of overtime
- Good workmates
- A supervisor who doesn't breathe down your neck

By contrast, Gordon Marshall (1988) used the following open-ended question in his study of social class:

When you hear someone described as 'working class', what sort of person do you think of?

a sociologist intends to study and hopes to achieve by carrying out the research. Often the aim will simply be to collect data on a particular topic, for example, people's leisure patterns, religious beliefs or attitudes to cohabitation. The Census of the entire population conducted by the government every ten years is designed to collect large quantities of data about many different aspects of British society.

Other surveys seek to test one or more hypotheses. A hypothesis is more specific than an aim. It is a possible explanation that can be tested by collecting evidence to prove it true or false.

For example, we may be interested in the topic of educational achievement. We may have a hunch or suspicion that achievement is affected by family size. If so, we can formulate a specific hypothesis in the form of a statement, such as: 'differences in educational achievement are the result of differences in family size'. We can then collect evidence to see whether or not this is true.

The advantage of a hypothesis is that it gives direction to our research. It will give a focus to the questions that we ask in our questionnaires or interviews, since their purpose is to gather information that will either confirm (prove) or refute (disprove) our hypothesis.

Creating a hypothesis requires imagination, because we have to think up a possible explanation first. Often, sociologists develop a hypothesis by studying previous work on the subject, but it could come to them from anywhere. The important thing is whether the evidence gathered in our survey supports it. If the hypothesis turns out to be false, we must discard it.

Discarding a hypothesis might seem like a bad thing, but in fact it means we have made some progress. In our example of educational achievement, if the survey reveals no link with family size, we have learned something new and we can now direct our attention to another possible cause instead. Perhaps the cause is parental attitudes, or income; we simply formulate a new hypothesis and set out to test it.

Operationalising concepts

Suppose we have the hypothesis that working-class pupils achieve lower qualifications than middle-class pupils because of lower parental income. Before we can test it, we need a working definition of our key ideas or concepts – in this case, the concept of social class. The reason is simple: without a working definition, we won't be able to count the numbers of working-class pupils who have or don't have qualifications.

Now, 'social class' is a fairly abstract idea, so we need a way of measuring or indicating what class each pupil belongs to. Most sociologists would probably use parental occupation as an indicator of a pupil's social class, both because it is easily identifiable and because it seems to be the best single indicator of all those other aspects of our lives that make up our 'class' (such as income, housing etc).

Once we have a working or 'operational' definition of our concept, we can set about writing questions that measure it. In our example, we might ask the parent, 'what is your job?' This will allow us to see what social class each pupil belongs to. We can then correlate this with information we collect about their qualifications to find out whether our hypothesis is true or false.

Before we can do research, then, we need to define our sociological ideas in such a way that they can be measured. This process of converting a concept (e.g. social class) into something that can be measured is called 'operationalisation'.

Operationalising a concept may seem straightforward, but a problem can arise when different sociologists operationalise the same concept differently. For example, we might agree that occupation is a useful operational definition of class, but disagree about whether a routine office worker is working-class or middle-class. Disagreements like these can make it hard to compare the findings of different pieces of research.

▲ Apart from family size, what other variables might influence children's achievement?

Activity

In small groups, discuss how you might operationalise the following concepts so you could use them in researching education: poverty; homelessness; disability; achievement. What problems might you encounter in operationalising them?

The pilot study

Once we have a hypothesis we want to test, the next stage is to produce a draft version of the questionnaire or interview schedule (the list of interview questions) that we intend to use, and to give this a trial run. This is known as a pilot study.

The basic aim of the pilot study is to iron out any problems, refine or clarify questions and their wording and give interviewers practice, so that the actual survey goes as smoothly as possible.

For example, Young and Willmott (1962) carried out just over 100 pilot interviews to help them decide on the design of their study, the questions to ask and how to word them.

A pilot study may reveal that some questions are badly worded and hard to understand, or that the answers are difficult to analyse. After carrying out the pilot study, it should be possible to finalise the questionnaire or interview schedule.

Sampling

Sociologists often aim to produce generalisations that apply to all cases of the topic they are interested in. For example, if we were interested in educational achievement, we would ideally want our theory to explain the achievement levels of *all* pupils, not just the ones who were in our study.

Obviously, however, we do not have the time or money to include every pupil in Britain in our survey, so we have to choose a sample of pupils to include. A sample is a smaller sub-group drawn from the wider group that we are interested in. The process of creating or selecting a sample is called sampling.

The basic purpose of sampling is usually to ensure that those people we have chosen to include in the study (such as pupils) are representative or typical of the research population, including all the people we have *not* been able to include in the study. (The research population refers to the whole group that we are interested in – all pupils, in this case.)

So long as our sample is representative, we should be able to generalise our findings to the whole research population. This is particularly attractive to positivist sociologists, who wish to make general, law-like statements about the wider social structure.

The sampling frame

To choose a sample, we first need a sampling frame. This is a list of all the members of the population we are interested in studying.

For example, Young and Willmott used the electoral register (the list of people entitled to vote) as their sampling frame. It is important that the list we use as a sampling frame is as complete and accurate as possible – otherwise the sample chosen from it may not be truly representative of the population.

Once we have obtained our sampling frame, we can choose our sample from it, for example by selecting every tenth name. In selecting the sample, we need to ensure it is representative of the wider population we are interested in.

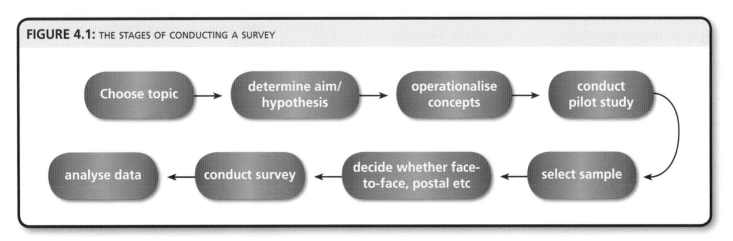

FIGURE 4.1: THE STAGES OF CONDUCTING A SURVEY

Choose topic → determine aim/hypothesis → operationalise concepts → conduct pilot study → select sample → decide whether face-to-face, postal etc → conduct survey → analyse data

Box 24	The biggest blunder in survey history?

The biggest blunder in survey history was probably the 1936 poll on voting intentions carried out by an American magazine, the Literary Digest. The poll asked respondents how they would vote in the forthcoming election: for Landon, the Republican Party candidate, or for Roosevelt, the Democratic Party candidate. Two million people responded to the poll. The great majority surveyed said they would vote for Landon and the magazine predicted a Republican victory. Yet when the election came, Roosevelt won by a landslide. How could the magazine have got it so wrong?

▶ *Roosevelt (left) celebrating his election victory*

The answer lies in the sampling frame used for the questionnaire. The magazine had used the telephone directory, wrongly assuming it would be a reasonably good list of all those who were entitled to vote. However, in 1936, telephones were still something of a luxury; many poorer voters were not telephone subscribers and did not appear in the directory. Since in America, poorer voters have tended to be Democrats and richer voters Republicans, using the directory to draw the sample was bound to over-represent the intentions of rich Republican voters and under-represent those of poor Democrats.

Activity

A good sampling frame should be: complete (covering all the population concerned); without duplications; accurate; up to date and all in one place. Working in pairs, consider the following examples and decide how far each one meets these five criteria. Give reasons for your answers.

(a) The annual register of electors as a sampling frame for all people entitled to vote.

(b) A telephone directory as a sampling frame for all the people in the area it covers.

(c) Members of a football team's supporters' club as a sampling frame for all fans of that team.

Sampling techniques

Sociologists use various sampling techniques to achieve a representative sample:

- **Random sampling** is the simplest technique, where the sample is selected purely by random chance. For example, names may be drawn out of a hat.
- **Quasi-random sampling** is similar, for instance every tenth or hundredth name on a list is selected. Young and Willmott used every thirty-sixth name on the electoral register for their general sample.

However, with both techniques, there is always the chance that the sample obtained is not truly representative. Imagine we have a city of 100,000 people, where half the population is male and half female. Suppose we take a 1 per cent sample (one person in every hundred). This will give us a sample of 1,000 people. Yet by chance it could happen that our sample contains, say, 600 females and only 400 males, rather than 500 of each sex.

Other more sophisticated techniques of sampling can reduce the chance of getting an unrepresentative sample like the one above. These include the following:

- **Stratified random sampling:** by first dividing ('stratifying') the population into males and females, and then taking

a 1 per cent sample of each, we can ensure that we end up with equal numbers of each sex, and that the sample is thus representative of the population as a whole. This process can be repeated for any other important variable such as people's age, income etc.

- **Quota sampling** is similar to stratified random sampling, but instead of choosing the samples for each category (e.g. male and female) randomly, the researchers go out looking for the right number (the quota) of each sort of person

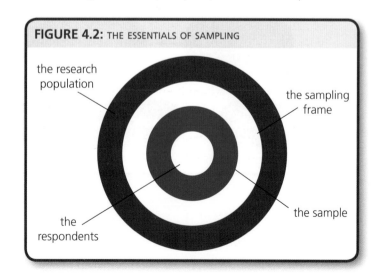

FIGURE 4.2: THE ESSENTIALS OF SAMPLING

the research population

the sampling frame

the respondents

the sample

required in each category. In our example, the researchers would have a quota of 500 males and 500 females to find.

Whatever sampling technique is actually used, researchers will often compile a reserve sample, so that if anyone in the original sample cannot be contacted, their counterpart from the reserve list can be used as a substitute.

Non-representative sampling

As we have seen, the purpose of sampling is usually to ensure that the people we include in our study are representative of the research population. However, for both practical and theoretical reasons, not all studies use representative sampling techniques.

practical reasons

There are several practical reasons why it may not be possible to create a representative sample, even when the researcher wishes to do so.

- The social characteristics of the research population, such as age, gender and class may not be known. It would thus be impossible to create a sample that was an exact cross-section of the research population.

- It may be impossible to find or create a sampling frame for that particular research population. For example, not all criminals are convicted, so there is no complete list available from which to select a sample.

- Potential respondents may refuse to participate in the survey. For example, some criminals may refuse for fear that their responses may be passed to the police.

In cases where it is not possible to obtain a representative sample, sociologists sometimes use snowball or opportunity samples.

- Snowball sampling involves collecting a sample by contacting a number of key individuals, who are asked to suggest others who might be interviewed, and so on, adding to the sample 'snowball' fashion, until enough data has been collected. Although not representative, this can be a useful way to contact a sample of people who might otherwise be difficult to find or persuade to take part, such as criminals.

- Opportunity sampling, sometimes called convenience sampling, involves choosing from those individuals who are easiest to access. Examples include selecting from passers-by in the street or from a captive audience such as a class of pupils. In neither case is the sample likely to be representative of the target research population.

theoretical reasons

Even where it is possible to create a representative sample, some researchers may not choose to do so, because of their sociological perspective. Interpretivists believe that it is more important to gain valid data and an authentic understanding of social actors' meanings than to discover general laws of behaviour. Because interpretivists are less concerned to make generalisations, they have less need for representative samples.

Once we have finalised the questionnaire or interview schedule and selected the sample, we can begin to collect data about the topic. To do so, we can use either questionnaires or interviews.

For more activities on Social surveys...

Go to www.sociology.uk.net

Summary

Surveys gather data by asking questions. Before conducting the survey, the researcher needs a **hypothesis** (a testable statement) or aim, and concepts need to be **operationalised** (defined so that they are measurable). A **pilot study** may be used to iron out problems. A **representative sample** is essential if findings are to be generalised.

QuickCheck Questions

1 Explain the difference between an open-ended and a closed-ended question.

2 State one advantage of having a hypothesis before starting research.

3 Explain the difference between an aim and a hypothesis.

4 What is a pilot study?

5 What does operationalisation of concepts mean?

6 How may a sample be stratified?

Check your answers at www.sociology.uk.net

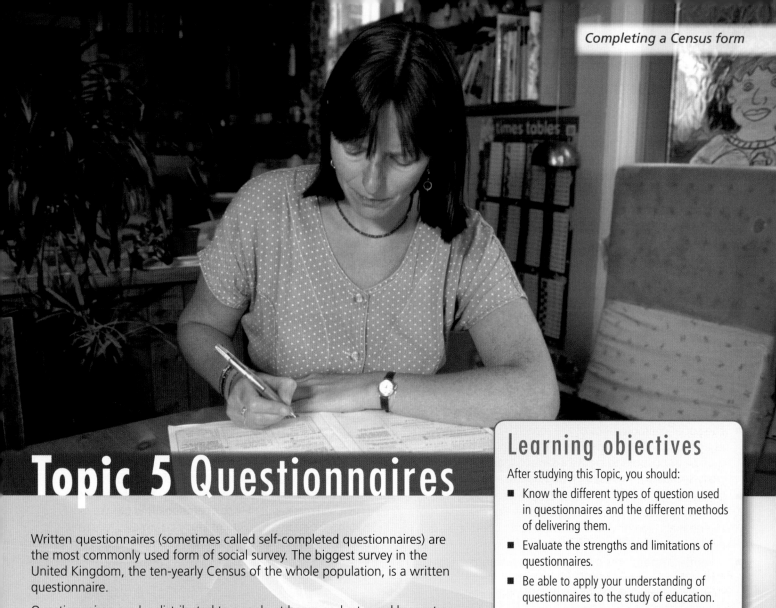

Topic 5 Questionnaires

Learning objectives

After studying this Topic, you should:

■ Know the different types of question used in questionnaires and the different methods of delivering them.

■ Evaluate the strengths and limitations of questionnaires.

■ Be able to apply your understanding of questionnaires to the study of education.

Written questionnaires (sometimes called self-completed questionnaires) are the most commonly used form of social survey. The biggest survey in the United Kingdom, the ten-yearly Census of the whole population, is a written questionnaire.

Questionnaires can be distributed to people at home and returned by post or in person, e-mailed or completed and collected on the spot, for example in a classroom or office.

Questionnaires ask respondents (the people who complete them) to provide answers to pre-set questions. Questions tend to be closed-ended, often with pre-coded answers, but open-ended questions can also be used. Written questionnaires are a relatively cheap and quick way to collect information from large samples of people.

Advantages of questionnaires

The popularity of questionnaires is undoubtedly due to the considerable range of advantages they offer to researchers.

1 Practical advantages

Questionnaires offer several major practical advantages:

- They are a quick and cheap means of gathering large quantities of data from large numbers of people, widely spread geographically, especially if a postal questionnaire is used. For example, Helen Connor and Sara Dewson (2001) posted nearly 4,000 questionnaires to students at 14 higher education institutions around the country in their study of the factors influencing the decisions of working-class students to go to university.
- There is no need to recruit and train interviewers or observers to collect the data, because respondents complete and return the questionnaires themselves.
- The data are usually easy to quantify, particularly where pre-coded, closed-ended questions are used, and can be processed quickly by computer to reveal the relationships between different variables.

Box 25	Positivism, interpretivism and questionnaires

Positivists favour questionnaires because they achieve the main positivist goals of reliability, generalisability and representativeness:

- Standardised questions and answers produce reliable data because other researchers can replicate the questionnaire.
- Pre-coded responses allow us to produce quantitative data, identify and measure behaviour patterns, and establish cause-and-effect relationships.
- Questionnaires are often large scale and thus more representative.

Interpretivists reject the use of questionnaires because they impose the researcher's framework of ideas on respondents. This tells us little about the meanings held by social actors. Questionnaires fail to achieve the main interpretivist goal of validity.

See Box 20 on page 166 for more about positivism, interpretivism and research methods.

2 Reliability

Questionnaires are seen as a reliable method of collecting data. That is, if repeated by another researcher, a questionnaire should give similar results to those gained by the first researcher. There are two reasons for this:

- When the research is repeated, a questionnaire identical to the original one is used, so new respondents are asked exactly the same questions, in the same order, with the same choice of answers, as the original respondents.
- With postal questionnaires, there is no researcher present to influence the respondent's answers (different researchers might influence respondents to give different answers) – unlike interviews, where interaction with the interviewer may affect the answer given.

In other words, the questionnaire is a fixed yardstick that can be used by any researcher to obtain the same results (provided that later researchers use a similar sample). This means one researcher's study can easily be repeated and checked by another.

The reliability of questionnaires also means that if we do find differences in the answers that respondents give, we can assume that these are the result of real differences between the respondents and not simply the result of different questions.

A related advantage of questionnaires is that they allow comparisons to be made, both over time and between different societies. By asking the same questions, we can compare the results obtained in two different societies or at two different times.

Suggest three reasons why questionnaires may be high in reliability.

3 Hypothesis testing

Questionnaires are particularly useful for testing hypotheses about cause-and-effect relationships between different variables. For instance, using our earlier example of educational achievement, analysis of respondents' answers could show whether there is a correlation between children's achievement levels and family size. We might find, for example, that most low achievers come from large families.

From this analysis, we can make statements about the possible causes of low achievement and predictions about which children are most likely to under-achieve.

Because questionnaires enable us to identify possible causes, they are very attractive to positivist sociologists. As we saw earlier, positivists take a scientific approach and seek to discover laws of cause and effect.

4 Detachment and objectivity

Positivists also favour questionnaires because they are a detached and objective (unbiased) form of research, where the sociologist's personal involvement with their respondents is kept to a minimum. For example, postal questionnaires are completed at a distance and involve little or no personal contact between researchers and respondents. For this reason, positivists see them as a good way of maintaining detachment and objectivity.

5 Representativeness

Because questionnaires can collect information from a large number of people, the results stand a better chance of being truly representative of the wider population than with other methods that study only very small numbers of people, such as participant observation.

In addition, researchers who use questionnaires tend to pay more attention to the need to obtain a representative sample. For these reasons, the findings of questionnaires are more likely to allow us to make accurate generalisations about the wider population from which the sample was drawn.

6 Ethical issues

Questionnaires pose fewer ethical problems than most other research methods. Although questionnaires may ask intrusive or sensitive questions, respondents are generally under no obligation to answer them. Nevertheless, researchers should gain their informed consent, guarantee respondents' anonymity and make it clear that they have a right not to answer any of the questions that they do not wish to.

Disadvantages of questionnaires

Despite their advantages, questionnaires have been subject to some sharp criticisms, especially in relation to the validity of the data they produce.

1 Practical problems

The data from questionnaires tend to be limited and superficial. One practical reason for this is that they need to be fairly brief, since most respondents are unlikely to complete and return a long, time-consuming questionnaire. This limits the amount of information that can be gathered from each respondent.

Similarly, although questionnaires are a relatively cheap means of gathering data, it may sometimes be necessary to offer incentives – such as entry into a prize draw – to persuade respondents to complete the form. This will obviously add to the cost.

With postal questionnaires, there are two additional problems. The researcher cannot be sure:

- Whether the potential respondent has actually received the questionnaire
- Whether a returned questionnaire was actually completed by the person to whom it was addressed

2 Response rate

Although questionnaires have the potential to collect data from large, representative samples, very low response rates can be a major problem, especially with postal questionnaires. This is because few of those who receive a questionnaire bother to complete and return it. For example,

Shere Hite's (1991) study of 'love, passion and emotional violence' in America sent out 100,000 questionnaires, but only 4.5 per cent of them were returned.

A higher response rate can be obtained if follow-up questionnaires are sent and if questionnaires are collected by hand. However, this adds to the cost and time.

The problem of non-response is sometimes caused by faulty questionnaire design. For example, a questionnaire that uses complex language may only be completed by the well educated.

The great danger with a low response rate is that those who return their questionnaires may be different from those who don't. For example, busy people in full-time employment or with young children may fail to respond, whereas the unemployed or socially isolated with time on their hands may be more likely to fill in their questionnaires. Similarly, those with strong views on a subject are more likely to respond than those who have little knowledge or interest in it. If the respondents are different from the non-respondents, this will produce distorted and unrepresentative results, from which no accurate generalisations can be made.

1 We are often asked to return questionnaires by magazines, or to telephone, text or email a radio or television programme to give our views. Suggest two reasons why those who respond to such requests are unlikely to be representative of the population as a whole.

2 Explain in your own words why non-response is a problem for sociologists.

3 Inflexibility

Questionnaires are a very inflexible method. Once the questionnaire has been finalised, the researcher is stuck with the questions they have decided to ask and cannot explore any new areas of interest should they come up during the course of the research.

This contrasts with more flexible methods of research such as unstructured interviews, where the researcher can change the direction of the interview to ask new questions if they seem relevant.

4 Questionnaires as snapshots

Questionnaires are snapshots. They give a picture of social reality at only one moment in time: the moment when the respondent answers the questions.

Questionnaires therefore fail to produce a fully valid picture because they do not capture the way people's attitudes and behaviour change. This snapshot contrasts with the moving image of social life that methods like participant observation can provide.

5 Detachment

Interpretivist sociologists such as Aaron Cicourel (1968) argue that data from questionnaires lack validity and do not give a true picture of what has been studied. They argue that we can only gain a valid picture by using methods that allow us to get close to the subjects of the study and share their meanings. Ideally, the method should enable us to put ourselves in the subject's place and see the world through their eyes.

Questionnaires fail to do this because they are the most detached of all primary methods. For example, postal questionnaires involve no direct contact between researcher and respondent.

This lack of contact means there is no opportunity to clarify what the questions mean to the respondent or to deal with misunderstandings. There is no way of knowing whether the respondent and researcher both interpret the questions, or the answers, in the same way. This can be a serious problem where there are cultural or language differences between researcher and respondent.

6 Lying, forgetting and 'right answerism'

All methods that gather data by asking questions depend ultimately on their respondents' willingness and ability to provide full and accurate answers. Problems of validity are created when respondents give answers that are not full or frank.

For example, respondents may lie, forget, not know, not understand (and not wish to admit that they don't

understand), or try to please or second-guess the researcher. Some may give 'respectable' answers they feel they ought to give, rather than tell the truth.

These problems put questionnaires at a disadvantage when compared with observational methods, since the observer can see for himself or herself what the subjects actually do, rather than what they say they do.

7 Imposing the researcher's meanings

A valid method is one that gives a truthful picture of people's meanings and experiences. Yet interpretivists argue that questionnaires are more likely to impose the researcher's own meanings than to reveal those of the respondent.

- By choosing which questions to ask, the researcher, not the respondent, has already decided what is important and what is not.
- If we use closed-ended questions, respondents then have to try to fit their views into the ones on offer. If they feel some other answer to be important, they have no opportunity of giving it, thus producing a distorted and invalid picture of their reality.
- On the other hand, if we use open-ended questions, respondents are free to answer as they please, but when the researcher comes to code them to produce quantitative data, similar but non-identical answers may get lumped together into the same category.

As Marten Shipman (1997) says, when the researcher's categories are not the respondent's categories, 'pruning and bending' of the data is inevitable. The questionnaire imposes a straitjacket that distorts the respondents' meanings and undermines the validity of the data.

In Michael Schofield's (1965) research on the sexual behaviour of teenagers. a young girl was asked in a questionnaire, 'Are you a virgin?' she answered, 'No, not yet'.

Identify the problems of questionnaire research that this suggests.

For more activities on Questionnaires...

Go to www.sociology.uk.net

Summary

Questionnaires are lists of written questions, usually **closed-ended** and often posted. They can gather data on **large numbers** cheaply and quickly. Positivists favour them because they are **reliable** and objective. However, **low response** rates can make findings unrepresentative. Interpretivists claim they **lack validity**: they are inflexible, superficial snapshots and don't give a true account of respondents' meanings.

QuickCheck Questions

1 What is the Census?

2 What is a respondent?

3 Suggest one reason why data from questionnaires often tends to be limited and superficial.

4 Why might a low response rate result in the findings of a study being unrepresentative?

5 Suggest one reason why questionnaires are seen as an inflexible method.

6 Suggest two reasons why the data from questionnaires may lack validity.

7 Explain what is meant by a correlation.

8 Why might questionnaires be described as 'snapshots' of social reality?

9 Identify one practical problem researchers might face when using postal questionnaires.

10 Explain why positivist sociologists might prefer to use questionnaires in their research.

11 Suggest two reasons why questionnaires might be regarded as a reliable method of sociological research.

 Check your answers at www.sociology.uk.net

Examining surveys and questionnaires

(a) Explain what is meant by a hypothesis. (2 marks)

(b) Explain the difference between a sample and a sampling frame. (4 marks)

(c) Suggest **two** practical advantages of using questionnaires in sociological research. (4 marks)

(d) Examine the reasons why some sociologists choose not to use questionnaires when conducting research. (20 marks)

The examiner's advice

Part (d) is an 'Examine' question of the type you will see in the exam. It carries 10 AO1 marks (knowledge and understanding) and 10 AO2 marks (interpretation, application, analysis and evaluation).

Most of the AO1 marks are for knowledge of the *limitations* of questionnaires. Practical limitations include the fact that they are often brief and superficial and, with postal questionnaires, uncertainties about whether respondents have received the questionnaire or who completed it.

The main theoretical limitation is lack of validity. This can result from researchers deciding in advance what questions are important, and closed-ended questions preventing respondents expressing their meanings. Similarly, the detached nature of questionnaires prevents questions or answers being clarified, leading to invalid data. Respondents may also lie, forget or give 'respectable' answers. Another theoretical limitation is low response rate undermining representativeness and generalisability. Relate these points to the positivist-interpretivist debate (see Box 25). There are few ethical limitations, though researchers still need to obtain informed consent and guarantee anonymity.

You can gain AO2 marks by referring briefly to the *strengths* of questionnaires. Try to link each strength to a limitation as you go, rather than listing all the strengths at the end. For example, the absence of personal contact means questions may be misunderstood, but it also helps prevent the researcher influencing the answers. You can also gain AO2 marks by comparing questionnaires with other methods, and by applying examples from studies.

METHODS IN CONTEXT
using questionnaires to investigate education

Sociologists sometimes use questionnaires to study issues such as:

- Subject and university choice
- Bullying and the experience of schooling
- Achievement and school factors
- Parental attitudes to education

Before reading this section, re-visit Topic 2 to refresh your understanding of what is different about researching education.

Operationalisation of concepts

Operationalising concepts involves turning abstract ideas into a measurable form. This can be particularly difficult when creating a questionnaire for pupils. Because their grasp of abstract concepts is generally less than that of adults, it may be more difficult to turn sociological ideas such as 'deferred gratification' or 'cultural capital' into language that pupils will understand.

This may produce answers that are based on a misunderstanding of what the questions mean. Alternatively, the sociologist may have to over-simplify the questions so much that they cease to have any sociological value.

▼ *What problems might there be in using questionnaires to study students' reasons for their choice of university?*

Oxford University

Samples and sampling frames

Schools routinely keep lists of pupils, staff and parents. These can provide accurate sampling frames from which the sociologist can draw a representative sample. Schools also have ready-made opportunity samples of pupils and teachers, for example in the form of classes and teaching departments.

However, schools may not keep lists that reflect the researcher's interests. For example, the sociologist may wish to take a representative sample of pupils of a particular ethnic group, but the school may not keep lists of pupils sorted by ethnic origin, so there is no sampling frame available from which to draw the sample. Even where the relevant sampling frame does exist, gaining access to such confidential information may pose practical problems.

Access and response rate

Response rates for questionnaires are often low. Schools may be reluctant to allow sociologists to distribute questionnaires because of the disruption to lessons that it may cause, or because they object to the researcher's chosen topic. For example, some schools might object to questionnaires about under-age sexual activity.

However, when questionnaires are conducted in schools, response rates can often be higher than in other areas. This is because, once the head has given their consent and put their authority behind the research, teachers and pupils may be under pressure to cooperate. Similarly, the head may authorise time to be taken out of lessons so that the questionnaires can be completed. The higher response rate may produce more representative data from which generalisations can be drawn.

Another reason why response rates might be higher is that pupils, teachers and parents are accustomed to completing questionnaires issued by the school, such as student satisfaction surveys. On the other hand, teachers are often too busy to complete a lengthy questionnaire and this may reduce the response rate.

Practical issues

Questionnaires are very useful for gathering large quantities of basic educational information quickly and cheaply. For example, Michael Rutter (1979) used questionnaires to collect large quantities of data from 12 inner London secondary schools. From this, he was able to correlate achievement, attendance and behaviour with variables such as school size, class size and number of staff. It would have been very difficult to do this with more labour-intensive methods such as interviewing or observation.

However, the data generated by questionnaires is often limited and superficial. In Rutter's study, the data provided correlations between variables such as class size and achievement, but not explanations for these correlations.

There are particular problems in using questionnaires to study children. Questionnaires involve participants being able to read and understand the questions. Thus they are unsuitable for those who cannot read reasonably well, such as young children or those with certain learning difficulties.

> Suppose you had designed a questionnaire on school discipline for sixth formers to complete. In what ways would you need to change it if you wanted to use it with 11 year olds?

Children generally have a shorter attention span than adults and so questionnaires need to be relatively brief if they are to stand a chance of being completed. This limits the amount of information that can be gathered.

Children's life experiences are narrower and their memory patterns different from those of adults. This may mean that pupils, particularly those of primary school age, do not actually 'know the answers'. Consequently, questionnaires may be of little value.

Schools have very active informal communication channels. Word of the researcher's presence may spread rapidly. If the questionnaire is delivered class by class, its purpose and questions may become known throughout the school long before all pupils or teachers have been given it. This may affect the responses given by later participants and so reduce the validity of the data.

Anonymity and detachment

Questionnaires can be particularly useful when researching sensitive educational issues such as bullying, where their anonymity may overcome pupils' embarrassment or fear of retribution from bullies. As a result, response rates may be higher and pupils may be more likely to reveal details of their experience of being bullied. This may produce more valid data than would a face-to-face structured interview, for example.

However, much depends on whether pupils are reassured that their anonymity will be safeguarded. Yet this reassurance may be difficult to achieve with such a detached method as a questionnaire, where there is little or no personal contact with the researcher.

Interpretivist sociologists emphasise the importance of developing rapport and so they reject questionnaires as a means of researching young people. Because the lack of contact with respondents makes rapport difficult to establish, young people may be less likely to give full and honest responses.

Questionnaires are formal, official-looking documents and pupils may equate them with school and teacher authority – especially if they are completed in class, like a test. As a result, some pupils, particularly those in anti-school subcultures, may refuse to cooperate or to take the activity seriously.

Activity

The Scottish Office conducted a questionnaire entitled 'What you think about school'. Read the extract from it below and then answer questions (a) to (d) that follow.

We want to find out more about what children think of school. Please tick your choice for each question. There are no 'good' or 'bad' answers. We just want to know what you think.

1	I like coming to school.	True	In Between	False
2	I think school is important.	True	In Between	False
3	My parents think that teachers are usually right.	True	In Between	False
4	Homework is important.	True	In Between	False
5	My school is a good school.	True	In Between	False
6	My friends think school is a waste of time.	True	In Between	False
7	I wish I didn't have to come to school.	True	In Between	False
8	I haven't got a 'best' subject.	True	In Between	False
9	My parents think school is important.	True	In Between	False
10	I do not like reading very much.	True	In Between	False

(a) Are the questions accessible to secondary school age pupils?

(b) In your view, which of the questions 'lead' pupils to a particular response?

(c) How useful are the three response categories?

(d) How valid do you think the data from this questionnaire would be? Give your reasons.

Source: adapted from Greig et al (2007), *Doing Research with Children*

Examining questionnaires in context

Researching parental attitudes to education

Parental attitudes to education can be a key influence on pupils' achievement. Sociologists are interested in what these attitudes are and how far they affect achievement.

Many parents are willing to be involved in research because they believe that their children will benefit in some way. Parents are also used to being involved in their children's education, for example by coming to parents evenings, filling in forms and talking to teachers.

However, sociologists may find it more difficult to identify, contact and gain responses from parents than from teachers and pupils, because researchers cannot easily access a school's database of parents.   5

Parents may tend to represent themselves as 'good parents'. This can be a barrier to uncovering their real attitudes and values.

Question

Using material from **Item A** and elsewhere, assess the strengths and limitations of questionnaires for the study of parental attitudes to education.

(20 marks)

The examiner's advice

This question carries 8 A01 marks (knowledge and understanding) and 12 A02 marks (interpretation, application, analysis and evaluation). It requires you to **apply** your knowledge and understanding of questionnaires to the study of the **particular** issue of parental attitudes to education. It is not enough simply to discuss questionnaires in general.

Response rates to questionnaires are usually low, but using them to research parental attitides may bring a high response rate because, as Item A notes, they think their children will benefit and because they are used to filling in forms from school.

However, as Item A implies, data on parents held by the school is confidential and so it may be hard to obtain a sampling frame.

You should also consider issues such as the tendency of parents to represent themselves as 'good' ('right answerism'), accessing parents and responders versus non-responders. How useful might questionnaires be in dealing with these issues? Would it make a difference if they were delivered face to face rather than by post or Internet?

You need to keep a reasonable balance between the strengths and limitations of questionnaires. You can also refer to studies that have used this method (e.g. Connor and Dewson) and to any relevant research you have been involved in.

Topic 6 Interviews

While social surveys can be conducted by means of written questionnaires, an alternative that is widely used by sociologists is to conduct interviews instead. These can be carried out either face to face or by telephone.

Although both written questionnaires and interviews gather data by asking people questions, the obvious difference between the two methods is that interviews involve a social interaction between the interviewer and interviewee, whereas with written questionnaires the respondent usually answers the questions without the involvement of the researcher. For example, in a postal questionnaire, there will normally be no direct contact between the researcher and respondent.

Learning objectives

After studying this Topic, you should:

- Understand the differences between structured and unstructured interviews.
- Be able to evaluate the strengths and limitations of the different types of interview.
- Be able to apply your understanding of interviews to the study of education.

Types of interview

Sociologists use different types of interview in their research. These range from completely structured to completely unstructured interviews. The difference between them lies in how free the interviewer is to vary the questions and the way they are asked:

- Structured or formal interviews are very similar to a questionnaire: the interviewer is given strict instructions on how to ask the questions. The interview is conducted in the same standardised way each time, asking each interviewee precisely the same questions, word for word, in the same order, tone of voice and so on.
- Unstructured or informal interviews (also called discovery interviews) are like a guided conversation. The interviewer has complete freedom to vary the questions, their wording, order and so on from one interview to the next, pursuing whatever line of questioning seems appropriate at the time, asking follow-up questions or probing more deeply.

In between these two extremes lie semi-structured interviews. Each interview has the same set of questions in common, but the interviewer can also probe for more information. For example, Aaron Cicourel and John Kitsuse (1963) always followed up their questions with 'How do you mean?' as a way of gaining more information. Additional questions can be asked where the interviewer thinks it relevant.

Most interviews are one-to-one, but some are group interviews, with up to a dozen or so people being interviewed together. Paul Willis (1977) used group interviews as part of his research into the 'lads' and schooling.

Focus groups are a form of group interview in which the researcher asks the group to discuss certain topics (such as how well the government is performing) and records their views. Group interviews have their own particular strengths and limitations, as Box 26 shows.

Box 26	Group interviews

By comparison with one-to-one interviews, group interviews and discussions have certain distinctive strengths and limitations.

Strengths

- Participants may feel more comfortable being with others and thus more likely to open up.
- In a discussion, participants often throw ideas around the group, stimulating each other's thinking. This produces richer and more reflective data.
- They can be a useful way of generating initial ideas that can be followed up in later research.
- The researcher can combine questioning with the opportunity to observe group dynamics and norms.

Limitations

- One or two individuals may dominate the discussion, inhibiting others from contributing.
- Much depends on the researcher's ability to keep the group focused on the discussion topic.
- Peer group pressure to conform to group norms may lead to participants not saying what they really think.
- Data generated from group interaction is more complex and difficult to analyse.

1 Why might the data obtained from two semi-structured interviews on the same topic not be strictly comparable?

2 Suggest one advantage and one disadvantage of using group interviews rather than one-to-one interviews.

Structured interviews

Structured interviews are like questionnaires: both involve asking people a set of prepared questions. In both cases, the questions are usually closed-ended with pre-coded answers. The main difference is that in the interview, the questions are read out and the answers filled in by a trained interviewer rather than by the interviewee.

This basic similarity between structured interviews and questionnaires means that they share many of the same advantages and disadvantages. Where there are differences, these often come from the fact that structured interviews involve interaction between researcher and interviewee.

1 Practical issues

- Training interviewers is relatively straightforward and inexpensive, since all they are really required to do is follow a set of instructions. However, this is more costly than simply posting questionnaires to people.
- Surveys that use structured interviews can cover quite large numbers of people with relatively limited resources because they are quick and fairly cheap to administer (see Box 27). However, they still cannot match the potentially huge numbers reached by postal questionnaires.

- Structured interviews are suitable for gathering straightforward factual information such as a person's age or job (see Box 27).
- The results are easily quantified because they use closed-ended questions with coded answers. This makes them suitable for hypothesis testing.

2 Response rate

The large numbers who can be surveyed using structured interviews increase the chances of obtaining a representative sample of the population. Although the numbers that can be studied are lower than for questionnaires, structured interviews generally have a higher response rate. For example, of the 987 people Young and Willmott approached for their main sample, only 54 refused to be interviewed. This may be because people find it harder to turn down a face-to-face request, and some may welcome the opportunity to talk.

Response rates can be increased if the interviewer can make several call backs to pursue those who fail to respond initially. However, this increases the cost of the survey. High response rates help to produce a more representative result and therefore a better basis for making generalisations.

On the other hand, as with questionnaires, those with the time or willingness to be interviewed may be untypical (for example, they may be lonely or have time on their hands). If so, this will make for unrepresentative data and undermine the validity of any generalisations made from the findings.

Box 27	Using structured interviews

Young and Willmott (1962) used structured interviews in their research into the extended family in east London:

'The general sample being much larger – 933 people – we could not do the interviewing ourselves; these interviews were carried out by other interviewers we employed for the purpose. The interviews were formal and standardised, the questions precise and factual, with a limited range of alternative answers, on straightforward topics like people's age, job, religion, birthplace and on the whereabouts and last contact with parents, parents-in-law, brothers and sisters, and married children. The interviewers' task was to ring the appropriate code-number opposite the answer they received or, at a few points in the interview, to write in a fairly short and simple reply. Each interview took between about ten minutes and half an hour, depending on the number of relatives possessed by a particular informant.'

Activity

Using information from the above passage, explain three advantages of using structured interviews to collect data. Write at least one sentence for each advantage.

3 Reliability

If a method is reliable, another sociologist could repeat the research and get the same results. Structured interviews are seen as reliable because it is easy for the researcher to standardise and control them. They can ensure that each interview is conducted in precisely the same way, with the same questions, in the same order, with the same wording and tone of voice.

If each interviewer conducts every interview in exactly the same way, then any other researcher following the same interview procedures should get very similar results. The structured interview provides a 'recipe' for repeating the research: as in cookery, anyone who follows the recipe ought to get the same result. The fact that all interviewees are asked exactly the same questions also means that we can compare their answers easily to identify similarities and differences.

4 Validity

A valid method is one that provides a true, authentic picture of the topic being researched. Critics of structured interviews argue that, like questionnaires, they often produce a false picture of the subjects they are trying to study.

- Structured interviews usually use closed-ended questions that restrict interviewees to choosing from a limited number of pre-set answers. If none of these answers fits what the interviewee really wishes to say, the data obtained will be invalid.
- Structured interviews give interviewers very little freedom to explain questions or clarify misunderstandings. For example, they may be given one alternative form of words to use if the interviewee doesn't understand the question, but if this fails to do the trick the interviewer usually has to move on to the next question.
- People may lie or exaggerate. These responses will produce false data.

The interview is a social interaction and so there is always a risk that the interaction between interviewer and interviewee will influence the answers given. For example, gender and ethnic differences can affect the answers, as can the interviewee's desire to be seen in a favourable light (see page 200).

5 Inflexibility

Like self-completed questionnaires, structured interviews suffer from the inflexibility that comes from having to draw up the questions in advance. The researcher has already decided what is important – yet this may not coincide with what the interviewee thinks is important.

As a result, the findings may lack validity because they do not reflect the interviewee's concerns and priorities. In particular, establishing the questions beforehand and then sticking to them rigidly will make it impossible to pursue any interesting leads that emerge in the course of the interviews, thereby losing valuable insights.

Also like questionnaires, structured interviews are merely snapshots taken at one moment in time, so they fail to capture the flowing, dynamic nature of social life.

6 Feminist criticisms

Hilary Graham (1983) argues that survey methods such as questionnaires and structured interviews are patriarchal and give a distorted, invalid picture of women's experience. She argues that:

- The researcher is in control of the interview and decides the line of questioning to be followed. This mirrors women's subordination in wider society.

- Survey methods treat women as isolated individuals rather than seeing them in the context of the power relationships that oppress them.
- Surveys impose the researcher's categories on women, making it difficult for them to express their experiences and concealing the unequal power relationships between the sexes.

These feminist criticisms are similar to those put forward by interpretivist sociologists. Graham argues that sociologists need to use methods that allow the researcher to understand women's behaviour, attitudes and meanings. She therefore advocates the use of direct observation instead.

Feminists also ague that gender inequality is an important factor limiting the reliability of interviews (see Box 29).

Unstructured interviews

Whereas a structured interview follows a standardised format, in an unstructured interview the interviewer has complete freedom to vary the interview. Supporters argue that this brings a number of important advantages.

Advantages of unstructured interviews

While structured interviews are criticised for their lack of validity unstructured interviews are widely seen as a way of gathering valid data, enabling researchers to get a deeper understanding of the interviewee's world. There are several reasons for this, which we examine below.

1 Rapport and sensitivity

The informality of unstructured interviews allows the interviewer to develop a rapport (relationship of trust and understanding) with the interviewee. This is more likely to put the interviewee at their ease and encourage them to open up than a formal structured interview.

A good example of this is the work of William Labov (1973). When using a more formal interview technique to study the language of black American children, they appeared to be tongue-tied and 'linguistically deprived'. However, adopting a more relaxed, informal style – the interviewer sitting on the floor, the child allowed to have a friend present – brought a completely different response. The children opened up and spoke freely, showing that they were competent speakers.

Unstructured interviews are particularly useful when researching sensitive topics. The empathy and encouragement of the interviewer will help the interviewee to feel comfortable discussing difficult or personal subjects such as abuse.

2 The interviewee's view

Because there are no set questions, unstructured interviews allow the interviewee more opportunity to speak about those things they think are important. This contrasts with the structured interview, where the researcher decides in advance what questions are worth asking and limits interviewees to a fixed range of possible answers. By allowing them greater freedom to express their views, an unstructured interview is more likely to produce fresh insights and valid data. Similarly, the interviewer's probing can help formulate and develop interviewees' thoughts more clearly.

In their study of claimants' experiences of unemployment, Hartley Dean and Peter Taylor-Gooby (1992) used unstructured tape-recorded interviews, lasting up to 90 minutes, with 85 claimants. In their words:

'Questions were not put in any set order; the wording of questions was adapted to fit the circumstances of the respondent and/or the interview situation; questions which were evidently inappropriate were omitted altogether; additional questions or prompts were used at the interviewer's discretion to clarify or develop themes as they emerged.'

This approach gives interviewees the freedom to talk in their own terms about the issues that concern them.

3 Checking understanding

A great danger in structured interviews is that the interviewee misunderstands the question, or the interviewer misunderstands the answer.

A major advantage of unstructured interviews is that they make it much easier for interviewer and interviewee to check each other's meanings. If the interviewee doesn't understand a question, it can be explained. Similarly, if the interviewer is unsure what the interviewee's answer means, follow-up questions can be put to clarify matters.

4 Flexibility

Unstructured interviews are highly flexible. The interviewer is not restricted to a fixed set of questions in advance, but can explore whatever seems interesting or relevant. The researcher can formulate new ideas and hypotheses and then put them to the test as they arise during the course of the interview. There is no need to go away and draw up a new interview schedule, as there would be if using structured interviews.

5 Exploring unfamiliar topics

With structured interviews, researchers need to have some knowledge of the subject and preferably also a clear hypothesis before they start interviewing; otherwise, they would have little idea of what questions to ask.

However, where the subject is one that we don't yet know much about, unstructured interviews may be more useful, precisely because they are open-ended and exploratory. As with an ordinary conversation, we can start out knowing nothing and, by asking questions, learn as we go along. Some sociologists use unstructured interviews as a starting point to develop their initial ideas about a topic before going on to use more structured methods of investigation.

Disadvantages of unstructured interviews

Despite their strengths, using unstructured interviews as a method of collecting data has a number of disadvantages.

1 Practical problems

Being in-depth explorations, unstructured interviews take a long time to conduct – often several hours each. This limits the number that can be carried out and means that the researcher will have a relatively small sample compared with the larger numbers who can be studied using structured interviews or questionnaires.

Training also needs to be more thorough than for someone conducting structured interviews. The interviewer needs to have a background in sociology so they can recognise when the interviewee has made a sociologically important point and can probe further with an appropriate line of questioning. All this adds to the cost of conducting unstructured interviews.

Interviewers also need good interpersonal skills so they can establish the rapport that is essential if interviewees are to answer fully and honestly.

2 Representativeness

The smaller numbers involved mean a greater likelihood that the sample interviewed will not be representative. This means that it will be harder to make valid generalisations based on the findings of the interviews.

3 Reliability

Unstructured interviews are not reliable because they are not standardised. Each interview is unique: interviewers are free to ask different questions in each case if they feel it is relevant to do so. This makes it virtually impossible for another researcher to replicate the interviews and check the findings or compare them with their own.

4 Quantification

Because unstructured interviews use mainly open-ended questions, answers cannot be pre-coded. This makes it very difficult to count up and quantify the numbers of interviewees giving this or that answer. In turn, the lack of quantitative data makes unstructured interviews less useful for establishing cause-and-effect relationships and hypothesis testing that positivists prefer.

5 Validity

Unstructured interviews are generally seen as producing valid data. However, critics argue that the fact that they involve an interaction between interviewer and interviewee inevitably distorts the information obtained. As we have seen, structured interviews are also susceptible to the same problem, even if not to the same extent. We examine the problems of interviews as interactions next.

| Box 28 | Positivism, interpretivism and interviews |

Positivists favour *structured* interviews because they achieve the main positivist goals of reliability, generalisability and representativeness:

- Standardised questions and answers produce reliable data because other researchers can replicate the interview.
- Pre-coded responses allow us to produce quantitative data, identify and measure behaviour patterns, and establish cause-and-effect relationships.
- Structured interviews are often large scale and thus more representative.

Interpretivists reject structured interviews because they impose the researcher's framework of ideas on interviewees.

Interpretivists favour *unstructured* interviews because they achieve the main interpretivist goal of validity:

- Absence of a pre-set structure means interviewees can discuss what is important to them.
- Open-ended questions allow interviewees to express themselves in their own words, thereby producing qualitative data that gives us an insight into their meanings.

Positivists reject unstructured interviews because each one is unique and cannot be replicated.

See Box 20 on page 166 for more about positivism, interpretivism and research methods.

The interview as a social interaction

All interviews, whether structured or unstructured, involve a social interaction between interviewer and interviewee. The danger is that the interviewee may be responding not to the questions themselves but the social situation in which they are asked.

Social interactions can threaten the validity of interviews in several ways.

1 Interviewer bias

The interviewer may ask 'leading' questions, where the wording 'tells' the interviewee how to answer. For example, the question, 'Wouldn't you agree that women should not go out to work when they have young children?' clearly implies that the interviewer expects the answer, 'Yes'. This is a greater danger in unstructured than in structured interviews, where the interview schedule restricts the interviewer to a particular set of questions and fixed wording. Interviewers may also consciously or unconsciously influence the answer by their facial expression, body language or tone of voice.

Another source of interviewer bias is where the interviewer identifies too closely with the interviewees. For example, Ann Oakley (1982) admits that, as a mother herself, she found it difficult to remain detached and neutral when interviewing other women about maternity and childbirth.

2 Artificiality

Even the most relaxed of unstructured interviews is still an interview and not a normal conversation: both parties know it is an interview, in which one 'side' takes the initiative and asks the questions. Under these artificial conditions, it is doubtful whether truthful answers can be obtained.

3 Status and power inequalities

Inequalities between interviewer and interviewee may affect the interviewee's honesty or willingness to answer. In general, the bigger the status difference, the less valid the data. For example, Josephine Rich (1968) shows that when adults interview children, the child's need to please the interviewer will affect their answers.

Similarly, gender differences in power and status can shape the interview, as Box 29 shows, while ethnic inequalities between interviewer and interviewee may make interviewing very difficult. This led John Howard Griffin (1962) to abandon interviewing in favour of participant observation (see Box 32, page 210).

While all interviews risk distorting the data as a result of these factors, structured interviews may be less susceptible. This is because in a structured interview there are more controls over the nature of the interaction. For example, the interviewer has to follow a standard list of pre-set questions.

> Identify two ways in which gender differences might affect the relationship between interviewers and interviewees.

| Box 29 | Interviewing in patriarchal society |

In a patriarchal society, female sociologists interviewing men may find that the power difference between them undermines the conventional notion of the interviewer as the 'dominant' actor in the interview, as Lorna McKee and Margaret O'Brien (1983) discovered in their study of fathers.

The men frequently tried to manipulate the interview for their own ends: for example, lone fathers often used it to express grievances against their ex-wives. Sometimes the interview came to resemble a 'wooing process', with one lone father even going so far as to prepare a meal of cheese soufflé and wine.

Although the authors experienced no physical abuse, there were instances of being pestered for further contact, and McKee and O'Brien took conscious decisions about make-up and clothes, and about maintaining a professional manner during the interviews. For example, they used 'props' such as tape-recorder, clipboard and interview schedule to define themselves as detached and scientific researchers rather than as potential sexual partners.

It seems unlikely that male sociologists conducting similar research would have had to take such precautions, which suggests that gender is an important factor limiting the reliability of interviews: if gender affects interactions and responses in the interview, then sociologists of a different gender are likely to obtain different answers to the same questions.

The researchers also found that their interviews with fathers were generally shorter and more formal than those they conducted with mothers, reflecting what they call the 'legitimacy of the topic'. British culture prescribes a 'sturdy oak' role for men – 'the strong, silent male' – and this restricts their ability to talk about personal feelings.

As McKee and O'Brien show, gender inequalities can have an important bearing on the data produced by cross-gender interviewing. The wider patriarchal structure of gender relationships in society influences the way interviews are conducted and the kinds of responses they produce.

4 Cultural differences

These may also undermine validity. There may be misunderstandings as a result of different meanings being given to the same words.

The cultural gap may also mean that interviewers cannot tell when they are being lied to. For example, Margaret Mead's (1943) research on adolescents in Samoa in the western Pacific has been criticised on the grounds that Mead, who couldn't speak the language, was unable to spot that the girls she interviewed had deliberately misled her.

5 The social desirability effect

In social interaction, people often seek to win approval. This may be even truer in an interview, where interviewees may be on their best behaviour and give answers that present themselves in a favourable light.

They may also wish not to appear ignorant or uninteresting and so, instead of saying that they don't know or don't understand the question, they offer any answer at all rather than none.

6 Ethical issues

There are relatively few ethical problems with interviews. Nevertheless, because the interview is a social interaction, the interviewee may feel under some pressure to answer questions. Researchers should gain interviewees' informed consent, guarantee anonymity and make it clear that they have a right not to answer any of the questions that they do not wish to.

Improving the validity of interviews

Some researchers use techniques to improve the chances of obtaining valid data. For example, to reduce the chance of interviewees making up answers or telling lies, Alfred Kinsey's (1953) interviews on sexual behaviour asked questions rapidly, giving interviewees little time to think, and used some questions to check the answers given to others. Follow-up interviews 18 months later were also used as a way of checking earlier answers.

Howard Becker (1971) developed another approach in his interviews with 60 Chicago schoolteachers. He used aggression, disbelief and 'playing dumb' as ways of extracting sensitive information from them that they might not otherwise have revealed, about how they classified pupils in terms of their social class and ethnic background. It should be stressed, however, that the success of such tactics requires the researcher to have special skills. For the same reason, this approach might also prove difficult to replicate.

Other researchers have overcome the problem of cultural differences by ensuring that interviewers and interviewees are ethnically and language-matched. For example, the interviews for James Nazroo's (1997) survey of the health of Britain's ethnic minorities were carried out in the language of the interviewee's choice. Questions and other materials were translated and tested in pilot studies before being used in the main study.

All these techniques can help to improve the validity of answers.

For more activities on Interviews...

Go to www.sociology.uk.net

Summary

Structured interviews use closed-ended questions. They are quicker and cheaper than unstructured interviews, cover larger numbers and produce **reliable** data, but lack validity and flexibility.

Unstructured interviews use open-ended questions, producing **valid** data by allowing interviewees to express themselves fully. However, they are less representative, and quantification is difficult.

Interviews are **social interactions** and face problems of interviewer bias, status or cultural differences between interviewer and interviewee.

Group interviews are relatively unstructured; they can be useful in revealing group dynamics.

QuickCheck Questions

1 Which of the following do you associate with structured interviews and which with unstructured?

(a) rapport   (b) similar to a questionnaire
(c) informal   (d) pre-coded questions
(e) standardised   (f) probing
(g) quantitative data (h) findings easily analysed.
(i) freedom to vary the questions

2 What is a focus group?

3 Identify one similarity and one difference between structured interviews and postal questionnaires.

4 True or false? Structured interviews produce valid data whereas unstructured interviews produce reliable data.

5 Give two examples of ways that an interviewer might influence a interviewee's answer.

6 What is the social desirability effect?

 Check your answers at www.sociology.uk.net

Examining interviews

(a) Explain what is meant by 'rapport'. (2 marks)

(b) Suggest **one** advantage and **one** disadvantage of using group interviews rather than one-to-one interviews in sociological research. (4 marks)

(c) Suggest **two** ways in which sociologists can improve the validity of interviews as a source of data. (4 marks)

(d) Examine the reasons why some sociologists choose to use structured interviews when conducting their research. (20 marks)

The examiner's advice

Part (d) is an 'Examine' question of the type you will see in the exam. It carries 10 AO1 marks (knowledge and understanding) and 10 AO2 marks (interpretation, application, analysis and evaluation).

Most of the AO1 marks are for knowledge of the strengths of structured interviews. Practical *strengths* include the fact that, when compared to most other methods, they are quick and cheap to administer, can cover large numbers and often achieve a high response rate. They are useful for gathering basic factual information and closed-ended questions and coded answers make results easy to quantify.

The main theoretical strength of structured interviews is reliability. They are standardised measuring instruments, where all interviewees are asked exactly the same questions, in the same order etc. This makes them easy to replicate by other researchers. Also, because they study relatively large numbers, findings may be representative and generalisable. Relate these points to the positivist-interpretivist debate (see Box 28). There are few ethical limitations with structured interviews, though researchers still need to obtain informed consent and guarantee anonymity.

You can gain AO2 marks by referring briefly to the *limitations* of structured interviews. Try to link each limitation to a strength as you go, rather than listing all the strengths at the end. For example, standardised questions mean greater reliability, but may prevent interviewers clarifying misunderstandings and so reduce the validity of the answers. You can also gain AO2 marks by comparing structured interviews with other methods, such as questionnaires or unstructured interviews, and by applying examples from studies.

METHODS IN CONTEXT
using interviews to investigate education

Sociologists may use interviews to study issues such as:

- Pupil subcultures
- Pupils' experience of sex and health education
- Class, ethnicity and language
- Gender identity and the male gaze
- Class and parental choice of schools.

Before reading this section, re-visit Topic 2 to refresh your understanding of what is different about researching education.

Practical issues

Young people's linguistic and intellectual skills are less developed than those of adults and this may pose practical problems for interviewers. Young interviewees may

- Be more inarticulate or reluctant to talk.
- Not understand long, complex sentences or some abstract concepts.
- Have a more limited vocabulary and use words incorrectly.
- Have a shorter attention span and poorer memory retrieval than adults.
- Read body language differently from adults.

These factors may lead to misunderstandings and incorrect or incomplete answers and thus undermine the validity of the data obtained. Such communication difficulties also mean that unstructured interviews may be more suitable than structured ones, since they allow the interviewer more scope to clear up misunderstandings by re-wording questions or explaining their meaning.

However, children may also have more difficulty in keeping to the point, especially in unstructured interviews. As Janet Powney and Mike Watts (1987) note, young children tend to be more literal minded and often pay attention to unexpected details in questions, and may use a different logic from adult interviewers. Training therefore needs to be more thorough for someone interviewing children, which adds to the costs of the research.

However, given that young people tend to have better verbal than literacy skills, interviews may be more successful than written questionnaires as a method of obtaining valid answers.

Another practical problem is that schools have very active informal communication channels. This means that the content of the interview – possibly an inaccurate version of it – may get around most pupils and teachers after only a few interviews have taken place. This can influence the responses given by later interviewees, thus reducing the validity of the data.

Reliability

Structured interviews produce reliable data because they are standardised: each interview is conducted in precisely the same way, with the same questions, in the same order, tone of voice and so on.

1 What is meant by 'response rate'?

2 What is meant by 'validity'?

3 What effect might age, gender or ethnic differences between the interviewer and interviewee have on the response rate and on the validity of the answers given?

However, structured interviews may not produce valid data, since young people are unlikely to respond favourably to such a formal style – perhaps because it makes the interviewer appear too much like a teacher.

Instead of using this formal approach, therefore, Di Bentley (1987) began each interview by showing them a 'jokey' image of her fooling around with her daughter. During the interview, she maintained a relaxed atmosphere by showing listening behaviours such as nodding, smiling and eye contact.

However, this is a very personal interviewing style that cannot easily be standardised. Thus, different interviewers would be likely to obtain very different results and this would reduce the reliability and comparability of their findings.

Access and response rate

Schools are hierarchical institutions and this can cause problems when seeking to interview teachers or pupils. As Powney and Watts note, the lower down the hierarchy the interviewee is, the more approvals that have to be obtained. Thus, to interview a teacher, a researcher might first have to obtain the permission of both the local education authority and the head.

Schools may also be reluctant to allow sociologists to conduct interviews during lesson time because of the disruption it causes, or because they object to the researcher's chosen topic. For example, some schools might object to interviews about under-age sexual activity. Similarly, there may be problems conducting interviews after school hours, whether on the premises or in pupils' homes.

> What problems might there be in conducting interviews in pupils' own homes?

Parental permission may also be required to interview children. The likelihood of this being granted varies according to the subject of research. Field's (1987) study of pupils' experience of sex and health education in schools had a relatively high refusal rate of 29 per cent, mainly because of parents withholding consent.

On the other hand, if the researcher can obtain official support for the study, then the hierarchical nature of school may work in their favour. For example, heads can instruct teachers to release pupils from class for interviews and this may increase the response rate.

The interviewer as 'teacher in disguise'

Power and status inequalities can affect the outcome of interviews. If interviewees have less power than the interviewer, they may see it as being in their own interests to lie, exaggerate, conceal information or seek to please when answering questions. They may also be less self-confident and their responses less articulate. All this will reduce the validity of the data.

There are power and status inequalities between young people and adults. Interviewers are usually adults and children may see them as authority figures. This is even more likely in educational research, especially if the interviews are conducted on school premises. In this situation, Bell (1981) notes, pupils may see the interviewer as a 'teacher in disguise'.

This may affect the validity of the data in several ways. For example, pupils may seek to win the 'teacher's' approval by giving untrue but socially acceptable answers that show them in a favourable light, for example about how much time they spend on homework.

Similarly, pupils are accustomed to adults 'knowing better' and so may defer to them in interviews. For example, children are more likely than adults to change their original answer when the question is repeated because they think it must have been wrong.

The interview is a social interaction. The inequalities between children and adults, pupils and teachers, may influence this interaction and thus distort the data obtained.

Improving the validity of interviews with pupils

As we have seen, interviews may not produce valid data. That is, they may not give a true picture of young people's

---

Box 30   **A group interview**

In this extract from a group interview conducted by Paul Willis, four of the 'lads' are discussing teachers:

Joey   They're bigger than us, they stand for a bigger establishment than we do. Like, we're just little and they stand for bigger things, and you try to get your own back. It's, uh, resenting authority, I suppose.

Eddie   The teachers think they're high and mighty 'cos they're teachers, but they're nobody really, they're just ordinary people, ain't they?

Bill   Teachers think they're everybody. They are more, they're higher than us, but they think they're a lot higher and they're not.

Spanksy   Wish we could call them [by their] first names and that…[they] think they're God.

Source: adapted from Willis (1976), *Learning to Labour*

▲ *What would be the difficulties and the advantages of conducting group interviews with children like these?*

In general, unstructured interviews may be more suitable for overcoming barriers of power and status inequality. Their informality can put young interviewees at their ease and establish rapport more easily. As Labov's research shows (page 197), this can encourage interviewees to open up and respond more fully, thus producing more valid data. This can be particularly useful when dealing with sensitive topics such as bullying.

Group interviews

An alternative to the conventional one-to-one interview is the group interview. This has both strengths and limitations as a method of studying education.

attitudes and behaviour. However, researchers can adopt strategies to improve the validity of interviews with pupils and young people. For example, Sheila Greene and Diane Hogan (2005) argue that interviewers should:

- Use open-ended rather closed-ended questions.
- Not interrupt children's answers.
- Tolerate long pauses to allow children to think about what they want to say.
- Recognise that children are more suggestible and so it is particularly important to avoid asking leading questions.
- Avoid repeating questions, since this makes children change their first answer because they think it was wrong.

Activity

Questionnaires can be difficult to use with young children because they cannot read well. This makes interviews a more suitable method, but we can sometimes use pictures as stimulus material alongside an interview. For example, if you wished to investigate children's ideas about gender role differences, one method would be to show them pictures connected to different jobs (e.g. a fire engine, computer etc) and ask them who would do the associated job – male, female or both?

In pairs, suggest another question that could be put to young children using pictures. Then, if you know a young child you could interview, draw (or cut out) some of the pictures and try them out. How well did they work? How difficult was it to stop yourself 'leading' the child?

Pupils and young people are often strongly influenced by peer pressure and this may reduce the validity of data gathered in a group interview, where individuals may conform to peer expectations rather than express what they truly think.

For example, the exchange in Box 30 reads like an authentic statement of the boys' shared values. Yet it is difficult to know whether the views expressed are genuinely shared or simply the product of the boys egging each other on to say similar things. In addition, the free-flowing nature of group interviews makes it impossible to standardise the questions and this will reduce the reliability of the method and the comparability of findings.

On the other hand, Greene and Hogan argue that group interviews are particularly suitable for use with pupils. They create a safe peer environment and they reproduce the small group settings that young people are familiar with in classroom work. Peer support also reduces the power imbalance between adult interviewer and young interviewee found in one-to-one interviews.

Group interviews can also reveal the interactions between pupils. For example, Box 30 illustrates how the lads reinforce their opposition to authority. However, peer pressure may influence individuals to give answers that conform to the group's values, rather than expressing their true opinions. For example, Spanksy begins to express a different view of teachers from the other lads, but then conforms to the group's anti-authority values.

Examining interviews in context

Researching pupil subcultures

A pupil subculture is a group of pupils who share similar values and attitudes. While some subcultures share the values of the school, others oppose them. Sociologists are interested in the reasons why pupil subcultures develop, their characteristics and how they contribute to class, gender and ethnic differences in achievement.

One problem with researching pupil subcultures is that pupils holding anti-school values are unlikely to cooperate, for example because they see the researcher as just a 'teacher in disguise'. Even if they do agree to participate, such pupils may still not take the research seriously. 5

A pupil subculture has its own shared norms and group dynamics. Unstructured group interviews can be particularly useful in revealing these.

Question

Using material from **Item A** and elsewhere, assess the strengths and limitations of unstructured interviews for the study of pupil subcultures.

(20 marks)

The examiner's advice

This question carries 8 A01 marks (knowledge and understanding) and 12 A02 marks (interpretation, application, analysis and evaluation). It requires you to **apply** your knowledge and understanding of unstructured interviews to the study of the **particular** issue of pupil subcultures. It is not enough simply to discuss unstructured interviews in general.

For example, Item A suggests that one issue in studying pupil subcultures is that anti-school pupils are unlikely to cooperate. The researcher will need to find some way of overcoming this barrier if they are to uncover the pupils' world-view. Unstructured interviews are very useful for doing this as they allow trust to build, thus reducing any identification of the researcher with school authority. This allows the researcher to get closer to the real meanings held by pupils.

Similarly, Item A notes that group interviews can reveal subcultural norms and dynamics, and you could explain this strength. On the other hand, subcultural peer group pressure may prevent individuals from expressing themselves freely in these interviews, thus undermining validity.

Other problems with researching young people in pupil subcultures include their greater vulnerability, poorer linguistic skills and lower status in school. You need to link the strengths and limitations of unstructured interviews to issues such as these.

You need to keep a reasonable balance between the strengths and limitations of unstructured interviews. You can also refer to studies that have used this method (e.g. Willis, Hargreaves) and to any relevant research you have been involved in.

What problems might a sociologist face in using participant observation to study this group?

Topic 7 Participant observation

As we have seen, one problem of using survey methods such as interviews or questionnaires to study people is that what they say they do and what they actually do may be two quite different things. For example, in interviews, people may conceal information or lie about their real behaviour in order to please the interviewer, save face or create a better impression of themselves.

One way of overcoming this problem might be simply to see for ourselves what people really do by observing them in their normal everyday environment rather than questioning them in an artificial interview situation.

By using observational methods rather than questioning people, we might hope to get a truer, more valid picture of social reality. There are many techniques for observing people. In this Topic, we briefly look at some of the main types of observational method before focusing on the one that is used most often by sociologists – namely, participant observation.

Learning objectives

After studying this Topic, you should:

- Know the different types of observational methods.
- Be able to explain the main stages in conducting a participant observation study.
- Be able to evaluate the strengths and limitations of overt and covert participant observation.
- Be able to apply your understanding of observational methods to the study of education.

Types of observation

There are several different types of observation. Firstly, we can distinguish between:

- Non-participant observation: the researcher simply observes the group or event without taking part in it. For example, they may use a two-way mirror to observe children playing.
- Participant observation: the researcher actually takes part in the event or the everyday life of the group while observing it.

Secondly, we can distinguish between:

- Overt observation: the researcher makes their true identity and purpose known to those being studied. The sociologist is open about what they are doing.
- Covert observation: the study is carried out 'under cover'. The researcher's real identity and purpose are kept concealed from the group being studied. The researcher takes on a false identity and role, usually posing as a genuine member of the group.

However, actual research does not always fit neatly into one or other of these categories. For example, William Whyte's (1955) study of 'Street Corner Society' was semi-overt (partly open). He revealed his real purpose to a key member of the group, Doc, but not to others.

In sociology, most observation is unstructured participant observation. However, positivist sociologists in particular do occasionally use structured observation, which is normally non-participant. Here, the researcher uses a structured observational schedule to categorise systematically what happens.

The schedule is a pre-determined list of the types of behaviour or situations the sociologist is interested in. Each

1 What advantages might there be for the researcher in revealing their real purpose to a key member of the group?

2 What disadvantages might there be?

Activity

Look at the three examples of observational studies below and decide which one is most likely to be done using

(a) covert participant observation

(b) overt non-participant observation

(c) covert non-participant observation.

1 Observing the interactions of mothers and children using a hidden camera.

2 Joining a criminal gang.

3 Sitting in to observe a school class.

time an instance of such behaviour occurs, the sociologist records it on the schedule, for example, how often boys and girls in a nursery play with particular toys. The researcher adds up the number of times each event occurs. This produces quantitative data, from which patterns and correlations can then be established. (See page 215 for an example of a structured observational schedule.)

Finally, observation may be used in conjunction with other methods. For example, when interviewing, the researcher may observe interviewees' body language to gauge whether or not they are telling the truth.

Conducting a participant observation study

Sociologists face two main issues when conducting a participant observation study:

- getting in, staying in and getting out of the group being studied
- whether to use overt or covert observation. We examine these two issues below.

Getting in

To do the study, we must first gain entry to the group. Some groups are easier to enter than others. For example, joining a football crowd is likely to be easier than joining a criminal gang.

making contact

Making the initial contact with the group may depend on personal skills, having the right connections, or even pure chance. Ned Polsky (1971), who was a good pool player himself, found his skill useful in gaining entry to the world of the poolroom hustler. James Patrick (1973) – not his real name – was able to join a Glasgow gang because he looked quite young and knew one of its members from having taught him in approved school. Eileen Fairhurst (1977) found herself hospitalised by back trouble and used the opportunity to conduct a study on being a patient.

acceptance

To gain entry to a group, the researcher will have to win their trust and acceptance. It may help to make friends with a key individual, as Sarah Thornton (1995) did with Kate in her study of the clubbing and rave scene. Sometimes, though, the researcher's age, gender, class or ethnicity may prove an obstacle. Thornton found her age and nationality a barrier:

'I began my research when I was 23 and slowly aged out of the peer group I was studying. Also, as a Canadian investigating British clubs and raves, I was quite literally a stranger in a strange land.'

Thornton was met with suspicion at first. As Kate's brother put it, 'How do you know she won't sell this to the Daily Mirror?' However, such barriers can sometimes be overcome. A white researcher, Elliot Liebow (1967), succeeded in gaining acceptance by a black street-corner gang in Washington DC. Some researchers have gone to remarkable lengths to gain acceptance and pass as one of the group, but probably none more so than John Howard Griffin (1962) (see Box 32).

observer's role

'Getting in' poses the question of what role the researcher should adopt. Ideally, it should:

- be one that does not disrupt the group's normal patterns
- offer a good vantage point from which to make observations.

Whyte succeeded in achieving both these aims by refusing all leadership roles, with the one exception of secretary of the community club, a position that allowed him to take ample notes under the guise of taking the minutes of meetings.

However, it is not always possible to take a role that is both unobtrusive and a good vantage point. Some roles may also involve taking sides in conflicts, with the result that the researcher may become estranged from one faction or the other, making observation more difficult.

1 Suggest two reasons why characteristics such as a researcher's age, gender, social class, ethnicity or personal appearance may prove an obstacle to 'getting in' to a group.

2 Why might it be a good idea to avoid taking leadership roles when doing participant observation?

Staying in

Once accepted, the researcher needs to be able to stay in the group and complete the study. Here we can see a key problem for the participant observer: having to be both involved in the group so as to understand it fully, and yet at the same time detached from the group so as to remain objective and unbiased.

going native

One danger of staying in the group is that of becoming over-involved or 'going native'. By over-identifying with the group, the researcher becomes biased. When this happens, they have stopped being an objective observer and have simply become a member of the group.

For example, in his study of the Amsterdam police, Maurice Punch (1979) found that in striving to be accepted by the tightly-knit patrol group he was studying, he over-identified with them, even acting as a 'policeman' himself – chasing and holding suspects, searching houses, cars and people, and shouting at people who abused his police 'colleagues'.

At the other extreme, the researcher may preserve their detachment so as to avoid bias, but by remaining detached they risk not understanding the events they observe. Striking a balance between these two extremes is immensely difficult. As David Downes and Paul Rock (1989) put it:

Box 31	Positivism, interpretivism and observation

Interpretivists favour *unstructured participant* observation because it achieves their main goal of validity:

- Observation gives the researcher a true picture because it shows us what people do, rather than simply what they say they do.
- Participation in the group gives the researcher first hand insight into social actors' meanings and behaviour – especially if carried out covertly.

Positivists reject participant observation because its lack of structure means it cannot be replicated or results quantified.

Positivists favour *structured non-participant* observation because it achieves their main goals of reliability, generalisability and representativeness:

- Standardised behaviour categories produce reliable data because other researchers can replicate the observation.
- Pre-determined observational categories allow us to produce quantitative data, identify and measure behaviour patterns, and establish cause-and-effect relationships.
- Structured observation takes less time than unstructured observation, so a larger, more representative sample can be studied.

Interpretivists reject structured observation as it imposes the researcher's view of reality on those being observed, resulting in invalid data.

See Box 20 on page 166 for more about positivism, interpretivism and research methods.

'Participant-observers try to perform a most intricate feat. They are required to reach the probably unattainable state of one who is both insider and outsider, a person who sees a social world from within it in the manner of a member yet who also stands apart and analyses it in the manner of a stranger.'

A further problem of staying in is that the longer the researcher spends with the group, the less strange its ways come to appear. After a while, the researcher may cease to notice things that would have struck them as unusual or noteworthy at an earlier stage of the research: the observer becomes less observant. As Whyte put it, 'I started as a non-participating observer and ended as a non-observing participator'.

Getting out

In practical terms, getting out of the group at the end of the study generally presents fewer problems than getting in or staying in. If the worst comes to the worst, the researcher can simply call a halt and leave. This was Patrick's experience of studying a Glasgow gang when, sickened by the violence, he abandoned the study abruptly. Others can leave more gracefully, particularly if their observation has been overt.

Nevertheless, leaving a group with whom one has become close can be difficult.

Re-entering one's normal world can also be difficult. Whyte found that when he returned to Harvard University after his research, he was tongue-tied and unable to communicate with fellow academics. These problems can be made worse if the research is conducted on and off over a period of time, with multiple 'crossings' between the two worlds.

The researcher may also find that loyalty prevents them from fully disclosing everything they have learnt, for fear that this might harm members of the group. For example, in the case of criminal groups, exposure of their activities might lead to prosecution, or reprisals against the author. Clearly, such concealment of data will reduce the validity of the study.

1 Explain what is meant by 'going native'.

2 How might going native lead to invalid data?

Overt observation

Sociologists face the decision whether to use overt or covert observation. Many sociologists favour the use of overt observation, where the researcher reveals his or her true identity and purpose to the group and asks their permission to observe. This has several advantages:

- It avoids the ethical (moral) problem of obtaining information by deceit and, when studying deviant groups, that of being expected to join in their activities.

- It allows the observer to ask the kind of naive but important questions that only an outsider could ask. For example, the researcher could ask a gang member, 'Why do you rob and steal?'
- The observer can take notes openly.
- It allows the researcher to use interview methods to check insights derived from observations.

However, overt observation has two major disadvantages:

- A group may refuse the researcher permission to observe them, or may prevent them from seeing everything. As two of the Amsterdam police officers that Punch had done his research with later told him, 'When you were with us, we only let you see what we wanted you to see'.
- It risks creating the Hawthorne Effect (see page 174), where those who know they are being observed begin to behave differently as a result. This undermines the validity of the data.

Covert observation

Because of these disadvantages, some sociologists choose to carry out covert observation. However, the use of covert observation raises several practical and ethical issues.

Practical issues

The main practical advantage of covert observation is that it reduces the risk of altering people's behaviour, and sometimes it is the only way to obtain valid information. This is particularly true where people are engaged in activities that they would rather keep secret. As Laud Humphreys (1970), who studied gay men's sexual encounters in public toilets, notes: 'There is only one way to watch highly discreditable behaviour and that is to pretend to be in the same boat with those engaging in it.'

If they knew they were being observed, they would change or conceal their behaviour and so the main advantage of observation – that it preserves the naturalness of people's behaviour – would be lost.

On the other hand, covert participant observation can pose practical problems:

- It requires the researcher to keep up an act, and may call for detailed knowledge of the group's way of life even before joining it. There is always a risk of one's cover being 'blown' by even a trivial mistake. Patrick was almost found out when he bought his suit with cash instead of credit and when he fastened the middle button of his jacket rather than the top one – things the gang would never have done. This is likely to bring the research to an abrupt end and may, in the case of some criminal groups, lead to physical harm. As Polsky advises, therefore:

'You damned well better not pretend to be "one of them" because they will test this claim out and you will either find yourself involved in illegal activities, or your cover will be blown.'

This was something Patrick also discovered when the gang handed him an axe to use in an expected fight.

- The sociologist cannot usually take notes openly and must rely on memory and the opportunity to write them in secret. Both Leon Festinger et al (1956), studying a religious sect that had predicted the imminent end of the world, and Jason Ditton (1977), studying theft among bread deliverymen, had to use toilets as a place for recording their observations. In Ditton's case, this eventually aroused suspicion.

- The researcher cannot ask naive but important questions, or combine observation with other methods, such as interviews.

- Although pretending to be an insider rather than an outsider reduces the risk of the Hawthorne Effect, the addition of a new member (the researcher) can still change the group's behaviour, thus reducing validity.

Ethical issues

Covert participant observation raises serious ethical (moral) issues for researchers. These often conflict with the practical advantage it brings of observing natural behaviour.

- It is immoral to deceive people, obtaining information by pretending to be their friend or 'in the same boat'. Researchers should obtain the informed consent of their subjects, and reveal the purpose of the study and the use to which its findings will be put. With covert observation, this cannot normally be done.

- Covert observers may have to lie about their reasons for leaving the group at the end of their research. Others, such as Patrick, simply abandon the group without explanation. Critics argue that this is unethical.

- They may have to participate in immoral or illegal activities as part of their 'cover' role.

- Similarly, as witnesses to such activities, they may have a moral or legal duty to intervene or to report them to the police.

Activity

In pairs, look at the examples in this section of situations where participant observers may have felt under pressure to participate in illegal activities (e.g. Patrick, Polsky, Punch, Humphreys).

What consequences might there be for the research and the researcher if they refuse to participate?

Is it ever justifiable ethically to participate in illegal activities as part of the research? Give your reasons.

Box 32	John Howard Griffin: 'Black Like Me'

Some researchers have gone to great lengths to pass as one of the group. An extraordinary example is John Howard Griffin, a white man who in 1959 used medication and sun lamp treatments to change his skin colour and pass as black. He then travelled around the Deep South of the USA experiencing first hand the impact of white racism.

Griffin rejected the use of interviews because, 'Though we lived side by side, communication between the two races had simply ceased to exist. The Southern Negro [the term used at the time to describe black people] will not tell the white man the truth. He long ago learned that if he speaks a truth unpleasing to the white, the white will make life miserable for him'.

And so, 'the only way I could see to bridge the gap between us was to

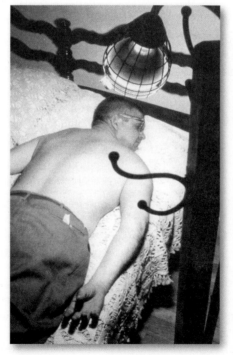

▲ *Griffin under the sun lamp*

▲ *Griffin working at a shoeshine stand, New Orleans*

become a Negro. I decided I would do this. With my decision to become a Negro I realised that I, a specialist in race issues, really knew nothing of the Negro's problems.'

▲ *Griffin with his key informant, Stirling Williams, in New Orleans. Though he told him he was really white, Williams was unconvinced.*

▲ *Griffin in a Negro diner. In the Deep South, public amenities such as schools, cafes, hotels, transport and toilets were all racially segregated.*

Advantages of participant observation

According to its supporters, participant observation offers a range of advantages.

1 Validity

What people say they do when filling in a questionnaire, and what they actually do in real life, are not always the same thing. By contrast, by actually observing them we can obtain a rich source of qualitative data that provides a picture of how they really live. Supporters of participant observation argue that this is the method's main strength, and most of its other advantages are linked to this.

2 Insight

The best way to truly understand what something is like is to experience it for ourselves. Sociologists call this personal or subjective understanding 'verstehen', a German word meaning 'empathy', or understanding that comes from putting yourself in another person's place.

Participant observation allows the researcher to gain empathy through personal experience. By actually living as a member of a group, we can gain insight into their way of life, their meanings and viewpoints, their values and problems. We can come to understand their 'life-world' as they themselves understand it. This closeness to people's lived reality means that participant observation can give uniquely valid, authentic data.

3 Flexibility

Survey methods involve beginning the research with a specific hypothesis and pre-set questions. Even before starting to collect the data, therefore, the researcher has already decided what questions are important. The obvious problem with this is that the questions the researcher thinks are important may not be the same as the ones the subjects think are important.

By contrast, participant observation is a much more flexible method. Rather than starting with a fixed hypothesis, it allows the sociologist to enter the situation with a relatively open mind about what they will find. As new situations are encountered, new explanations can be formulated and the sociologist can change direction to follow them up there and then. In this way, any theories that the researcher produces are 'grounded' in real life.

This open-mindedness allows the researcher to discover things that other methods may miss. As Whyte noted, simply by observing, 'I learned answers to questions that I would not have had the sense to ask if I had been using interviews.' Similarly, Polsky offers some sound, if blunt, advice: 'initially, keep your eyes and ears open but keep your mouth shut'.

4 Practical advantages

Sometimes participant observation may be the only method for studying certain groups, particularly those engaged in activities that wider society sees as deviant or disreputable. Such groups are likely to be suspicious of outsiders who come asking questions. As Lewis Yablonsky (1973) points out, a teenage gang is likely to see researchers who come armed with questionnaires as the unwelcome representatives of authority.

By contrast, because participant observation enables the sociologist to build a rapport with the group and gain its trust, it has proved a successful method of studying delinquent gangs, football hooligans, thieves, drug users, religious sects and other 'outsider' groups.

Participant observation can also be used in other situations where questioning would be ineffective. This is shown in Aaron Cicourel's (1968) study of how police and probation officers categorise juveniles by making unconscious assumptions about whether they are criminal 'types'. Precisely because they are unaware of their assumptions, it would be pointless for the sociologist to ask them questions about these. For Cicourel, therefore, the only way to get at these assumptions is to observe the police directly in their work.

Disadvantages of participant observation

Despite the advantages offered by participant observation, it also suffers from a number of disadvantages.

1 Practical disadvantages

There are several practical disadvantages in using participant observation:

- It is very time-consuming. Whyte's study took him four years to complete.
- The researcher needs to be trained so as to be able to recognise aspects of a situation that are sociologically significant and worth further attention.
- It can be personally stressful and demanding, especially if covert.
- It requires observational and interpersonal skills that not everyone possesses.
- Personal characteristics such as age, gender or ethnicity may restrict what kinds of groups can be studied. As Downes and Rock put it, 'not everyone would pass uneventfully into the world of punk rockers or Hell's Angels'.
- Many groups may not wish to be studied in this way, and some have the power to make access difficult. This is one reason why participant observation often focuses on relatively powerless groups who are less able to resist being studied, such as petty criminals.

2 Ethical problems

As we have seen, covert participant observation in particular raises serious ethical difficulties, including deceiving people in order to obtain information about them and participating in illegal or immoral activities in the course of their sociological research.

3 Representativeness

Sociologists who use quantitative survey methods usually study large, carefully selected representative samples that provide a sound basis for making generalisations. By contrast, in participant observation studies, the group studied is usually very small and the 'sample' is often selected haphazardly, for example by a chance encounter with someone who turns out to be a key informant.

This does not provide a sound basis for making generalisations. As Downes and Rock note, although participant observation may provide valid insights into the particular group being studied, it is doubtful how far these 'internally valid' insights are 'externally valid', that is, generalisable to the wider population.

4 Reliability

Reliability means that if another researcher repeats the method, they will obtain the same results. To achieve reliability, research procedures must be standardised so that other researchers can reproduce them. For example, in structured interviews all interviewers ask the same standard questions in the same way.

By contrast, in participant observation so much depends on the personal skills and characteristics of a lone researcher that it is unlikely any other investigator would be able to replicate the original study. For example, as Whyte recognised, his method was to some extent unique to him alone.

Also, because participant observation usually produces qualitative data, this can make comparisons with other studies difficult. As a result, it is unlikely to produce reliable data. Positivists, who see sociology as scientific, thus reject participant observation as an unsystematic method that cannot be replicated by other researchers.

5 Bias and lack of objectivity

Critics argue that participant observation studies lack objectivity.

- As the term 'going native' indicates, it can be difficult to remain objective and the sociologist may end up presenting a one-sided or biased view of the group.
- Sometimes, loyalty to the group or fear of reprisals leads the sociologist to conceal 'sensitive' information. This denies those who read the published study a full and objective account of the research.
- Participant observation often attracts sociologists whose sympathies lie with the underdog. Since it is seen as an effective method for 'telling it like it is' from the actor's point of view, some of those who use it may be biased in favour of their subjects' viewpoint.

6 Validity

According to its supporters, the great strength of participant observation lies in its validity. As a form of verstehen, allowing the sociologist to become an insider, it gives an authentic account of the actor's world.

Positivists reject this claim. They argue that the findings from such studies are merely the subjective and biased impressions of the observer. Rather than truly 'telling it like it is', participant observation simply tells it as the observer sees it.

Supporters of participant observation claim that it does not impose the sociologist's own categories and ideas on the facts, but positivists argue that in reality the researcher selects what facts they think are worth recording, and that these are likely to fit in with the researcher's pre-existing views and prejudices.

A further threat to validity comes from the Hawthorne Effect: the very presence of the observer may make the subjects act differently. This defeats the main aim of participant observation, to produce a 'naturalistic' account of human behaviour.

7 Lack of a concept of structure

Interactionists favour the use of participant observation. They see society as constructed through the small-scale, face-to-face interactions of its members and the meanings that individual actors give to their situation. In their view, participant observation is a useful tool for examining these micro-level interactions and meanings at first hand.

However, structural sociologists such as Marxists and functionalists see this as inadequate. They argue that because it focuses on the 'micro' level of actors' meanings, participant observation research tends to ignore the wider structural forces that shape our behaviour, such as class inequality or the norms and values into which we are socialised.

In the structuralist view, therefore, seeing things only through the actors' eyes will never give us the complete picture. For example, if the actors are unaware of the structural forces shaping their behaviour, then their own account of their lives, revealed through participant observation, will give us only a partial view.

For more activities on Participant observation...

Go to www.sociology.uk.net

Summary

Participant observation (PO) involves joining in with a group to gain **insight**, and can be overt or covert. Research goes through three phases: getting in, staying in and getting out. **Covert** PO may produce more **valid** data, but is **ethically** questionable and faces **practical** problems of maintaining one's cover. **Interpretivists** claim that PO produces valid data, but **positivists** argue that it is unreliable, unrepresentative and lacks objectivity. They prefer **structured observation**, which is usually non-participant and collects quantitative data.

QuickCheck Questions

1 What do sociologists mean by 'verstehen'?

2 Why can participant observation be described as a flexible method?

3 What problems might the observer have in leaving the group they have been observing?

4 State two advantages of using overt participant observation.

5 Why might participant observation not produce:

 (a) representative data

 (b) reliable data?

6 Suggest two reasons why participant observation may produce valid data.

Check your answers at www.sociology.uk.net

Examining participant observation

(a) Explain what is meant by a structured observational schedule. (2 marks)

(b) Suggest **two** reasons why participant observation may produce valid data. (4 marks)

(c) Suggest **two** ethical problems of using covert observation. (4 marks)

(d) Examine the reasons why some sociologists choose not to use overt observation when conducting research. (20 marks)

The examiner's advice

Part (d) is an 'Examine' question of the type you will see in the exam. It carries 10 AO1 marks (knowledge and understanding) and 10 AO2 marks (interpretation, application, analysis and evaluation).

Focus mainly on overt *participant* observation, but say something about overt *non-participant* observation too. Use examples from relevant studies.

Most of the AO1 marks are for knowledge of the *limitations* of overt observation. Practical limitations include the fact that some groups will not consent to being studied (or may not allow the researcher to observe everything) and the time involved especially in *participant* observation.

A major theoretical limitation of overt *participant* observation is lack of representativeness, since it is generally only possible to study small, perhaps untypical, groups. It is also likely to be unreliable, since participant observational procedures are very hard to standardise and so the research cannot be replicated. Both overt *participant* and *non-participant* observation may suffer from lack of validity because of the Hawthorne Effect: those being observed are aware of the observer and may act differently. Overt non-participant observation also produces superficial data lacking in insight because the observer is not personally involved in the group.

You should relate these points to the positivist-interpretivist debate (see Box 31).

There are few ethical limitations. However, researchers still need to obtain informed consent and guarantee anonymity to participants.

You can gain AO2 marks by referring briefly to the *strengths* of overt observation. Try to link each strength to a limitation as you go, rather than listing all the limitations at the end. For example, being overt may mean difficulties gaining access to a group but it means that the researcher will not be expected to act as one of them, which may involve participating in illegal activities. You can also gain AO2 marks by comparing overt observation with other methods, such as covert observation, or contrasting overt participant and non-participant observation, and by applying examples from studies.

METHODS IN CONTEXT
using observation to investigate education

The main use of observational techniques in the study of education is to investigate classroom interaction and the attitudes and values of teachers and pupils. Sociologists are interested in a range of possible classroom interaction issues. These include:

- Gender and classroom behaviour
- Teacher expectations and labelling
- Language codes in the classroom
- Pupil subcultures
- Racism
- The hidden curriculum

Before reading this section, re-visit Topic 2 to refresh your understanding of what is different about researching education.

types of observation

There are several types of observation. At one extreme are highly structured methods using pre-categorised observational schedules. Positivists prefer these methods because they enable them to identify and make quantitative measurements of behaviour patterns. These methods are usually non-participant.

At the other extreme are less structured, more open-ended and flexible methods. Interpretivists favour these methods because they enable them to understand the meanings held by teachers and pupils. These methods may be either participant or non-participant.

Structured observational methods

practical issues

One example of the structured observational schedules favoured by positivists is the Flanders system of interaction analysis categories (FIAC). This is used to measure pupil-pupil and pupil-teacher interaction quantitatively. The observer uses a standard chart to record interactions at three-second intervals, placing each observation in one of ten pre-defined behaviour categories. (See Box 33.)

Observations can thus easily be converted into quantitative data simply by counting the number of times each type of behaviour occurs. Thus, for example, N.A. Flanders (1970) found that in the typical American classroom, 68 per cent of the time is taken up by teacher talk, 20 per cent by pupil talk and 12 per cent lost in silence or confusion.

The relative simplicity of structured observational methods such as FIAC means that they are quicker, cheaper and require less training than less structured methods.

Box 33	Flanders interaction analysis categories (FIAC)

Teacher Talk

1 Teacher accepts pupils' feelings.

2 Teacher praises or encourages pupils.

3 Teacher accepts or uses ideas of pupils.

4 Teacher asks questions.

5 Teacher lectures.

6 Teacher gives directions.

7 Teacher criticises pupils or justifies authority.

Pupil Talk

8 Pupils talk in response to teacher.

9 Pupils initiate talk.

Silence

10 Silence or confusion.

Source: Delamont (1976), *Interaction in the Classroom*

Activity

Try applying the FIAC system to a classroom interaction. Sit at the back of a lesson, having first obtained permission to observe from the teacher. Work in pairs, one observing and recording, the other indicating every three seconds when to record. If you find this difficult, try recording at longer intervals, e.g. every five seconds. After 10 minutes, swop roles.

1 Immediately afterwards, make a list of the problems you experienced.

2 What did your results show? Were they similar to those of Flanders?

3 What are the advantages of using this method of studying classroom interaction?

4 Does your numerical data give a true reflection of what seemed to be happening?

reliability

Structured observational techniques such as FIAC are likely to be easily replicated. This is because FIAC uses only ten categories of classroom interaction, which makes it relatively easy for other researchers to apply in a standardised way. It also generates quantitative data, which makes the findings easy to compare with those of other studies.

validity

Interpretivist sociologists criticise structured observation of classroom interaction for its lack of validity. Sara Delamont (1984) argues that simply counting classroom behaviour and classifying it into a limited number of pre-decided categories ignores the meanings that pupils and teachers attach to it.

Less structured observational methods

Interpretivists favour the use of less structured, more open-ended, qualitative observational methods that allow them to gain access to the meanings that teachers and pupils give to situations. Sociologists use these observational methods more often than structured ones.

practical issues

Schools are complex places and more time-consuming to observe than many other settings. It took Lacey two months to familiarise himself with the school, while Eggleston (1976) needed over three months just to set up his cover role for his observations.

However, it may be easier to gain permission to observe lessons than to interview pupils and teachers. The head of the London school studied by Fuller decided not only that it would be good for the pupils to have a non-teaching adult around, but that permission from parents was not required for her to observe normal school behaviour – whereas it would have been if she had wanted to conduct interviews.

Personal characteristics such as age, gender and ethnicity affect the process of observation. At the time Wright (1992) was carrying out her research, there were few black teachers and she found that her African Caribbean ethnicity produced antagonistic reactions from some white teachers. On the other hand, she found that black pupils often held her in high esteem and would ask her for support.

Observation of interactions in school settings is limited by the restrictions of the school timetable, holidays, control over access, health and safety legislation and so on.

Schools are busy public places, so the observer may find it difficult to find the privacy needed to record observations. Hammersley found that noting down the staffroom conversations he overheard had to be done covertly and hurriedly, in one case on the back of his newspaper. More often, he jotted down notes after he had left the staffroom, trying to record the exact statements he had overheard. Hammersley acknowledges that he may well have made mistakes or relied on his own interpretation of the general sense of what was said.

ethical issues

The additional ethical issues relating to the observation of young people usually mean that a covert approach to studying pupils is not appropriate. Their greater vulnerability and limited ability to give informed consent means that observation normally has to be overt.

Delamont points out that every observer in a school learns things that could get pupils into trouble. In some cases, this may even involve the law, such as when pupils steal from school. What to do with this 'guilty knowledge' is an ethical problem.

Delamont also notes that, given the harm that can be done to pupils, teachers and schools, additional care should be taken to protect their identity. This is even more of an issue in a marketised education system where a good public image is essential to the success of a school.

validity

For interpretivists, the main strength of observation, especially participant observation, is its validity – it gives us an authentic understanding of the world-views of social actors. This understanding is particularly important when researching issues such as classroom interaction and labelling in schools.

The power difference between young people and adults is a major barrier to uncovering the real attitudes and behaviour of pupils. They may present a false image when being observed by an adult researcher, thus undermining validity. Nevertheless, observation is more likely than most methods to overcome this problem, because it gives the researcher the opportunity to gain acceptance by pupils.

A further factor limiting validity is that teachers may be quite skilled at disguising their feelings and altering their behaviour when being observed – for example, by inspectors and school managers.

There is also the problem that the language of the pupil is different from that of the researcher. This makes it difficult for researchers to be certain they understand pupils' meanings.

the Hawthorne Effect

It is very difficult to carry out covert observation of educational settings, especially classrooms. This is because there are few 'cover' roles the researcher can adopt and because he or she stands out as being much older than the pupils.

This means that most classroom observation has to be overt. However, this makes it very difficult to avoid the Hawthorne Effect, where the presence of the researcher influences the behaviour of those being observed.

For example, Ronald King (1984) tried to blend into the background in an infant school by initially spending short periods of time in the classroom to allow the children to become familiar with his presence. So as not to be seen as a teacher, he avoided eye contact and politely refused their requests for help. In an attempt to be unobtrusive, he even used the classroom's Wendy House as a 'hide'.

This example shows how difficult it is for an adult observer to reduce the effect of their presence on pupils' behaviour. As Ball (1993) asks, what did the children actually make of the tall man hiding in the Wendy House? In other words, the danger is that the children's awareness of King's presence may have changed their normal behaviour and so undermined the validity of his observations.

representativeness

The scale of the education system is vast. There are around 4,000 secondary and over 30,000 primary schools in England and Wales, as well as over 350 colleges. The average secondary school has around 70 classes taking place at any one time. The result is a huge amount of educational activity.

By contrast, most observational studies focus on a small number of pupils in just a single school. For example, Willis (1977) studied a core group of only twelve boys. The small scale of such studies results from the fact that it takes time to become familiar with the setting, gain the trust of teachers and pupils, and carry out the actual observations. The limited resources of the typical researcher, together with the sheer size of the education system, mean that observing school interaction is unlikely to produce representative data.

Hammersley considered that the data he collected in the school staffroom was more open than his classroom data to sample bias. This was because, although he sought a wide range of contacts among the teachers, he found that many treated him with suspicion. As a result, he tended to associate largely with one group of teachers with whom he had more in common. This made his sample less representative.

reliability

Participant observation studies of education tend to lack reliability. This is because data recording is often unsystematic and hard to replicate. For example, as we saw earlier, Hammersley found that on one occasion he had to write his notes on the back of a newspaper because he was observing staffroom conversations covertly.

Secondly, the personal characteristics of observers, such as their age, gender and ethnicity, mean that pupils may react differently to different researchers. For example, Wright found that as a black female, she was met with hostility by some white teachers, but was readily accepted by black pupils. A white male researcher may well have found the opposite.

Examining observation in context

Item A   Researching gender relations in schools

How male and female pupils and teachers act towards each other has a major effect on pupils' experiences of education. Sociologists are interested in the reasons why gender relations take the form they do and their relationship to classroom interaction, subject choice, achievement and identity.

Gender relations affect many areas of school life, such as parents' evenings, governors' meetings, senior management decision-making, appointments and promotions, as well interactions in the classroom and staffroom.   5

Schools have gender equality policies. As a result, pupils and teachers may disguise their real attitudes towards gender and this may make it difficult for the researcher to get at the truth.

Sociologists are interested in the reasons for gender differences in subject choice. These include primary socialisation in the home, peer group pressure, subject images and gendered career opportunities.

Question

Using material from **Item A** and elsewhere, assess the strengths and limitations of participant observation for the study of labelling in schools.   (20 marks)

The examiner's advice

This question carries 8 A01 marks (knowledge and understanding) and 12 A02 marks (interpretation, application, analysis and evaluation). It requires you to **apply** your knowledge and understanding of covert and overt participant observation (PO) to the study of the **particular** issue of gender relations in schools. It is not enough simply to discuss PO in general.

For example, Item A suggests that teachers may disguise their sexist attitudes (e.g. because they have a professional duty to treat all pupils equally). However, they may find it hard to sustain this 'front' when being observed over a prolonged period.

On the other hand, teachers are used to being inspected and 'putting on a show' for the observer. How effectively might the different types of PO deal with this? For example, covert PO might mean behaviour is unaffected, but what classroom roles could an observer occupy covertly?

Item A (paragraphs 2 and 4) indicates many other areas of school life affected by gender relations. Is PO equally useful for studying each of these areas? You could examine age and status/power differences between observers and pupils, particular ethical issues with observing young people (especially covertly), the researcher's own gender, the classroom as a closed social setting and the researcher's access to schools.

You need to keep a reasonable balance between the strengths and limitations of different types of PO. You can also refer to studies that have used this method (e.g. Hammersley) and to any relevant research you have been involved in.

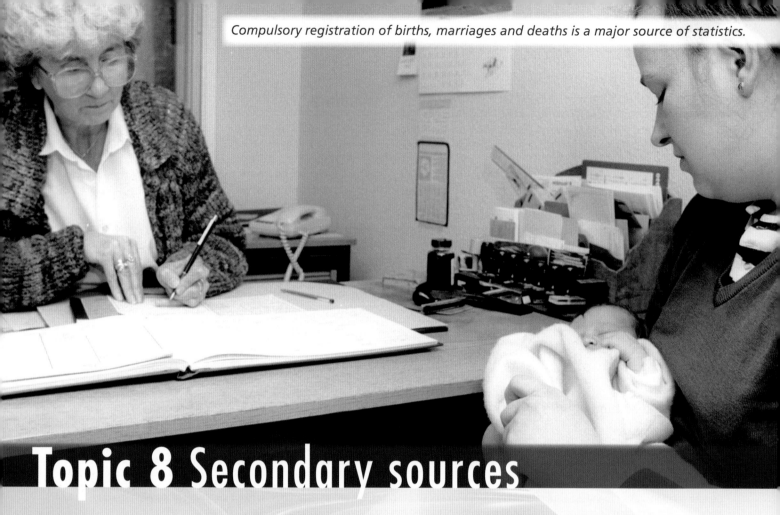

Compulsory registration of births, marriages and deaths is a major source of statistics.

Topic 8 Secondary sources

Sociologists not only use data they have gathered themselves by primary methods such as observation or surveys. They also make use of information that other people have already created or gathered.

For example, governments collect data on the number of births, marriages and deaths, and private individuals often keep diaries as a record of their experiences. Sociologists often make use of information from such sources. Similarly, research findings previously made by one sociologist become secondary data when used by another sociologist.

These are known as secondary sources, and the information from them is called secondary data. Secondary data are therefore data gathered or produced by other people for their own particular purposes, but which sociologists make use of in their research. For example, we could use birth rate statistics to develop or test hypotheses about the family, or use diaries to gain a sense of what life was like for people in the past.

There are two main sources of secondary data:

- **Official statistics**
- **Documents.**

In this Topic, we shall examine the strengths and limitations of these two sources of secondary data in sociology.

Learning objectives

After studying this Topic, you should:

- Know the different types of secondary data.
- Evaluate the strengths and limitations of official statistics and documents.
- Be able to apply your understanding of secondary data to the study of education.

Official statistics

Official statistics are quantitative data gathered by the government or other official bodies. Examples include statistics on births, deaths, marriages and divorces, exam results, school exclusions, crime, suicide, unemployment and health. The ten-yearly Census of the whole UK population is a major source of official statistics. Examples of many other official statistics can be found in the annual publication, Social Trends.

The government collects official statistics to use in policy-making. For example, statistics on births help the government to plan the number of school places for the future. Similarly, the Department for Children Schools and Families (DCSF) and Ofsted use statistics to monitor the effectiveness of schools and colleges.

There are two ways of collecting official statistics:

- Registration – for example, the law requires parents to register births
- Official surveys, such as the Census or the General Household Survey.

In addition to official statistics produced by government, organisations and groups such as trade unions, businesses and churches also produce various kinds of statistics. For example, the educational pressure group, the National Grammar Schools Association, produces statistics on the comparative performance of grammar and non-selective schools.

Both the advantages and the disadvantages of official statistics stem largely from the fact that they are secondary data. That is, they are not collected by sociologists but by official agencies for their own particular purposes – which may not always be the same as those of the sociologist.

> Despite the legal requirement for every household to complete the Census form, in inner city areas there are often lower rates of completion than elsewhere. Suggest two reasons for this.

1 Practical advantages and disadvantages

Official statistics offer several practical advantages.

They are a free source of huge amounts of quantitative data. Only the state can afford to conduct large-scale surveys costing millions of pounds, such as the ten-yearly Census covering every household in the UK. Likewise, only the government has the power to compel citizens to provide it with information, for example by requiring parents to register births. Sociologists can make use of this data, saving them both time and money.

- Statistics allow comparisons between groups. For example, we can compare statistics on educational achievement, crime rates or life expectancy between classes, genders or ethnic groups.
- Because official statistics are collected at regular intervals, they show trends and patterns over time. This means sociologists can use them for 'before and after' studies to show cause-and-effect relationships. For example, we can compare divorce statistics before and after a change in the divorce law to measure what effect the new legislation has had.

However, official statistics can have practical disadvantages.

- The government collects statistics for its own purposes, and not for the benefit of sociologists, so there may be none available on the topic we are interested in. For example, Durkheim in his study of suicide found that there were no statistics specifically on the religion of suicide victims, presumably because the state had no use for the information. However, this was crucial to Durkheim's hypothesis about integration and suicide.
- The definitions that the state uses in collecting the data may be different from those that sociologists would use. For example, they may define 'poverty' or 'truancy' differently. In turn, this may lead to different views of how large the problem is.

FIGURE 4.3: SECONDARY SOURCES

Quantitative
- Official statistics
- Non–official statistics
- Existing quantitative sociological research

Qualitative
- Existing qualitative sociological research
- Public documents
- Personal documents
- Historical documents

See Box 20 on page 166 for more about positivism, interpretivism and research methods.

> **Box 34** **Positivism, interpretivism and official statistics**
>
> **Positivists** favour official statistics as objective social facts that achieve the main positivist goals of reliability, generalisability and representativeness.
> - They provide reliable data because their standardised categories and collection techniques can be easily replicated.
> - Because they are collected at regular intervals, they show trends in behaviour over time.
> - They provide quantitative data, allowing us to identify and measure behaviour patterns and establish cause-and-effect relationships.
> - They are usually large scale and thus very representative.
>
> **Interpretivists** reject official statistics, particularly 'soft' ones, as social constructs and not social facts. They fail to achieve the main interpretivist goal of validity.

- If definitions change over time, it may make comparisons difficult. For example, the official definition of unemployment changed over 30 times during the 1980s and early 1990s – so the unemployment statistics are not comparing like with like.

2 Representativeness

Because official statistics often cover very large numbers (even the entire population), and because care is taken with sampling procedures, they often provide a more representative sample than surveys conducted with the limited resources available to the sociologist. They may thus provide a sounder basis for making generalisations and testing hypotheses.

However, some statistics may be less representative than others. For example, statistics gathered by compulsory registration, such as birth and death statistics or the number of pupils in school, are likely to cover virtually all cases and therefore be 'representative'.

By contrast, statistics produced from official surveys, such as the British Crime Survey or the General Household Survey, may be less representative because they are only based on a sample of the relevant population. Nonetheless, such official surveys are usually much bigger than most sociologists could carry out themselves. For example, the British Crime Survey in 2002 used a sample of 33,000 adults.

3 Reliability

Official statistics are generally seen as a reliable source of data. They are compiled in a standardised way by trained staff, following set procedures. For example, government statisticians compile death rates for different social classes following a standard procedure

that uses the occupation recorded on each person's death certificate to identify their class. Official statistics are therefore reliable because, in principle, any person properly trained will allocate a given case to the same category.

However, official statistics are not always wholly reliable. For example, census coders may make errors or omit information when recording data from census forms, or members of the public may fill in the form incorrectly.

4 Validity: the 'dark figure'

A major problem with using official statistics is that of validity. Do they actually measure the thing that they claim to measure?

▲ *Not all crimes get reported or recorded.*

Some 'hard' official statistics do succeed in doing this. For example, statistics on the number of births, deaths, marriages and divorces generally give a very accurate picture (although a small number of births and deaths do go unrecorded). However, other 'soft' statistics give a much less valid picture. For example, police statistics do not record all crimes. Similarly, educational statistics do not record all racist incidents occurring in schools.

Attempts have been made to compensate for the shortcomings of police statistics by using self-report or victim studies to give a more accurate picture of the amount of crime. For example, the British Crime Survey (BCS) asks people what crimes they have been victims of.

By comparing the BCS results with the police statistics, we can see that the latter underestimate the 'real rate' of crime and from this we can make a more accurate estimate of the extent of crime. For example, the 2002 BCS found that only 42 per cent of crimes were reported to the police and of these, the police only recorded three-fifths.

FIGURE 4.4: CRIME STATISTICS – THE OFFICIAL VIEW

In the official view, statistics give a relatively accurate and true picture of society The flow chart below indicates the official view of how crime statistics are created.

A crime is committed.

It is observed by witnesses or victims

The crime is reported to the police

Police record the crime

Police investigate

Police arrest the suspect

The suspect is charged with the crime

Suspect appears in court and, if found guilty, offender and crime are counted in the official crime statistics.

Activity

Suggest reasons why the process above may not be a true reflection of how official crime statistics are created. Write a sentence summarising why official crime statistics may not give a valid picture of the amount and types of crime. Explain how some crimes are 'lost' to the statistics at different stages.

1 Suggest three types of crime that may not be reported to the police.

2 For each example, suggest why this may be so.

3 Suggest three reasons why the police do not record all the crimes reported to them.

5 Official statistics: facts, constructs or ideology?

Whether we see official statistics as useful or not also depends in part on which theoretical perspective we adopt.

positivism

Positivists such as Emile Durkheim (1897) see statistics as a valuable resource for sociologists. They take for granted that official statistics are 'social facts'; that is, true and objective measures of the real rate of crime, suicide etc. They see sociology as a science and they develop hypotheses to discover the causes of the patterns of behaviour that the statistics reveal.

Positivists often use official statistics to test their hypotheses. For example, Durkheim put forward the hypothesis that suicide is caused by a lack of social integration. Using the comparative method (see page 175), he argued that Protestant and Catholic religions differ in how well they integrate individuals into society. Using official suicide statistics, he was able to show that Protestants had a higher suicide rate than Catholics, and so was able to argue that this statistical evidence proved his hypothesis correct.

interpretivism

By contrast, interpretivists such as Maxwell Atkinson (1971) regard official statistics as lacking validity. They argue that statistics are not real things or 'social facts' that exist out there in the world. Instead, statistics are socially constructed – they merely represent the labels some people give to the behaviour of others.

In this view, suicide statistics do not represent the 'real rate' of suicides that have actually taken place, but merely the total number of decisions made by coroners to label some deaths as suicides. The statistics therefore tell us more about the way coroners label deaths than about the actual causes of deaths.

Rather than taking statistics at face value, therefore, interpretivists argue that we should investigate how they are socially constructed. For example, Atkinson uses qualitative methods such as observing the proceedings of coroners' courts to discover how coroners reach their decisions to label some deaths as suicides, others as accidents and so on.

Marxism

Marxists such as John Irvine (1987) take a different view. Unlike interpretivists, they do not regard official statistics as merely the outcome of the labels applied by officials such as coroners. Instead they see official statistics as serving the interests of capitalism.

Marxists see capitalist society as made up of two social classes in conflict with each other, the capitalist ruling class and the working class. In this conflict, the state is not neutral, but serves the interests of the capitalist class. The statistics that the state produces are part of ruling class ideology – part of the ideas and values that help to maintain the capitalist class in power.

Unemployment statistics are a good example of this process. The state has regularly changed the definition of unemployment over the years. This has almost always reduced the numbers officially defined as unemployed, thus disguising the true level of unemployment.

Documents

The term 'document' refers to any written text, such as personal diaries, government reports, medical records, novels, newspapers, letters, parish registers, train timetables, shopping lists, bank statements – the list is almost endless. In fact, we can also take the term to include 'texts' such as paintings, drawings, photographs, maps and so on.

We can also include sounds and images from film, television, radio and the Internet and other media output.

Public and personal documents

We can distinguish between public and personal documents:

public documents

Public documents are produced by organisations such as government departments, schools, welfare agencies, businesses and charities. Some of this output may be available for researchers to use. It includes documents such as Ofsted reports of school inspections, minutes of council meetings, published company accounts and records of parliamentary debates.

Public documents also include the official reports of public enquiries such as the Black Report (1980) into inequalities in health, which has become a major source of information for sociologists.

personal documents

Personal documents include items such as letters, diaries, photo albums and autobiographies. These are first-person accounts of social events and personal experiences, and they generally also include the writer's feelings and attitudes.

An early example of a study using personal documents is William Thomas and Florian Znaniecki's (1919) The Polish Peasant in Europe and America, a study of migration and social change. As interactionists, they were particularly interested in people's experiences of these events.

They used personal documents to reveal the meanings and interpretations that individuals gave to their experience of migration. The documents included 764 letters bought after an advertisement in a Polish newspaper in Chicago, as well as several autobiographies.

Thomas and Znaniecki also used public documents, such as newspaper articles and court and social work records. With these documents, they were able to explore the experiences of social change of some of the thousands of people who migrated from rural Poland to the United States of America in the early 20th century.

Box 35	Positivism, interpretivism and documents

Interpretivists tend to favour documents because they achieve the main interpretivist goal of validity:

- They are not usually written with research in mind and can thus be an authentic statement of their author's views.
- They provide qualitative data that gives us insight into the author's world-view and meanings.

Positivists tend to reject documents because they fail to achieve the main positivist goals of reliability, generalisability and representativeness:

- They are often unstandardised and unreliable; for example, every person's diary is unique. This also makes it difficult to draw generalisations from them.
- They are often unrepresentative; for example, only literate groups can write diaries and letters.
- In interpreting documents, researchers may impose their own meanings on them.

However, positivists do sometimes carry out content analysis on documents to produce quantitative data from them.

See Box 20 on page 166 for more about positivism, interpretivism and research methods.

Historical documents

A historical document is simply a personal or public document created in the past. If we want to study the past, historical documents are usually the only source of information (although in the case of the recent past, there may still be people alive who can be interviewed).

We can use the study of families and households to illustrate some of the types of historical documents that have been used:

- Peter Laslett used parish records in his study of family structure in pre-industrial England.
- Michael Anderson used parliamentary reports on child labour, as well as statistical material from the 1851 Census, to study changes in family structure in 19th century Preston.
- Tamara Hareven's study of kinship networks among French Canadian migrants in the textile industry in New Hampshire, USA, from 1880 to 1930, used local government and insurance records and company employee files.
- Philippe Aries used child-rearing manuals and paintings of children in his study of the rise of the modern notion of childhood.

Assessing documents

As John Scott (1990) argues, when it comes to assessing documentary sources, the general principles are the same as those for any other type of sociological evidence. He puts forward four criteria for evaluating documents: authenticity, credibility, representativeness and meaning.

authenticity

Is the document what it claims to be? Are there any missing pages, and if it is a copy, is it free from errors? Who actually wrote the document? For example, the so-called 'Hitler Diaries' were later proven to be fakes.

credibility

Is the document believable? Was the author sincere? Politicians may write diaries intended for publication that inflate their own importance. Thomas and Znaniecki's

Polish immigrants may have lied in their letters home about how good life in the USA was, to justify their decision to emigrate.

Is the document accurate? For example, was the account of a riot written soon after the event, or years later?

representativeness

Is the evidence in the document typical? If we cannot answer this question, we cannot know whether it is safe to generalise from it:

- Not all documents survive: are the surviving documents typical of the ones that get destroyed or lost?
- Not all surviving documents are available for researchers to use. The 30-year rule prevents access to official documents for 30 years and, if classified as official

Activity

Working in pairs and using Scott's four criteria assess the value of each of the following documents as a source of evidence

(a) crime reports in newspapers

(b) letters from soldiers at war

(c) photographs of a riot

(d) a novel about schooldays

(e) notes passed around in class by pupils

(f) *The Diary of Anne Frank* (www.annefrank.com is a useful source of information).

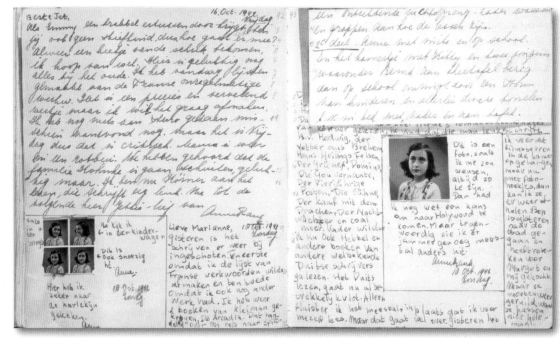

▲ *The diary of Anne Frank, a Jewish schoolgirl in Amsterdam during World War Two. She kept a diary while hiding from the Nazis but was discovered shortly before the end of the war and died in a concentration camp.*

secrets, they may not be available at all. Private documents such as diaries may never become available.

■ Certain groups may be unrepresented: the illiterate, and those with limited leisure time, are unlikely to keep diaries.

meaning

The researcher may need special skills to understand a document. It may have to be translated from a foreign language; words may change their meaning over time.

We also have to interpret what the document actually means to the writer and the intended audience. Different sociologists may interpret the same document differently. Thomas later admitted that the interpretations he and Znaniecki had offered in the book were not based on the data from the documents.

Advantages of documents

Although documents need to be assessed carefully by the sociologist before they are used as sources of evidence, nevertheless they have several important advantages:

■ Personal documents such as diaries and letters enable the researcher to get close to the social actor's reality, giving insight through their richly detailed qualitative data. Interactionists favour them for this reason.

■ Sometimes documents are the only source of information, for example in studying the past.

■ By providing another source of data, documents offer an extra check on the results obtained by primary methods.

■ They are a cheap source of data, because someone else has already gathered the information.

■ For the same reason, using existing documents saves the sociologist time.

Content analysis

Content analysis is a method for dealing systematically with the contents of documents. It is best known for its use in analysing documents produced by the mass media, such as television news bulletins or advertisements.

Although such documents are usually qualitative, content analysis enables the sociologist to produce quantitative data from these sources.

Ros Gill (1988) describes how content analysis works as follows. Imagine we want to measure particular aspects of a media message; for example, how many female characters are portrayed as being in paid employment.

■ First we decide what categories we are going to use, such as employee, full-time housewife etc.

■ Next, we study the source (television broadcast, magazine article etc) and place the characters in it into the categories we have decided upon.

■ We can then count up the number in each category, for

example to compare how often women are portrayed as full-time housewives rather than employees.

We might then go on to compare the results of our content analysis with the official statistics for female employment to see if the media were presenting a false or stereotypical picture of women's roles.

Glenys Lobban (1974) used content analysis to analyse gender roles in children's reading schemes, while Gaye Tuchman (1978) used it to analyse television's portrayal of women. Both studies found that females were portrayed in a range of roles that was both limited and stereotyped. For example, Lobban found that female characters were generally portrayed playing domestic roles. (See page 129.)

Content analysis has several advantages:

■ It is cheap.

■ It is usually easy to find sources of material in the form of newspapers, television broadcasts and so on.

■ Positivists see it as a useful source of objective, quantitative, scientific data.

However, interpretivist sociologists argue that simply counting up the number of times something appears in a document tells us nothing about its meaning.

Activity

Working in small groups, carry out a content analysis of one of the following to find out how men and women are portrayed:

1 One episode of a soap

2 The adverts from one or two commercial breaks on television

3 Stories in women's magazines.

You will need to devise some appropriate categories in advance, such as different roles played by males and females, where they play them etc. Carry out your analysis following the steps outlined by Gill above.

Did everyone in your group agree on which categories to use and on where to put different characters?

 For more activities on Secondary sources, go to www.sociology.uk.net

Summary

Secondary data include **official statistics** and **documents.** Secondary sources save time and money and provide useful data, but they may not always be available. Statistics may lack validity, measuring officials' decisions rather than real events. Documents, such as diaries, letters and government reports, may not be authentic or representative. Some sociologists apply **content analysis** to documents.

QuickCheck Questions

1 What does the term 'secondary data' mean?

2 What are the two main ways that official statistics are collected?

3 Give three examples of official statistics.

4 Apart from government, name three other types of organisation that produce statistics.

5 State three advantages of official statistics to sociologists.

6 A major problem with using official statistics is that of validity. Explain (a) what validity means (b) why official statistics may lack validity.

7 State three other disadvantages of official statistics apart from lack of validity.

8 Give two examples of personal documents.

9 Give two examples of sociological studies that have used historical documents.

 Check your answers at www.sociology.uk.net

Examining secondary sources

(a) Explain what is meant by content analysis. (2 marks)

(b) Suggest **two** examples of personal documents. (4 marks)

(c) Identify **two** problems of using documents in sociological research. (4 marks)

(d) Examine the reasons why some sociologists choose to use official statistics when conducting research. (20 marks)

The examiner's advice

Part (d) is an 'Examine' question of the type you will see in the exam. It carries 10 AO1 marks (knowledge and understanding) and 10 AO2 marks (interpretation, application, analysis and evaluation).

Most of the AO1 marks are for knowledge of the *strengths* of official statistics. Examine practical strengths such as that they are quick and cheap, cover large numbers, are useful for providing factual information, already quantified, and show patterns and trends over time.

Their main theoretical strength is reliability: they are compiled in a standardised way by trained officials, making them easy to replicate. Also, because they cover large numbers, findings may be representative and generalisable, particularly as the state can compel people to provide information. They can also be used to test hypotheses and identify cause-and-effect relationships, making them attractive to positivists. You should relate these points to the positivist-interpretivist debate (see Box 34).

Ethical strengths include the fact that, being in the public domain already, official statistics require no consent for their use and cannot be used to identify individuals personally.

You can gain AO2 marks by referring briefly to the *limitations* of official statistics. Try to link each limitation to a strength as you go, rather than listing all the limitations at the end. For example, the fact that they are collected by the state saves the researcher time and money, but it means that they are only collected on issues that the state considers important. You can also gain AO2 marks by comparing official statistics with other methods, and by applying examples of the use of official statistics in sociological research.

METHODS IN CONTEXT
using secondary sources to investigate education

Sociologists use secondary sources to study a variety of educational issues. The main secondary sources that they use are official statistics and a variety of documents, both personal and official. We shall examine the usefulness of each of these in turn.

Before reading this section, re-visit Topic 2 to refresh your understanding of what is different about researching education.

Using official statistics to investigate education

Education is one of the key services provided by the state and as such is closely monitored. As a result, schools, colleges, local education authorities (LEAs) and the Department for Children, Schools and Families (DCSF) collect a wide range of official statistics on education. These cover many issues that sociologists are interested in, including:

- Ethnicity, class, gender and educational achievement
- School attendance, truancy and inclusion
- League tables, marketisation and school performance
- Gender and subject choice
- Education, work and training

practical issues

Much of this data is published and thus available to the sociologist, saving them both time and money. For example, the government collects statistics on over 30,000 primary and 4,000 secondary schools in England and Wales. In practice, it would be too costly and time-consuming for a sociologist to gather information on so many schools themselves.

Educational statistics allow sociologists to make comparisons between the achievements of different social groups based on ethnicity, gender and social class. Also, because educational statistics are collected at regular and frequent intervals, sociologists can make comparisons over time. For example, annually gathered exam statistics enable the sociologist to see trends in results.

Governments gather statistics to monitor the effectiveness of their educational policies, such as those dealing with the curriculum, subject choice, raising standards and reducing inequality of achievement. Such issues are also of great relevance to sociologists, so the statistics produced by government may be very useful to researchers.

However, governments collect statistics for their own purposes and these may not be the same as those of sociologists. For example, sociologists are very interested in the relationship between language, social class and achievement, but there are no official statistics available on this.

Even where the state collects educational statistics of sociological interest, the definitions of key concepts may differ from those that sociologists use. For example, official definitions of pupils' social class are based on parental occupation, whereas Marxist sociologists define class in terms of property ownership.

representativeness

Some official statistics on education are highly representative. For example, all state schools have to complete a school census three times a year. This collects information on pupils' attendance, ethnicity and gender, the numbers receiving free school meals and so on. Because these statistics cover virtually every pupil in the country, they are highly representative.

reliability

Positivists favour official statistics because their reliability means that they can be used to test and re-test hypotheses and thus discover cause and effect relationships. For example, statistics on exam results showing class differences in educational achievement may correlate with statistics on parental income. From this, positivists may conclude that poverty causes under-achievement.

Although it is possible for errors to creep into the production of official statistics on education, they are generally very reliable. This is because the government imposes standard definitions and categories for their collection, which all schools must use. This enables the process to be replicated from year to year, allowing direct comparisons to be made, for example of school performance.

However, governments may change the definitions and categories. For example, when the Conservatives first introduced league tables of school performance in 1988, a school's position was based purely on its exam results. This generally meant that schools with middle-class pupils were placed higher than those with working-class intakes.

However, in 2006, the Labour government introduced a new measure of school performance called Contextual Value Added (CVA). This took into account not just exam results, but also the level of deprivation pupils suffer.

Activity

Look again at your answer to the activity on crime statistics on page 221. Now construct a flow chart showing how absences from school become truancy statistics.

Using documents to investigate education

▲ *A wide variety of documents about education is available to the researcher.*

In many cases, CVA 'turns the tables' and results in schools with disadvantaged pupils being placed higher than those with middle-class intakes. Changing the definitions on which educational statistics are based makes it difficult for sociologists to draw comparisons over time.

Activity

Imagine you are a parent wishing to compare the performance of local schools. Visit the website of the Department for Children, Schools and Families and follow the links for parents. Find the percentage of pupils gaining five or more A*-C GCSEs for your own school and other schools in your area.

 Go to www.dcsf.gov.uk

validity

Interpretivists question the validity of educational statistics. They argue that such statistics are socially constructed. For example, they see truancy statistics as the outcome of a series of definitions and decisions made by a variety of social actors, such as parents, teachers and pupils.

Schools may manipulate their attendance figures by re-defining poor attenders as being on 'study leave' or additional work experience. They may be tempted to do so because, in an education market, there is pressure on schools to present themselves in the best possible light in order to maintain their funding and parental support. However, this deliberate distorting of attendance figures undermines the validity of educational statistics.

Schools, colleges, local education authorities and the Department for Children, Schools and Families (DCSF) generate a wide range of public documents. Also, because pupils produce large amounts of paper-based work, there is the opportunity for the researcher to use personal educational documents. But these are not the only documents that sociologists can use, as Box 36 shows.

Documents cover many educational issues that sociologists are interested in, including:

- Ethnicity, class, gender and differences in achievement
- The official curriculum
- Gender stereotyping in school books
- Racist incidents in schools
- Special educational needs

Box 36	Examples of documents in education

Public documents	*Personal documents*
School websites	Pupil's written work
DCSF guidance to schools and colleges	School reports on pupils
School prospectuses	Pupils and teachers' diaries
Government enquiries	Pupils and teachers' autobiographies
Novels about school life	Graffiti on school buildings, desks etc
School textbooks	
Recordings of playground songs and games	Notes passed between pupils in class
Media reports, films etc about education	Letters from parents e.g. explaining absences
Ofsted inspection reports	Text messages between pupils

practical issues

Public documents on education are often easily accessible to the researcher. Partly because of government policies emphasising parental choice, schools make a large amount of information available to the public, which researchers may then use. There is also a cost saving since it would take a long time for researchers to compile this information for each school themselves.

For example, David Gillborn (1995), in his study of racism and schooling, was able to access a wide range of school documents, including school policy statements, local authority guidelines on anti-racism and the minutes of staff meetings and working parties.

These documents gave Gillborn the 'official' picture of what was happening in terms of racism and anti-racism in the schools he studied. Gillborn then compared this with the data he collected from interviews and observation.

Similarly, Gewirtz et al (1995), in their study of marketisation and education, found that school brochures and prospectuses were a useful free source of information about how schools presented themselves in the education 'marketplace'.

Personal documents can be more difficult to access. Valerie Hey (1997) made use of the notes girls passed to each other in class to understand their friendship patterns. However, the notes were not always easy to obtain, as the girls were experts at hiding them from teachers.

ethical issues

There are few ethical concerns with public documents produced by schools. Having been placed in the public domain by the organisation that produced them, permission for their use is not required.

However, there are more ethical problems with personal documents. For example, Hey collected in the notes that girls had passed to each other in class. In some cases, the girls offered her the notes freely, but in others Hey collected them from desks at the end of the lesson or, in one case, a teacher took them from the wastepaper bin and offered them to her. Thus in some cases, informed consent for their use had not been obtained.

representativeness

Some official documents are legally required of all schools and colleges, such as records of racist incidents. This makes it more likely that we can form a representative picture of racism in schools across the land. However, of course, not all racist incidents may be documented.

Personal documents are often less representative. For example, Hey collected about 70 notes, but the unsystematic way in which she came by them makes it likely that her sample was unrepresentative.

reliability

Many public documents, for example attendance registers, are produced in a systematic format. This enables researchers to make direct comparisons of the absence rates of pupils in different schools.

However, deliberate falsifications or accidental mistakes made when filling in registers reduce their reliability because teachers are not applying the measure of attendance consistently.

Some educational documents can also be used in ways that other researchers can replicate. Lobban examined 179 stories from six school reading schemes looking for gender stereotyping.

She analysed the content of each story using the same set of categories, counting the number of times images fell into each category. Future researchers can easily apply systematic content analysis of this kind to create comparative data from educational documents.

validity

Documents can provide important insights into the meanings held by teachers and pupils and can therefore be high in validity. For example, Hey initially examined girls' friendships in schools through observation and interviews.

Eventually, however, she realised that she was ignoring a useful source of insight into girls' feelings and actions – the notes they passed to each other in class.

Although teachers considered these notes to be 'bits of silliness', Hey found that they offered valuable insights into the nature of girls' friendships. This is because they were spontaneous expressions of the girls' feelings and attitudes.

However, all documents are open to different interpretations. For example, we cannot be sure that Hey's interpretation of the meaning of the notes was the same as that of the girls.

Also, because the girls sometimes handed Hey the notes after the class, it is possible that they were written with her in mind and may not have been spontaneous.

Examining official statistics in context

Researching ethnicity and educational achievement

Sociologists seek to identify and measure the relationship between ethnicity and educational achievement. They also aim to explain why some ethnic groups are less successful in school than others.

One problem with studying ethnicity and achievement is that, in a multi-cultural society like Britain, there are many ethnicities, based for example on religion, culture, language or country of origin. This makes it difficult to decide which ethnic categories to use.

Many sociologists are interested in identifying and explaining society-wide ethnic patterns of achievement. However, identifying these   5
patterns is one thing, understanding and explaining them is another. This would require investigation of the effect of factors such as home background, teacher labelling and racism in wider society.

Question

Using material from **Item A** and elsewhere, assess the strengths and limitations of official statistics for the study of ethnicity and educational achievement.

(20 marks)

The examiner's advice

This question carries 8 A01 marks (knowledge and understanding) and 12 A02 marks (interpretation, application, analysis and evaluation). It requires you to **apply** your knowledge and understanding of official statistics to the study of the **particular** issue of ethnicity and educational achievement. It is not enough simply to discuss official statistics in general.

Item A suggests that it is difficult to decide which ethnic categories to use when identifying patterns of achievement. For example, in the 1970s, official statistics on achievement often used only three categories, whereas today over 90 are commonly used. This makes it difficult to compare achievement patterns over time. You could also discuss whether it is better to use the official categories or pupils' own definition of their ethnicity, as well as issues of mixed heritage and overlapping categories.

Official statistics can identify the 'society-wide ethnic patterns of achievement' referred to in Item A. Because all schools and colleges are legally required to collect and report exam results by ethnic group, this makes official educational statistics a source of cheap, comprehensive data on ethnicity and achievement. However, you need to consider how useful these statistics are in explaining the patterns.

You need to keep a reasonable balance between the strengths and limitations of official statistics. You can also refer to studies that have used this source of data (e.g. the Swann Report) and to any relevant research you have been involved in.

Case studies have been used to investigate events such as strikes.

Topic 9 Other types of research

So far in this chapter, we have looked at a range of specific primary and secondary methods and sources. In this final section, we look at three other types of research:

- **Case studies**
- **Longitudinal studies**
- **Life histories.**

As we shall see, in each of these types of sociological research, one or more different methods or sources of data may be used in carrying out the study.

Finally in this Topic, we look at the idea of 'triangulation' or the combination of different methods to give a fuller picture of social reality.

Learning objectives

After studying this Topic, you should:

- Understand the uses that sociologists may make of case studies, longitudinal studies and life histories.
- Be able to evaluate the usefulness of each of these methods of research.
- Understand why sociologists may use a combination of methods in their research.

Case studies

A case study involves the detailed examination of a single case or example, such as a school, family or workplace. It may even be the study of one individual. For example, Elizabeth Burn (2001) carried out a case study of Jenny, an inner-city primary school teacher from a working-class background. Tony Lane and Ken Roberts (1971) studied a single strike at Pilkington's glass factory in Warrington.

Because case studies examine only one or at most a few cases, they cannot claim to be representative or typical. Their main limitation is that we cannot generalise from our findings: whatever we may have discovered to be true of that one case, we cannot guarantee it will be true of other cases. Nevertheless, case studies have many different uses:

- To provide a detailed insight into a particular group. Studies that use qualitative methods such as participant observation studies are usually case studies.
- To study exceptional cases. An example is Max Weber's (1905) famous study of the role of the Calvinist religion in the rise of capitalism in Western Europe, which he saw as unique.
- In a large-scale quantitative study, case studies can be used to illustrate general points in more detail and give the study a qualitative dimension. Peter Townsend's (1979) national survey of poverty also includes cases of individual families to show what living in poverty means for those affected by it.
- To test a theory. The Kendal Project (2004) is an ongoing case study of religious belief and practice focused on one town, which is being used to test a range of different theories about religion.
- To suggest hypotheses in the early stages of a research project. Looking closely at one case may give us ideas that can be tested on a larger group. Questions asked later are more likely to be relevant if they emerge from an initial case.

Longitudinal studies

A longitudinal study is one that follows the same sample or group over an extended period of time. We can use the study of education and families and households to see how longitudinal studies have been used:

- J.W.B. Douglas' (1964) study followed a sample of 5,632 children who were all born in the first week of March 1946 through their schooling.
- The National Child Development Study (NCDS) has been running since 1958. It is a birth cohort study tracing the lives of all those born in Great Britain in the same week in 1958. It has collected extensive information on them at regular intervals from birth, through childhood into adulthood. This has provided the basis for other studies.

For example, Ferri and Smith's (1998) study of step parenting used a sample of almost 6,000 adults, drawn from the NCDS.

- Many participant observation studies are longitudinal. For example, Colin Lacey spent four years studying pupils at Hightown grammar school.

An example of a longitudinal study from a different area is David Gauntlett and Annette Hill's (1999) study of television viewing. This ran for five years and used an original sample of 509 respondents, who were each asked to complete three questionnaire diaries per year on their viewing habits.

By the end of the study, 427 of the sample were still involved. One reason for this was that the researchers maintained regular contact by sending Christmas and birthday cards and even writing personally when diaries indicated events such as illness or bereavement. The research produced over 3.5 million words of material for analysis.

Longitudinal studies have both advantages and disadvantages:

- Their major advantage is that they trace developments over a period of time, rather than just offering a 'snapshot' of one moment in time. This also allows a more detailed picture to be built up.
- By making comparisons between groups over time, we can identify causes. For example, Douglas followed children of different class backgrounds but similar ability to discover why middle-class children did better at school.
- There can be problems keeping track of the sample. The NCDS lost a third of its sample of 17,400 between 1958 and 1999. This is called sample attrition. Reasons for sample attrition include death, loss of contact or participants refusing to continue. However, using methods like Gauntlett and Hill's to keep in touch can reduce sample attrition.
- A further problem is that those who drop out may not be typical of those who stay in, making the remaining sample less representative.
- Demographic changes in the research population may mean that the original sample is no longer representative. For example, if over time migration patterns alter the proportion of different ethnic groups in the population, the original sample will cease to be representative of the population's ethnic mix.
- The large amount of data produced can be difficult to analyse and, by definition, results cannot be obtained quickly.
- They can be costly. Howard Parker's (1998) five-year study of illegal drug use among 1,125 adolescents in Greater Manchester and Merseyside cost £380,000.
- The Hawthorne Effect may occur: those in the sample may act differently as a result of the prolonged attention they receive through being in the study.

Activity

Working in groups of two or three, imagine you are conducting a large-scale longitudinal study of members of Alcoholics Anonymous groups from different social backgrounds who have given up alcohol. Your aim is to find out why some people are more successful than others at giving up alcohol.

1 What would be the advantages of re-interviewing your sample every year for five years?

2 What problems might you face in carrying out this longitudinal study?

Life histories

Life histories are often used in case studies of individuals. They are a qualitative method used mainly by interpretivist sociologists to understand how individuals construct and interpret their 'life worlds'. They involve collecting and recording individuals' experiences. This can be done either:

- By the individual writing down their own life story (an autobiography). For example, Mann (1998) collected the educational life histories of 60 female sixth formers.

- By a semi-structured or unstructured interview, which the researcher then writes up as a life story. For example, Chamberlain and Goulbourne (Silva, 1999) carried out biographical life story interviews with three generations of 60 families who had originated in the Caribbean and migrated to Britain in the 1950s and 1960s.

Life histories are a rich source of insight into both a person's individual experiences, presented from their own point of view, and into the wider social forces that affect their lives. For example, they can give us insight into how war affects those who live through it.

According to Graham Hitchcock (1995), the life history adds a historical dimension to our understanding of individuals and social structures. It 'enables the researcher to build up a mosaic-like picture of the individual and the events and people surrounding them, so that relations, influences and patterns may be observed'.

However, life histories conducted through interviews require the ability to empathise with the subject, and good listening skills. They are also very time-consuming and labour-intensive.

Triangulation

In practice, many sociological studies use a combination of methods. For example, a study may begin with a limited number of in-depth, unstructured interviews to gain insights; these can then be used to develop questions for a questionnaire administered to a larger sample.

The term 'triangulation' is sometimes used to describe this process. Fiona Devine and Sue Heath (1999) define triangulation as a technique that aims to obtain a more rounded picture by studying the same thing from more than one viewpoint, using a number of different sources or methods.

The idea is that different methods can complement each other – the weaknesses of one can be countered by the strengths of the other. For example, Howard Newby's (1977) study of Suffolk farm workers uses a variety of methods and sources including participant observation and a survey. He argues that these two methods complement each other:

'Insights gained from participant observation could be checked against survey data, while on the other hand, much of this data only became meaningful through the experiences gained from living with a farm worker and his family in their cottage for six months.'

By combining different methods in this way, we can get the best of both worlds: both reliable quantitative data covering large numbers of cases, as favoured by positivists, and valid qualitative data looking at a smaller number of cases in depth, as preferred by interpretivists.

Summary

Case studies involve the detailed examination of a single case or example. **Longitudinal studies** follow the same sample over an extended period of time. **Life histories** involve collecting and recording individuals' experiences. Sociologists often use **triangulation**, where two or more methods complement one another. Often this involves combining a qualitative with a quantitative source of data.

QuickCheck Questions

1 True or false? A case study follows the same group over an extended period of time.

2 Give two examples of research that has been carried out by means of case studies.

3 True or false? Case studies can be used to suggest hypotheses that can then be tested on a larger sample.

4 Give two examples of longitudinal studies.

5 What is 'sample attrition' in a longitudinal study?

6 Identify one advantage of longitudinal studies.

 Check your answers at www.sociology.uk.net

Exam questions and student answers

Examining sociological methods

(a) Explain what is meant by triangulation. (2 marks)

(b) Explain the difference between reliability and validity. (4 marks)

(c) Suggest **one** advantage and **one** disadvantage of life histories. (4 marks)

(d) Examine the ways in which practical, ethical and theoretical factors may influence sociologists' choice of research methods. (20 marks)

The examiner's advice

Part (d) is an 'Examine' question of the type you will see in the exam. It carries 10 AO1 marks (knowledge and understanding) and 10 AO2 marks (interpretation, application, analysis and evaluation).

To maximise your marks, you need to show your knowledge and understanding of all three factors – practical, ethical and theoretical. Practical factors include time, cost, access to the group you wish to study, funding bodies, the researcher's personal skills and characteristics, and research opportunity (including pure chance).

Ethical factors in relation to the research participants include issues of deceit and informed consent (e.g. in relation to covert observation), confidentiality and privacy, harmful effects (especially in relation to vulnerable groups), anonymity and the use to which findings are put.

Theoretical factors include reliability, representativeness and validity. Ensure you know what these terms mean and can apply them to particular methods. You should relate these issues to the positivist-interpretivist debate (see Box 20).

You can gain AO2 marks by considering the relative importance of different factors or how, for instance, a theoretical strength may involve ethical or practical limitations. For example, covert participant observation may produce valid data, but it involves deceit and it may also be difficult to maintain one's cover. Try to link practical, theoretical and ethical factors in this way, rather than just dealing with each one separately. You can also gain AO2 marks by comparing different methods in terms of their theoretical, practical or ethical strengths or limitations – and by using examples from studies employing different methods and sources. Include examples of primary and secondary sources of data and of quantitative and qualitative methods.

Answer by Andy

Many factors can influence the sociologist's choice of what method to use in their work. These include practical, theoretical and ethical factors. When deciding, much depends on the topic and group being investigated.

> Too general. The last sentence needs developing.

The type of perspective is vital for the method a sociologist prefers to use. For example, a positivist would use quantitative methods such as questionnaires because they fundamentally believe that society is a real thing, just like the natural world.

> Andy should explain further why positivists prefer this method.

Some sociologists will choose to carry out a comparative study because they want to examine a particular issue to see trends and patterns over time. For example, Durkheim used official statistics to see if he could see links between the likelihood of suicide and a person's religion.

> Appropriate example of a research study, but needs to be applied more clearly.

Alternatively, interpretivists would want to use qualitative data collected through participant observation and other methods. This is because they believe that the right approach to sociology is to look at the social world through the eyes of those involved. They want to understand the thoughts and meanings people hold about social behaviour and this cannot be measured in the way positivists think it can be.

> Explains the link between theoretical preference and types of method.

Practical factors include time and money. If the sociologist wants to carry out a longitudinal study over a long period of time, then they will need a lot of funding to do so. It takes time to identify a representative sample and to return to it every so often. Alternatively, a short PO study such as that by Patrick carried out over a few weekends, is cheaper and much more cost effective.

> Sound knowledge, plus use of a concept and an appropriate example.

There are many methods that could be used. One that is not used very often is the experiment. Even when used as a field experiment, this technique is not well suited to studying most types of social behaviour. Experiments are too artificial, although not as much as the laboratory experiment. They also have ethical problems such as often they do not get the informed consent of those being studied.

> Not really very relevant except for the last, undeveloped sentence.

The examiner's comments

Andy presents a sound range of knowledge about choice of methods, with only the last paragraph moving away from the question. However, although Andy covers methodological issues quite well and deals with practical factors in a more basic manner, he only makes a passing mention of ethical issues.

However, the main weakness is a lack of analysis and evaluation. Appropriate points are often made fairly well, but then not developed. Andy needs to explain why the factors he presents affect choice of method. He could also gain AO2 marks by assessing the relative importance of each of the three types of factor.

12/20

Examining methods in context

Item A   Researching teachers' attitudes

Teachers may hold different attitudes towards different groups of pupils based on their ethnicity, class or gender. They may well judge different groups of pupils against an image of the 'ideal pupil'. Teachers' attitudes are likely to be an important influence on pupils' examination performance.

Sociologists want to know what these attitudes are, where they come from, how they are transmitted to pupils and what effects they have on educational achievement.

5

However, measuring the attitudes of a large, geographically dispersed social group such as teachers is not easy. Furthermore, attitudes are not easy to identify and measure. For example, teachers are used to 'putting on an act' in front of pupils, inspectors and others. This may make it difficult to see teachers' 'real' attitudes towards pupils.

Question

Using material from **Item A** and elsewhere, assess the strengths and limitations of questionnaires for the study of teachers' attitudes.

(20 marks)

The examiner's advice

As with all 'methods' essays, you need to relate strengths and limitations to positivism and interpretivism. You must also use the key concepts of reliability, representativeness and validity. Use the 'PET' technique to organise strengths and limitations in terms of Practical, Ethical and Theoretical issues.

However, because this is a 'methods in context' question, you must keep relating the strengths and limitations of questionnaires to the study of the **particular** issue of teachers' attitudes. Think about teachers as a group to be researched – what is different about them? What do sociologists want to find out about teachers' attitudes? (The Item gives you some ideas.) How useful are questionnaires likely to be in researching teachers' attitudes? What barriers are there to investigating this issue?

Each time you identify a strength or limitation, try to link it in some way to studying teachers and their attitudes. It may not be possible to do this every time but the more you do so, the more application marks will come your way.

Answer by Brendan

The usefulness of questionnaires in researching teachers' attitudes depends on your theoretical perspective. Positivists in particular see questionnaires as useful because they produce statistical data from which correlations and cause-and-effect relationships can be drawn.

As Item A suggests, one of the particular issues with researching teachers is that they are a large, geographically scattered group. The only way to reach a large number of teachers in a wide range of schools is by posting questionnaires to them. Positivists see this as useful because they want to be able to make generalisations about the attitudes of all teachers by using a representative sample.

Questionnaires are also especially useful for researching sensitive issues such as teachers' attitudes. Teachers are required to treat all pupils fairly and may therefore conceal their real attitudes. Questionnaires offer anonymity so teachers would be more likely to reveal any negative attitudes they hold about certain groups of students because there would be no 'comeback' on them. However, interpretivists would argue that rapport is necessary to uncover a social actor's meanings and questionnaires are simply too detached to be able to do this.

Data from questionnaires is usually easy to quantify because they use pre-coded, closed-ended questions. In turn, this reveals relationships between different variables. It is also quite easy to find a sample of teachers to send your questionnaire to as schools offer several ready-made sampling frames.

Teachers' attitudes, their expectations and labelling of different groups of pupils are not easy issues to research. This issue is all about the meanings teachers hold about their pupils and interpretivists would argue that questionnaires tell us little about the real meanings. They argue that expectations and labels cannot be measured quantitatively. Fixed questions with limited, pre-conceived response categories limit responses.

Questionnaires often have low response rates. Schools may refuse permission to give out a questionnaire on this issue because they do not believe their teachers would act unfairly towards different groups of pupils. Even if the questionnaire is distributed, will teachers answer the questions honestly? In any survey, respondents may lie, not know the answer or not understand the questions. In this case, when asked about their attitudes to pupils, teachers may well give 'respectable' answers - the ones they feel they ought to give - rather than tell the truth. This undermines the validity of responses, which is why interpretivists do not use them. They argue that a researcher might get closer to the truth by observing how teachers act towards their pupils.

> Theory is a good way to start – although focusing on the particular research issue would also be effective.

> Uses the Item to pick something specific to teachers, then develops it – good interpretation and application skills.

> Good application skill again – explains why teacher attitudes are a sensitive issue. Some evaluation too.

> Needs to explain link to teachers' attitudes – missed opportunity to gain application marks.

> Begins to unpack the particular research issue – but needs to link points about questionnaires in general (e.g. fixed questions) to researching teachers' attitudes.

> Identifies limitations and applies them to studying teachers' attitudes – but should explain why teachers might give 'respectable' answers to such questions.

The examiner's comments

This is a balanced answer that deals with both strengths and limitations of questionnaires. Crucially, in some cases, Brendan also applies these to the specific study of teachers' attitudes. Picking out some of the characteristics of teachers as a research group, and their attitudes as a research issue, are both good ways to gain application marks. However, he doesn't do this consistently and there are some lost opportunities to gain further marks.

Brendan presents a good range of strengths and limitations, but this could be broader. He makes use of theory and key methodological concepts such as validity and representativeness. He could also discuss practical problems, inflexibility, the imposition of researcher's meanings, ethical issues etc. Brendan could also compare the usefulness of questionnaires to other methods for this particular issue. His answer also lacks a conclusion.

Preparing for the Exam

CHAPTER 5

Tackling the AS sociology exam

This chapter focuses on the examination itself. It deals with:

- The knowledge and skills you have to show in your exams
- The format of the exam papers
- The different types of question and how to tackle them.

This chapter also includes mock exam papers for each of the two AS Sociology units, along with the examiner's advice on how to tackle the essay questions on these papers.

The Assessment Objectives

In AS sociology exams, your answers are assessed in terms of two aims or 'assessment objectives'. These are:

- **Assessment Objective 1** (AO1): Knowledge and Understanding
- **Assessment Objective 2** (AO2): the skills of Interpretation, Application, Analysis and Evaluation.

Roughly half the marks in the exam are for AO1 and half for AO2, so it's very important that you show evidence of both of them to the examiner. Let's take a closer look at the kind of knowledge, understanding and skills you need to demonstrate in your answers.

Knowledge and Understanding

You need to know about and understand some of the main theories, methods and concepts (ideas) that sociologists use in their work.

You also need to be familiar with some of the studies they have carried out and what these studies have found.

Interpretation

The skill of interpretation is about being able to select only the material that is relevant to the particular question you are answering, and avoiding writing an 'everything I know about this whole topic' answer. Interpretation includes:

- Explaining what an essay question involves.
- Using material from an Item when the question tells you to, linking it to your own knowledge and to the question.
- Using relevant examples, e.g. from studies, news and current events, personal experience, other topics you have studied in sociology etc.

Application

The skill of application includes:

- Linking ideas, concepts, theories, studies, methods etc to each other and to the question.
- Showing how the material you have selected is relevant to the question.
- In questions on methods, connecting the strengths and limitations of a method to the characteristics of a particular research issue.

Analysis

The skill of analysis includes:

- Breaking down an argument or explanation into the ideas that make it up and showing how they fit together.
- Comparing and contrasting ideas to show their similarities and differences.
- Organising your essays with a well-focused introduction and a clear, logical line of reasoning from paragraph to paragraph, leading to an appropriate conclusion.

Evaluation

Evaluation is about weighing things up, giving informed opinions or making balanced judgements about something. The 'something' could be different evidence, ideas, views, theories or methods. In exams, evaluation is often signalled by the word 'assess'.

The skill of evaluation includes:

- Looking at the arguments and evidence for and against a particular view.
- Examining a theory's assumptions or linking it to a particular perspective.
- Putting forward alternative views and perspectives.
- Discussing the strengths (or advantages) and limitations (or disadvantages) of a research method.

In practice, the two assessment objectives often overlap. For example, in order to select and apply the right information (AO2), you first need to know some sociology and understand the set question (AO1).

The exam papers

For AS level Sociology, you will take two written exam papers. These take the format described below.

Unit 1

- This is a one-hour exam worth 40% of the AS level (20% of the A level).
- There are **three** sections on this paper, each covering a different topic: *Families and Households, Culture and Identity, and Wealth, Poverty and Welfare*.
- You must choose **one** of these sections, e.g. Families and Households.
- Each section consists of two Items of stimulus material, plus five questions labelled (a) to (e).
- Questions (a) to (c) are short questions, while questions (d) and (e) are essays.

Before reading on, turn to page 242 and take a look at the mock exam paper for Unit 1. Focus on the overall structure of the paper rather than trying to figure out the answers to the questions, and check the paper against the list above.

(You will see we have only included Section B – Families and Households.)

Unit 2

- This is a two-hour exam worth 60% of the AS level (30% of the A level)
- There are **two** sections on this paper: Section A – *Education and Research Methods*, and Section B – *Health and Research Methods*. There are three questions in each section.
- You must choose **one** of these sections. Let us assume you have chosen Section A.
- **Question 1** is on Education. It has one Item and four parts. Parts (a) to (b) are short questions, part (c) is a mini-essay, while part (d) is an essay.
- **Question 2** is on Research Methods in the context of Education. It has one Item and one essay.
- **Question 3** is on Research Methods. It has four parts. Parts (a) to (c) are short questions, while part (d) is an essay question. There is no Item for this question.

Now look at the mock exam for Unit 2 on page 243. Focus again on its overall structure and check it against the list above. (You will see we have only included Section A – *Education and Research Methods*.)

Further details of the different types of question are given below, along with advice on how to tackle them.

How long to spend on each question

Unit 1

First of all, allow a few minutes to read the Items and questions. Then divide the remainder of your time roughly as follows: about 10 minutes for answering (a) to (c), 20-25 minutes for (d) and 20-25 minutes for (e). However, since (a) to (c) can be answered quite briefly, you may find you have a little longer for the essays (d) and (e).

Unit 2

AQA (the exam board) advises you to spend about 50 minutes on Question 1, 25 minutes on Question 2 and 40 minutes on Question 3. This leaves you 5 minutes for checking your answers.

However, Questions 1 and 3 are both in four parts, so you will need to sub-divide the above timings when answering these:

- **Question 1:** spend about half the time (25 minutes) reading the Item and answering questions (a) to (c). Spend the other half answering the essay question (d).
- **Question 2:** spend 25 minutes reading the Item and answering the essay question.

- **Question 3:** spend about 12-15 minutes answering questions (a) to (c). Spend about 25 minutes answering the essay question (d).

However, the short questions can often be answered more quickly, so you may be able to spend a little longer on the 20-mark essays and the 12-mark mini-essay.

For both Units, remember that these time allocations also include planning time. Spend a couple of minutes making a brief plan for the essay questions. You should also read through each answer as you finish it and make any necessary alterations.

Answering the short questions

The short questions carry two, four or six marks. Some are based on an Item and in this case you should read the Item carefully before answering.

A good performance on these short questions can get you halfway to a pass mark even before you tackle the longer questions. But it's important not to spend too much time writing long answers to them – you're not expected or required to do so. And as well as wasting time, long answers are often less clear and may end up scoring lower marks.

Two-mark questions

These questions ask you to explain the meaning of a term or concept. For example:

Explain what is meant by 'meritocracy'.

points to remember

- To get the two marks available, you must give a clear explanation or definition of the term. Simply giving an example may sometimes gain one mark, but it's not enough for both marks.
- Avoid repeating the word or phrase you're being asked about in your explanation – e.g. simply writing, 'Meritocracy is a system of rewards based on merit' doesn't show the examiner that you understand the term clearly. It would be better to write, 'It is a system of rewards based on the individual's effort and ability'. Put it in different words to make the meaning clear.

Four-mark and six-mark questions

'Identify' and 'Suggest' questions

These ask you either to 'identify' or to 'suggest' two things (for four marks) or three things (for six marks). These things can be reasons, examples, criticisms, advantages, ways, functions, causes etc. For example:

Identify two criticisms of the functionalist view of the family.

Suggest two functions that the extended family might perform today.

Suggest three advantages of using structured interviews in sociological research.

'Identify' means 'state from your knowledge'. For example, two criticisms of the functionalist view are that it ignores conflict in the family and that it ignores family diversity.

'Suggest' means you can put forward possible functions, ways etc. There does not have to be definite evidence, but your suggestions must be reasonably plausible (likely or convincing). For example, you could reasonably suggest, 'Helping out with the care of grandchildren while their mother goes out to work' as one function the extended family might perform today.

points to remember

- For these questions, your answers can be quite short. One sentence for each point will be enough.
- If you're not sure whether all your points are right but you can think of an extra one, put this down too – you won't be penalised. If you're asked for three reasons but give four, any three that are right will get the marks, even if the other one is wrong. But remember, the more points you give, the more time you use up.

'Explain the difference' questions

Some four-mark questions ask you to explain the difference (or the similarity) between two things. For example:

Explain the difference between ascribed status and achieved status.

You need to define or explain each term so as to bring out the difference between them. For example, you could say, 'Ascribed status is a position fixed at birth that you can't alter, whereas achieved status is a position that you gain through your own efforts'.

Answering the longer questions

There are three kinds of question that require longer answers:

- **'Assess'** questions
- **'Examine'** questions
- **'Outline'** questions

'Assess' questions

These are essays. They are worth 24 marks in Unit 1 and 20 marks in Unit 2. They ask you to assess something – often a view, theory, method or explanation. For example:

Using material from Item B and elsewhere, assess the view that husbands and wives are now more equal than in the past.

Using material from Item A and elsewhere, assess the Marxist view of the role of education.

Using material from Item A and elsewhere, assess the strengths and limitations of participant observation as a method of studying classroom behaviour.

'Assess' means the same as 'evaluate', so you need to focus on the AO2 skills by analysing and evaluating the material you use, rather than just describing or listing information. As Box 37 shows, 'Assess' questions give more marks for AO2 than for AO1.

the Items

The other key feature of these questions is that they will tell you to use material from an Item.

The Items are a very important source of help, so read them through very carefully at least twice, and check back to the question in between readings. Highlight or underline any words or phrases that seem important. Sometimes, line references are given in the questions. Use these to find key terms in the Item.

You will be rewarded for selecting and using material from the Item – so it's a good idea to draw the examiner's attention to the fact that you have done so by using a phrase like, 'as Item A says'.

You can quote from the Item or put it in your own words, but always try to build on it by linking it to the question and to your own knowledge.

Remember, too, that if you don't use the Item when told to, you won't be able to gain the higher marks. Box 38 gives an example of how you might use an Item.

You will also see that 'Assess' questions ask you to use 'material from elsewhere'. This is a signal that you must apply your own knowledge as well. In other words, you won't find everything in the Item that you need to answer the question.

| Box 37 | AO1 and AO2 marks for essays | | |

Question type	AO1	AO2	Total
Unit 1			
Examine	14	10	24
Assess	10	14	24
Unit 2			
Outline	8	4	12
Examine	10	10	20
Assess	8	12	20

Note: AO1 marks are for knowledge & understanding. AO2 marks are for interpretation, application, analysis & evaluation

'Examine' questions

These are essays. They are worth 24 marks in Unit 1 and 20 marks in Unit 2. They ask you to examine something. For example:

Examine the ways in which processes within schools may cause differences in educational achievement.

Examine the reasons why sociologists sometimes use written questionnaires in their research.

Examine the extent of and reasons for family diversity in Britain today.

'Examine' means you need to look closely at something, to consider its different aspects or features in detail. You therefore need to show you have a good knowledge and understanding of relevant material and of the issues raised by the question.

Some questions ask you to examine one kind of thing (e.g. reasons, ways, factors, causes), but others may ask you to examine two kinds of thing (e.g. extent of and reasons for, causes and effects). Make sure you deal with both aspects if asked to do so, even if you don't cover them equally.

Questions often ask for 'the reasons', 'the ways' etc. You may well be able to think of many more reasons or ways than you could possibly write about in the time available. Don't worry; so long as you can write about a range of reasons, you don't have to cover every possible one under the sun.

Write a solid paragraph for each main point that you are examining, using your knowledge of studies, theories, methods and examples as relevant to the question.

This type of question is not linked to an Item – it is always 'free standing'. This means that the information you use to answer it needs to come solely from your own knowledge.

As Box 37 shows, 'Examine' questions give a bigger share of the marks to AO1 Knowledge and Understanding than 'Assess' questions do.

'Outline' questions

These are mini-essays. They are worth 12 marks and are only found in Unit 2. They ask you to outline something. For example:

Outline some of the ways in which processes within the education system may lead to differences in achievement between ethnic groups.

Outline some of the policies that governments have introduced to reduce ethnic inequalities in educational achievement.

'Outline' means you need to identify the different aspects of the issue in the question and cover some of these in some detail. This means you need to show a good knowledge and understanding of relevant material.

These questions are like a shorter version of the 'Examine' questions described above. They usually ask you to outline just one kind of thing (e.g. policies, ways, factors). Questions usually ask for 'some of' the reasons, 'some of' the ways etc.

You may well be able to think of many more policies, ways etc than you could write about in the time available. Don't worry; so long as you can write about a range of reasons, you can gain full marks. You do not need the same range and detail as for 'Examine' questions. Write a solid paragraph for each main point you are considering, using your knowledge of studies, theories and examples as relevant to the question.

This type of question is not linked to an Item – it is always 'free standing'. This means that the information you use to answer it needs to come solely from your own knowledge.

As Box 37 shows, 'Outline' questions give more marks for AO1 than for AO2. However, you still need to show some AO2 skills – for example, by analysing the reasons, policies etc that the question asks about, and by briefly mentioning one or two criticisms.

points to remember for essay questions

- Read the question carefully until you understand it; then make a brief plan.
- Write a short introduction linking to key aspects of the question.
- Stick to the question. Don't write 'All I know about the family' (or education, or methods) answers.
- Discuss a range of concepts, explanations, theories/ perspectives and/or methods. Use evidence from sociological studies.
- Use the Items when instructed to, and use examples.
- Write a brief conclusion following logically from the main points in your essay.
- For 'Assess' questions, focus on showing the AO2 skills of Interpretation, Application, Analysis and Evaluation.
- For 'Examine' questions, there are more marks for Knowledge and Understanding, but you still need to show some AO2 skills.

Box 38   **Using an item**

The Item and question below are from 'Examining childhood' on page 37. We have highlighted some of the key words and phrases you could use as a starting point in answering the question. We have suggested how you could connect these ideas to other material on the topic and to the question. When using an Item, always try to find ways to link it to what you already know and to the question you have been asked.

Item A   According to some sociologists, children in today's supposedly child-centred society lead lives that are segregated and controlled, but childhood was not always like this. For example, Ariès describes a medieval world in which, if children were not actually the equals of adults, they nevertheless mixed freely with adults in both work and leisure. Little distinction was drawn between adults and children.

According to this view, however, industrialisation brought major changes to the position of children. The development of industrial society meant that their lives were increasingly confined, disciplined and regulated by adults. The result is that in the West today, adults exercise a control over children's time, space and bodies that would have been unimaginable to medieval society.

5

Not all sociologists share this view of modern childhood, however. Some argue that the distinction between childhood and adulthood is once again becoming blurred.

Essay   Using material from **Item A** and elsewhere, assess sociological explanations of changes in the status of childhood.

(24 marks)

Here are some examples of how you could use the highlights to stimulate your thinking and make links to other material and to the question:

- What does child-centred society mean? Why and how are we child-centred?
- What else do you know about Ariès' work? Medieval world… work and leisure. Little distinction… between adults and children. Why not? What evidence is there?
- How might industrialisation have changed children's position? Mention laws, policies, new ideas about children's rights. Link this to the 'march of progress' view.
- Give examples of how children are segregated and controlled … confined, disciplined and regulated…and of adults' control over children's time, space and bodies. Link this to age patriarchy and the child liberationist view and discuss these.
- Not all sociologists share this view … blurred. Use this to introduce contrasting views, e.g. Postman. Explain why he thinks the distinction is blurred or disappearing.

Unit 1 mock exam

Read Items A and B below and answer parts (a) to (e) that follow.   **Time allowed: 1 hour**

Item A

The structure and composition of families and households has changed considerably over the last century. For example, average household size has halved, and there has been a great increase in the number of households containing only one person. In 1901, only about one in 20 was of this type, whereas today it accounts for almost three in ten households. One reason for this is the increased divorce rate.

There has also been a steady decline in the proportion of 'traditional' households made up of a married couple and their own   5
dependent children. For example, in the early 1960s, this type accounted for almost 40% of households, but by 2006 it stood at only 22% - barely half the earlier figure. Such changes are partly the result of policies or laws introduced by government, but other social factors are also responsible.

Item B

According to some sociologists, social policy plays a positive role by helping the family to fulfil its functions and meet its members' needs more effectively. For example, free schooling and the National Health Service assist families in educating their children and caring for their members when they fall ill.

However, feminist sociologists argue that the role of social policy is to maintain patriarchy, especially in the form of the heterosexual nuclear family. For example, feminists point to the fact that maternity leave is much more generous than paternity   5
leave, thus reinforcing the notion that it is the mother's responsibility rather than the father's to care for babies. Feminists reject the view put forward by the New Right, that social policies have actually undermined the traditional nuclear family.

(a) Explain the difference between a family and a household (**Item A**).   (4 marks)

(b) Suggest two reasons for the increase in one-person households, apart from the increased divorce rate
(**Item A**, line 2).   (4 marks)

(c) Suggest two reasons for the decline in the proportion of households made up of a married couple and their own
dependent children (**Item A**, lines 5-6).   (4 marks)

(d) Examine the reasons for changes in the size and structure of the population of the United Kingdom since the
beginning of the 20th century.   (24 marks)

(e) Using material from **Item B** and elsewhere, assess the extent to which social policies on the family serve to
maintain patriarchy.   (24 marks)

Unit 2 mock exam

Answer all the questions. **Time allowed: 2 hours**

You are advised to spend approximately 50 minutes on Question 1, 25 minutes on Question 2, and 40 minutes on Question 3.

1 Read Item A below and answer parts (a) to (d) that follow.

Item A

There are marked differences in the educational achievement of pupils from different ethnic backgrounds. For example, whites and Asians on average do better than blacks. However, there are significant variations among Asians. For example, Indians do better than Pakistanis and Bangladeshis.

Although white pupils' achievements are very close to the national average, this is mainly because they make up about 85% of all pupils. When we look more closely, we find major class differences in the performance of white pupils. 5

Sociologists have explained the poorer performance of some ethnic groups in terms of home background factors. For example, New Right thinkers such as Murray have argued that a high rate of lone parenthood among black families is a primary cause of the under-achievement of black pupils. Others, such as Bereiter and Engelmann, have suggested that the language of black American pupils is inadequate for educational development.

(a) Explain what is meant by 'material deprivation.' (2 marks)

(b) Suggest three reasons why girls and boys often choose different subjects to study. (6 marks)

(c) Outline some of the current education policies that affect the achievement of social classes. (12 marks)

(d) Using material from **Item A** and elsewhere, assess the view that ethnic differences in achievement are primarily the result of home background factors. (20 marks)

2 This question requires you to **apply** your knowledge and understanding of sociological research methods to the study of this **particular** issue in education.

Read Item B below and answer the question that follows.

Item B

Researching teachers' attitudes

Teachers may hold different attitudes towards different groups of pupils based on their ethnicity, class or gender. They may well judge different groups of pupils against an image of the 'ideal pupil'. Teachers' attitudes are likely to be an important influence on pupils' examination performance.

Sociologists want to know what these attitudes are, where they come from, how they are transmitted to pupils and what effects they have on educational achievement. 5

However, measuring the attitudes of a large, geographically dispersed social group such as teachers is not easy. Furthermore, attitudes are not easy to identify and measure. For example, teachers are used to 'putting on an act' in front of pupils, inspectors and others. This may make it difficult to see teachers' 'real' attitudes towards pupils.

Using material from **Item B** and elsewhere, assess the strengths and limitations of unstructured interviews for the study of teachers' attitudes. (20 marks)

3 This question permits you to draw examples from **any areas** of sociology with which you are familiar.

(a) Explain what is meant by 'representative data'. (2 marks)

(b) Identify two ethical considerations that influence a sociologist's choice of research method. (4 marks)

(c) Suggest two practical problems of using participant observation in sociological research. (4 marks)

(d) Examine the problems of using official statistics in sociological research. (20 marks)

The examiner's advice: Unit 1 families and households

Part (d) carries 14 AO1 marks (knowledge and understanding) and 10 AO2 marks (interpretation, application, analysis and evaluation). The emphasis is on showing a sound, detailed sociological knowledge, but to score high marks you must also demonstrate AO2 skills.

Deal with both the size and structure of the population since 1900. Give some figures for growth in size and then examine the reasons. For these, first look at natural increase – outline patterns of births, deaths and life expectancy, and give the reasons for these (e.g. declining infant mortality, children as an economic liability, nutrition etc). Next look at the effect of net migration on population growth. Describe immigration and emigration patterns and 'push' and 'pull' factors that affect them. For population structure, describe changes in age structure and ethnic composition. You can explain these in terms of life expectancy and migration patterns. Write a separate conclusion.

Part (e) carries 10 AO1 and 14 AO2 marks. The emphasis is on showing well-developed AO2 skills, but to score high marks you must also show a good sociological knowledge. You must also make sure you use the Item.

Begin by defining patriarchy, then explain the feminist view of policy's role in maintaining it, using relevant examples from Item 2B and elsewhere. Also use the Item to illustrate other perspectives (e.g. New Right, functionalist). Ensure you use the key concepts of each perspective – e.g. instrumental and expressive roles, dependency culture, reserve army of labour etc. Evaluate the feminist view by considering alternative perspectives and examples of policies that promote non-patriarchal families, e.g. Civil Partnership Act, access to contraception and abortion etc. Also consider the New Right claim that policy undermines rather than supports the traditional family. Write a separate conclusion.

The examiner's advice: Unit 2 education

Q1 part (c) carries 8 AO1 and 4 AO2 marks. A good way to organise your answer might be to structure it in two parts – policies that may widen class differences in achievement and policies that may narrow them. You could explain how marketisation policies (the 1988 ERA, exam league tables, business sponsorship of schools etc) widen class differences. By contrast, you could explain how other policies (e.g. EMAs, EAZs, Aim Higher etc) may reduce inequalities. Focus on current policies – avoid giving accounts of the 1944 Education Act etc. Finish with an assessment of which policies have had most impact.

Q1 part (d) carries 8 AO1 and 12 AO2 marks. You should identify the differences in ethnic achievement – between and within ethnic groups. Explain the range of possible home background reasons for these differences such as cultural deprivation, linguistic factors, material deprivation and racism. Use material from Item A such as the references to New Right thinkers. Evaluate these explanations by referring to internal, school factors or by showing the way gender and class interact with ethnicity to create ethnic differences in achievement.

The examiner's advice: Unit 2 research methods

Q2 carries 8 AO1 and 12 AO2 marks. You need to relate strengths and limitations to positivism and interpretivism. You must also use the key concepts of reliability, representativeness and validity. Use the 'PET' technique to organise strengths and limitations in terms of practical (P), ethical (E) and theoretical (T) issues.

Because this is a 'methods in context' question, you must keep relating the strengths and limitations of unstructured interviews to the study of the *particular* issue of teachers' attitudes. Think about teachers as a group to be researched – what's different about them? What do sociologists want to find out about their attitudes? (Item B gives you some ideas.) How useful are unstructured interviews likely to be in researching this issue?

Each time you identify a strength or limitation, try to link it to investigating teachers and their attitudes. It may not be possible to do this every time but, the more you do so, the more application marks you will gain.

Q3 part (d) carries 10 AO1 and 10 AO2 marks. Keep the focus of your answer on the problems that sociologists find with using official statistics, such as social construction, problems of definition, relevance etc. Link these problems to validity, reliability and representativeness as well as placing them in the context of the theoretical debate between positivists and interpretivists. Also consider the practical problems of using statistics. You can make reference to the strengths of official statistics, but do so by linking these to each problem in turn.

Key Concepts

The following is an alphabetical list of some of the key concepts you need to know for AS level Sociology. You can use the list as:

- **a handy reference** to find a quick definition of a term you're not sure of
- **a revision aid** to ensure you know and understand important sociological ideas.

When you look up a concept in the list, you may find other terms in the explanation printed *in italics*. This means you will find a separate entry for these terms elsewhere in the list. You will also find that a lot of entries give you a 'see also' reference. Following these up will show you some of the links between concepts and broaden your understanding of them.

age patriarchy: *see* patriarchy.

ageism: the negative stereotyping of people on the basis of their age; e.g. the old are often portrayed as vulnerable, incompetent or irrational, and as a burden to society.

alienation: where an individual or group feels socially isolated and estranged because they lack the power to control their lives and realise their true potential. Marx describes workers in capitalist society as alienated because they are exploited and lack control of the production process. *See also* **Marxism.**

banding: a form of streaming.

birth rate: the number of live births per thousand of the population per year. *See also* **infant mortality rate**.

bourgeoisie: a Marxist term for the capitalist class, the owners of the means of production (factories, machinery, raw materials, land etc). Marx argues that the bourgeoisie's ownership of the means of production also gives them political and ideological power. *See also* **exploitation; ideology; Marxism; proletariat.**

capitalism: *see* **Marxism**.

case study: research that examines a single case or example, such as a single school, family or workplace, often using several methods or sources.

childhood: a socially defined age-status. There are major differences in how childhood is defined, both historically and between cultures. Western societies today define children as vulnerable and segregate them from the adult world, but in the past they were part of adult society from an early age. These differences show that childhood is a social construction. *See also* **patriarchy**.

civil partnership: the 2004 Civil Partnership Act has given same-sex couples similar legal rights to married couples in respect of pensions, inheritance, tenancies and property.

class: *See* **social class**.

closed-ended questions: questions used in a social survey that allow only a limited choice of answers from a pre-set list. They produce quantitative data and the answers are often pre-coded for ease of analysis. An example is 'Will you vote in the next election?' where the choices are Yes, No, Don't know. *See also* **open-ended questions**.

comparative method: a research method that compares two social groups that are alike apart from one factor. For example, Durkheim compared two groups that were identical apart from their religion in order to find out the effect of religion on suicide rates. The method is often used as an alternative to experiments.

compensatory education: government education policies such as Operation Headstart in the USA that seek to tackle the problem of under-achievement by providing extra support and funding to schools and families in deprived areas. *See also* **cultural deprivation.**

comprehensive system: a non-selective education system where all children attend the same type of secondary school. It was introduced in England and Wales from 1965. *See also* **tripartite system.**

conjugal roles: the roles played by husband and wife. Segregated conjugal roles are where the husband is breadwinner and the wife is homemaker, with leisure spent separately. In joint conjugal roles, husband and wife each perform both roles and spend their leisure time together. *See also* **symmetrical family**.

content analysis: a method of analysing the content of documents and media output to find out how often and in what ways different types of people or events appear. For example, the Glasgow University Media Group (1976) used content analysis to reveal bias in how television news reported strikes.

control group: in *experiments*, scientists compare a control group and an experimental group that are identical in all respects. Unlike the experimental group, the control group is not exposed to the variable under investigation and so provides a baseline against which any changes in the experimental group can be compared.

correlation: when two or more factors or *variables* vary together; e.g. there is a correlation between low social class and low educational achievement. However, the existence of a correlation between two variables does not necessarily prove that one causes the other. It may simply be coincidence. *See also* **experiments**.

correspondence principle: Bowles and Gintis' concept describing the way that the organisation and control of schools mirrors or 'corresponds to' the workplace in capitalist society. For example, the control teachers exert over pupils mirrors the control managers exert over workers. *See also* **reproduction**.

covert participant observation: *see* **participant observation**.

cultural capital: the knowledge, attitudes, values, language, tastes and abilities that the middle class transmit to their children. Bourdieu argues that educational success is largely based on possession of cultural capital, thus giving middle-class children an advantage. *See also* **reproduction; speech codes**.

cultural deprivation: the theory that many working-class and black children are inadequately socialised and therefore lack the 'right' culture needed for educational success; e.g. their families do not instil the value of *deferred gratification*. *See also* **compensatory education**.

culture: all those things that are learnt and shared by a society or group of people and transmitted from generation to generation through socialisation. It includes shared norms, values, knowledge, beliefs and skills. *See also* **subculture**.

curriculum: those things taught or learnt in educational institutions. The overt or official curriculum includes the subjects, courses etc offered (e.g. the National Curriculum), while the hidden curriculum includes all those things learnt without being formally taught and often acquired simply through the everyday workings of the school, such as attitudes of obedience, conformity and competitiveness. *See also* **ethnocentric**.

death rate: the number of deaths per thousand of the population per year.

deferred gratification: postponing immediate rewards or pleasures, generally with the aim of producing a greater reward at a later date, e.g. staying in to revise rather than going out with friends, which will bring success in exams. It is seen as a characteristic of middle-class *culture*. *See also* **immediate gratification; values**.

demography: the study of population, including birth, death, fertility and infant mortality rates, immigration and emigration, and age structure, as well as the reasons for changes in these.

dependency culture: where people assume that the state will support them, rather than relying on their own efforts and taking responsibility for their families. The *New Right* see *the welfare state* as over-generous, encouraging people to remain unemployed and dependent on benefits, and as responsible for the growing number of lone-parent families and rising crime rate. *See also* **underclass**.

dependency ratio: the relationship between the size of the working population and the non-working or dependent population.

deviance: behaviour that does not conform to the *norms* of a society or group. Deviance is a *social construction* (defined or created by social groups). Deviance is relative: what counts as deviant varies between groups and cultures and over time.

differentiation: distinguishing or creating differences between individuals or groups. In education, *streaming* is a form of differentiation that distinguishes between pupils on the basis of ability. In the study of *stratification*, differentiation refers to the process of distinguishing between people on the basis of class, gender, ethnic, age etc differences. *See also* **labelling**.

discrimination: treating people differently, whether negatively (disadvantaging them) or positively (advantaging them), usually because they are members of a particular social group. It can occur on grounds of *gender*, *ethnicity*, age, disability, *sexuality*, religion etc. *See also* **racism; sexism; ageism**.

documents: are of two types. Public documents are produced by organisations such as governments, schools, media etc. They include Acts of Parliament, school prospectuses, newspaper articles etc. Personal documents are created by individuals and often provide first-person accounts of events and experiences. They include diaries, letters, autobiographies etc. Both types are used as secondary sources of qualitative data in sociological research.

domestic labour: work performed in the home, such as childcare, cooking, and cleaning. Functionalists see it as part of the *expressive role* performed by women, while feminists regard it as a major source of women's oppression. *See also* **dual burden**.

dual burden: when a person is responsible for two jobs. Usually applied to women who are in paid work but also responsible for *domestic labour*. *See also* **emotion work**.

educational triage: the process whereby schools sort pupils into 'hopeless cases', 'those who will pass anyway', and 'those with potential to pass', and then concentrate their efforts on the last of these groups as a way to boost the school's exam league table position. Sorting may be based on stereotypical ideas about pupils' ability. *See also* **selection**.

emotion work: the work involved in meeting the emotional needs of other people, e.g. looking after a sick child involves responding to emotional as well as physical needs. Some sociologists argue that women carry a triple burden of housework, paid work and emotion work. *See also* **dual burden**.

empathy: an understanding of how another person thinks, feels or acts, achieved by putting oneself in their place. Interactionists advocate the use of qualitative methods such as participant observation as a way of achieving empathy and obtaining data high in *validity*. *See also* **interactionism; objectivity; subjectivity**.

empty shell marriage: a marriage in name only, where a couple continues to live under the same roof but as separate individuals. It may occur where divorce is difficult for legal, religious or financial reasons, or where a couple decides to stay together for the sake of the children.

ethics: issues of right and wrong; moral principles or guidelines. There are ethical objections to research that deceives or harms its participants or fails to obtain their *informed consent*.

ethnic group: people who share the same heritage, culture and identity, often including the same language and religion, and who see themselves as a distinct group, e.g. the Bangladeshi community in Britain. As well as having ethnic minority groups, societies such as Britain have an ethnic majority. *See also* **culture; racism; stratification**.

ethnocentric: seeing or judging things in a biased way from the viewpoint of one particular culture; e.g. the National Curriculum has been described as an ethnocentric curriculum since it tends to value white, western music, literature, languages, history, religion etc and disregards or does not value black and Asian cultures.

exchange theory: the idea that people create, maintain or break off relationships depending on the costs and benefits of doing so; e.g. a person may provide a relative with accommodation (cost) in return for help with childcare (benefit).

experiments: a laboratory experiment is a test carried out in controlled conditions in an artificial setting (a laboratory) to establish a cause-and-effect relationship between two or more variables. A field experiment has the same aim but is carried out in a natural setting (e.g. a street or workplace) not a laboratory. *See also* **control group; positivism**.

experimental group: see **control group**.

exploitation: paying workers less than the value of their labour. According to Marxists, it is the process whereby the *bourgeoisie* extract surplus value or profit from the labour of the *proletariat*. Feminists see men as exploiting the *domestic labour* of women. *See also* **Marxism; feminism**.

expressive role: the caring, nurturing, 'homemaker' role in the family. Functionalists argue that women are biologically suited to performing this role, but feminists reject this. *See also* **instrumental role**.

extended family: any group of kin (people related by blood, marriage or adoption) extended beyond the *nuclear family*. The family may be extended vertically (e.g. grandparents), horizontally (e.g. aunts, uncles, cousins), or both. *See also* **family structure**.

family diversity: the idea that there is a range of different family types, rather than a single dominant one (such as the nuclear family). It is associated with the postmodernist idea that in today's society, increasing choice about relationships is creating greater family diversity.

family practices: the routine actions through which we create our sense of 'being a family member', such as doing

the shopping or the DIY. Morgan prefers the term to that of *family structure* because it conveys the idea that families are not 'things', but what their members actually do.

family structure: the composition of a group of people who live together as a family unit. Structures include the *nuclear family*, *extended family*, *reconstituted family*, lone-parent and same-sex families.

fertility rate: the total fertility rate (TFR) is the average number of children women will have during their fertile years. For statistical purposes, this is defined as age 15-44.

feminism: a sociological perspective and political movement that focuses on women's oppression and the struggle to end it. Feminists argue that sociology has traditionally taken a 'malestream' viewpoint that ignores women. Instead, they examine women's experiences and study society from a female perspective. There are different strands of feminism, including Marxist, radical, liberal and difference feminism. *See also* **patriarchy**.

Fordism: a type of industrial production based on a detailed division of labour, using closely supervised, low-skilled workers and assembly-line technology to mass-produce standardised goods. Named after the car manufacturing techniques first introduced by the Ford Motor Company in the early 20th century. *See also* **alienation; post-Fordism**.

function: the contribution that a part of society makes to the stability or well-being of society as a whole. For example, according to Durkheim, one function of religion is to give individuals a sense of belonging to something greater than themselves and so integrate them into society. *See also* **functionalism**.

functional fit: Parsons' theory that, with *industrialisation*, the structure of the family becomes nuclear to fit the needs of industrial society for a geographically and socially mobile labour force. *See also* **functionalism; mobility**.

functionalism: a consensus perspective in sociology that sees society as based on shared values into which members are socialised. It sees society as like an organism, each part performing functions to maintain the system as a whole; e.g. the family and education system perform *socialisation* functions. *See also* **function; value consensus**.

gender: the social and cultural characteristics of men and women. Unlike sex differences, which are biological and inborn, gender differences in behaviour are cultural in origin and learned through gender role *socialisation*. Definitions of masculinity and femininity are socially constructed and vary between cultures and social groups. *See also* **feminism; patriarchy**.

geographical mobility: see **mobility**.

globalisation: the idea that the world is becoming increasingly interconnected and barriers are disappearing, e.g. as a result of instantaneous communication systems, deregulation of trade, the creation of global markets and global media and culture. Many see it as creating new risks, uncertainties and choices, and an increased rate of social change.

Hawthorne Effect: where the subjects of a research study know they are being studied and begin to behave differently as a result, thereby undermining the study's *validity*. The term comes from Elton Mayo's studies at the Hawthorne electrical plant.

hidden curriculum: see **curriculum**.

hierarchy: an organisation or social structure based on a 'pyramid' of senior and junior positions and top-down control; e.g. an army with its different ranks and command from above. *See also* **stratification**.

household: a group of people who live together and share things such as meals, bills, facilities or chores, or one person living alone.

hypothesis: an untested theory or explanation, expressed as a statement. Sociologists seek to prove or disprove hypotheses by testing them against the evidence. *See also* **experiments**.

identity: the individual's sense of self, influenced by *socialisation* and interactions with others; a sense of belonging to a community. Postmodernists see identity as a choice that individuals make from among different sources of identity, such as *gender*, *ethnic group*, religion, *sexuality*, leisure interests, nationality etc. *See also* **postmodernism**.

ideology: originally a Marxist idea meaning a set of beliefs that serve the interests of a dominant social group by justifying their privileged position. The term usually implies that the beliefs are false or only partially true; e.g. Bowles and Gintis argue that meritocracy is a 'myth', i.e. untrue. *See also* **legitimation**; **Marxism**.

immediate gratification: a preference for immediate pleasure or reward, without regard for the longer-term consequences; e.g. going out with friends instead of doing one's homework. *Cultural deprivation* theorists argue that working-class children are socialised into the value of immediate gratification and that this explains their educational failure. *See also* **deferred gratification; values**.

industrialisation: the shift from an agricultural economy to one based on factory production. In Britain, industrialisation occurred from about the late 18th to the mid-19th centuries. Industrialisation often occurs along with *urbanisation*.

individualism: the belief that the individual is more important than the group or community. In modern and postmodern society, individualism becomes more important than in traditional society and individuals' actions are influenced more by calculations of their own self-interest than by a sense of obligation to others.

infant mortality rate: the number of infants who die before their first birthday, per thousand live births per year. *See also* **birth rate; death rate**.

informed consent: where those taking part in a study have agreed to do so and understand the purpose of the study, the uses to which its findings may be put, and its possible effects. *See also* **ethics**.

instrumental role: the breadwinner or provider role in the family. Functionalists see this as the man's role. *See also* **expressive role**.

interactionism: a sociological perspective that focuses on small-scale (micro-level) interactions between individuals and groups, rather than on the large-scale workings of society. Interactionists seek to understand the meanings that social actors give to actions and situations, usually by using qualitative research methods. *See also* **interpretivism; labelling; self-fulfilling prophecy**.

interpretivism: a term covering a range of perspectives including *interactionism*. Interpretivists focus on how we construct our social worlds through the meanings we create and attach to events, actions and situations. They favour qualitative methods and see human beings as fundamentally different from the natural phenomena studied by scientists, in that we have free will, consciousness and choice. *See also* **positivism; subjectivity**.

interview schedule: the list of questions to be asked in an interview. It is useful because it allows some standardisation of the interviewing process, since all interviewers will use the same schedule of questions.

interviews: a method of gathering information by asking questions orally, either face-to-face or by telephone. Structured (or formal) interviews use pre-set, standardised, usually *closed-ended questions* producing *quantitative data*. Unstructured (informal or depth) interviews are more like a guided conversation and use *open-ended questions* producing *qualitative data*. Semi-structured interviews include both types of question. *See also* **questionnaires**.

labelling: the process of attaching a definition or meaning to an individual or group; e.g. teachers may label a pupil as a 'trouble maker'. Often the label is a stereotype that defines all members of a group in the same way. The concept is widely used in the study of *deviance*, mental illness and education. *See also* **self-fulfilling prophecy**.

legitimation: justifying something by making it seem fair and natural. This is the main function of *ideology*. Marxists argue that institutions in capitalist society such as education, the media and religion are 'ideological state apparatuses' whose function is to legitimate inequality. *See also* **meritocracy**.

life chances: the chances that different social groups have of obtaining those things society regards as desirable (e.g. educational qualifications) or of suffering those things regarded as undesirable (e.g. low income). Statistics on education, health, income etc show that such opportunities vary by *class, gender* and *ethnic group*. *See also* **stratification**.

life course analysis: an approach focusing on the meanings family members give to life events and choices, e.g. deciding to leave home, get divorced etc. It uses unstructured interviews to uncover these meanings and understand people's choices about relationships and how these may lead to family diversity.

life expectancy: how long on average people who are born in a given year can expect to live.

living apart together ('LATs'): couples who are in a significant relationship, but not married or cohabiting. Some sociologists suggest that LATs may reflect a trend towards less formalised relationships.

longitudinal study: study of a *sample* of people (sometimes called a panel) in which information is collected at regular intervals over an extended period of time; e.g. the National Child Development Study has been running since 1958. These studies usually use *questionnaires or interviews*, but other methods may also be employed.

macro-level: theories such as *functionalism* and *Marxism* that focus on the large scale, i.e. on the social structure as a whole or on the relationships between social institutions like the education system and the economy. These theories see the individual as shaped by society. *See also* **micro-level; positivism**.

marketisation: the policy of introducing market forces of supply and demand into areas run by the state, such as education and the National Health Service. The 1988 Education Reform Act began the marketisation of education by encouraging competition between schools and choice for parents. *See also* **New Right**.

Marxism: a conflict perspective based on the ideas of Karl Marx (1818-83). It sees society as divided into two opposed classes, one of which exploits the labour of the other. In capitalist society, the *bourgeoisie* exploits the *proletariat*. Marx predicted the proletariat would unite to overthrow capitalism and create a classless society. Marxist sociologists argue that institutions such as education and the media function to maintain capitalism. *See also* **alienation; exploitation; ideology; modernism; polarisation; reproduction**.

material deprivation: poverty; a lack of basic necessities such as adequate diet, housing, clothing or the money to buy these things. In education, material deprivation theory explains working-class under-achievement as the result of the lack of such resources; e.g. parents are unable to afford educational aids, overcrowding deprives children of a quiet study area etc.

means of production: *see* **bourgeoisie**.

meritocracy: an educational or social system where everyone has an equal opportunity to succeed and where individuals' rewards and status are achieved by their own efforts rather than ascribed by their *gender, class* or *ethnic group*. *See also* **myth of meritocracy**.

micro-level: theories such as interactionism that focus on small-scale, face-to-face interaction, e.g. between teacher and pupils in a classroom. These theories see individuals constructing society through their interactions. *See also* **interpretivism; macro-level**.

mobility: movement; change of position. Sociologists distinguish between geographical mobility, in which people move from one place to another (e.g. in search of work), and social mobility, in which they change position or status in a *hierarchy* or *stratification* system. Functionalists argue that the geographical and social mobility of the *nuclear family* enable it to meet the needs of industrial society. *See also* **industrialisation**.

modernism: modernist perspectives (e.g. *functionalism*, *Marxism* and *positivism*) believe that society has a fairly clear-cut, predictable structure and that it is possible to gain true and certain scientific knowledge of how society functions. This knowledge can be used to achieve progress to a better society. *See also* **postmodernism**.

multicultural: a society or institution that recognises and gives value to different cultures and/or ethnic groups; e.g. multi-cultural education teaches children about the cultures of other groups, not just the dominant or majority *culture*.

myth of meritocracy: Functionalists argue that the education system is meritocratic, but Bowles and Gintis claim that meritocracy is an *ideology* legitimating inequality by falsely claiming that everyone has equal opportunity and that unequal rewards are the 'natural' result of unequal ability. *See also* **legitimation; meritocracy**.

natural change: the difference between the number of births and the number of deaths in a population, resulting in either a natural increase or a natural decrease.

net migration: the difference between the number of immigrants entering a country and the number of emigrants leaving it.

New Right: a conservative political perspective whose supporters believe in self-reliance and individual choice, rather than dependence on the state. They believe in applying free market principles, e.g. the *marketisation* of education, and argue that generous welfare benefits encourage the growth of an *underclass*.

new vocationalism: the idea that education should be primarily about meeting the needs of the economy, especially by equipping young people with the knowledge, skills, attitudes and *values* needed to prepare them for work. Since the 1970s it has given rise to educational initiatives such as the Youth Training Scheme, BTEC and vocational GCSEs.

non-participant observation: a primary research method where the observer records events without taking part in them; e.g. a sociologist might observe and record how gender roles influence children's play without taking part. In sociology, *participant observation* is used much more often.

Key Concepts

norms: social rules, expectations or standards that govern the behaviour expected in particular situations. Norms may be formal (e.g. written laws or rules) or informal (e.g. rules of politeness). Each *culture* has detailed norms governing every aspect of behaviour. *See also* **values**.

nuclear family: a two-generation family of a man and woman and their dependent children, own or adopted. *See also* **family structure**.

objectivity: the absence of bias or preconceived ideas. It implies that we can look at things as they really are, without our opinions or *values* getting in the way (and thus we can get at the truth). Positivists believe sociology can achieve objectivity by modelling itself on the natural sciences, using methods that keep sociologists detached from their research subjects. *See also* **positivism; subjectivity**.

official statistics: *quantitative data* collected by the government. They can be gathered either by registration (e.g. the law requires parents to register births) or by official surveys (e.g. the ten-yearly Census of the entire population).

open-ended questions: questions in a *social survey* that allow respondents to answer as they wish, in their own words (e.g. 'How did you feel about being excluded from school?'). Answers are harder to analyse because they cannot be pre-coded. *See also* **closed-ended questions**.

operationalisation: the process of turning a sociological concept or theory into something measurable. For example, a sociologist studying the effect of *social class* on educational achievement might use parental occupation to measure the concept 'social class'.

overt participant observation: *see* **participant observation**.

parentocracy: literally, 'rule by parents'. The concept is associated with marketised education systems, which are based on an ideology of parental choice of school. Middle-class parents may benefit from parentocracy because they have more economic and *cultural capital* and are better placed to exercise choice. *See also* **marketisation**.

participant observation: a primary research method in which the sociologist studies a group by taking a role within it and participating in its activities. It may be overt, where other participants are aware of the researcher's true identity and motive. Alternatively, it may be covert ('undercover'), where the sociologist's identity and purpose are kept secret.

patriarchy: literally, rule by the father. Feminists use the term to describe a society based on male domination; a system or *ideology* of male power over women. Child liberationists argue that children are victims of 'age patriarchy' – the domination of fathers, or adults generally. *See also* **feminism**.

pilot study: a small-scale trial run, usually of a social survey, conducted before the main study. Its basic aim is to iron out any problems, clarify questions and their wording, give

interviewers practice etc, so that any necessary changes can be made before the main study is carried out.

polarisation: a process that results in the creation of two opposite extremes, e.g. pupils' responses to *labelling* and *streaming* in schools can create a pro-school and an anti-school *pupil subculture*. In the study of *stratification*, Marx describes how in capitalist society the class structure becomes polarised into a wealthy bourgeoisie and impoverished proletariat. *See also* **differentiation; self-fulfilling prophecy; Marxism**.

population: in a *social survey*, the population (sometimes called the 'survey population') is all the members of the group that the researcher is interested in; e.g. in a study of political opinions, the population may be the entire electorate. *See also* **demography; sampling frame**.

positivism: the belief that society is made up of 'social facts' that can be studied scientifically to discover laws of cause and effect. Durkheim took *official statistics* on suicide as social facts and tried to produce a law explaining why suicide rates vary between groups. With such knowledge, sociologists would be able to find solutions to social problems. *See also* **comparative method; experiments; interpretivism; objectivity**.

post-Fordism: a type of industrial production. A highly skilled, adaptable workforce, combined with computerised technology, means that production takes the form of 'flexible specialisation', able to respond swiftly to changing consumer demands and to produce for a variety of small, customised 'niche' markets. *See also* **Fordism**.

postmodernism: a perspective that rejects the modernists' belief in progress and their view that we can have certain, true knowledge of society that will enable us to improve it. Society has become so unstable and diverse that it is now impossible to produce any absolute explanations. No one theory is 'truer' than any other; theories such as *Marxism* and *functionalism* are merely viewpoints. Instead, sociology should concentrate on reflecting and celebrating social diversity. *See also* **modernism**.

primary data: information collected first hand by sociologists themselves for their own research purposes. Methods such as *participant observation*, *social surveys* and *experiments* are sources of primary data. *See also* **secondary data**.

primary socialisation: *see* **socialisation**.

privatised family: a *nuclear family* whose lifestyle and leisure patterns centre on the home rather than the extended family, workmates or wider community. In Young and Willmott's study, many families who moved out of Bethnal Green to the suburbs became privatised.

proletariat: the working class in capitalist society They own no means of production and are 'wage slaves', forced to sell their labour-power to the *bourgeoisie* in order to survive. *See also* **exploitation; Marxism**.

pure relationship: one which exists solely to meet each partner's needs. Couples stay together for love, happiness or sexual attraction, rather than because of tradition or duty, or for the sake of the children. According to Giddens, it is increasingly regarded as the only acceptable basis for a relationship.

qualitative data: information, usually expressed in words, about people's thoughts, feelings, motivations, attitudes, values etc. It is obtained from qualitative methods and sources such as *participant observation, unstructured interviews*, diaries and letters. It aims to give an insight into what it is like to be in another person's 'shoes'. *See also* **empathy; interactionism.**

quantitative data: information in numerical form (percentages, tables, graphs etc). *Official statistics* and the results of *social surveys* are two important sources of quantitative data. See also **closed-ended questions; positivism.**

questionnaires: lists of questions. Written or self-completion questionnaires are widely used in large-scale social surveys, where they may be sent out and returned by post. Questionnaires tend to use mainly *closed-ended questions* with pre-coded answers for ease of analysis. *See also* **quantitative data; response rate.**

racism: a system of beliefs that defines people as superior or inferior, and justifies their unequal treatment, on the basis of biological differences such as skin colour. Individual racism refers to the prejudiced views and discriminatory behaviour of individuals. Institutional racism exists when the routine ways an organisation operates have racist outcomes regardless of the intentions of the individuals within it.

reconstituted family: a stepfamily, in which one or both partners has children from a previous relationship. *See also* **family structure.**

reliability: a piece of research is reliable if it produces exactly the same results (a replica) when repeated using identical methods and procedures. In general, quantitative methods such as *experiments* and *questionnaires* are more reliable than qualitative methods because they use standardised procedures that are easier to replicate; e.g. a questionnaire asking all respondents the same set of questions.

representative: typical; a cross-section. A researcher may choose to study a sample of a larger group. If the sample is representative, those in it will be typical of the larger group. This will allow the findings to be generalised, i.e. applied to all members of the group, not just those in the *sample*.

reproduction: the re-creation or continuation of something into future generations; e.g. Marxists argue that schooling reproduces the class structure by failing working-class pupils so that they take working-class jobs. *See also* **correspondence principle; Marxism.**

reserve army of labour: a Marxist concept describing groups who can be brought into the workforce when there is a labour shortage as the capitalist economy expands during a boom, and discarded when it contracts. Women were used as a reserve army of labour during the two world wars, returning afterwards to their primary domestic role. *See also* **Marxism.**

response rate: the proportion of those people included in a social survey who actually reply or respond to the questions asked. A high response rate is important to help ensure that findings are *representative*.

role: how someone who occupies a particular *status* is expected to act; e.g. someone playing the role of bus driver is expected to drive safely, stop for passengers, charge the correct fare etc.

sample: a smaller group selected from the larger survey *population* to take part in a study. It may be too costly or time-consuming to study the whole population in which we are interested, so we choose a sample to study instead. *See also* **sampling; sampling frame.**

sampling: the process of selecting a *sample*. The aim of sampling is usually to select a sample that is representative of the wider survey *population*, so as to allow the study's findings to be generalised. There are several types of sampling, e.g. random, stratified random, quota and snowball sampling. *See also* **sampling frame.**

sampling frame: the list of people from which a *sample* for a *social survey* is selected, e.g. a school roll could be the sampling frame for a survey of pupils. It should list all the members of the survey *population* that the sociologist is interested in studying, though this is not always possible; e.g. there is no complete list of all criminals (since some are not caught).

sanctions: *see* **social control.**

secondary data: information collected not by sociologists themselves for their own research purposes, but by other people or organisations for non-sociological purposes. Sociologists make extensive use of this 'second hand' information because it is often free or cheap, readily available and covers large numbers. Secondary sources of data include *official statistics*, the media and *personal documents*. *See also* **primary data.**

secondary socialisation: *see* **socialisation.**

secularisation: the decline of religion; the process whereby religious beliefs, practices and institutions lose their importance or influence; e.g. fewer couples now marry in church and many people disregard religious teachings on issues like divorce, homosexuality etc.

selection: in education, the process of choosing and allocating pupils to a particular school, class, stream etc; e.g. in the *tripartite system* after 1944, the 11-plus exam selected

Key Concepts

pupils supposedly on the basis of ability for either grammar or secondary modern school. *See also* **educational triage**.

self-fulfilling prophecy: where a prediction made about a person or group comes true simply because it has been made. For example, in predicting that some pupils will do badly, teachers treat them in line with these lower expectations. This will discourage the pupils from trying and make the prediction come true. The prediction is a form of *labelling*. It works by changing the individual's self-image to bring it in line with the expectations that others have of him/her. *See also* **interactionism; streaming**.

separatism: a radical feminist idea that women should live independently of men as the only way to free themselves from the patriarchal oppression of the heterosexual family.

sexism: prejudice and *discrimination* on the grounds of sex; e.g. seeing girls as better suited for courses in 'caring' subjects. *See also* **patriarchy**.

sexuality: sexual orientation; a person's sexual preference; e.g. heterosexual, homosexual (gay or lesbian).

social action theories: see individuals as having free will and choice, and the power to create society through their actions and interactions, rather than being shaped by society. *Interactionism* is the best-known theory of this type, *postmodernism* also has certain features in common with social action theories. *See also* **structural theories**.

social class: social groupings or hierarchy based on differences in wealth, income or occupation. Marx identified two opposed classes in capitalist society, the *bourgeoisie* and *proletariat*. Many sociologists use occupation to distinguish between a manual working class and a non-manual middle class. Some also identify an *underclass* beneath the working class. *See also* **life chances; Marxism**.

social construction: where something is created by social processes, rather than simply occurring naturally. For example, interpretivists argue that official crime statistics are socially constructed through the interactions of police and suspects. When something is socially constructed, it is likely to vary historically and between cultures. Sociologists see *childhood, gender, identity* etc as social constructs.

social control: the means by which society tries to ensure that its members behave as others expect them to. Control can be formal (e.g. the law) or informal (e.g. peer pressure). Negative sanctions (punishments) may be threatened or positive sanctions (rewards) offered to encourage individuals to conform to society's *norms* and *values*.

social mobility: *see* **mobility**.

social policy: the actions, plans and programmes of government bodies and agencies that aim to deal with a problem or achieve a goal, e.g. raising levels of educational attainment. Policies are often based on laws that provide the framework within which these agencies operate. *See also* **welfare state**.

social survey: any research method that involves systematically collecting information from a group of people (either a *sample* or the whole target *population*, e.g. the Census) by asking them questions. Usually, this involves using written *questionnaires* or structured *interviews* and the questions are standardised.

socialisation: the process by which an individual learns or internalises the *culture* of society. Primary socialisation occurs largely within the family and involves acquiring basic skills and *values*, while much secondary socialisation takes place within educational institutions and includes acquisition of knowledge and skills needed for work. Other agencies of socialisation include peer groups, the mass media and religion.

speech codes: patterns or ways of using language. Bernstein argues that the working class use only the context-bound restricted code, with short, grammatically simple sentences and limited vocabulary. The middle class use the context-free elaborated code, with complex sentences and able to describe abstract ideas. This code is used in education, giving middle-class children an advantage. *See also* **cultural capital**.

stabilisation of adult personalities: according to Parsons, one of the two functions of the nuclear family along with primary *socialisation*. It is a place where adults can relax and release tensions, enabling them to return to the workplace ready to meet its demands. This is functional for the efficiency of the economy.

status: a position in society. Ascribed status occurs where our position in society is determined by fixed characteristics that we are born with and cannot normally change, e.g. *gender*, ethnicity or family of origin. Achieved status occurs where an individual's position is the result of their effort and ability, e.g. getting into university. *See also* **meritocracy**.

stereotype: a simplified, one-sided and often negative image of a group or individual which assumes that all members of that group share the same characteristics; e.g. the image that all black boys are disruptive and unruly. *See also* **labelling**.

stigma: a negative label or mark of disapproval, discredit or shame attached to a person, group or characteristic. The stigma is used to justify the exclusion of the individual from normal social interaction; e.g. in the past, divorcees were often stigmatised and excluded from 'respectable' company. *See also* **labelling**.

stratification: the division of society into a hierarchy of unequal groups. The inequalities may be of wealth, power and/or status. Stratification systems may be based on differences in *social class, ethnic group*, age, *gender*, religion etc. Members of different groups usually have different *life chances*.

stratified diffusion: the spread of beliefs and practices from one social class to another; e.g. Young and Willmott claim that the *symmetrical family* developed first among the middle class and then spread down the class structure eventually to become the norm for the working class as well.

streaming: where children are separated into different ability groups or classes ('streams') and then each ability group is taught separately from the others for all subjects; the opposite of mixed-ability teaching. *See also* **differentiation; self-fulfilling prophecy**.

structural theories: see individuals as entirely shaped by the way society is structured or organised; e.g. *functionalism* sees society as socialising individuals into shared norms and values that dictate how they will behave. *Marxism* and most types of *feminism* are usually regarded as structural theories. *See also* **social action theories**.

subculture: a group of people within society who share *norms*, *values*, beliefs and attitudes that are in some ways different from or opposed to the mainstream *culture*; e.g. an anti-school subculture formed by pupils in lower streams.

subjectivity: bias, lack of *objectivity*, where the individual's own viewpoint influences their perception or judgement. Interpretivists believe sociology is inevitably subjective, since it involves understanding other humans by seeing the world through their eyes. *See also* **empathy; interpretivism**.

survey: *see* **social survey**.

symmetrical family: Young and Willmott's 'stage three' privatised nuclear family with more equal and *joint conjugal roles*, in which husbands participate in domestic labour as well as being breadwinners, and wives go out to work as well as being homemakers. The couple spend their leisure time together and are more home-centred.

triangulation: the use of two or more different methods or sources of data so that they complement each other, the strengths of one countering the weaknesses of the other and vice versa; e.g. using both a qualitative method such as *participant observation* and a quantitative method such as structured *interviews*.

tripartite system: the system of secondary education created by the 1944 Education Act, based on three types of school. The 11+ exam was used to identify pupils' aptitudes and abilities. Those identified as having academic ability (mainly middle-class) went to grammar schools; most working-class children went to secondary modern schools. Although replaced in most areas after 1965, the tripartite system still continues in some. *See also* **comprehensive system**.

triple shift; triple burden: *see* **emotion work**.

underclass: those at the lowest level of the class structure; a class below the working class with a separate, deviant *subculture* and lifestyle, including a high rate of lone-parent families, male unemployment and criminality. *See also* **dependency culture; New Right**.

unit of consumption: unlike the pre-industrial family, the modern family no longer works together, but still consumes together as a single unit or group the income that its members earn, e.g. on food, housing and leisure activities. *See also* **unit of production**.

unit of production: where family members work together as economic producers, said to be more common in pre-industrial society; e.g. *an extended family* that works together on a farm. *See also* **unit of consumption**.

urbanisation: the process of change from a rural society where the majority of the population lives in the countryside to an urban society where most people live in towns and cities. It often occurs along with *industrialisation*.

validity: the capacity of a research method to measure what it sets out to measure; a true or genuine picture of what something is really like. A valid method is thus one that gives a truthful picture. Methods such as participant observation that produce *qualitative data* are usually seen as high in validity. *See also* **empathy; interactionism**.

value consensus: agreement among society's members about what values are important; a shared culture. According to functionalists, it integrates individuals into society by giving them a sense of solidarity or 'fellow feeling' with others and enables them to agree on goals and cooperate harmoniously. *See also* **functionalism**.

values: ideas or beliefs about general principles or goals. They tell society's members what is good or important in life and what to aim for, and they underlie more detailed *norms* of conduct. Functionalists see shared values as vital in holding society together. *See also* **functionalism; value consensus**.

variables: any factor that can change or vary; such as age, gender, occupation or income. Sociologists seek to discover *correlations* between variables; e.g. between *social class* and educational achievement. Laboratory *experiments* are occasionally used to control variables and measure their effect.

vocational: connected to a career. Vocational education and training transmits knowledge, skills and attitudes needed to pursue particular careers, e.g. courses in engineering, health and social care, IT or hairdressing. *See also* **new vocationalism**.

welfare state: where the government or state takes responsibility for people's well being, especially their basic minimum needs. In Britain, today's welfare state was created largely in the late 1940s. It includes various benefits to provide a minimum income, as well as the NHS, state education and council housing. *See also* **dependency culture; underclass**.

Bibliography

Adonis A and Pollard S (1998) *A Class Act*, Penguin

Allan G (1985) *Family Life*, Blackwell

Allan G (1996) *Kinship and Friendship in Modern Britain*, Oxford University Press

Allan G and Crow G (2001) *Families, Households and Society*, Palgrave

Althusser L (1971) *Lenin and Philosophy and Other Essays*, New Left Books

Amato P (2000) 'The consequences of divorce for adults and children', *Journal of Marriage and Family*

Anderson M (1980) *Approaches to the History of the Western Family*, Macmillan

Ansley F (1972) cited in Bernard J (1976)

Arber S and Ginn J (1995) 'The Mirage of Gender Equality', British Journal of Sociology

Aries P (1960) *Centuries of Childhood*, Penguin

Arnot C (2004) 'Where White Liberals Fear to Tread', The Guardian

Askew S and Ross C (1988) *Boys Don't Cry*, Open University

Atkinson M (1971) 'Societal Reactions to Suicide', in Cohen S (ed) *Images of Deviance*, Penguin

Ball S J (1981) *Beachside Comprehensive*, Open University

Ball S J (1993) in Burgess R *The Research Process in Educational Settings: Ten Case Studies,* Falmer

Ball S J (1994) *Education Reform*, Open University

Ball S J, Bowe R and Gewirtz S (1994), 'Market forces and parental choice', in Tomlinson S (ed), *Education Reform and its Consequences*, IPPR/Rivers Oram Press

Ballard R (1982) 'South Asian Families', in Rapoport R and Rapoport R (ed) *Families in Britain*, RKP

Barrett M and McIntosh M (1991) *The Anti-Social Family*, Verso

Bartlett W (1993) 'Quasi-Markets and Educational Reform', in Le Grand et al (ed) *Quasi-Markets and Social Policy*, Macmillan

BBC (2006), 'Schools "too feminine for boys"', 13 June, www.bbc.co.uk

Beck U (1992) *Risk Society*, Sage

Beck U and Beck-Gernsheim E (1995) *The Normal Chaos of Love*, Polity

Becker H et al (1961) *Boys in White*, University of Chicago Press

Becker H (1971) 'Social Class Variations in the Teacher-Pupil Relationship', in Cosin B et al (ed) *Education Structure and Society*, Penguin

Beijin A (1985) *Western Sexuality*, Blackwell

Bell C (1968) *Middle Class Families*, RKP

Benedict R (1934) *Patterns of Culture*, Houghton Mifflin

Benson H (2006) *The conflation of marriage and cohabitation in government statistics – a denial of difference rendered untenable by an analysis of outcomes*, Bristol Community Family Trust

Bentley D (1987) 'Interviewing in the context of non-verbal research' in Powney J and Watts M *Interviewing in Educational Research*. Routledge and Kegan Paul

Bereiter C and Engelmann S (1966) *Teaching Disadvantaged Children in Pre-school,* Prentice Hall

Bernard J (1976) *The Future of Marriage*, Penguin

Bernstein B and Young D (1967) 'Differences in Conceptions on the Use of Toys', Sociology

Bernstein B (1975) *Class, Codes and Control*, Schocken

Bernstein B (1976) 'Education Cannot Compensate for Society', in Butterworth E et al (ed) *The Sociology of Modern Britain*, Fontana

Best L (1993) '"Dragons, dinner ladies and ferrets": sex roles in children's books', *Sociology Review*

Beynon J and Atkinson P (1984) ' "Sussing out" teachers: pupils as data gatherers' in Hammersley M and Woods P (eds) *Life in School: the sociology of pupil culture*, Open University

Bhatti G (1999) *Asian Children at Home and at School: an Ethnographic Study*, Routledge

Bilton T et al (1987) *Introductory Sociology*, Macmillan

Black D et al (1980; 1992) 'The Black Report', in Whitehead M et al (ed) *Inequalities in Health,* Penguin

Blackstone T and Mortimore J (1994) 'Cultural factors in child-rearing and attitudes to education', in Moore B and Mayes AS (ed) *Teaching and Learning in the Secondary School,* Routledge

Blau P and Duncan O (1978) *The American Occupational Structure*, Free Press

Blauner R (1964) *Alienation and Freedom*, University of Chicago Press

Blundell J and Griffiths J (2003) *Sociology Since 1995*, Connect

Boaler J (1998) 'Mathematical Equity', in Epstein D et al (ed) *Failing Boys?* Open University

Bonke J (1999) 'Children's household work: is there a difference between girls and boys?' Working Paper, Danish National Institute of Social Research.

Bott E (1957) *Family and Social Network*, Tavistock

Boulton M (1983) *On Being a Mother*, Tavistock

Bourdieu P (1984) *Distinction*, RKP

Bourne J (1994) *Outcast England*, Institute of Race Relations

Bowker G (1968) *The Education of Coloured Immigrants*, Longman

Bowles S and Gintis H (1976) *Schooling in Capitalist America*, RKP

Brannen J et al (1994) *Young People, Health and Family Life*, Open University

Brass W and Kabir M (1978) 'Regional Variations in Fertility and Child Mortality during the Demographic Transition in England and Wales' in Hobcraft J and Rees P (eds) *Regional Demographic Development*, Croom Helm

British Crime Survey (2000; 2002) www. homeoffice.gov.uk

British Household Panel Survey (1998) www.iser.essex.ac.uk/bhps

British Social Attitudes (2000) www.esds.ac.uk

Browne N and Ross C (1991) 'Girls' Stuff, Boys' Stuff', in Browne N (ed) *Science and Technology in the Early Years*, Open University

Bull D (1980) *What Price Free Education?* Child Poverty Action Group

Burn E (2001) 'Battling Through The System', International Journal of Inclusive Education

Byrne E (1979) *Women and Education*, Routledge

Cameron M (1964) *The Booster and the Snitch*, Free Press

Cashmore E (1985) *Having to. The World of One Parent Families*, Allen and Unwin

Chaikin A, Sigler E and Derlega V (1975) 'Non-verbal mediators of teacher expectancy effects', *Journal of Personality and Social Psychology*

Chamberlain M (1999) 'Brothers and Sisters, Uncles and Aunts', in Silva et al (ed) *The New Family?* Sage

Chapman K (1994) *The Sociology of Schools*, Routledge

Cheal D (1991) *Family and the State of Theory*, Harvester

Cheal D (1993) 'Unity and Difference in Postmodern Families', *Journal of Family Issues*

Cheal D (2002) *Sociology of Family Life*, Palgrave Macmillan

Chester R (1985) 'The Rise of the Neo-Conventional Family', *New Society*

Chubb J and Moe T (1990) *Politics, Markets and America's Schools*, Brookings

Clarke A (2006) *Referrals, assessments and children and young people on child protection registers, England (First Release)*, DfES

Cicourel A and Kitsuse J (1963) *The Education Decision-Makers*, Bobbs Merill

Cicourel A (1968) *The Social Organisation of Juvenile Justice*, Wiley

Coard B (1971) *How the West Indian Child is Made Educationally Subnormal in the British School System*, New Beacon

Coard B (2005) 'Why I wrote the ESN Book", The Guardian, 5 February

Coast E (2006) 'Currently cohabiting: relationship attitudes, intentions and behaviour' *Royal Geographical Society annual conference*

Cockburn C (1987) *Two Track Training*, Macmillan

Coleman K, Jansson K, Kaiza P and Reed E (2007) *Homicides, Firearm Offences and Intimate Violence 2005/06 (Supplementary volume 1 to Crime in England and Wales 2005/06)* Home Office Statistical Bulletin 02/07

Colley A (1998) 'Gender and Subject Choice in Secondary Education', in Radford J (ed) *Gender and Choice in Education and Occupation*, Routledge

Commission for Racial Equality (1992) *Set to Fail*, CRE

Commission for Racial Equality (1993) *Draft Circular on Admission Arrangements*, CRE

Condry R (2007) 'Families Shamed', *LSE Magazine*, Winter

Connell RW (1995), *Masculinities*, Polity

Connolly P (1988) *Racism, Gender Identities and Young Children*, Routledge

Connolly P (2006) 'The effects of social class and ethnicity on gender differences in GCSE attainment: a secondary analysis of the Youth Cohort Study of England and Wales 1997-2001', *British Educational Research Journal*

Connor H and Dewson S (2001) *Social Class and HE*, DfES Research Report

Crompton R (1997) *Women and Work in Modern Britain*, Oxford University Press

Crystal D (2003) *The Cambridge Encyclopaedia of Language*, Cambridge University Press

Cumberbatch G and Negrine R (1992) *Images of Disability on Television*, Routledge

Cunningham H (2007) 'Social constructions of childhood', *Sociology Review*

Curtis P (2007), 'Private schools prepare to face tests on keeping their charity tax breaks', The Guardian, 29 October

David M (1993) *Parents, Gender and Education Reform*, Polity

Davis K and Moore W (1945; 1967) 'Some Principles of Social Stratification', in Bendix and Lipset (ed) *Class Status and Power*, RKP

De Mause L (1974) *The History of Childhood*, Psychohistory Press

Dean H and Taylor-Gooby P (1992) *Dependency Culture*, Wheatsheaf

Delamont S (1976) *Interaction in the Classroom*, Methuen

Devine F and Heath S (1999) *Sociological Research Methods in Context*, Macmillan

Dewar A (1990) 'Oppression and Privilege in Physical Education', in Kirk D et al (ed) *Physical Education, Curriculum and Culture*, Falmer

Department for Education and Skills (2005) *Ethnicity and education*, DfES

Department for Education and Skills (2006), *School Workforce in England data*, DfES

Department for Education and Skills (2007) *Gender and education: the evidence on pupils in England*, DfES

Ditton J (1977) *Part-time Crime*, Macmillan

Dobash R and Dobash R (1979) *Violence against Wives*, Open Books

Donzelot J (1977) *The Policing of Families*, Hutchinson

Douglas J (1964) *The Home and the School*, Penguin

Downes D and Rock P (1989) *Understanding Deviance*, Oxford University Press

Drew E et al (1995) *Families, Labour Markets and Gender Roles*, www.eurofound.eu.int

Driver G (1977) *Cultural Power, Social Power and School Achievement*, New Community

Duncombe J and Marsden D (1995) 'Women's Triple Shift', Sociology Review

Bibliography

Dunne G (1999) 'A Passion for Sameness', in Silva E et al (ed) *The New Family?* Sage

Durkheim E (1893; 1985) *The Division of Labour in Society*, Penguin

Durkheim E (1897; 2002) *Suicide*, Routledge

Durkheim E (1903; 2002) *Moral Education,* Dover

Edgell S (1980) *Middle Class Couples*, Allen and Unwin

Elwood J and Murphy P (1998) 'Gendered Learning Outside and Inside School', in Epstein D et al (ed) *Failing Boys?* Open University

Elwood J (2005), 'Gender and achievement: what have exams got to do with it?' *Oxford Review of Education*

Engels F (1978) *Origin of the Family, Private Property and the State*, Foreign Languages Press, Peking

Epstein D et al (1998) 'Boys' Underachievement in Context', in Epstein D et al (ed) *Failing Boys?* Open University

Economic and Social Research Council (2007) 'Men's housework could reduce divorce' *Britain in 2008,* ESRC

Evans G (2006) *Educational Failure and Working Class White Children in Britain*, Palgrave Macmillan

Fairhurst E (1977) 'On Being a Patient in an Orthopaedic Ward', in Horobin G et al (ed) *Medical Encounters*, Croom Helm

Feinstein L (1998) 'Which Children Succeed and Why?', New Economy

Ferri E and Smith K (1996) *Parenting in the 1990s*, Family Policy Studies Centre

Ferri E and Smith K (1998) *Step-parenting in the l990s*, Family Policy Studies Centre

Festinger L et al (1956) *When Prophecy Fails*, Harper and Row

Field J (n.d.) 'An interview survey of teenagers and parents', quoted in Powney J and Watts M (1987) *Interviewing in Educational Research*, Routledge & Kegan Paul

Finch J (1983) *Married to the Job*, Allen and Unwin

Finch J and Mason J (1989) *Family Obligations and Social Change*, Polity

Finch J and Mason J (1993) *Negotiating Family Responsibilities*, Routledge

Finn D (1984) 'Leaving School and Growing Up', in Bates I et al (ed) *Schooling for the Dole*, Macmillan

Firestone S (1970) *The Dialectics of Sex*, Paladin

Firestone S (1979) 'Down with Childhood', in Hoyles M (ed) *Changing Childhood*, Writers and Readers

Firth R (1970) *Rank and Religion in Tikopia*, Routledge

Fitz J et al (1997) 'Opting into the Past?' in Glatter P et al (ed) *Choice and Diversity in Schooling*, Routledge

Flaherty J et al (2004) *Poverty – the Facts,* 5th edition, CPAG

Flanders NA (1970) *Analysing Teacher Behaviour*, Addison Wesley

Fletcher R (1966) *The Family and Marriage in Britain*, Penguin

Flew A (1984) *Education, Race and Revolution*, Centre for Policy Studies

Foster P (1990) *Policy and Practice in Multicultural and Anti-Racist Education*, Routledge

Foucault M (1976) *The Birth of the Clinic*, Routledge

Francis B (2001), *Boys, Girls and Achievement: Addressing the Classroom Issues*, Routledge/Falmer

Francis B et al (2006) 'A Perfect Match? Pupils' and Teachers' Views of the Impact of Matching Educators and Learners By Gender', *Research Papers in Education Journal*

Frank A (1965) *The Diary of Anne Frank*, Pan

French J and French P (1993) 'Gender Imbalances in the Primary Classroom', in Woods P et al (ed) *Gender and Ethnicity in Schools*, Routledge

Fuller M (1984) 'Black Girls in a London Comprehensive School', in Deem R (ed) *Schooling for Women's Work*, RKP

Furlong J (1984) 'Interaction Sets in the Classroom', in Hammersley M et al (ed) *Life in Schools*, Open University

Future Foundation (2000) *Complicated Lives*, John Wiley & Sons

Gauntlett D and Hill A (1999) *TV Living,* Routledge

Gershuny J et al (1994) 'The Domestic Labour Revolution', in Anderson M et al (ed) *The Social and Political Economy of the Household*, Oxford University Press

Gewirtz S et al (1995) *Markets, Choice and Equity in Education*, Open University

Giddens A (1992) *The Transformation of Intimacy*, Polity

Gill R (1988) 'Altered Images', Social Studies Review

Gillborn D (1990) *Race, Ethnicity and Education*, Unwin Hyman

Gillborn D (1997) 'Race and Ethnicity in Education 14-19', in Tomlinson S (ed) *Education 14-19 Critical Perspectives*, Athorne

Gillborn D and Mirza H S (2000) *Educational Inequality: Mapping Race, Gender and Class: a Synthesis of Research*, Ofsted

Gillborn D and Youdell D (2000) *Rationing Education: Policy, Practice, Reform and Equity,* Open University

Gittins D (1998) *The Child in Question*, Macmillan

Glasgow University Media Group (1976) *Bad News*, RKP

Goldthorpe J and Lockwood D et al (1969) *The Affluent Worker in the Class Structure*, Cambridge University Press

Goode W (1964) *The Family*, Prentice Hall

Graham H (1983) 'Do Her Answers Fit His Questions?', in Gamarnikow E et al (ed) *The Public and the Private*, Heinemann

Graham H (1984) *Women, Health and the Family*, Prentice Hall

Greene S and Hogan D (2005) *Researching Children's Experiences: Approaches and Methods,* Sage

Greer G (2000) *The Whole Woman*, Anchor

Gregson N and Lowe M (1994) *Servicing the Middle Classes*, Routledge

Greig A et al (2007) *Doing Educational Research*, Sage

Griffin J (1962) *Black Like Me*, Collins

Griffiths R (1988) *Community Care: Agenda for Action*, HMSO

Hardill I et al (1997) 'Who Decides What?', Work, Employment and Society

Hareven T (1999) *Families, History and Social Change*, Westview

Hargreaves D (1967) *Social Relations in a Secondary School*, RKP

Harvey D and Slatin G (1976) 'The relationships between child's SES and teacher expectations, *Social Forces*

Hastings S (2006) 'White underachievement', Times Educational Supplement, 28 April

Hatcher R et al (1996) *Racial Equality and the Local Management of Schools*, Warwick Papers on Education Policy

Haywood C and Mac an Ghaill M (1996) 'Schooling Masculinities', in Mac an Ghaill M (ed) *Understanding Masculinities*, Open University

Hey V (1997) *The Company She Keeps: an ethnography of girls' friendship*, Open University Press

Hillman M (1993) *Children, Transport and the Quality of Life*, Policy Studies Institute

Hirsch D (2005) 'Paying for ourselves as we get older: rethinking resource allocation', Institute of Actuaries

Hitchcock G (1995) 'Writing Lives', Sociology Review

Hite S (1991) *The Hite Report on Love, Passion and Emotional Violence*, Penguin

Hochschild A (1983) *The Managed Heart*, University of California Press

Hochschild A (1997) *The Time Bind*, Metropolitan Books

Hockey J and James A (1993) *Growing Up and Growing Old*, Sage

Holdsworth C and Morgan D (2005) *Transitions in Context: Leaving Home, Independence and Adulthood*, Open University Press

Holmes L (1974) *Samoan Village*, Thompson

Holt J (1974) *Escape from Childhood*, Penguin

Howard M et al (2001) *Poverty the Facts*, Child Poverty Action Group

Hugo R (1982) *The Hitler Diaries*, William Morrow

Humphreys C and Thiara R (2002) *Routes to Safety*, Women's Aid Federation

Humphreys L (1970) *The Tea Room Trade*, Duckworth

Hyman H (1967) 'The Value Systems of Different Classes', in Bendix R and Lipset S (ed) *Class, Status and Power*, RKP

Irvine J (1987) *Demystifying Social Statistics*, Pluto

Jackson D (1998) 'Breaking the Binary Trap', in Epstein et al (ed) *Failing Boys?* Open University

Jenkins R (1986) *Racism and Recruitment*, Cambridge University Press

Kan M-Y (2001) 'Gender Asymmetry in the Division of Domestic Labour', *BHPS 2001 conference*, Institute for Social and Economic Research

Katz C (1993) 'Growing Girls', in Katz C et al (ed) *Full Circles*, Routledge

Keddie N (1971) 'Classroom Knowledge', in Young M (ed) *Knowledge and Control*, Macmillan

Keddie N (1973) *Tinker, Tailor: the Myth of Cultural Deprivation*, Penguin

Kelly A (1987) *Science for Girls*, Open University

Kempson E et al (1994) *Hard Times?*, Family Policy Studies Centre

Kendal Project (2004) www.lancs.ac.uk

Khan V (1979) *Minority Families in Britain*, Macmillan

King R (1984) 'The Man in the Wendy House, in Burgess R *The Research Process in Educational Settings: Ten Case Studies*, Falmer

Kinsey A et al (1953) *Sexual Behaviour in the Human Female*, WB Saunders

Labov W (1973) 'The Logic of Nonstandard English', in Keddie N (ed) *Tinker, Tailor: the Myth of Cultural Deprivation*, Penguin

Lacey C (1970) *Hightown Grammar*, Manchester University Press

Lancet (2002) www.thelancet.com

Land H (1978) 'Who Cares for the Family?' Journal of Social Policy

Lane T and Roberts K (1971) *Strike at Pilkingtons*, Fontana

Laslett P (1972) *Household and Family in Past Time*, Cambridge University Press

Lawrence E (1982) 'The Sociology of Black Pathology', in CCCS (ed) *The Empire Strikes Back*, Hutchinson

Lawson T and Garrod J (2000) *The Complete A to Z Sociology Handbook*, Hodder

Leach E (1967) *Runaway World?* BBC

Lees S (1986) *Losing Out*, Hutchinson

Lees S (1993) *Sugar and Spice*, Penguin

Leonard D (1978) 'The Regulation of Marriage', in Littlejohn G et al (ed) *Power and the State*, Croom Helm

Leonard D (2006) 'Single-sex schooling', in Francis B et al (eds) *Handbook of Gender And Education*, Sage

Liebow E (1967) *Tally's Corner*, Little Brown

Litwak E (1960) 'Occupational Mobility and Extended Family Cohesion', *American Sociological Review*

Liverpool Victoria (2007) *Annual 'Cost of a Child' survey 2007*, www.lv.com

Lobban G (1974) 'Data Report on British Reading Schemes', Times Educational Supplement

Lupton R (2004) "Schools in Disadvantaged Areas", Centre for Analysis of Social Exclusion

Lyotard J (1984) *The Postmodern Condition*, Manchester University Press

Bibliography

Mac an Ghaill M (1994) *The Making of Men*, Open University

MacDonald M (1980) 'Socio-cultural Reproduction and Women's Education', in Deem R (ed) *Schooling for Women's Work*, RKP

Macklin E (1980) 'Non-Marital Heterosexual Cohabitation', in Skolnick A et al (ed) *The Intimate Environment*, Little Brown

Macrae S et al (1997) 'Competition, Choice and Hierarchy in the post-16 Market', in Tomlinson S (ed) *Education 14—19 Critical Perspectives*, Athorne

Malinowski B (1957) *The Sexual Life of Savages*, RKP

Margo J and Dixon M (2006) *Freedom's Orphans,*, IPPR

Marshall G (1988) *Social Class in Modern Britain*, Harper Collins

Marx K (1848; 2002) *The Communist Manifesto*, Penguin

Mason D (1995) *Race and Ethnicity in Modern Britain*, Oxford University Press

Mason E J (1973) 'Teachers' observations of boys and girls as influenced by biased psychological reports and knowledge of the effects of bias', Journal of Educational Research

Mayo E (1927; 2003) *Human Problems of an Industrial Civilisation*, Routledge

McKee L and O'Brien M (1983) 'Interviewing Men', in Gamarnikow E et al (ed) *The Public and the Private*, Heinemann

McKeown T et al (1972) 'An Interpretation of the Modern Rise in Population in Europe', *Population Studies*

McRobbie A (1978) 'Working Class Girls and the Culture of Femininity', in Hall S et al (ed) *Resistance Through Ritual*, Hutchison

McRobbie A (1994) *Postmodernism and Popular Culture*, Routledge

McVeigh T (2001) 'Boys Lagging in Class for Years', The Observer

Mead M (1943) *Coming of Age in Samoa*, Penguin

Meighan R (1981) *A Sociology of Educating,* Cassell Education

Merton R (1949) *Social Theory and Social Structure*, Free Press

Milgram S (1974) *Obedience and Authority*, Harper Collins

Millett K (1970) *Sexual Politics*, Doubleday

Mirlees-Black C (1999) *Domestic Violence*, The Home Office

Mirza H (1992) *Young Female and Black*, Routledge

Mirza H (1997) *Black British Feminism*, Routledge

Mirza H (2005) 'The more things change, the more they stay the same', in Richardson B (ed) *Tell It Like It Is,* Bookmarks Publications and Trentham Books

Mitchell J and Goody J (1997) 'Feminism, Fatherhood and the Family in Britain', in Oakley A and Mitchell J (ed) *Who's Afraid of Feminism*, Penguin

Mitsos E and Browne K (1998) 'Gender Differences in Education', Sociology Review

Moore D and Davenport S (1990) 'Choice: the New Improved Sorting Machine', in Boyd W et al (ed) *Choice in Education,* McCutchan

Morgan D (1996) *Family Connections*, Polity

Morgan D (1997) 'Risk and Family Practices', in Silva E et al (ed) *The New Family*, Sage

Morgan D (2007) *Passing Acquaintances*, Open University Press

MORI (2004) *Schools Omnibus 2004: A Research Study Among 11-16 Year Olds on behalf of The Sutton Trust*, www.suttontrust.com

Morris L (1990) *The Workings of the Household*, Polity

Morrow R and Torres C (1998) 'Education and the Reproduction of Class, Gender and Race', in Torres C et al (ed) *Sociology of Education: Emerging Perspectives*, University of New York Press

Mortimore P and Whitty G (1997) *Can School Improvement Overcome the Effects of Disadvantage?* Institute of Education

Moynihan D (1965) *The Negro Family*, US Department of Labor

Murdock G P (1949) *Social Structure*, Macmillan

Murphy P (1991) 'Gender Differences in Pupils' Reactions to Practical Work', in Woolnough B (ed) *Practical Science*, Open University

Murphy P and Elwood J (1998) 'Gendered Learning Outside and Inside School', in Epstein D et al (ed) *Failing Boys?* Open University

Murray C (1984) *Losing Ground*, Basic Books

Myhill D and Jones S (2006) 'She Doesn't Shout at No Girls, *Cambridge Journal of Education*

National Audit Office (2002) www.nao.gov.uk

Nazroo J (1997) *The Health of Britain's Ethnic Minorities*, Policy Studies Institute

Newby H (1977) *The Deferential Worker*, Allen and Unwin

Noon M (1993) 'Racial Discrimination in Speculative Applications', Human Resources Management Journal

Norman F et al (1988) 'Look, Jane, Look', in Weiner G (ed) *Just a Bunch of Girls*, Open University

O'Brien M and Jones D (1996) 'Revisiting Family and Kinship', Sociology Review

Oakley A (1973) *Sex, Gender and Society*, Temple Smith

Oakley A (1974) *The Sociology of Housework*, Martin Robertson

Oakley A (1982) *Subject Women*, Penguin

Oakley A (1997) 'A Brief History of Gender', in Oakley A and Mitchell J (ed) *Who's Afraid of Feminism*, Penguin

Opie I (1993) *The People in the Playground*, Oxford University Press

Paetcher C (1998) *Educating the Other*, Falmer

Pahl J and Vogler C (1993) 'Social and Economic Change and the Organisation of Money within Marriage', Work, Employment and Society

Palmer S (2006) *Toxic Childhood*, Orion

Papworth J (2000) 'Millions of Children Work: Most are Exploited', The Guardian

Parker A (1996) 'Sporting Masculinities', in Mac an Ghaill M (ed) *Understanding Masculinities*, Open University

Parker H (1974) *View From the Boys*, David and Charles

Parker H et al (1998) *Illegal Leisure*, Routledge

Parsons T (1951; 1991) *The Social System*, Routledge

Parsons T (1955) 'The American Family', in Parsons T and Bales R (ed) *Family Socialisation and Interaction Process,* Free Press

Parsons T (1961) 'The School Class as a Social System', in Halsey A et al (ed) *Education, Economy and Society*, Free Press

Patrick J (1973) *A Glasgow Gang Observed*, Methuen

Pilcher J (1995) *Age and Generation in Modern Britain*, Oxford University Press

Pirie M (2000) 'How Exams are Fixed in Favour of Girls', The Spectator

Pollock L (1983) *Forgotten Children*, Cambridge University Press

Polsky N (1971) *Hustlers, Beats and Others*, Penguin

Postman N (1994) *The Disappearance of Childhood*, Vintage

Powney J and Watts M (1987) *Interviewing in Educational Research*, Routledge and Kegan Paul

Prosser M (2006) 'Shaping a Fairer Future', Women and Work Commission

Pryce K (1979) *Endless Pressure*, Penguin

Punch M (1979) *Policing the Inner City*, Macmillan

Punch S (2001) 'Negotiating autonomy: childhoods in rural Bolivia' in L. Alanen and B. Mayall (eds) *Conceptualising Child-Adult Relations*, Routledge Falmer

Qualifications and Curriculum Authority (1999) www.qca.org.uk

Qvortrup J (1990) *Childhood a Social Problem*, Centre for Study of Adult Life

Ramos X (2003) 'Domestic Work Time and Gender Differentials in Great Britain 1992-1998' *BHPS 2003 conference*, Institute for Social and Economic Research

Rapoport R and Rapoport R (1971) *Dual Career Families*, Penguin

Rapoport R and Rapoport R (1982) *Families in Britain*, RKP

Redman P and Mac an Ghaill M (1997) 'Educating Peter', in Steinberg D et al (ed) *Border Patrols*, Cassell

Renvoize J (1985) *Going Solo*, Routledge

Rex J (1986) *Race and Ethnicity*, Open University

Reynolds T (1997) 'Mis-representing the Black Super-woman', in Mirza S (ed) *Black British Feminism*, Routledge

Ribbens McCarthy J et al (2003) *Making Families: Moral Tales of Parenting and Step-Parenting*, Sociology Press

Rich J (1968) *Interviewing Children and Adolescents*, Macmillan

Ridge T (2002), *Childhood Poverty and Social Exclusion: from a child's perspective*, The Bailey Press

Rist R (1970) 'Student Social Class and Teacher Expectations', Harvard Educational Review

Robertson Elliot F (1996) *Gender, Family and Society*, Macmillan

Robinson P (1997) *Literacy, Numeracy and Economic Performance*, London School of Economics

Rosenhan D (1973) 'On Being Sane in Insane Places', Science

Rosenthal R and Jacobson L (1968) *Pygmalion in the Classroom*, Holt Rinehart and Winston

Roulstone A (1998) 'Researching a Disabling Society', in Shakespeare T (ed) *The Disability Reader*, Cassell

Rutter M et al (1979) *Fifteen Thousand Hours*, Open Books

Schofield M (1965) *The Sexual Behaviour of Young People*, Longman

Schor J (1993) *The Overworked American,* Basic Books

Scott J (1990) *A Matter of Record*, Polity

Scruton R (1986) 'The Myth of Cultural Relativism', in O'Keefe D (ed) *Anti-Racism: an Assault on Education and Value*, Sherwood

Sewell T (1998) 'Loose Cannons', in Epstein D et al (ed) *Failing Boys?* Open University

Sharp R and Green A (1975) *Education and Social Control*, RKP

Sharpe S (1994) *Just Like a Girl*, Penguin

Shaw C (1930) T*he Jack-Roller*, University of Chicago Press

Shelton B and John D (1993) 'Does Marital Status Make a Difference?', Journal of Family Issues

Shipman M (1997) *Limitations of Social Research*, Longman

Shorter E (1975) *The Making of the Modern Family*, Fontana

Silver H (1987) 'Only So Many Hours in a Day', Service Industries Journal

Sissons M (1970) *The Psychology of Social Class*, Open University

Skeggs B (1997) *Formations of Class and Gender*, Sage

Slee R (1998) 'High Reliability Organisations and Liability Students', in Slee R et al (ed) *School Effectiveness for Whom?* Falmer

Smithers R (2001) 'Today's Special', The Guardian

Somerville J (2000) *Feminism and the Family*, Macmillan

Spender D (1983) Invisible Women, Women's Press

Stables A and Wikeley F (1996) 'Pupil Approaches to Subject Option Choices', Conference Papers cited in Epstein D et al (1998)

Stacey J (1998) *Brave New Families*, University of California Press

Steel L and Kidd W (2001) *The Family*, Palgrave

Stein P (1976) *Single*, Prentice-Hall

Stone M (1981) *The Education of the Black Child in Britain*, Fontana

Sugarman B (1970) 'Social Class Values and Behaviour in Schools', in Craft M (ed) *Family Class and Education*, Longman

Sullivan A (2001) 'Cultural capital and educational attainment', *Sociology*

Sullivan O (2000) 'The Division of Domestic Labour: Twenty Years of Change?' *Sociology*

Swann J and Graddol D (1994) 'Gender inequalities in classroom talk', in Graddol et al (eds) *Researching Language and Literacy in Social Contexts*, Clevedon

Swann J (1998) 'Language and Gender', in Epstein D et al (ed) *Failing Boys?* Open University

Swann Report (1985) *Education For All*, HMSO

Bibliography

Tanner E et al (2003) *The Costs of Education*, Child Poverty Action Group

Thomas W and Znaniecki F (1919; 1995) *The Polish Peasant in Europe and America*, University of Illinois Press

Thompson K (1992) 'Social Pluralism and Postmodernity', in Hall S et al (ed) *Modernity and its Futures*, Polity

Thomson K et al (eds) (2008) *British Social Attitudes: the 24th Report*, Sage

Thornton S (1995) *Club Cultures*, Polity

Townsend P (1979) *Poverty in the United Kingdom*, Penguin

Townsend P (1981) 'The structured dependency of the elderly', *Ageing and Society*, vol 1

Tranter NL (1996) *British Population in the Twentieth Century*, Macmillan

Troyna B and Williams J (1986) *Racism, Education and the State*, Croom Helm

Tuchman G (1978) *Hearth and Home*, Oxford University Press

Tuckett D (2001) *An Introduction to Medical Sociology*, Routledge

Tumin M (1967) *Social Stratification*, Prentice Hall

Usher R et al (1997) *Adult Education and the Postmodern Challenge*, Routledge

Vogler C (1994) 'Money in the Household', in Anderson M et al (ed) *The Social and Political Economy of the Household*, Oxford University Press

Wagg S (1992) 'I Blame the Parents', Sociology Review

Walford G et al (1991) *City Technology College*, Open University

Warde A and Hetherington K (1993) 'A Changing Domestic Division of Labour?" Work, Economy and Society

Weber M (1905; 2002) *The Protestant Ethic and the Spirit of Capitalism*, Routledge

Weeks J et al (1999) 'Everyday Experiments', in Silva E et al (ed) *The New Family?*, Sage

Weeks J (2000) *Making Sexual History*, Polity

Weiner G (1993) 'Shell-shock or Sisterhood', in Arnot M et al (ed) *Feminism and Social Justice in Education*, Falmer

Weiner G et al (1995) *Equal Opportunities in Colleges and Universities*, Open University

Weston K (1992) 'The Politics of Gay Families', in Thorne B and Yallom M (ed) *Rethinking the Family*, Northeastern University Press

Westwood S and Bhachu P (1988) *Images and Realities*, New Society

Whitty G et al (1998) *Devolution and Choice in Education*, Open University

Whyte W (1955) *Street Corner Society*, University of Chicago Press

Wilkinson R (1996) *Unhealthy Societies*, Routledge

Willis P (1977) *Learning to Labour*, Saxon House

Willmott P (1988) *The Evolution of a Community*, Routledge

Wilson A (1985) *Family*, Routledge

Womack S (2007) 'Can we make childhood less "toxic"?' *The Edge*, Autumn, ESRC

Women's Aid Federation (1999; 2003) www.womensaid.org.uk

Woodroffe C et al (1993) *Children, Teenagers and Health*, Open University

Woods P (1979) The Divided School, RKP

Wright C (1992) 'Early Education', in Gill D et al (ed) *Racism in Education*, Sage

Wrong D (1961) 'The Oversocialised Conception of Man', *American Sociological Review*

Yablonsky L (1973) *The Violent Gang*, Penguin

Yearnshire S (1997) 'Analysis of Cohort', in Bewley et al (ed) *Violence Against Women*, RCOG Press

Youdell D (2001) 'Engineering school markets, constituting schools and subjectivating students', *Journal of Educational Policy*

Yougov (2007), 'Primary School Kids', www.yougov.com

Young M and Willmott P (1962) *Family and Kinship in East London*, Penguin

Young M and Willmott P (1973) *The Symmetrical Family*, Penguin

Zaretsky E (1976) *Capitalism, The Family and Personal Life*, Pluto Press

Index

Index

Index

Index

Index